樋口大輔

"Why am I alive?"
There are not many things we can do in this short life. Wouldn't it be great if you pursued your passions so that it made you feel glad to be alive? When I realized that, I quit my company job and dived into this world.

Nothing will change if you don't take action yourself. It's your life, after all.

— Daisuke Higuchi

Daisuke Higuchi's manga career began in 1992 when the artist was honored with third prize in the 43rd Osamu Tezuka Award. In that same year, Higuchi debuted as creator of a romantic action story titled *Itaru*. In 1998, *Weekly Shonen Jump* began serializing *Whistle!* Higuchi's realistic soccer manga became an instant hit with readers and eventually inspired an anime series, debuting on Japanese TV in May of 2002.

WHISTLE!
VOL. 16: FEEL THE DESTINY

The SHONEN JUMP Manga Edition

STORY AND ART BY
DAISUKE HIGUCHI

English Adaptation/Drew Williams
Translation/Naomi Kokubo
Touch-up Art & Lettering/Jim Keefe
Cover, Graphics & Layout/Sean Lee
Editor/Jonathan Tarbox

Managing Editor/Frances E. Wall
Editorial Director/Elizabeth Kawasaki
Editor in Chief, Books/Alvin Lu
Editor in Chief, Magazines/Marc Weidenbaum
Sr. Director of Acquisitions/Rika Inouye
Sr. VP of Marketing/Liza Coppola
Exec. VP of Sales & Marketing/John Easum
Publisher/Hyoe Narita

Printed in the U.S.A.

Published by VIZ Media, LLC
P.O. Box 77010
San Francisco, CA 94107

SHONEN JUMP Manga Edition
10 9 8 7 6 5 4 3 2 1
First printing, May 2007

THE WORLD'S
MOST POPULAR MANGA

www.shonenjump.com

Vol. 16

FEEL THE DESTINY

Story and Art by
Daisuke Higuchi

jGRAPHIC
NOVEL

SHŌ KAZAMATSURI

● **JOSUI JUNIOR HIGH SOCCER TEAM FORWARD**

AKIRA SAIONJI

TSUBASA SHIINA

TATSUYA MIZUNO

● **JOSUI JUNIOR HIGH SOCCER TEAM MIDFIELDER**

CHARACTERS

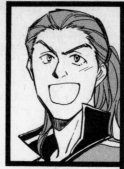

TAKI SUGIHARA

TAKANAWA JUNIOR HIGH

MIDFIELDER

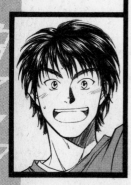

TAKASHI NARUMI

MEISEI JUNIOR HIGH

FORWARD

MASAHIRO SUŌ

J2 PANTERA FUCHŪ

FORWARD

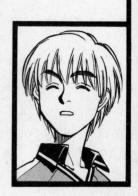

STORY

TO REALIZE HIS DREAM, SHŌ KAZAMATSURI, A BENCHWARMER AT SOCCER POWERHOUSE MUSASHI-NOMORI, TRANSFERRED TO JOSUI JUNIOR HIGH SO HE COULD PLAY THE GAME HE LOVES.

JOSUI'S SOCCER TEAM WAS A JOKE UNTIL SOUJŪ MATSUSHITA, A FORMER JAPAN LEAGUE PLAYER, TOOK ON THE COACHING DUTIES. UNDER MATSUSHITA'S GUIDANCE, THE TEAM HAS BECOME A FORCE TO BE RECKONED WITH. THEY BLASTED THROUGH THE DISTRICT PRIMARY TOURNAMENT, AND NOW THEY ARE DETERMINED TO ADVANCE THROUGH THE MAIN TOURNAMENT.

MEANWHILE, SHŌ, TATSUYA AND DAICHI WERE INVITED TO THE SELECTION CAMP FOR THE TOKYO SELECT TEAM. ON THE LAST DAY OF CAMP, A RED VS. WHITE MATCH DETERMINED THE FINAL TEAM ROSTER. SHŌ MANAGED TO SCORE DURING THE MATCH, AND WAS CHOSEN FOR THE TEAM...AS A SUBSTITUTE. EVEN THOUGH HE'S MADE THE CUT, HE'S BEGINNING TO QUESTION HIS ROLE ON THE TEAM...

WHISTLE!

**Vol. 16
FEEL THE
DESTINY**

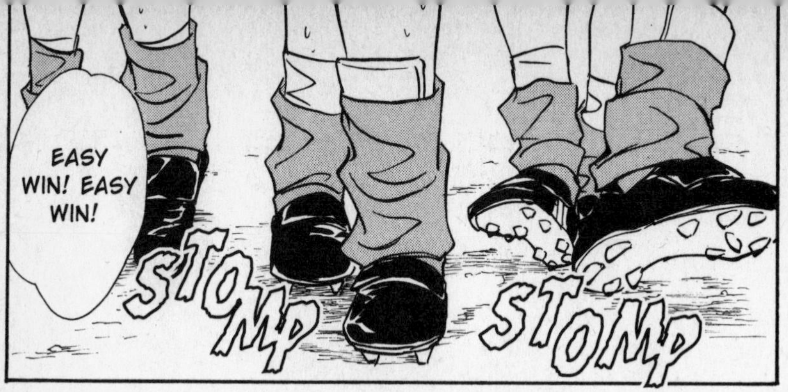
EASY WIN! EASY WIN!
STOMP
STOMP

STAGE.135 Running in Place

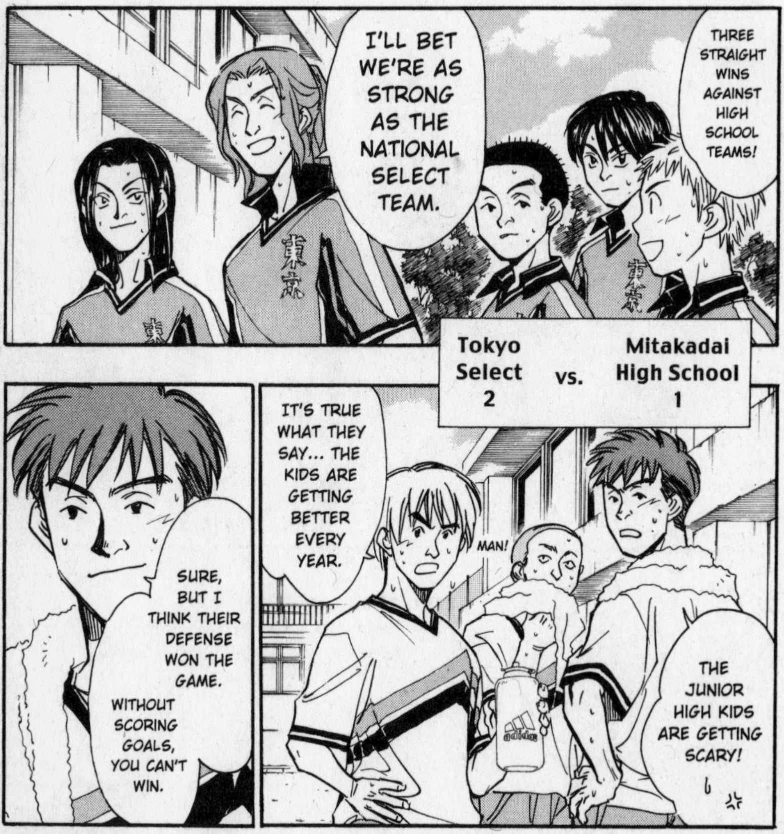
THREE STRAIGHT WINS AGAINST HIGH SCHOOL TEAMS!
I'LL BET WE'RE AS STRONG AS THE NATIONAL SELECT TEAM.
Tokyo Select 2 vs. Mitakadai High School 1
IT'S TRUE WHAT THEY SAY... THE KIDS ARE GETTING BETTER EVERY YEAR.
MAN!
THE JUNIOR HIGH KIDS ARE GETTING SCARY!
SURE, BUT I THINK THEIR DEFENSE WON THE GAME.
WITHOUT SCORING GOALS, YOU CAN'T WIN.

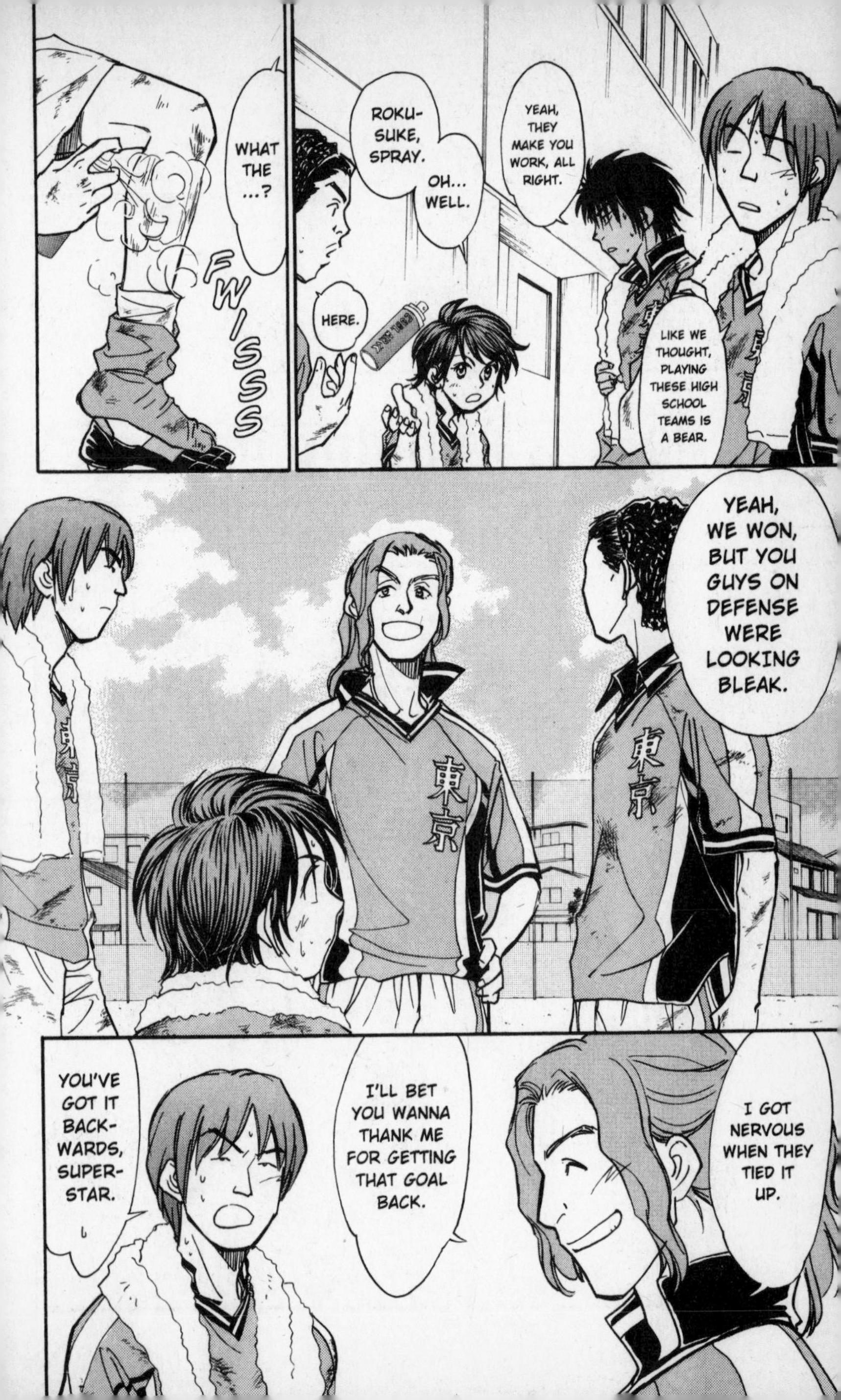

LIKE WE THOUGHT, PLAYING THESE HIGH SCHOOL TEAMS IS A BEAR.
YEAH, THEY MAKE YOU WORK, ALL RIGHT.
ROKU-SUKE, SPRAY.
OH... WELL.
HERE.
WHAT THE ...?
FWISSS
YEAH, WE WON, BUT YOU GUYS ON DEFENSE WERE LOOKING BLEAK.
I GOT NERVOUS WHEN THEY TIED IT UP.
I'LL BET YOU WANNA THANK ME FOR GETTING THAT GOAL BACK.
YOU'VE GOT IT BACK-WARDS, SUPER-STAR.

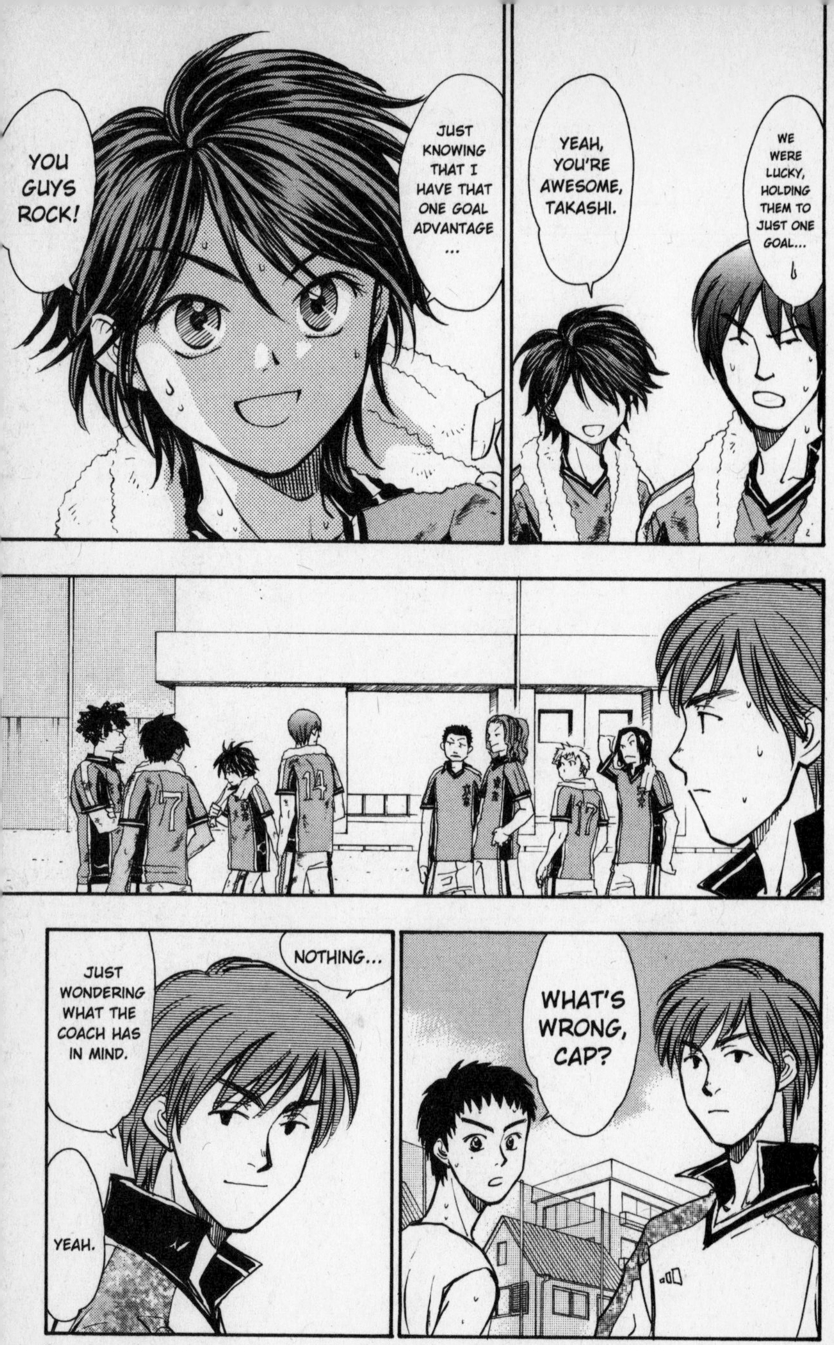
WE WERE LUCKY, HOLDING THEM TO JUST ONE GOAL...
YEAH, YOU'RE AWESOME, TAKASHI.
JUST KNOWING THAT I HAVE THAT ONE GOAL ADVANTAGE ...
YOU GUYS ROCK!
WHAT'S WRONG, CAP?
NOTHING...
JUST WONDERING WHAT THE COACH HAS IN MIND.
YEAH.

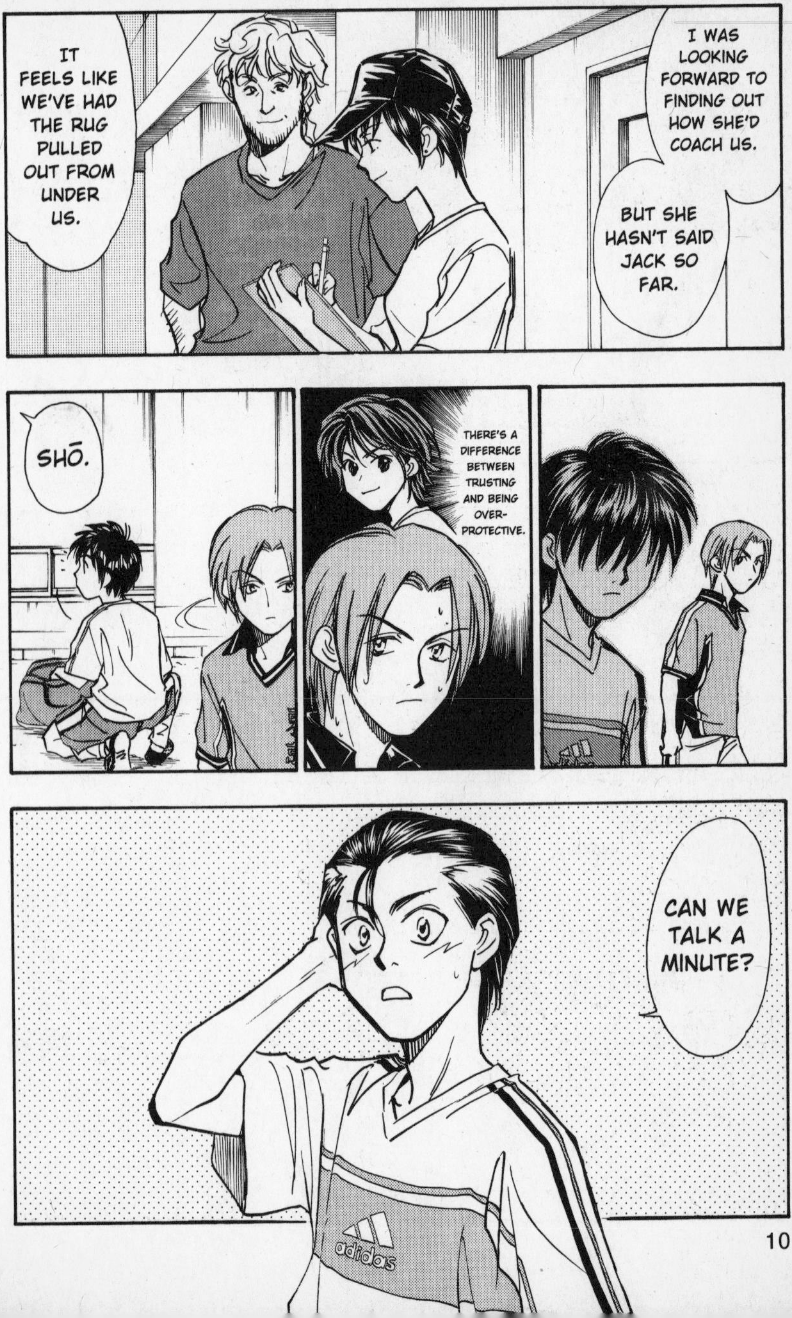
I WAS LOOKING FORWARD TO FINDING OUT HOW SHE'D COACH US.
BUT SHE HASN'T SAID JACK SO FAR.
IT FEELS LIKE WE'VE HAD THE RUG PULLED OUT FROM UNDER US.
THERE'S A DIFFERENCE BETWEEN TRUSTING AND BEING OVER-PROTECTIVE.
SHŌ.
CAN WE TALK A MINUTE?

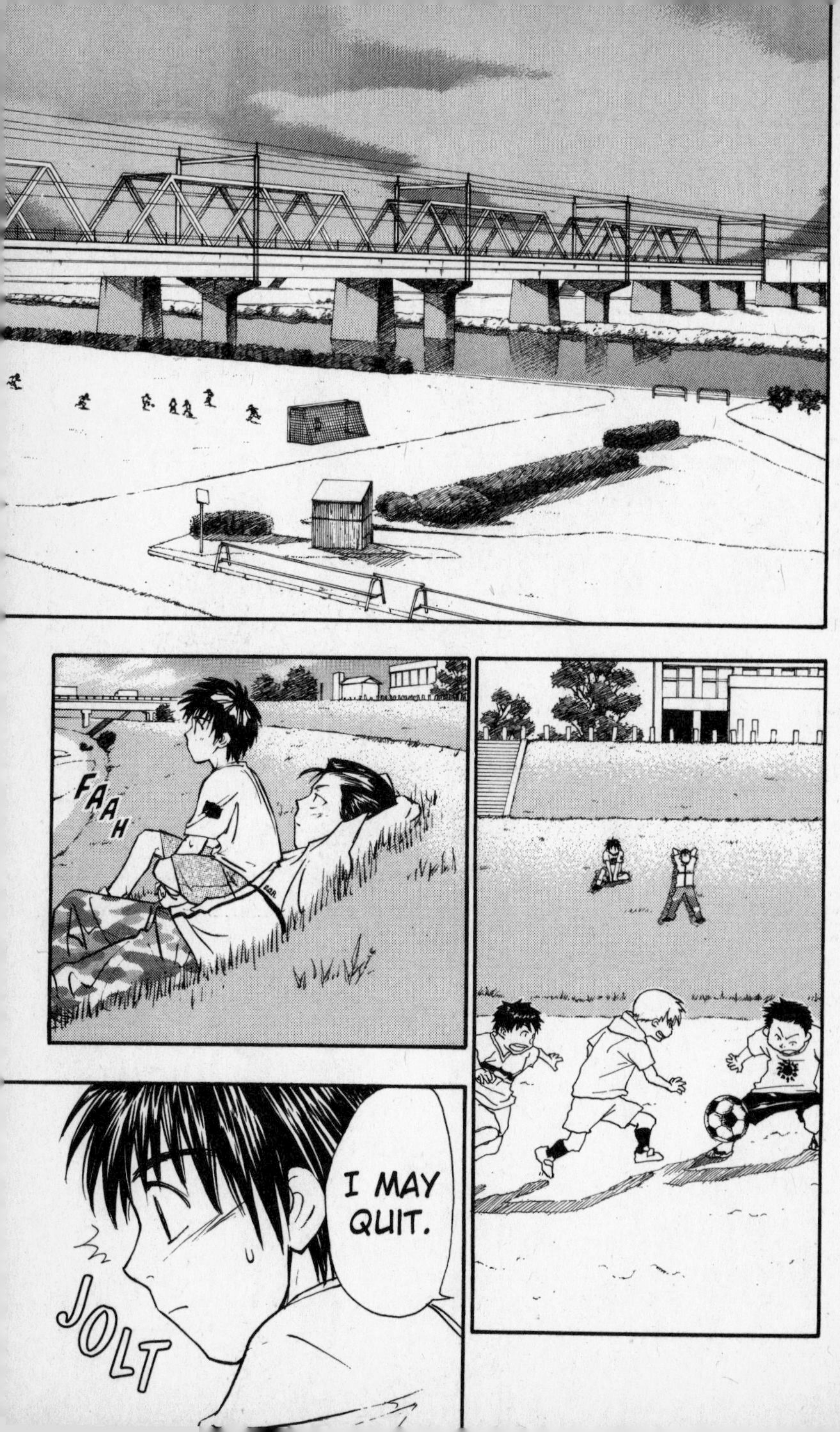
FAAH
I MAY QUIT.
JOLT

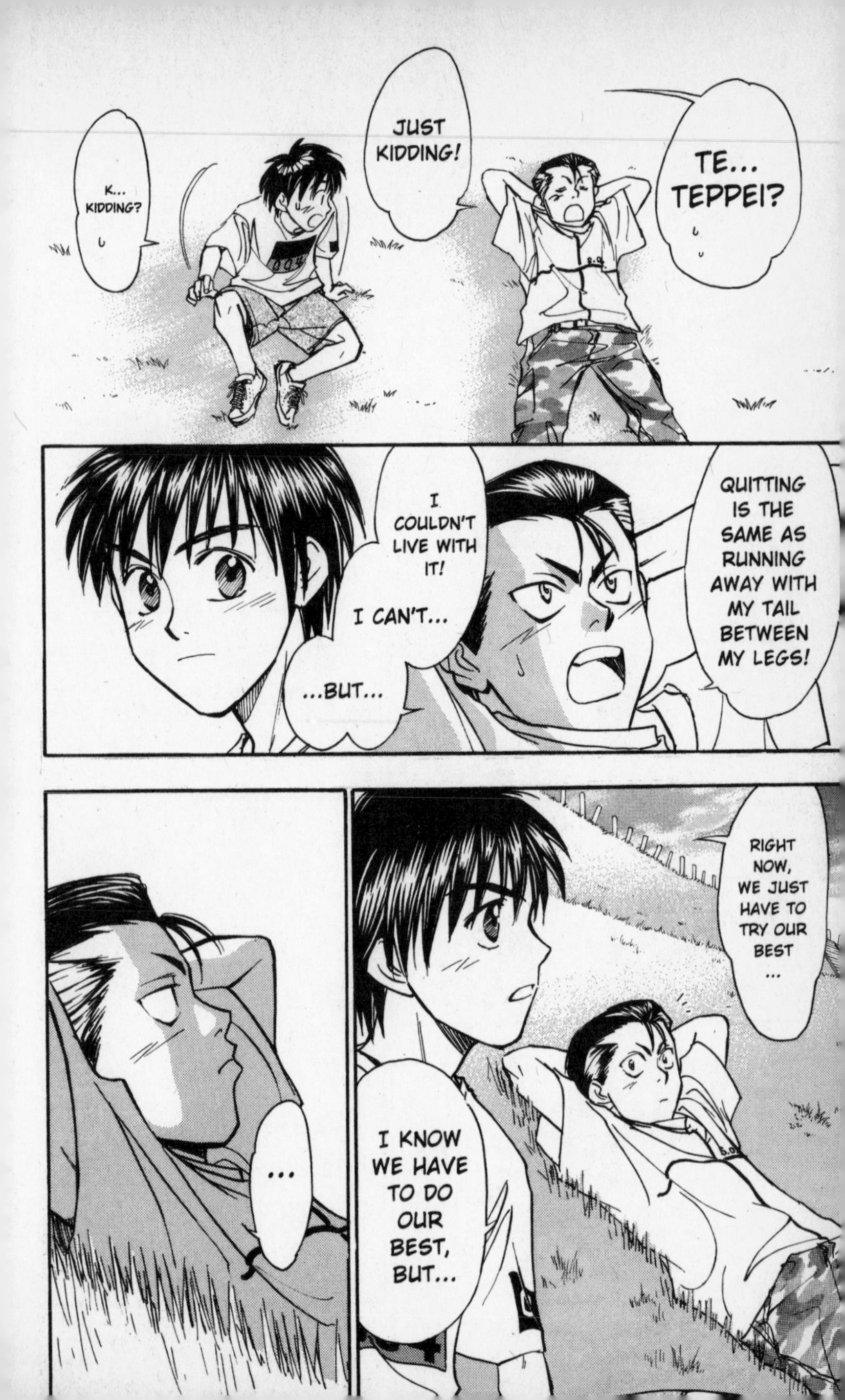
TE... TEPPEI?
JUST KIDDING!
K... KIDDING?
QUITTING IS THE SAME AS RUNNING AWAY WITH MY TAIL BETWEEN MY LEGS!
I COULDN'T LIVE WITH IT!
I CAN'T...
...BUT...
RIGHT NOW, WE JUST HAVE TO TRY OUR BEST ...
I KNOW WE HAVE TO DO OUR BEST, BUT...
...

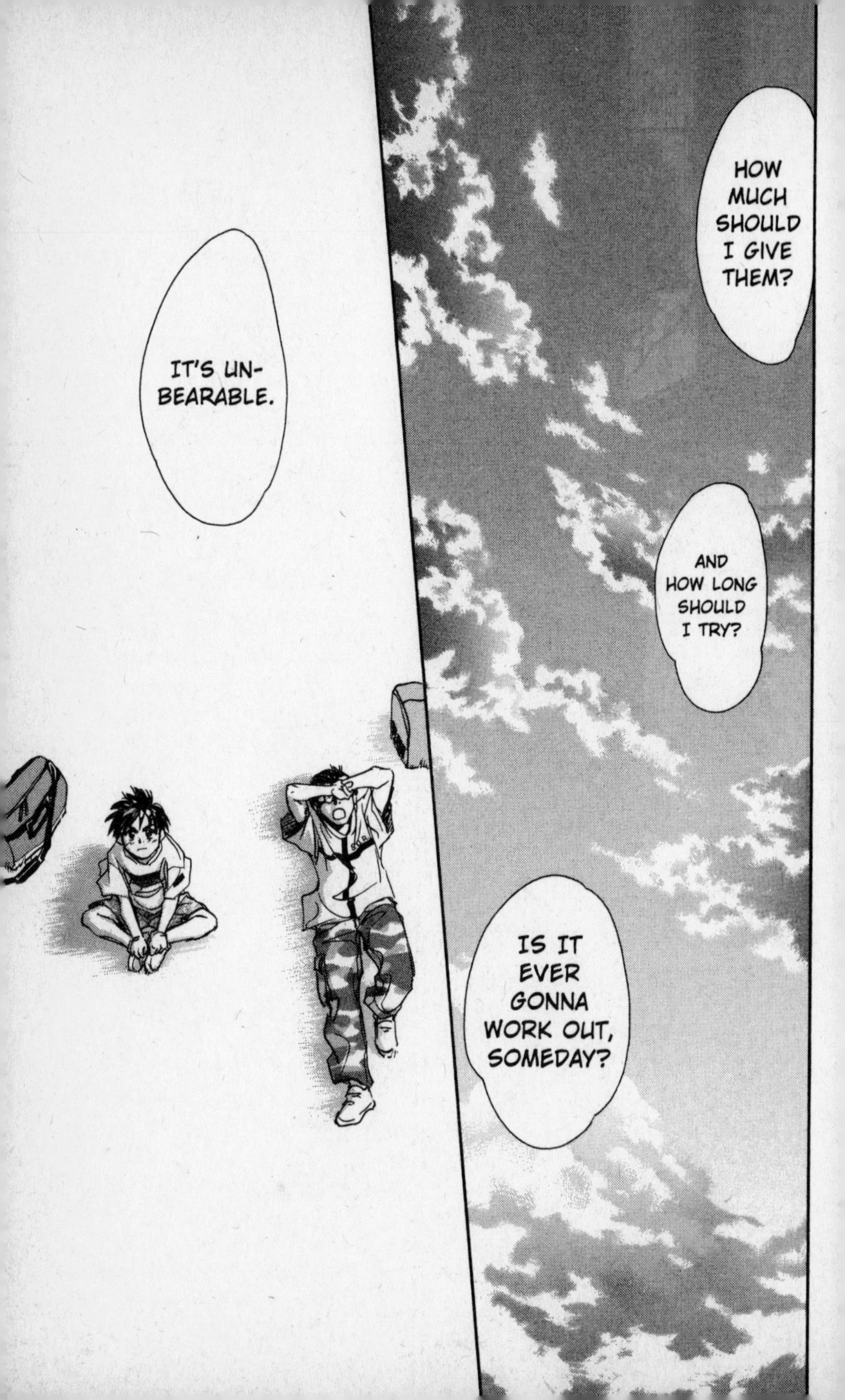
HOW MUCH SHOULD I GIVE THEM?
AND HOW LONG SHOULD I TRY?
IS IT EVER GONNA WORK OUT, SOMEDAY?
IT'S UN-BEARABLE.

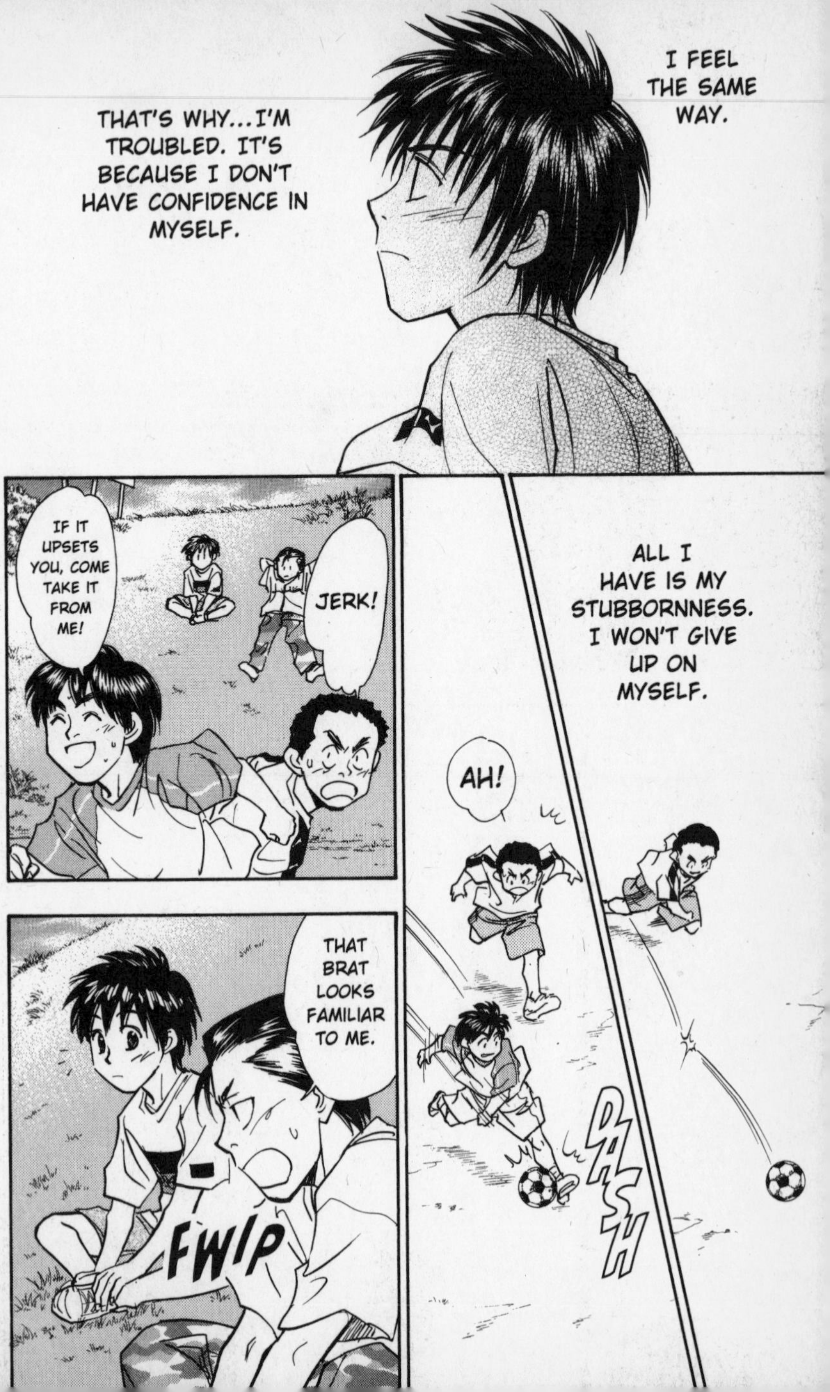

I FEEL THE SAME WAY.
THAT'S WHY...I'M TROUBLED. IT'S BECAUSE I DON'T HAVE CONFIDENCE IN MYSELF.
ALL I HAVE IS MY STUBBORNNESS. I WON'T GIVE UP ON MYSELF.
AH!
DASH
IF IT UPSETS YOU, COME TAKE IT FROM ME!
JERK!
THAT BRAT LOOKS FAMILIAR TO ME.
FWIP

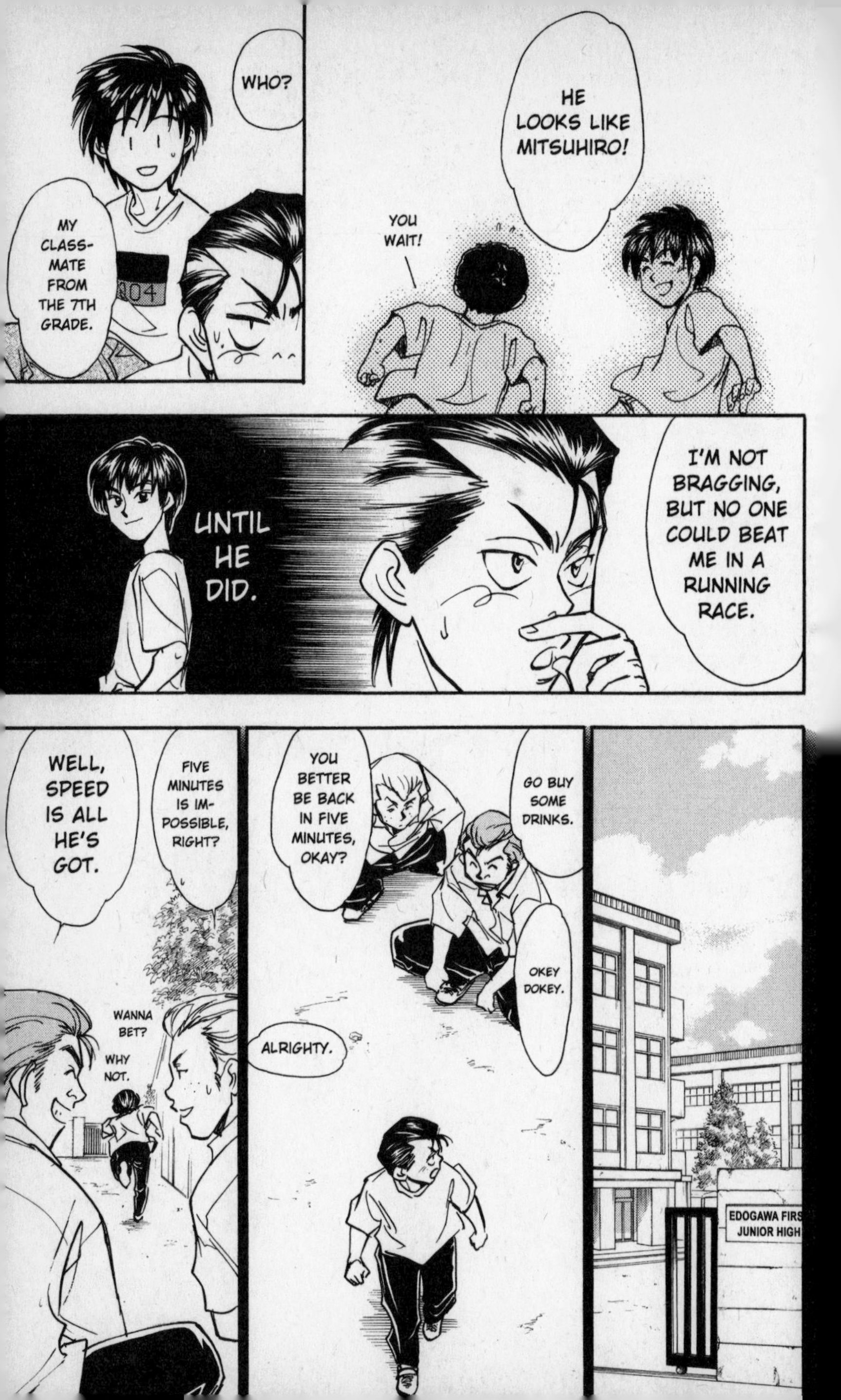
HE LOOKS LIKE MITSUHIRO!
YOU WAIT!
WHO?
MY CLASSMATE FROM THE 7TH GRADE.
I'M NOT BRAGGING, BUT NO ONE COULD BEAT ME IN A RUNNING RACE.
UNTIL HE DID.
EDOGAWA FIRS
JUNIOR HIGH
GO BUY SOME DRINKS.
YOU BETTER BE BACK IN FIVE MINUTES, OKAY?
OKEY DOKEY.
ALRIGHTY.
FIVE MINUTES IS IMPOSSIBLE, RIGHT?
WELL, SPEED IS ALL HE'S GOT.
WANNA BET?
WHY NOT.

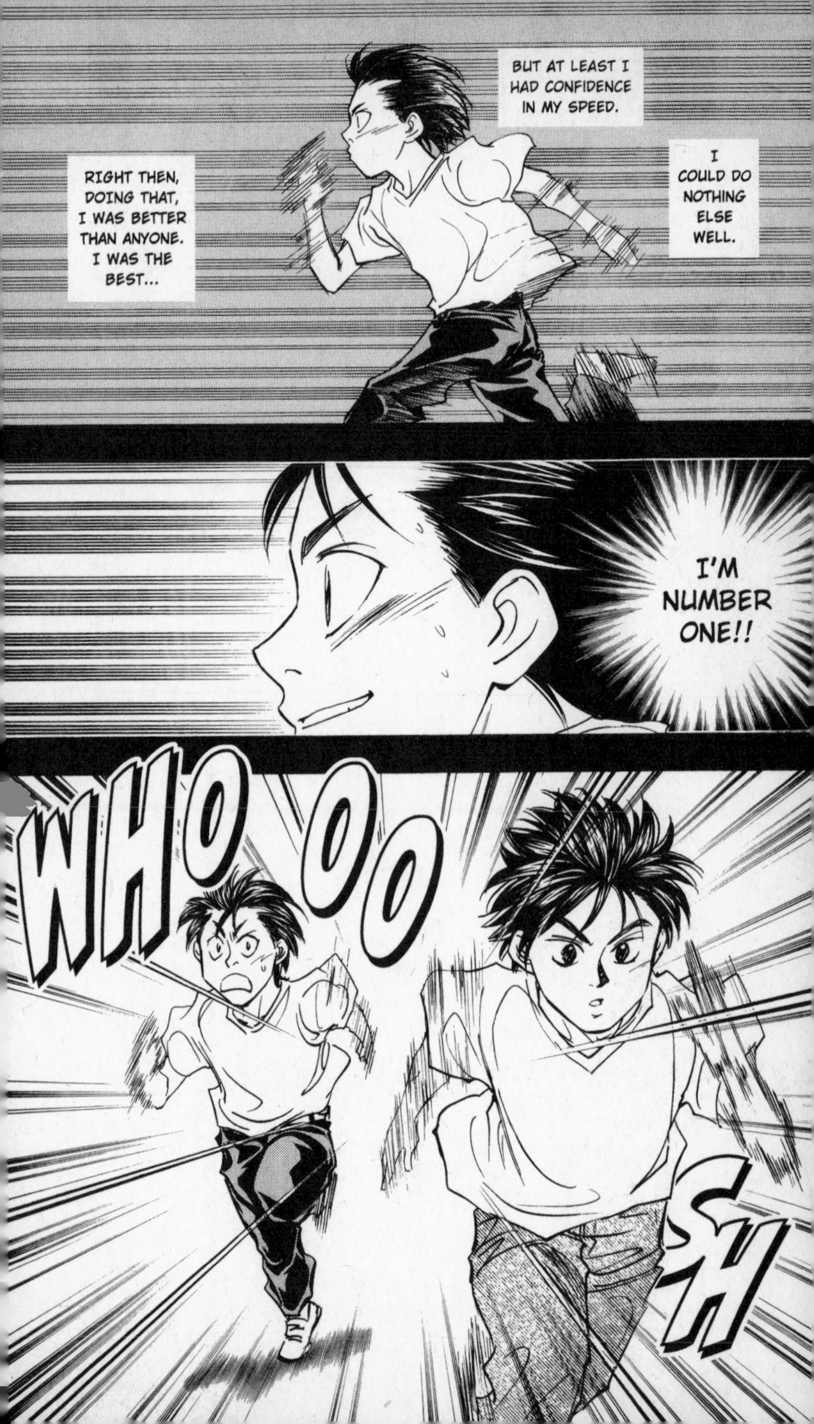
BUT AT LEAST I HAD CONFIDENCE IN MY SPEED.
I COULD DO NOTHING ELSE WELL.
RIGHT THEN, DOING THAT, I WAS BETTER THAN ANYONE. I WAS THE BEST...
I'M NUMBER ONE!!
WHOOOO
SH

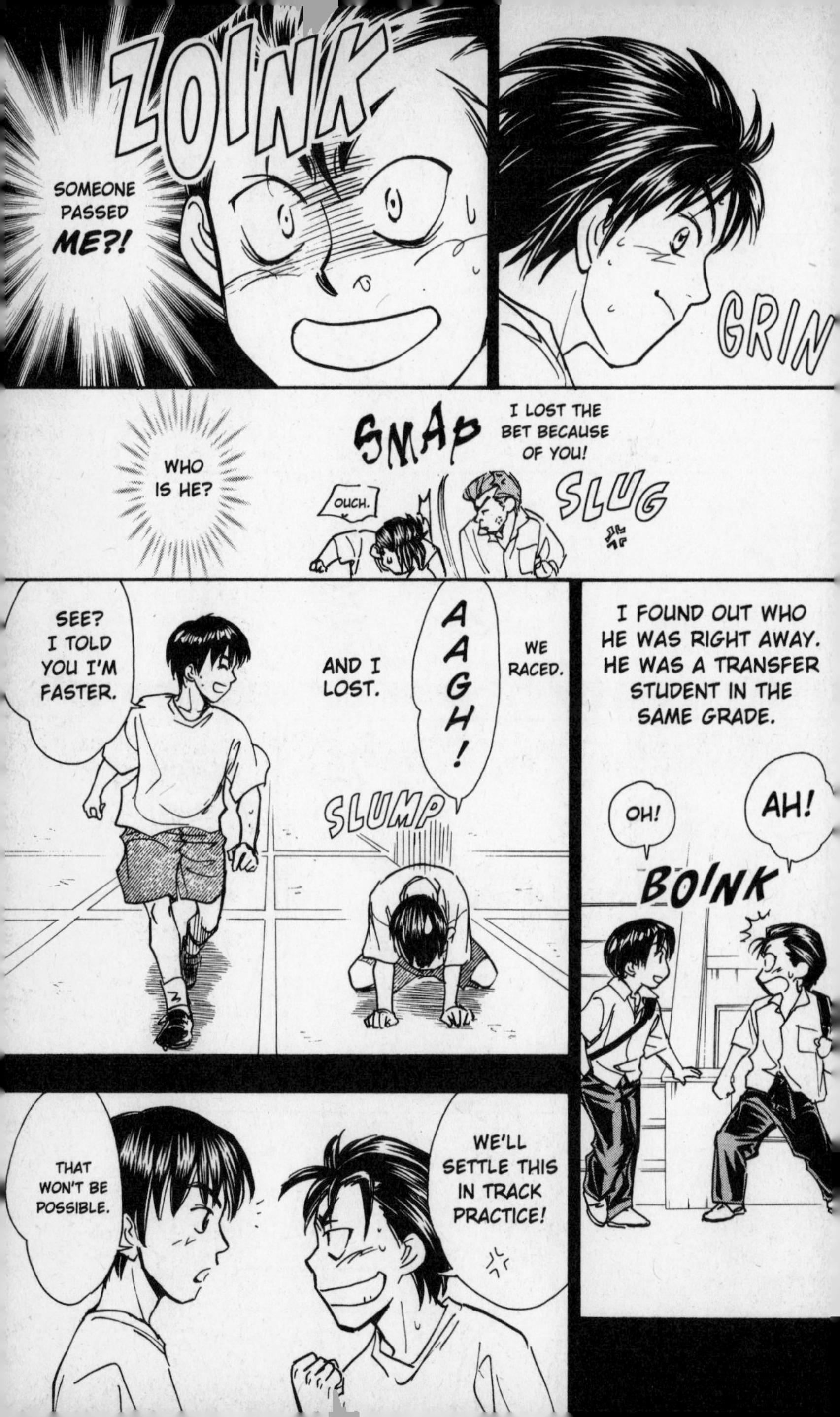
GRIN
ZOINK
SOMEONE PASSED ME?!
I LOST THE BET BECAUSE OF YOU!
SLUG
SMAP
OUCH.
WHO IS HE?
I FOUND OUT WHO HE WAS RIGHT AWAY. HE WAS A TRANSFER STUDENT IN THE SAME GRADE.
AH!
OH!
BOINK
WE RACED.
AAGH!
AND I LOST.
SLUMP
SEE? I TOLD YOU I'M FASTER.
WE'LL SETTLE THIS IN TRACK PRACTICE!
THAT WON'T BE POSSIBLE.

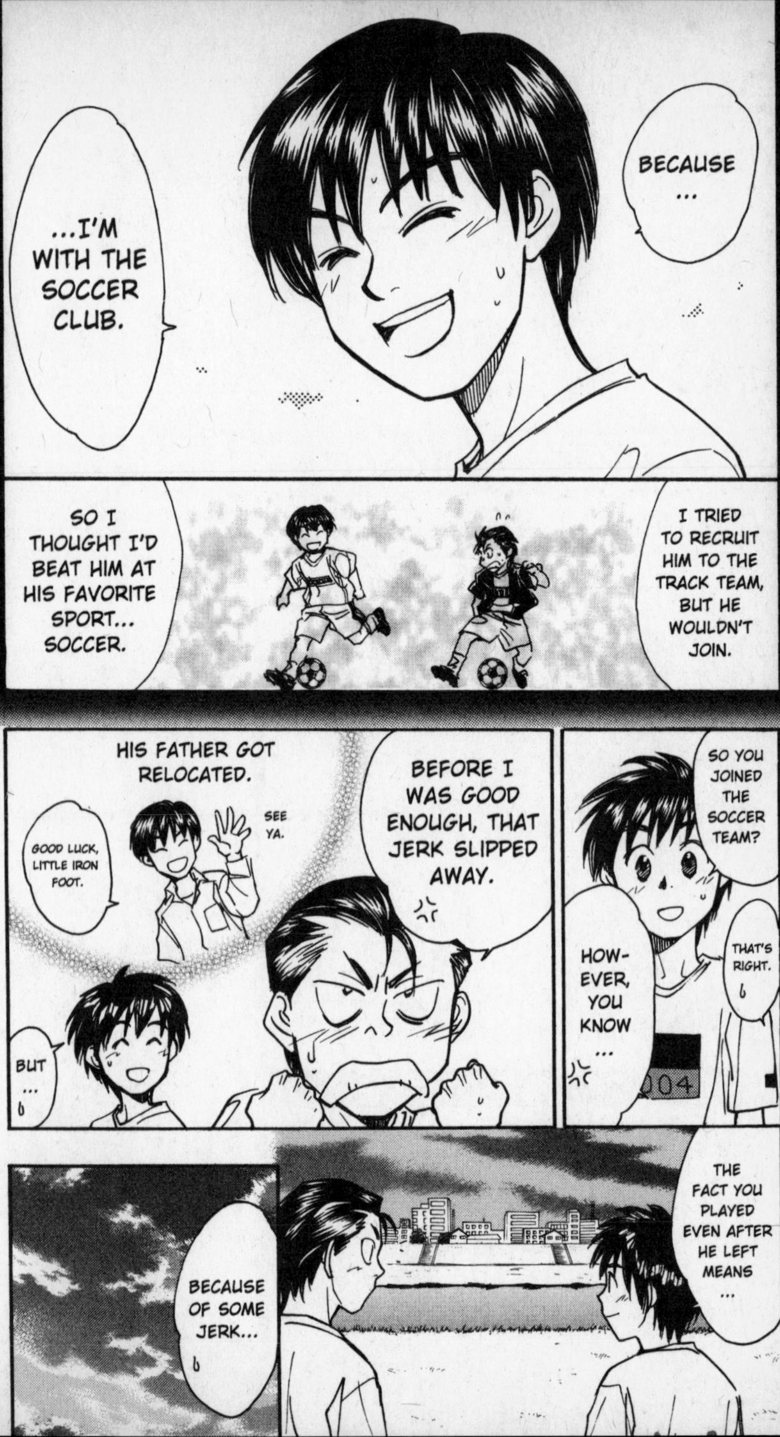
BECAUSE ...
...I'M WITH THE SOCCER CLUB.
I TRIED TO RECRUIT HIM TO THE TRACK TEAM, BUT HE WOULDN'T JOIN.
SO I THOUGHT I'D BEAT HIM AT HIS FAVORITE SPORT... SOCCER.
SO YOU JOINED THE SOCCER TEAM?
THAT'S RIGHT.
HOW-EVER, YOU KNOW ...
BEFORE I WAS GOOD ENOUGH, THAT JERK SLIPPED AWAY.
HIS FATHER GOT RELOCATED.
SEE YA.
GOOD LUCK, LITTLE IRON FOOT.
BUT ...
THE FACT YOU PLAYED EVEN AFTER HE LEFT MEANS ...
BECAUSE OF SOME JERK...

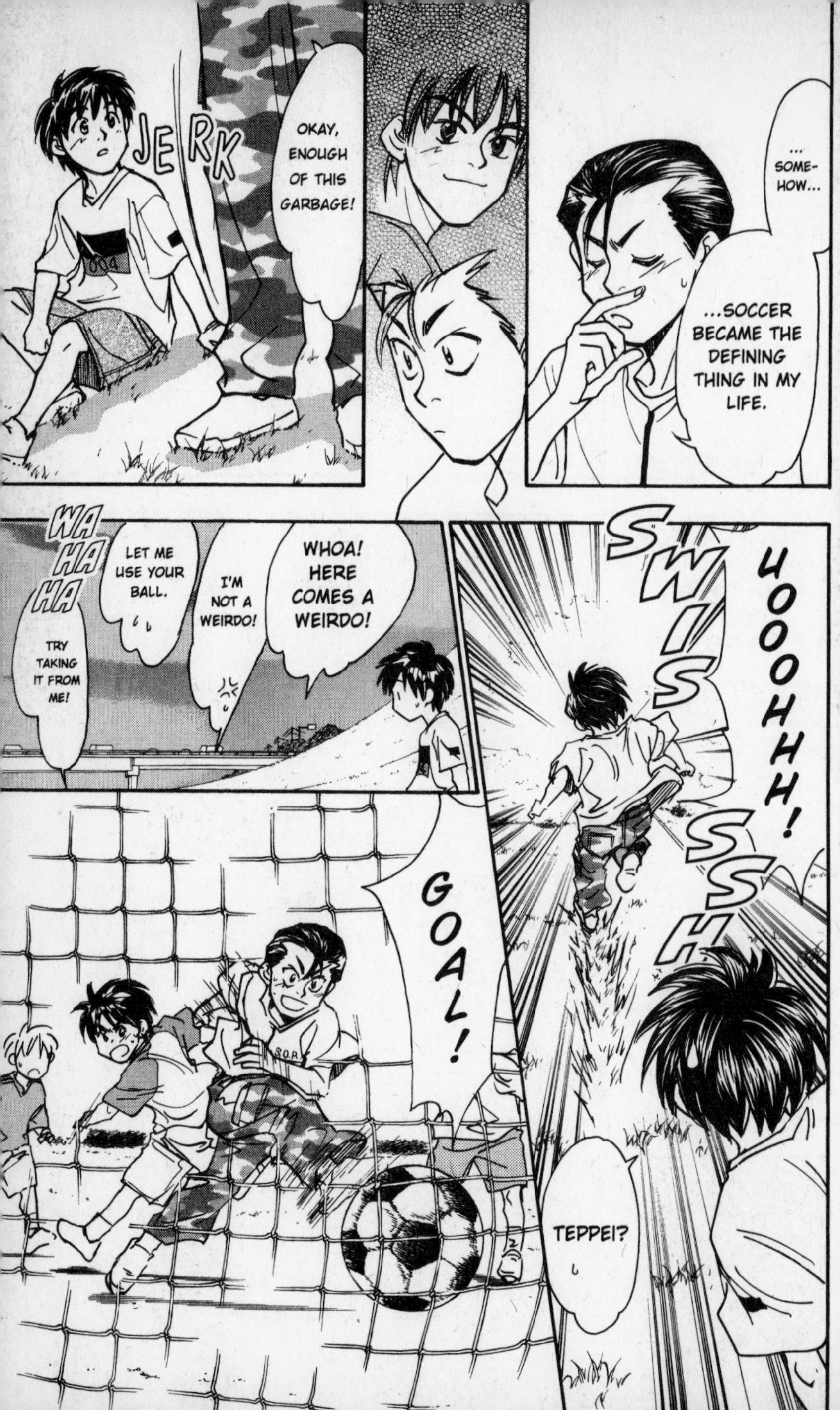
... SOME-HOW...
...SOCCER BECAME THE DEFINING THING IN MY LIFE.
OKAY, ENOUGH OF THIS GARBAGE!
JERK
UOOOHHH!
SWISSSH
TEPPEI?
WHOA! HERE COMES A WEIRDO!
I'M NOT A WEIRDO!
LET ME USE YOUR BALL.
WA HA HA HA
TRY TAKING IT FROM ME!
GOAL!

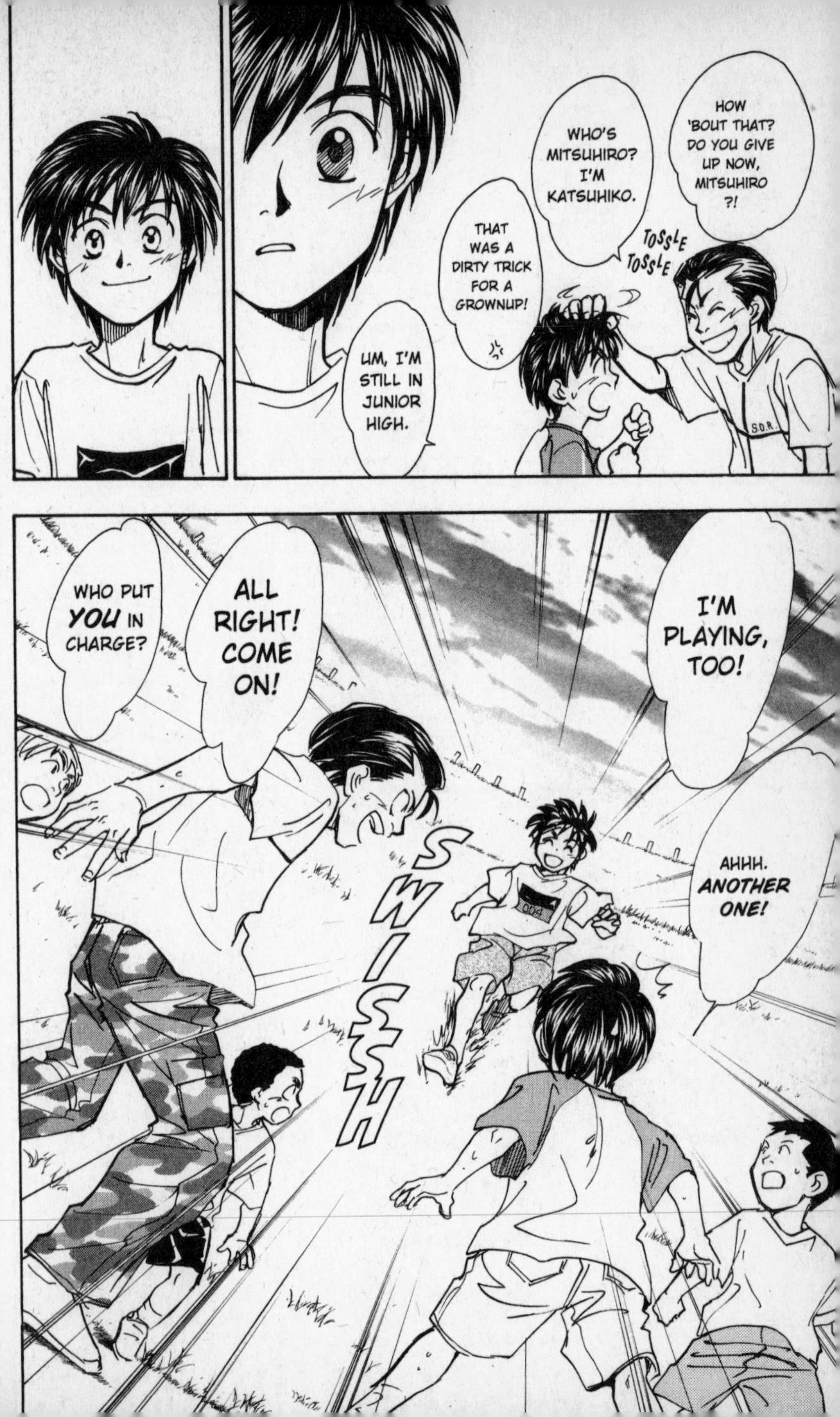
HOW 'BOUT THAT? DO YOU GIVE UP NOW, MITSUHIRO ?!
WHO'S MITSUHIRO? I'M KATSUHIKO.
TOSSLE TOSSLE
THAT WAS A DIRTY TRICK FOR A GROWNUP!
UM, I'M STILL IN JUNIOR HIGH.
I'M PLAYING, TOO!
ALL RIGHT! COME ON!
WHO PUT **YOU** IN CHARGE?
AHHH. **ANOTHER ONE!**
SWISH

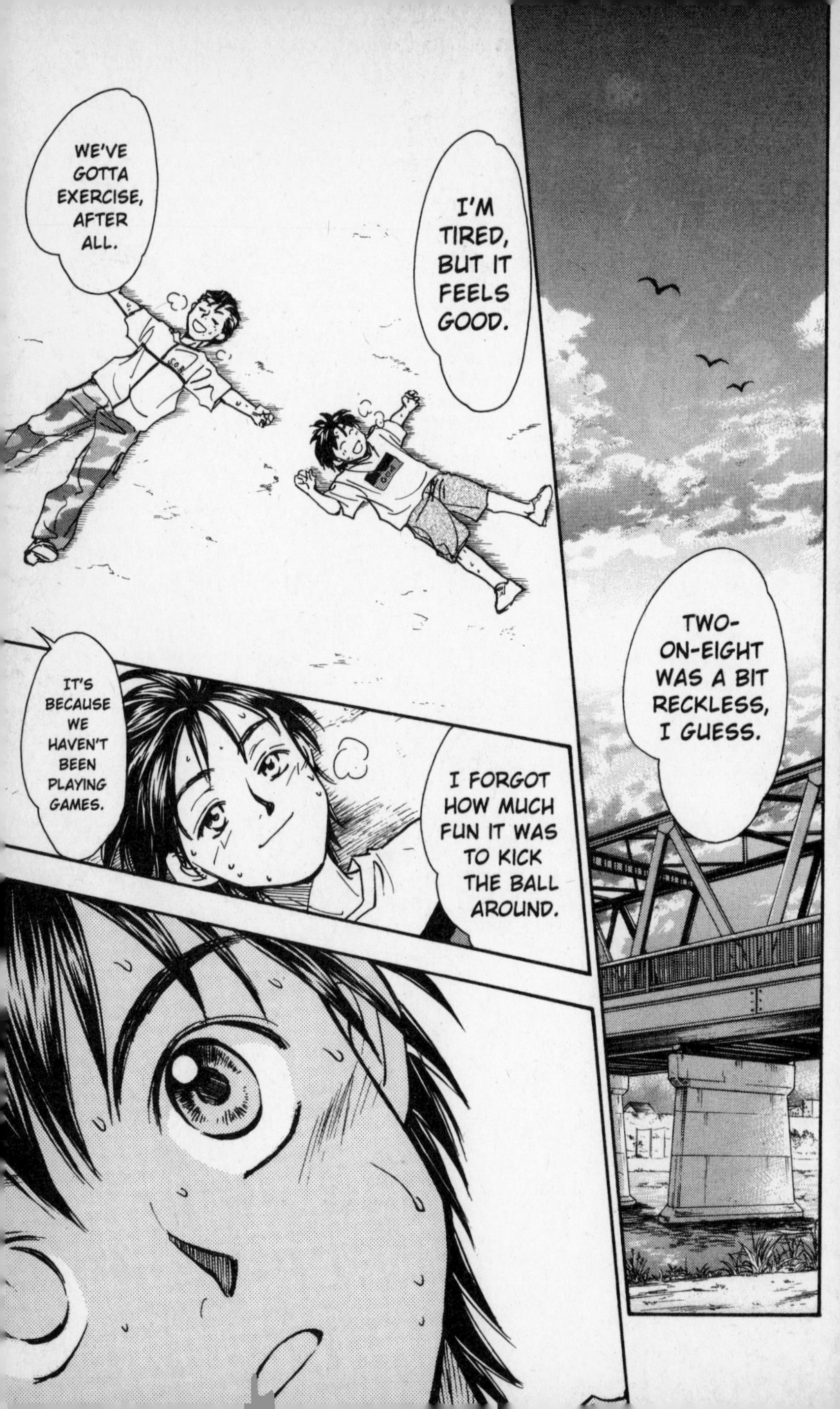
TWO-ON-EIGHT WAS A BIT RECKLESS, I GUESS.
I'M TIRED, BUT IT FEELS GOOD.
WE'VE GOTTA EXERCISE, AFTER ALL.
I FORGOT HOW MUCH FUN IT WAS TO KICK THE BALL AROUND.
IT'S BECAUSE WE HAVEN'T BEEN PLAYING GAMES.

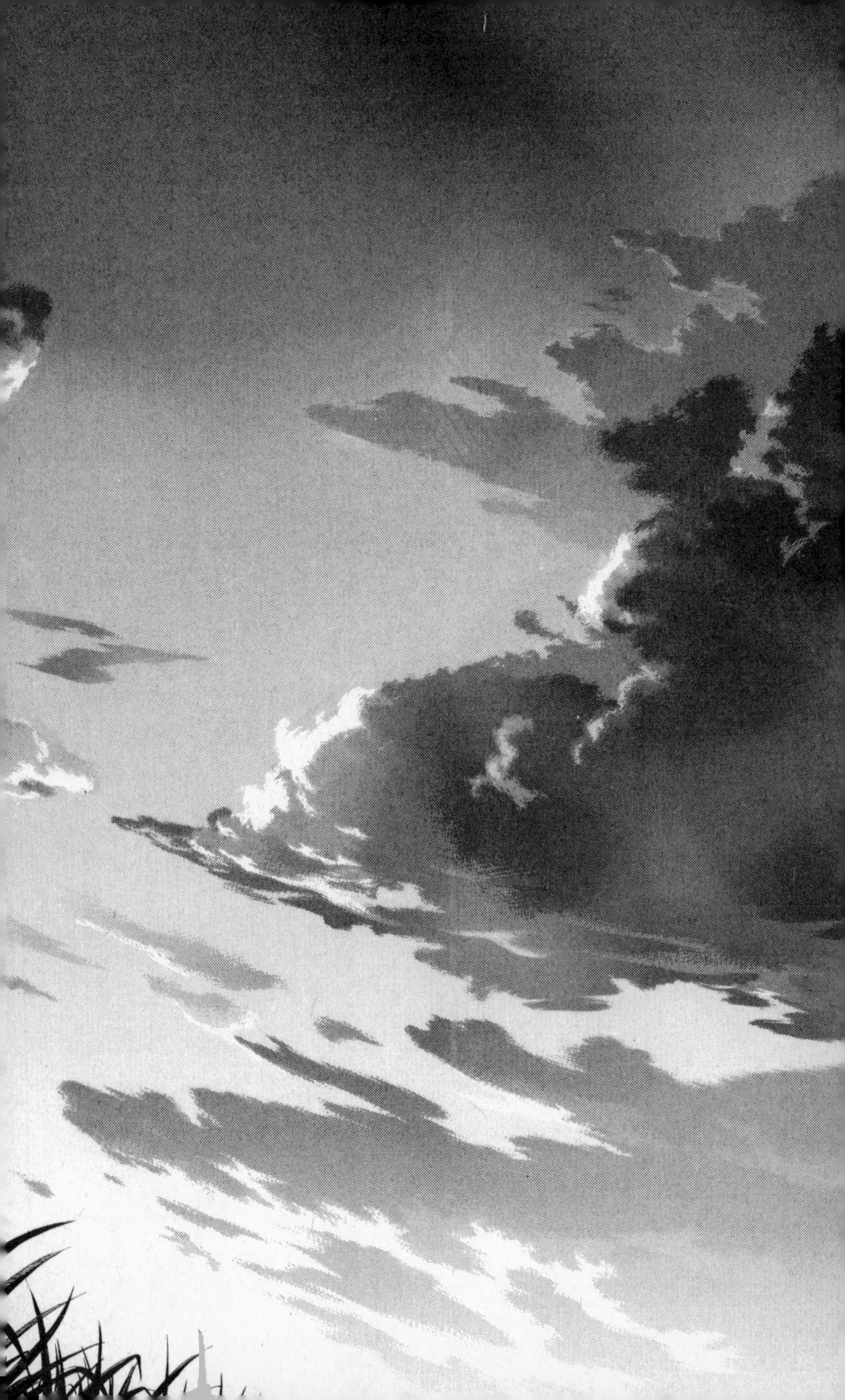

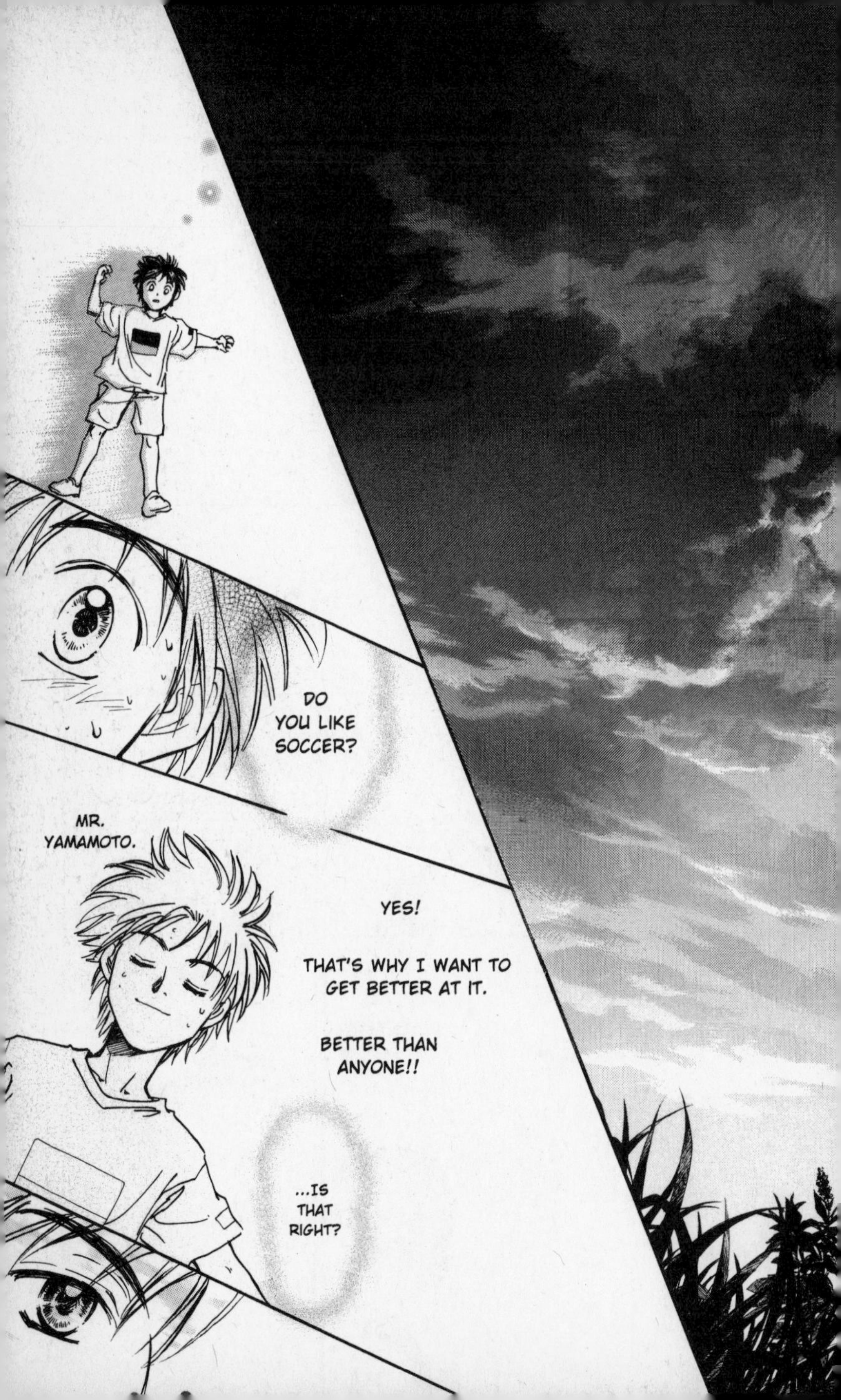
DO YOU LIKE SOCCER?
MR. YAMAMOTO.
YES!
THAT'S WHY I WANT TO GET BETTER AT IT.
BETTER THAN ANYONE!!
...IS THAT RIGHT?

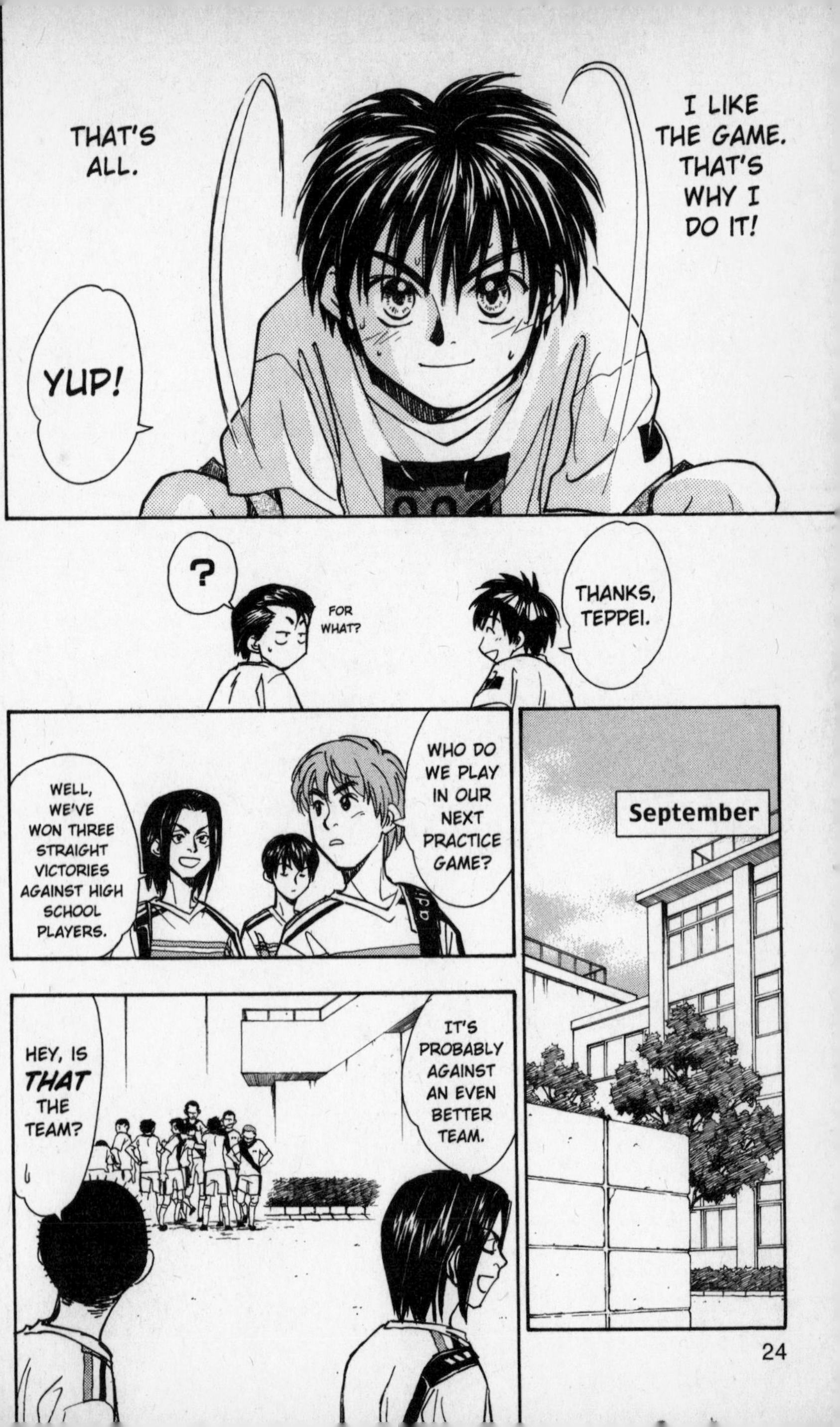
I LIKE THE GAME. THAT'S WHY I DO IT!
THAT'S ALL.
YUP!
THANKS, TEPPEI.
?
FOR WHAT?
September
WHO DO WE PLAY IN OUR NEXT PRACTICE GAME?
WELL, WE'VE WON THREE STRAIGHT VICTORIES AGAINST HIGH SCHOOL PLAYERS.
IT'S PROBABLY AGAINST AN EVEN BETTER TEAM.
HEY, IS *THAT* THE TEAM?

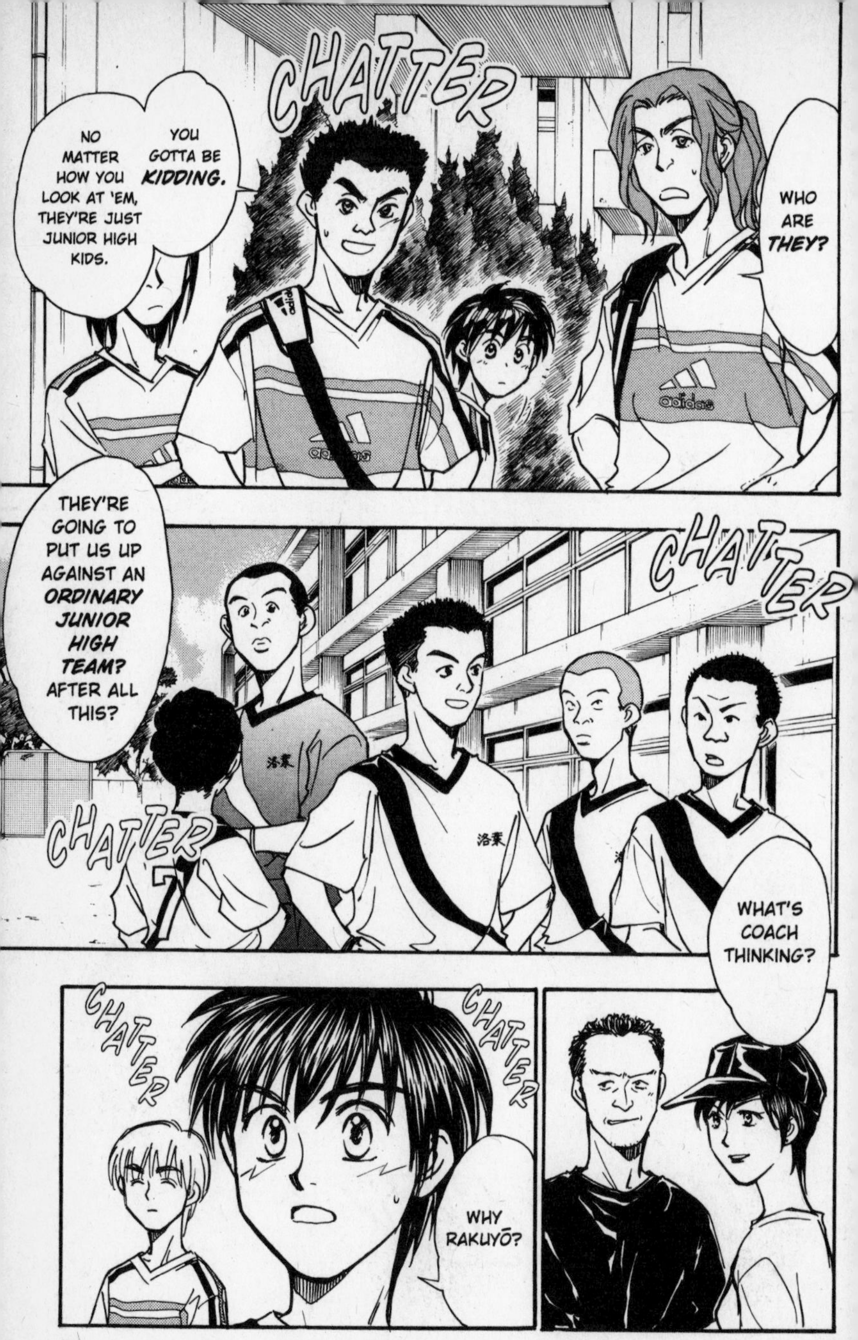
CHATTER
WHO ARE THEY?
YOU GOTTA BE KIDDING.
NO MATTER HOW YOU LOOK AT 'EM, THEY'RE JUST JUNIOR HIGH KIDS.
CHATTER
THEY'RE GOING TO PUT US UP AGAINST AN ORDINARY JUNIOR HIGH TEAM? AFTER ALL THIS?
CHATTER
WHAT'S COACH THINKING?
CHATTER
CHATTER
WHY RAKUYŌ?

WHISTLE!™

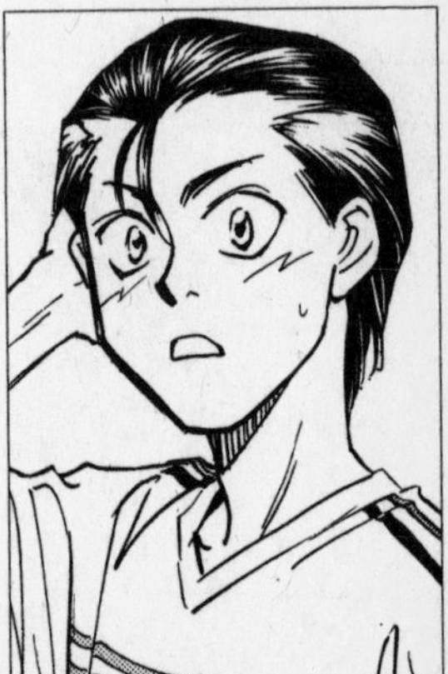

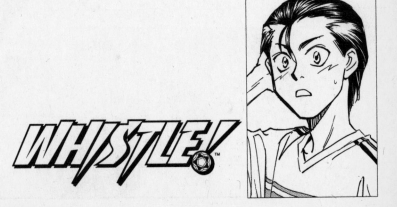

STAGE.136 Dissonant Hearts

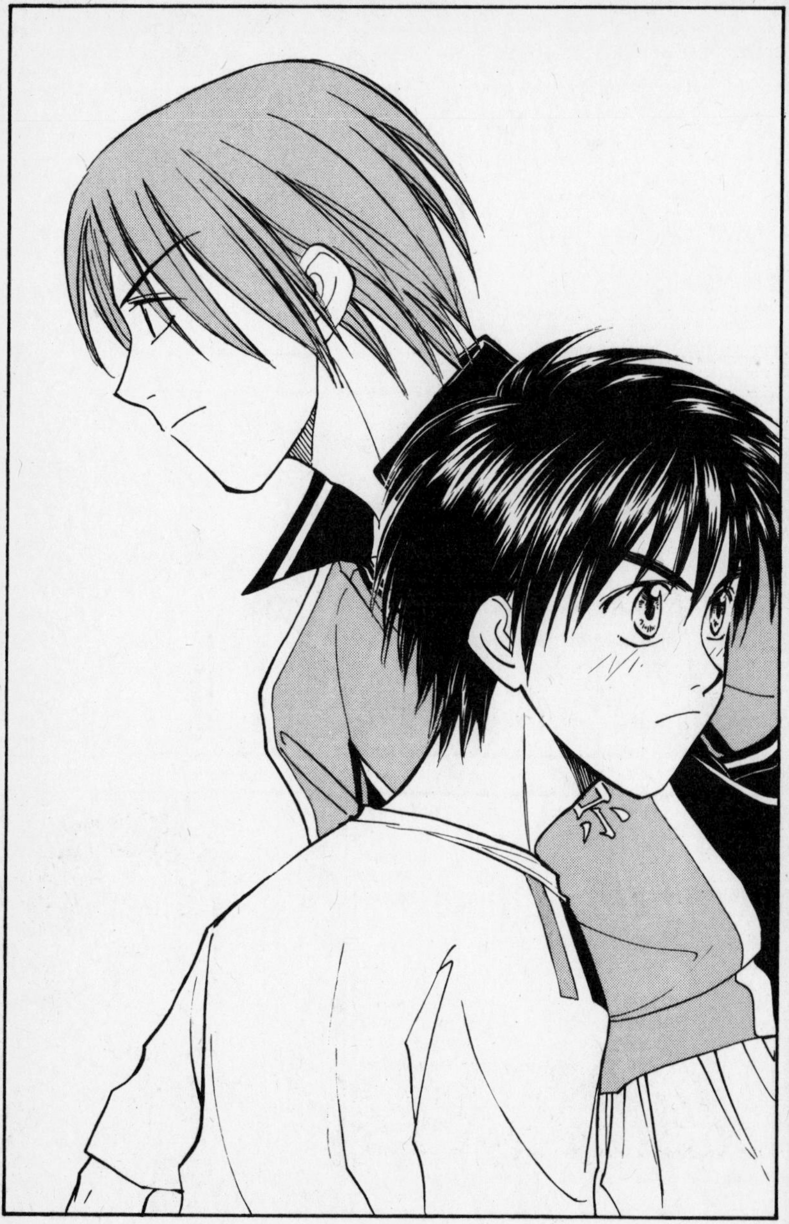

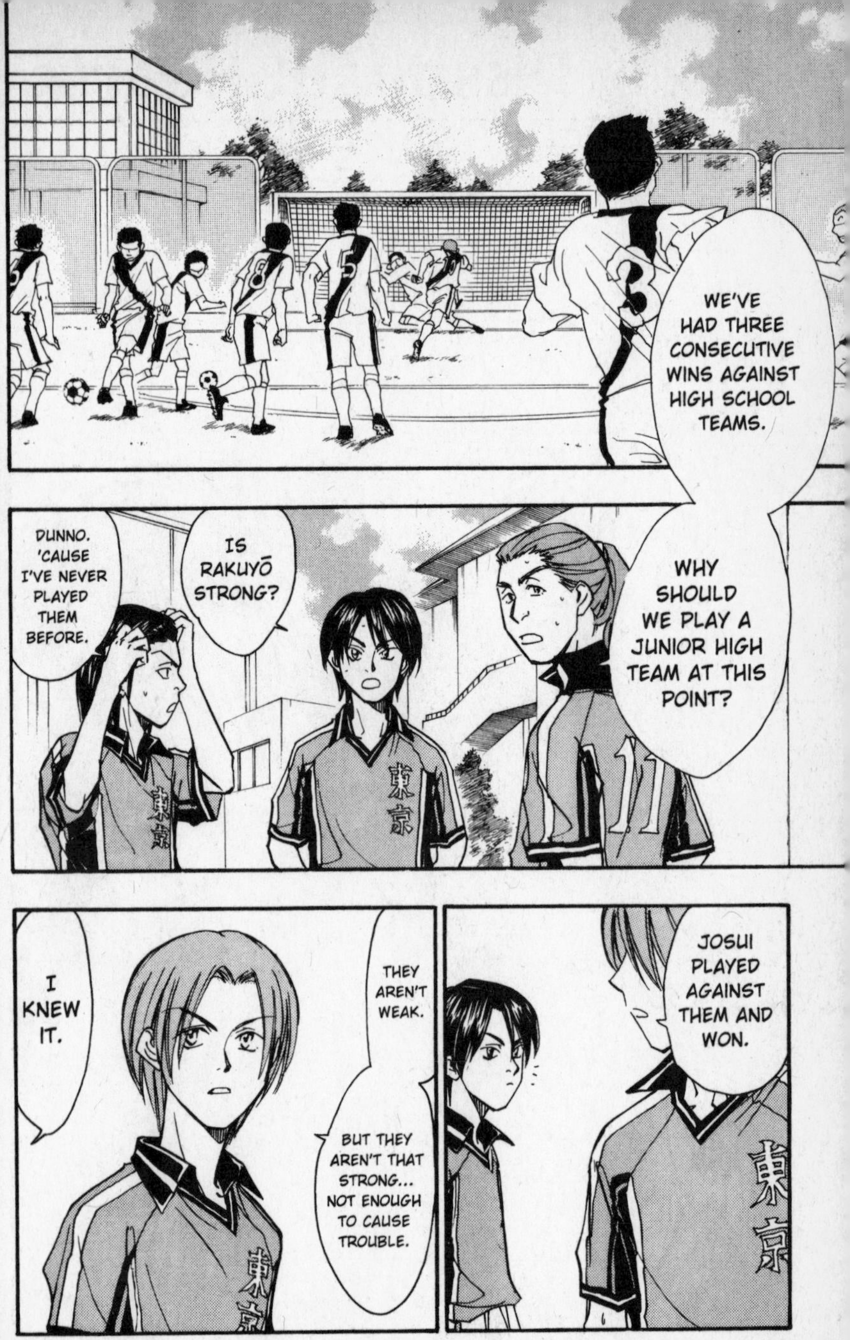
WE'VE HAD THREE CONSECUTIVE WINS AGAINST HIGH SCHOOL TEAMS.
WHY SHOULD WE PLAY A JUNIOR HIGH TEAM AT THIS POINT?
IS RAKUYŌ STRONG?
DUNNO. 'CAUSE I'VE NEVER PLAYED THEM BEFORE.
JOSUI PLAYED AGAINST THEM AND WON.
THEY AREN'T WEAK.
BUT THEY AREN'T THAT STRONG... NOT ENOUGH TO CAUSE TROUBLE.
I KNEW IT.

READ THIS WAY

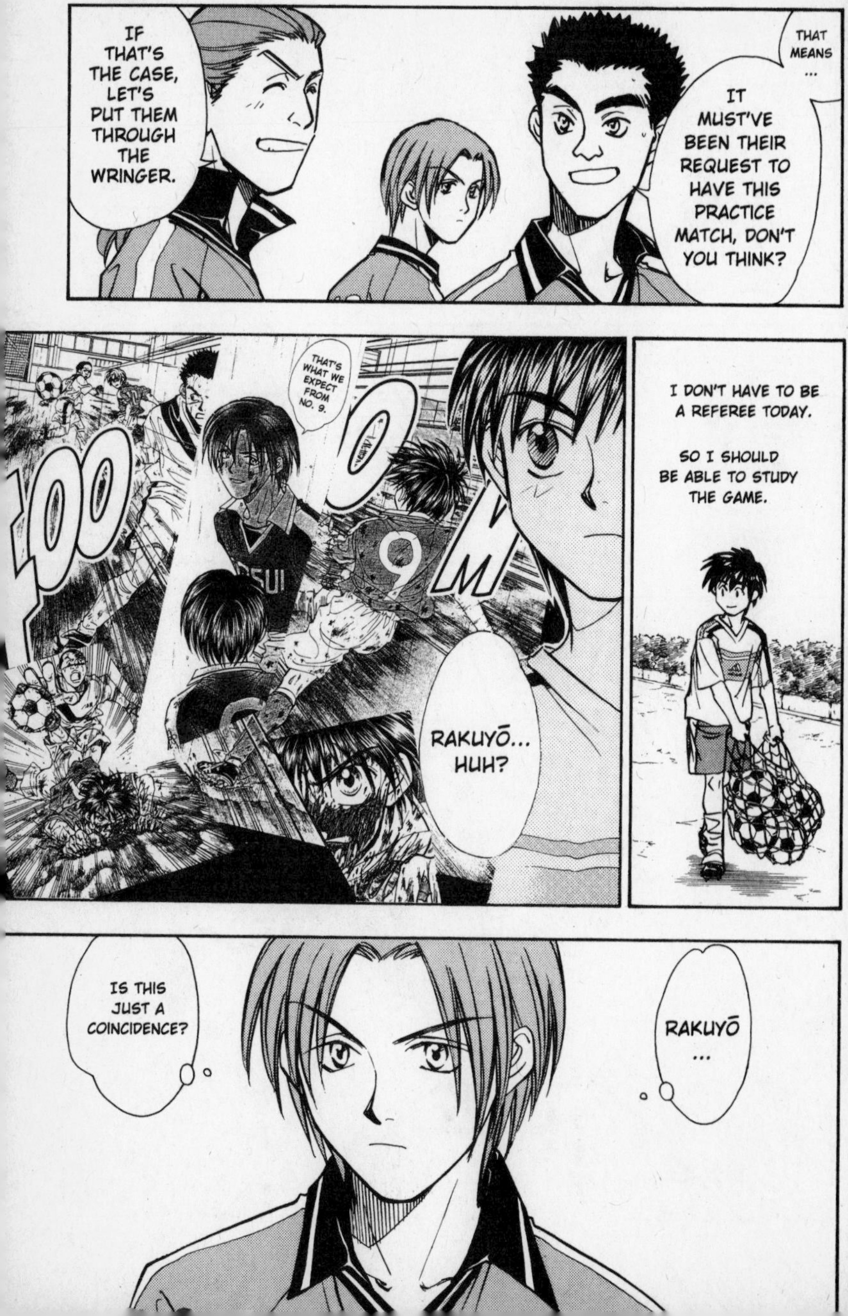
THAT MEANS ...
IT MUST'VE BEEN THEIR REQUEST TO HAVE THIS PRACTICE MATCH, DON'T YOU THINK?
IF THAT'S THE CASE, LET'S PUT THEM THROUGH THE WRINGER.
I DON'T HAVE TO BE A REFEREE TODAY.
SO I SHOULD BE ABLE TO STUDY THE GAME.
RAKUYŌ... HUH?
THAT'S WHAT WE EXPECT FROM NO. 9.
RAKUYŌ ...
IS THIS JUST A COINCIDENCE?

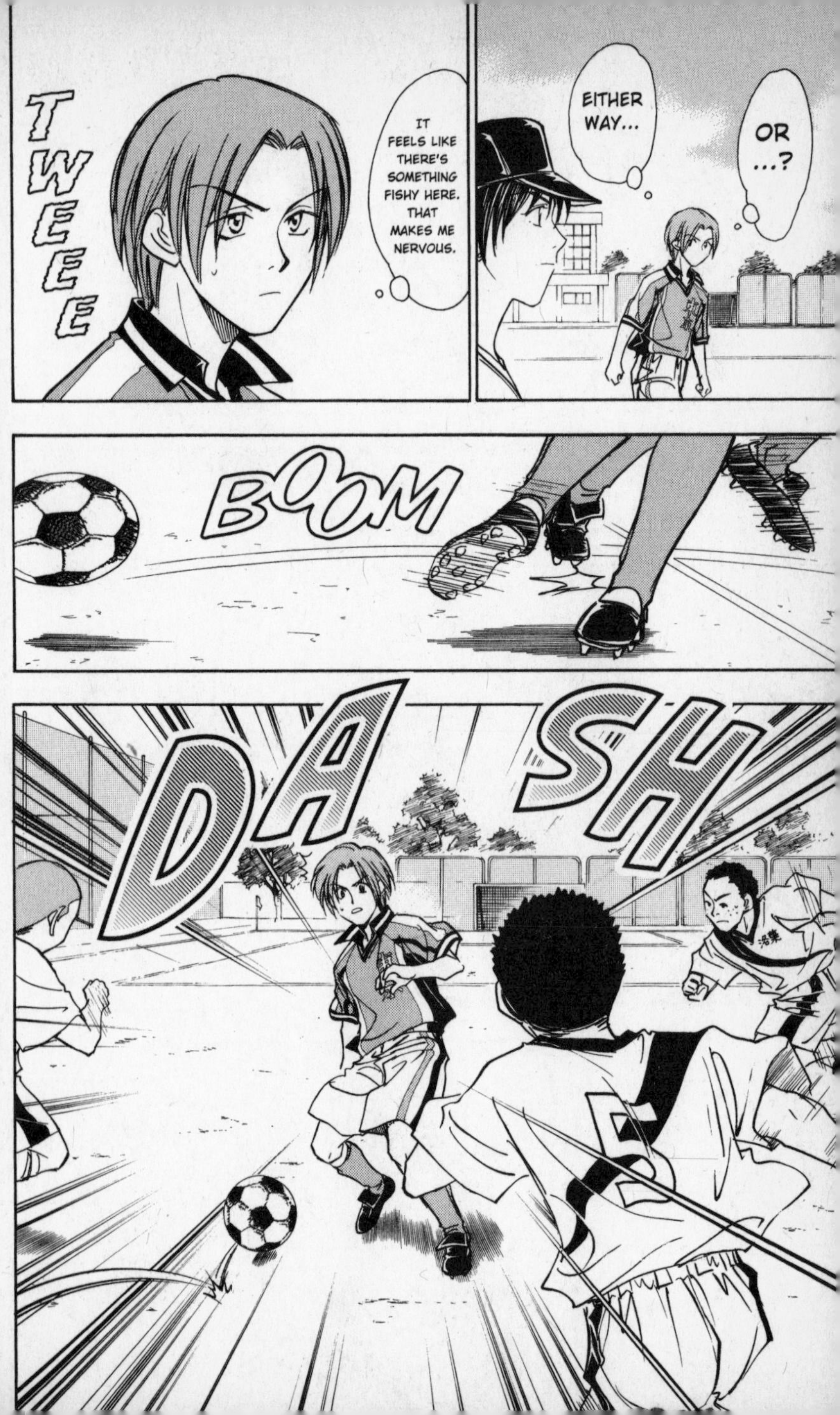
EITHER WAY...
OR ...?
TWEEE
IT FEELS LIKE THERE'S SOMETHING FISHY HERE. THAT MAKES ME NERVOUS.
BOOM
DASH

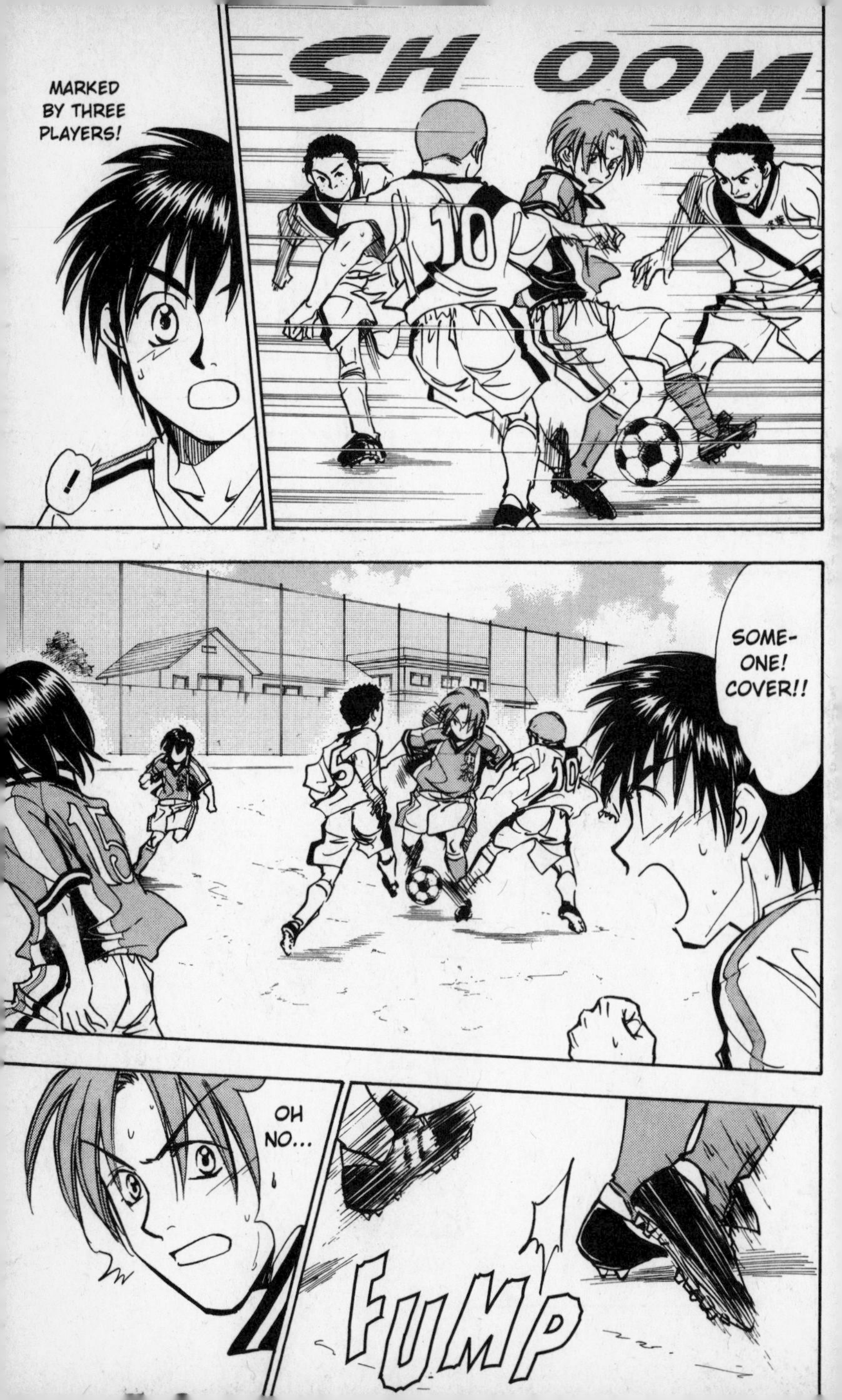
SH OOM
MARKED BY THREE PLAYERS!
!
SOME-ONE! COVER!!
FUMP
OH NO...

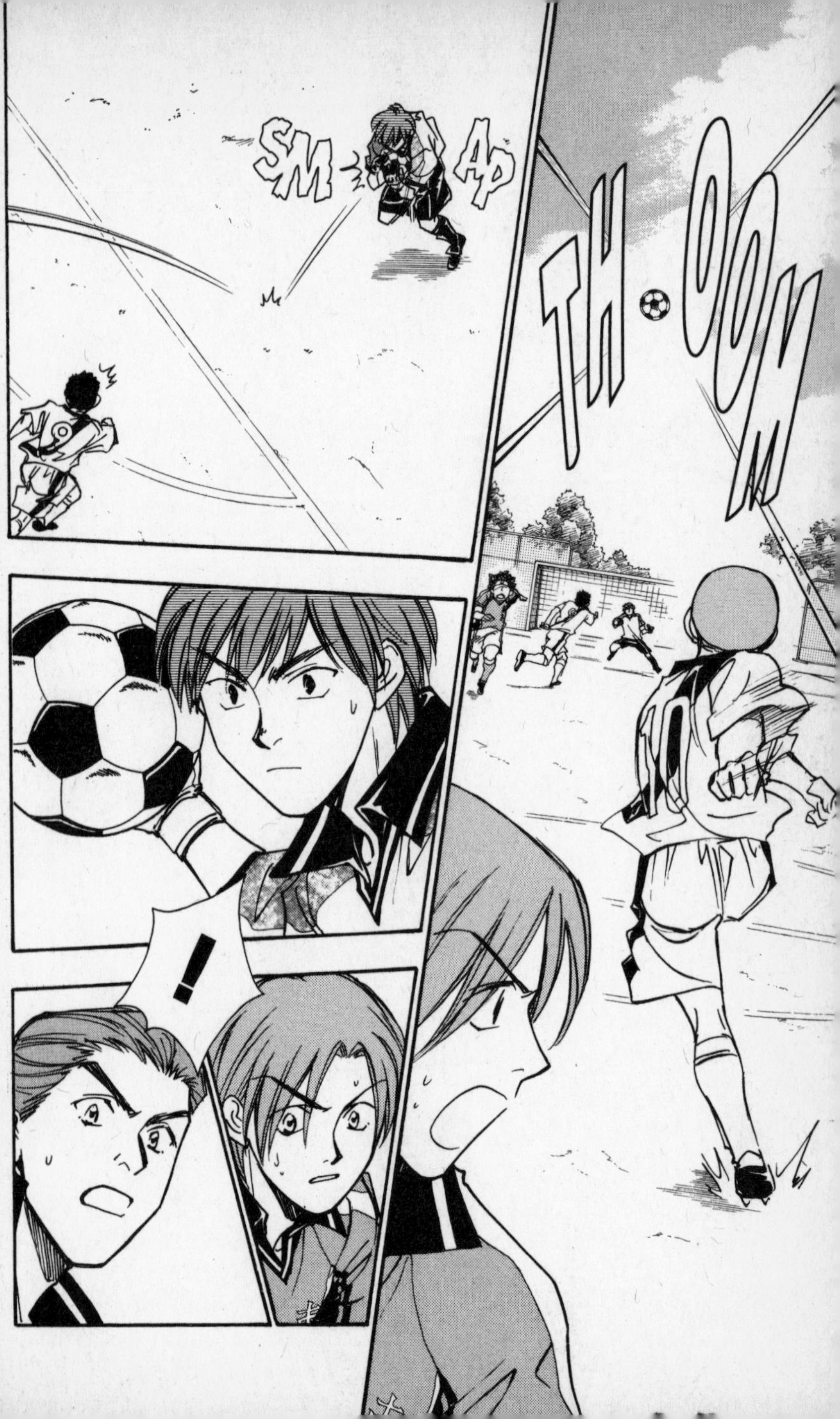
TH-OOOM
SM-AP
!

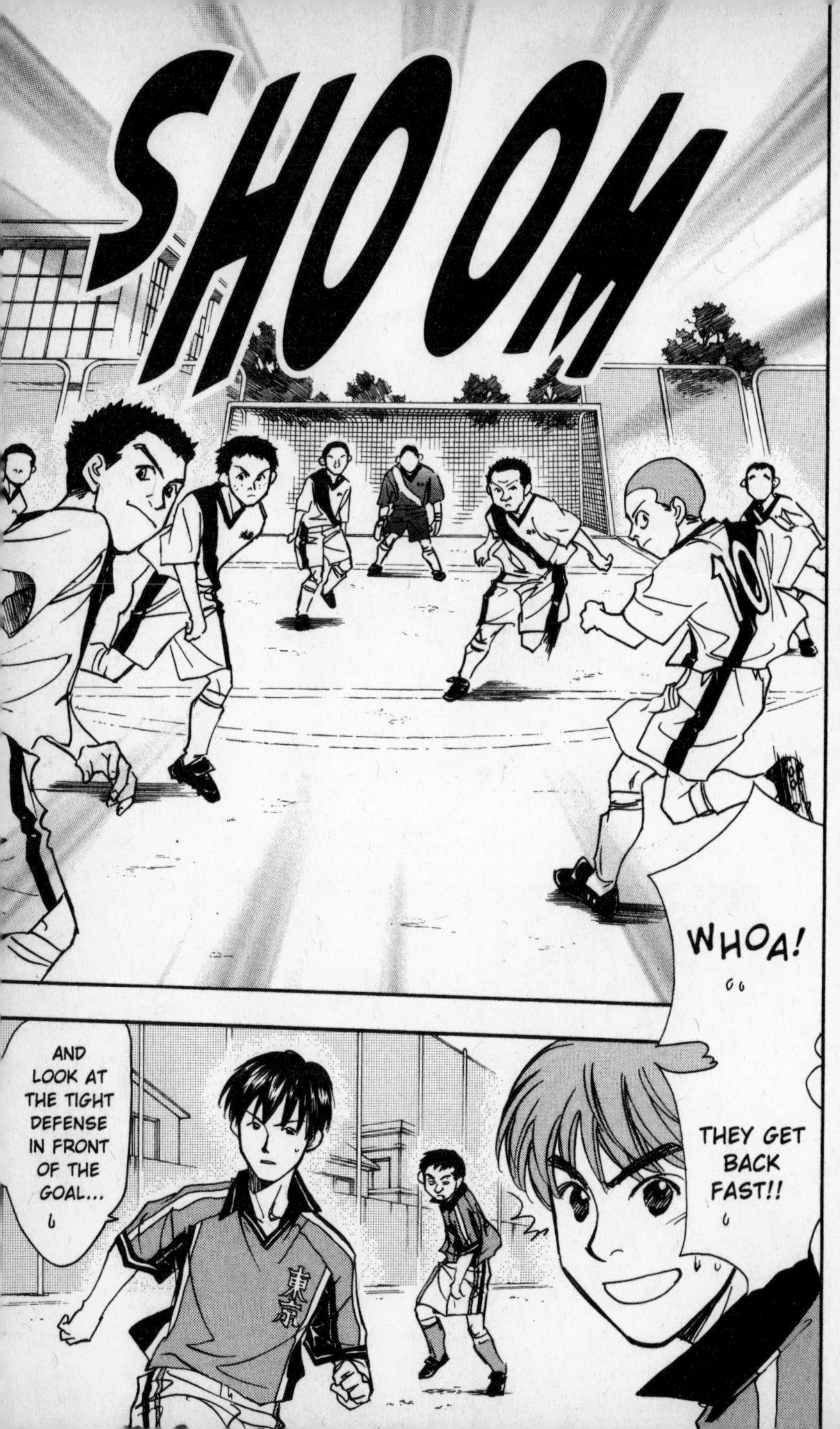
SHOOM
WHOA!
THEY GET BACK FAST!!
AND LOOK AT THE TIGHT DEFENSE IN FRONT OF THE GOAL...

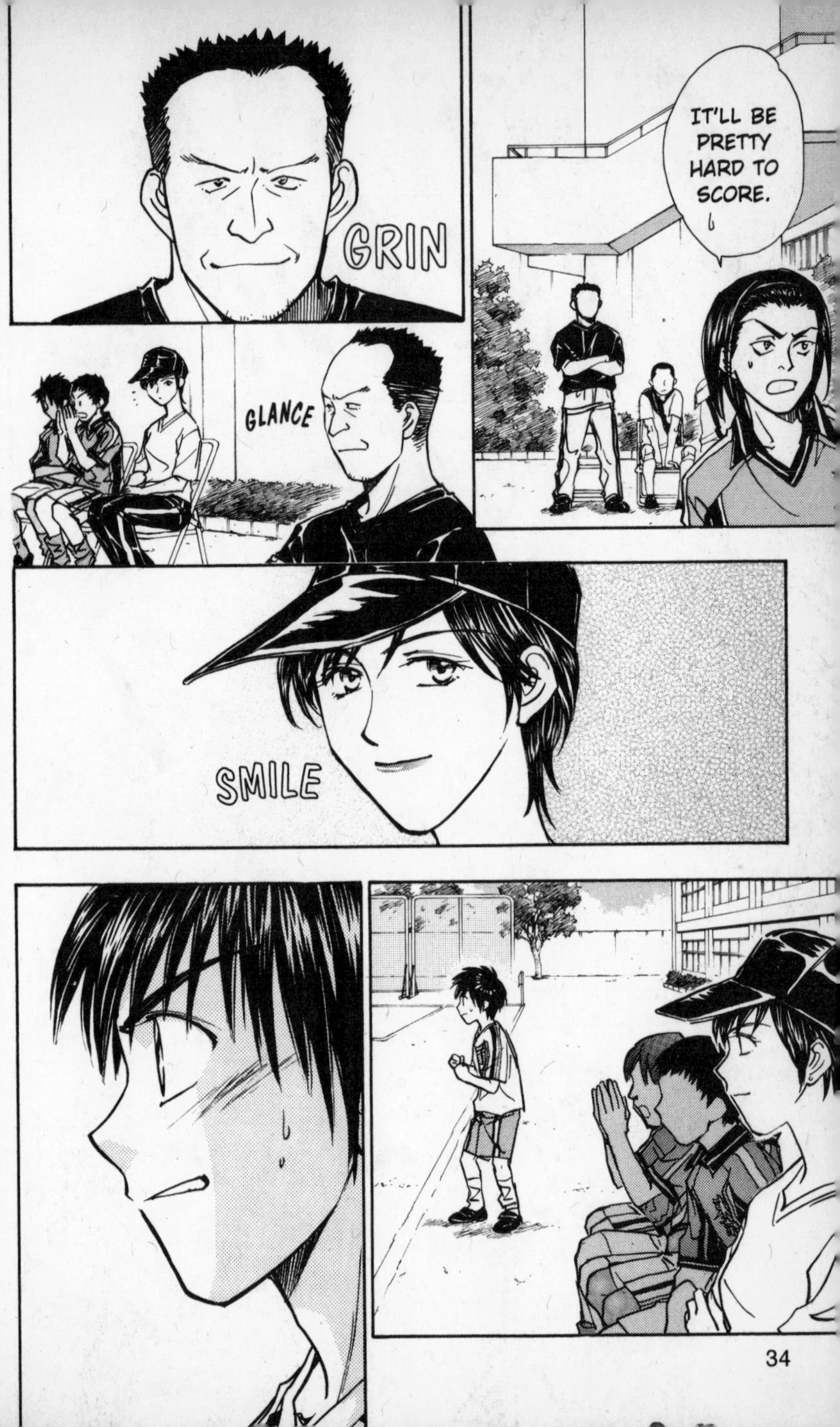
IT'LL BE PRETTY HARD TO SCORE.
GRIN
GLANCE
SMILE

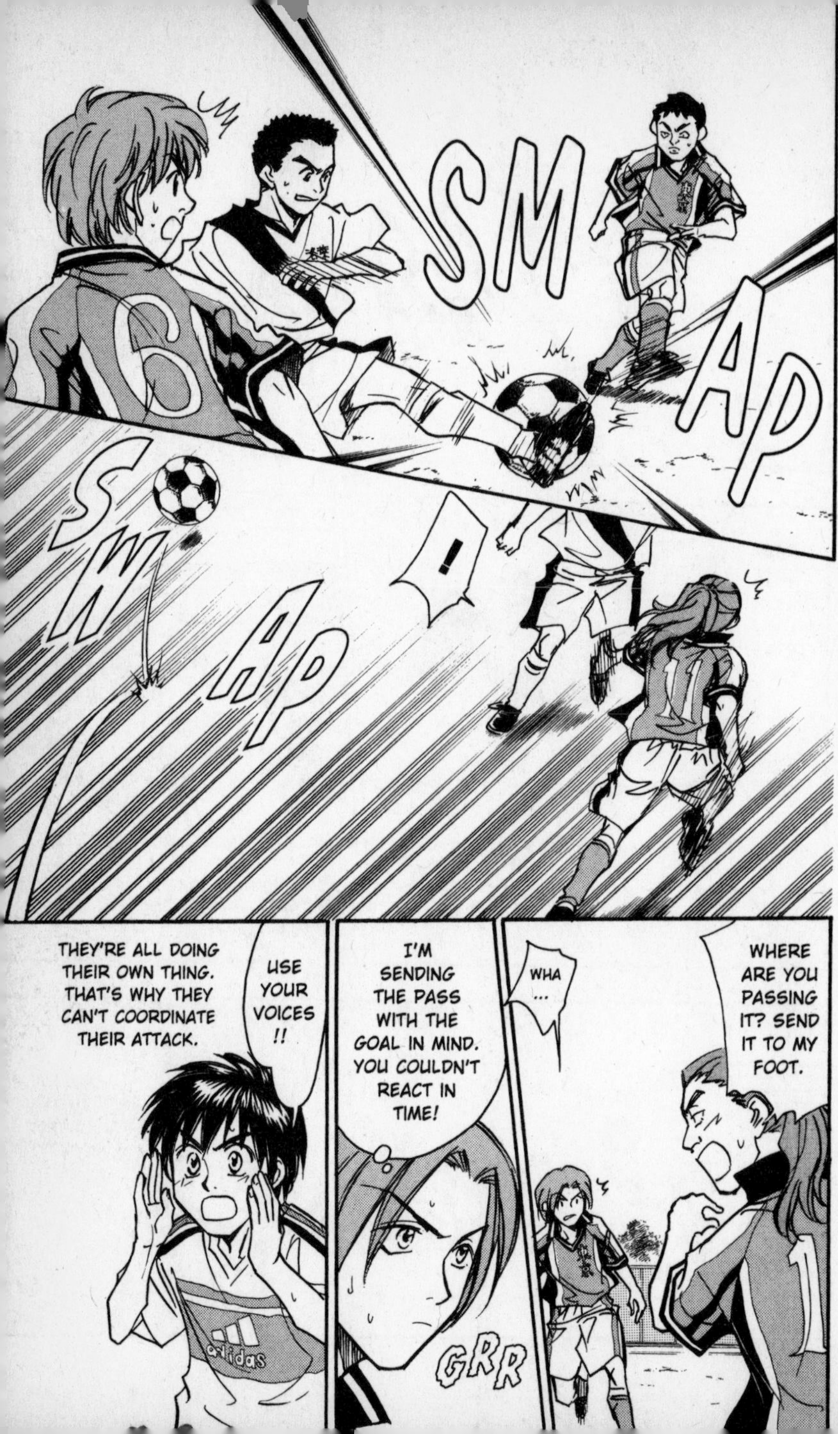
SMAP
SWAP
!
WHERE ARE YOU PASSING IT? SEND IT TO MY FOOT.
WHA ...
I'M SENDING THE PASS WITH THE GOAL IN MIND. YOU COULDN'T REACT IN TIME!
GRR
USE YOUR VOICES !!
THEY'RE ALL DOING THEIR OWN THING. THAT'S WHY THEY CAN'T COORDINATE THEIR ATTACK.
adidas

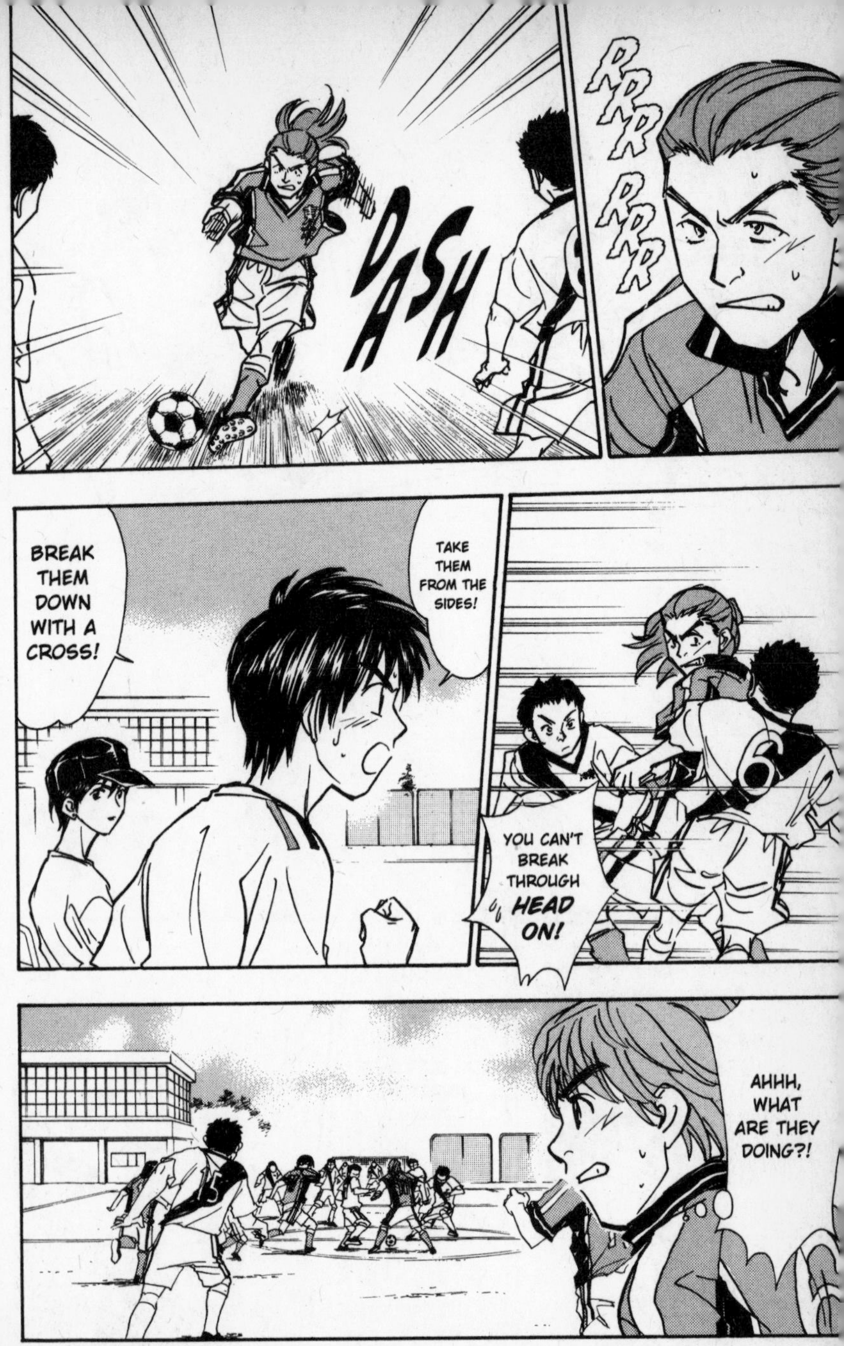
RRRRRR
DASH
YOU CAN'T BREAK THROUGH HEAD ON!
TAKE THEM FROM THE SIDES!
BREAK THEM DOWN WITH A CROSS!
AHHH, WHAT ARE THEY DOING?!

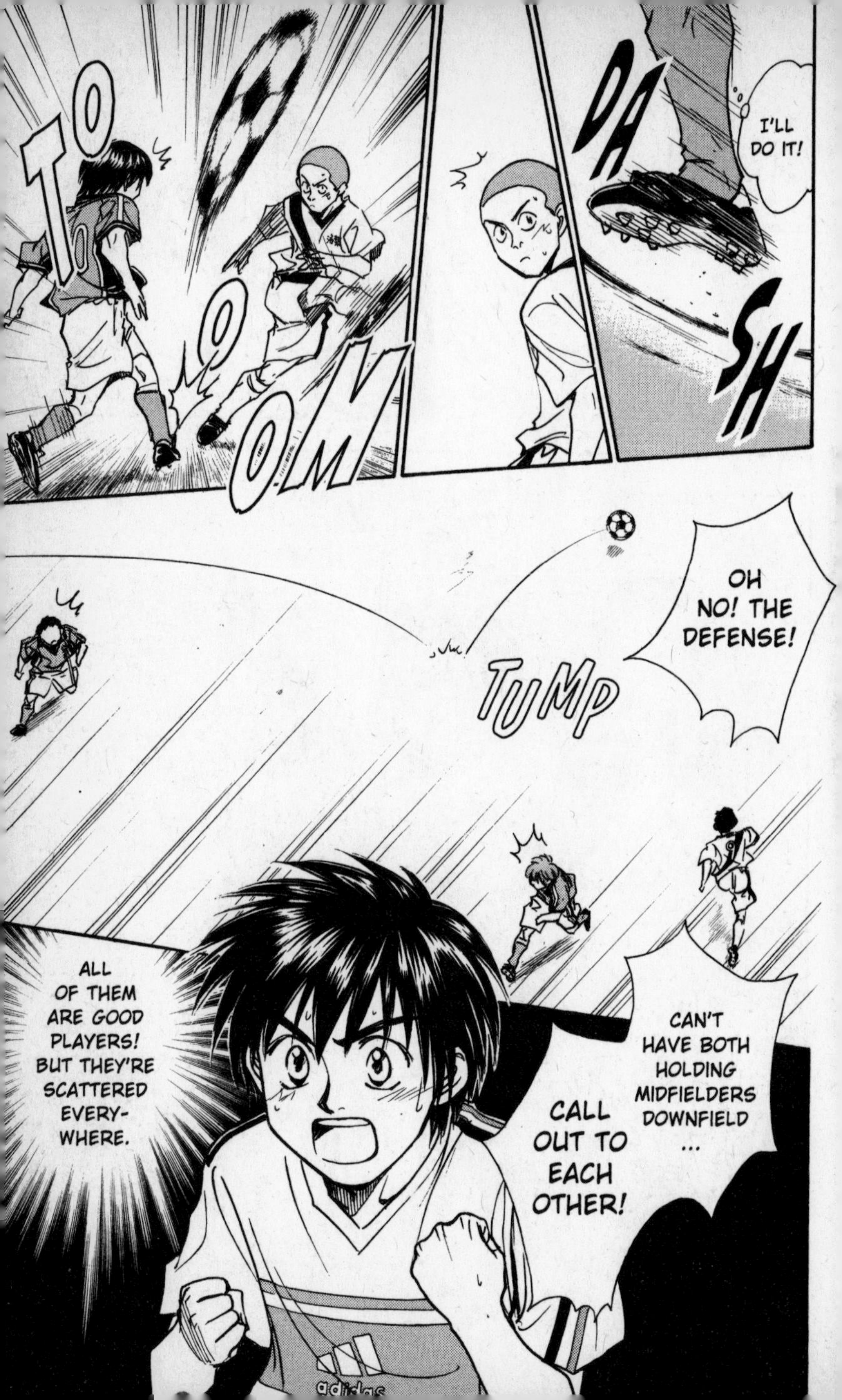
DA
I'LL DO IT!
SH
TOOOM
OH NO! THE DEFENSE!
TUMP
CAN'T HAVE BOTH HOLDING MIDFIELDERS DOWNFIELD ...
CALL OUT TO EACH OTHER!
ALL OF THEM ARE GOOD PLAYERS! BUT THEY'RE SCATTERED EVERY-WHERE.

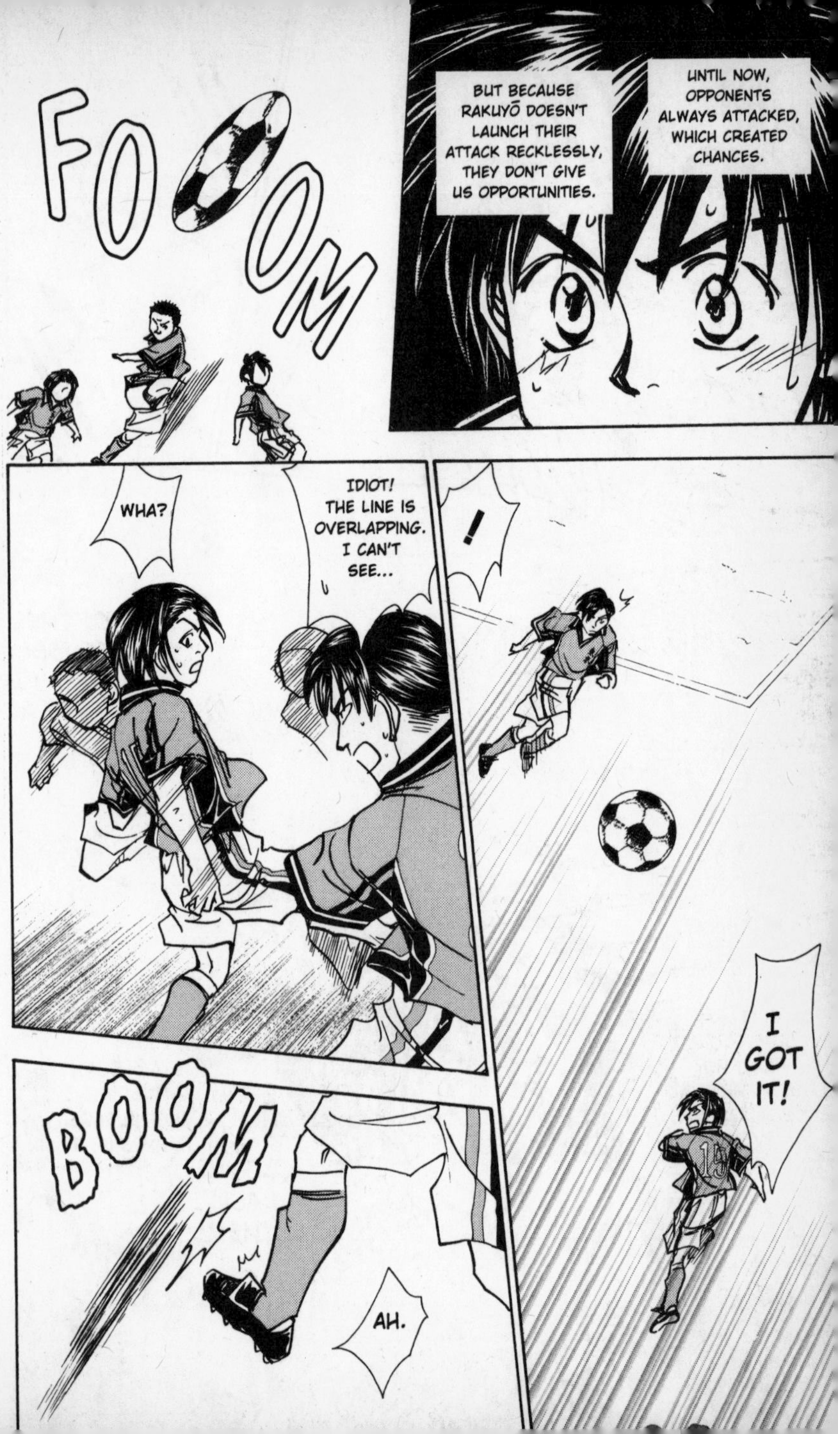

UNTIL NOW, OPPONENTS ALWAYS ATTACKED, WHICH CREATED CHANCES.
BUT BECAUSE RAKUYŌ DOESN'T LAUNCH THEIR ATTACK RECKLESSLY, THEY DON'T GIVE US OPPORTUNITIES.
FOOOM
!
I GOT IT!
IDIOT! THE LINE IS OVERLAPPING. I CAN'T SEE...
WHA?
BOOM
AH.

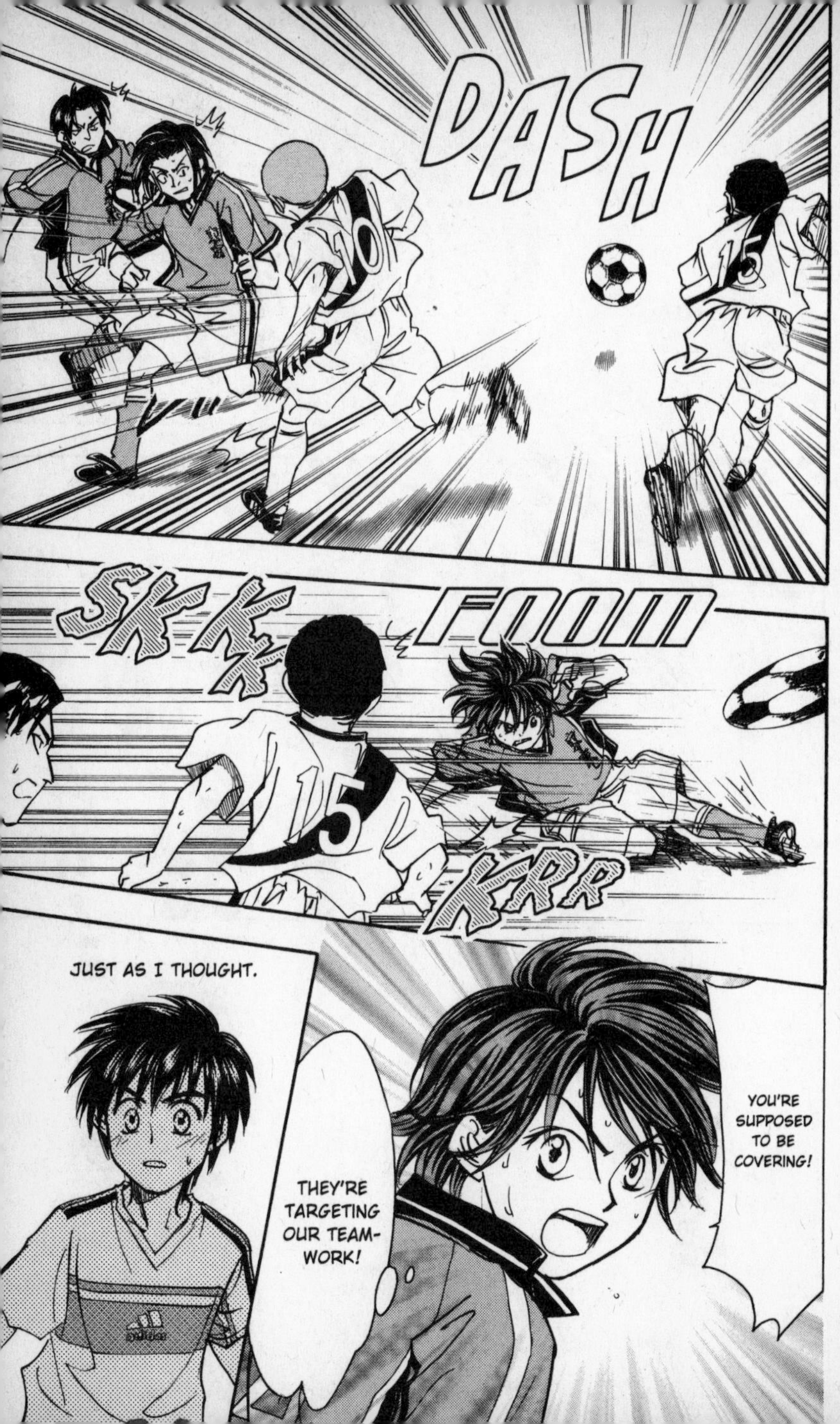
DASH
FOOM
SKK
KRR
YOU'RE SUPPOSED TO BE COVERING!
THEY'RE TARGETING OUR TEAM-WORK!
JUST AS I THOUGHT.

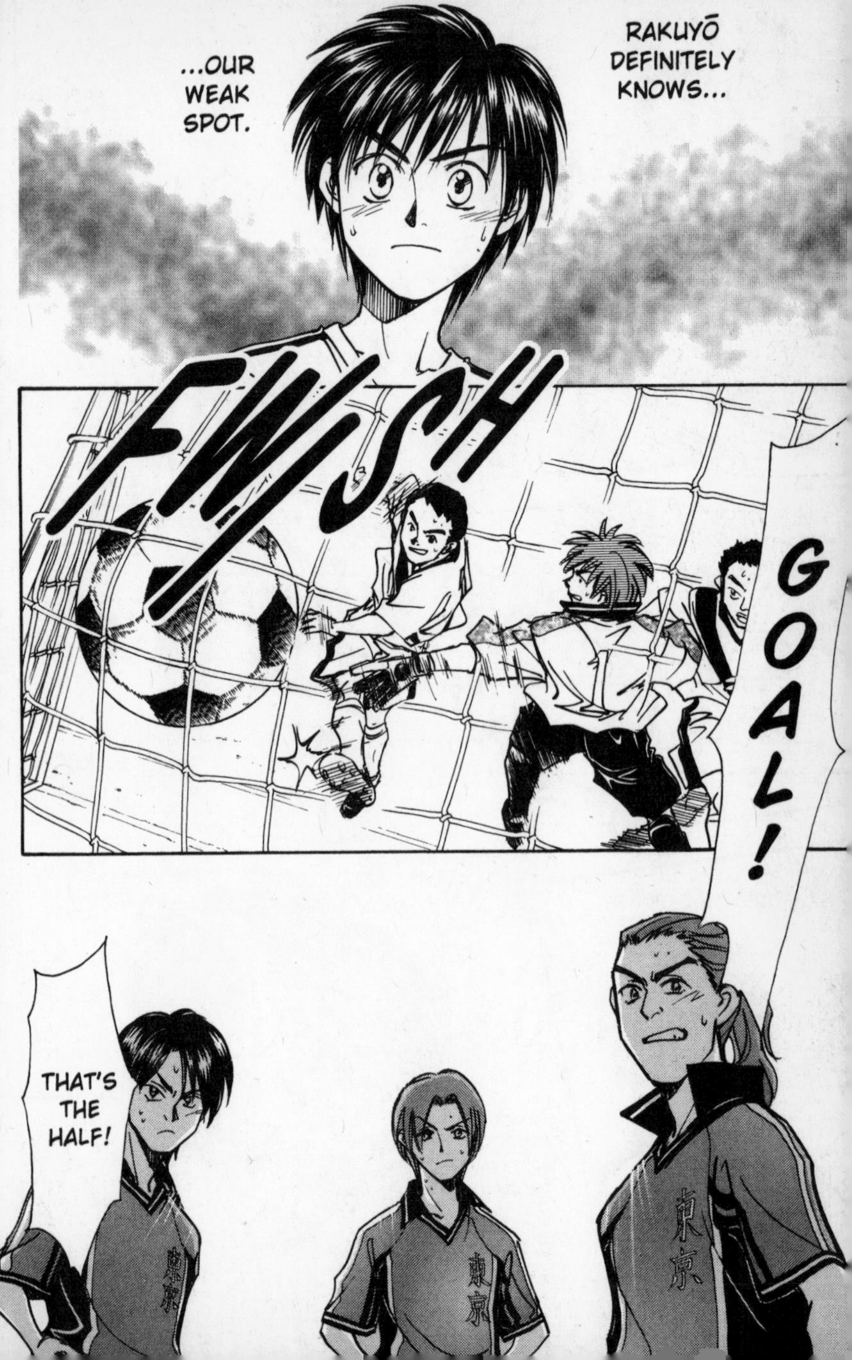
RAKUYŌ DEFINITELY KNOWS...
...OUR WEAK SPOT.
FWISH
GOAL!
THAT'S THE HALF!

READ THIS WAY

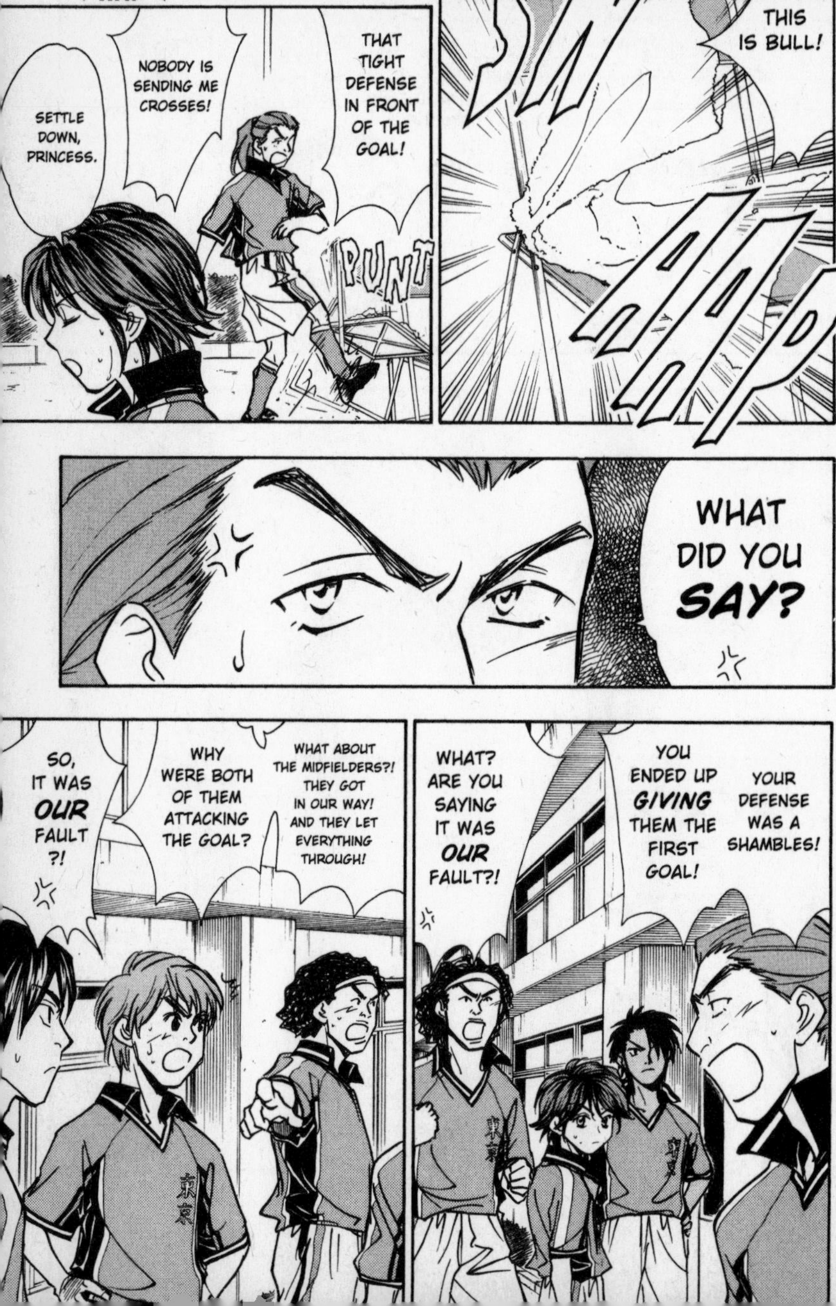

SHHP
THIS IS BULL!
THAT TIGHT DEFENSE IN FRONT OF THE GOAL!
NOBODY IS SENDING ME CROSSES!
SETTLE DOWN, PRINCESS.
PUNT
WHAT DID YOU SAY?
YOUR DEFENSE WAS A SHAMBLES!
YOU ENDED UP GIVING THEM THE FIRST GOAL!
WHAT? ARE YOU SAYING IT WAS OUR FAULT?!
WHAT ABOUT THE MIDFIELDERS?! THEY GOT IN OUR WAY! AND THEY LET EVERYTHING THROUGH!
WHY WERE BOTH OF THEM ATTACKING THE GOAL?
SO, IT WAS OUR FAULT?!

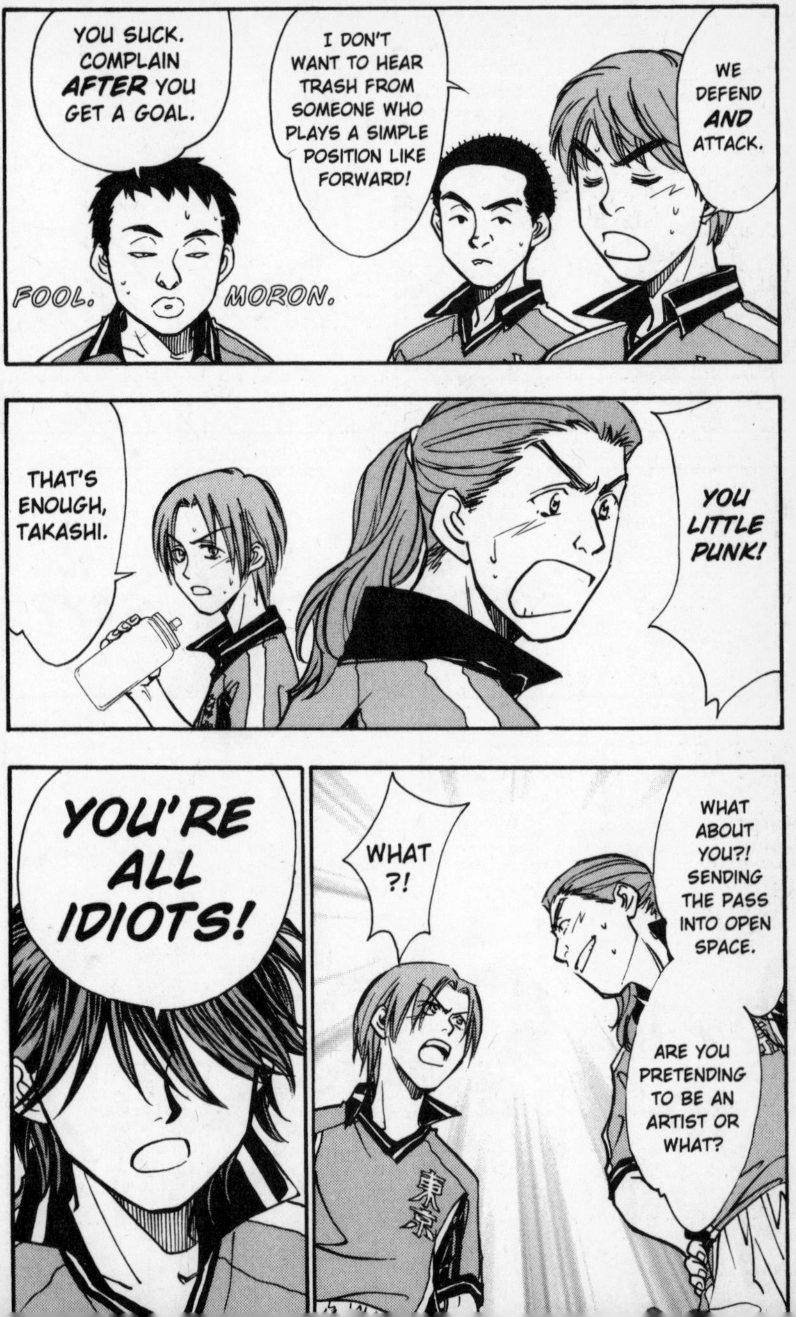
WE DEFEND AND ATTACK.
I DON'T WANT TO HEAR TRASH FROM SOMEONE WHO PLAYS A SIMPLE POSITION LIKE FORWARD!
YOU SUCK. COMPLAIN AFTER YOU GET A GOAL.
MORON.
FOOL.
YOU LITTLE PUNK!
THAT'S ENOUGH, TAKASHI.
WHAT ABOUT YOU?! SENDING THE PASS INTO OPEN SPACE.
ARE YOU PRETENDING TO BE AN ARTIST OR WHAT?
WHAT ?!
YOU'RE ALL IDIOTS!

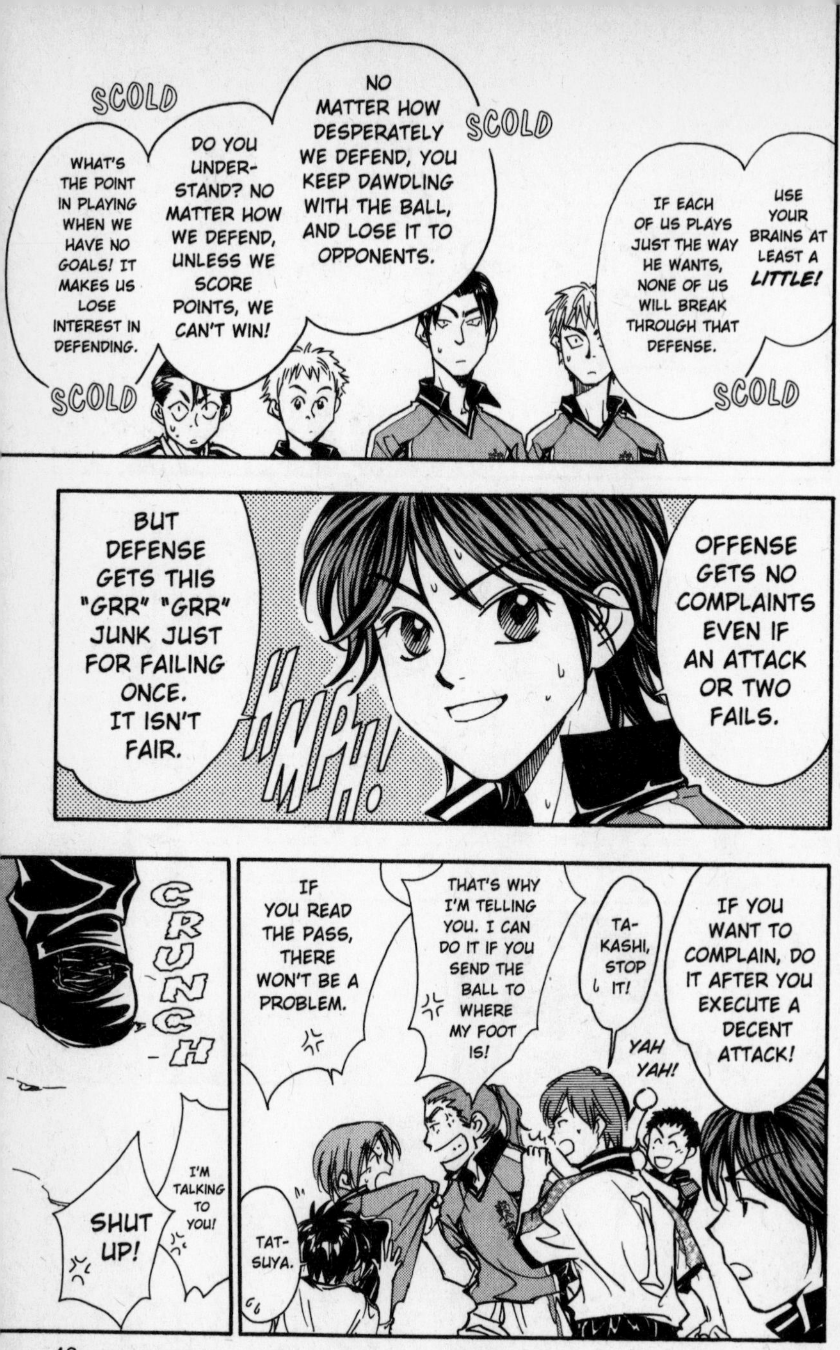
USE YOUR BRAINS AT LEAST A *LITTLE!*
IF EACH OF US PLAYS JUST THE WAY HE WANTS, NONE OF US WILL BREAK THROUGH THAT DEFENSE.
SCOLD
SCOLD
NO MATTER HOW DESPERATELY WE DEFEND, YOU KEEP DAWDLING WITH THE BALL, AND LOSE IT TO OPPONENTS.
DO YOU UNDERSTAND? NO MATTER HOW WE DEFEND, UNLESS WE SCORE POINTS, WE CAN'T WIN!
SCOLD
WHAT'S THE POINT IN PLAYING WHEN WE HAVE NO GOALS! IT MAKES US LOSE INTEREST IN DEFENDING.
SCOLD
OFFENSE GETS NO COMPLAINTS EVEN IF AN ATTACK OR TWO FAILS.
HMPH!
BUT DEFENSE GETS THIS "GRR" "GRR" JUNK JUST FOR FAILING ONCE. IT ISN'T FAIR.
IF YOU WANT TO COMPLAIN, DO IT AFTER YOU EXECUTE A DECENT ATTACK!
TA-KASHI, STOP IT!
YAH YAH!
THAT'S WHY I'M TELLING YOU. I CAN DO IT IF YOU SEND THE BALL TO WHERE MY FOOT IS!
IF YOU READ THE PASS, THERE WON'T BE A PROBLEM.
TAT-SUYA.
CRUNCH
I'M TALKING TO YOU!
SHUT UP!

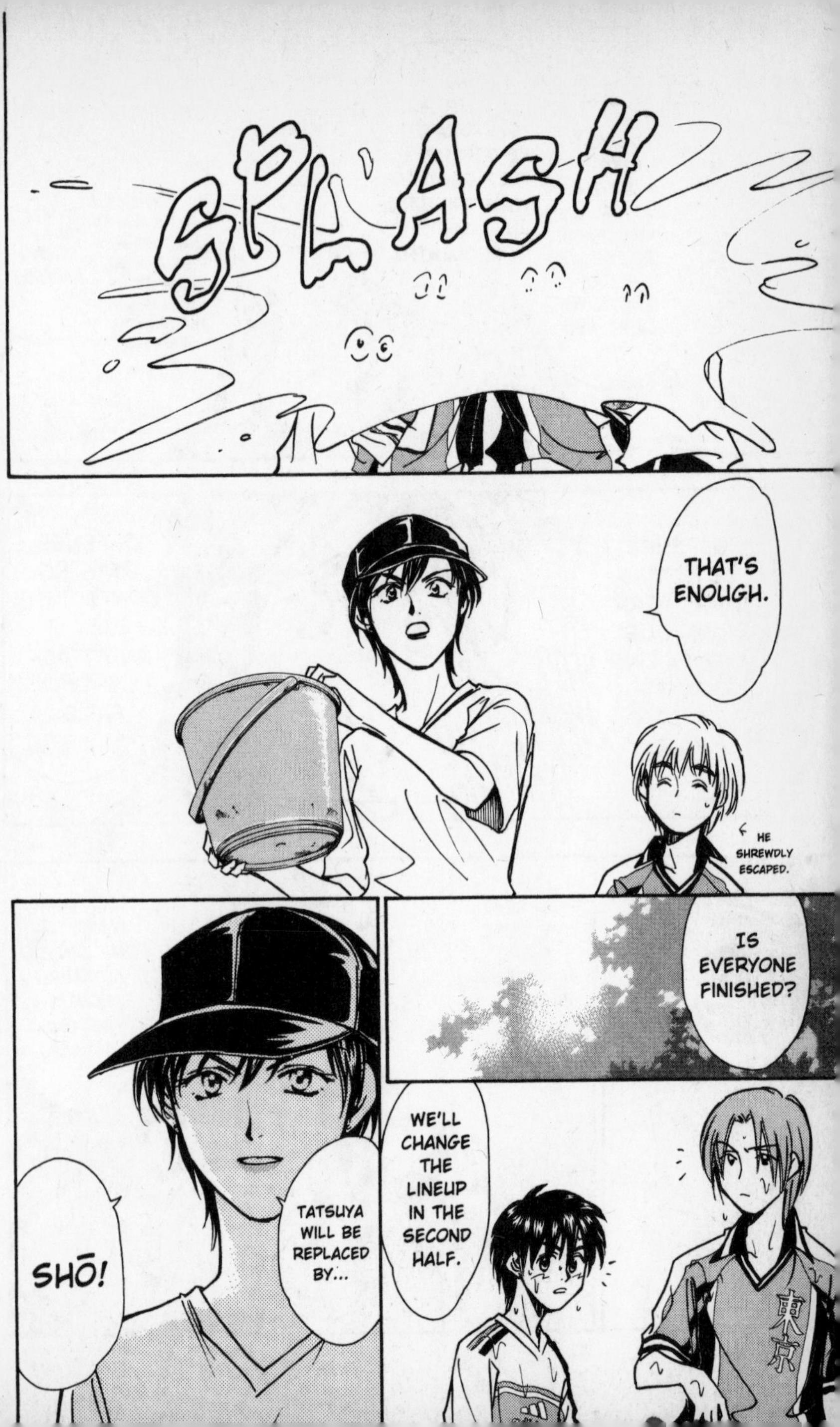
SPLASH
THAT'S ENOUGH.
HE SHREWDLY ESCAPED.
IS EVERYONE FINISHED?
WE'LL CHANGE THE LINEUP IN THE SECOND HALF.
TATSUYA WILL BE REPLACED BY...
SHŌ!

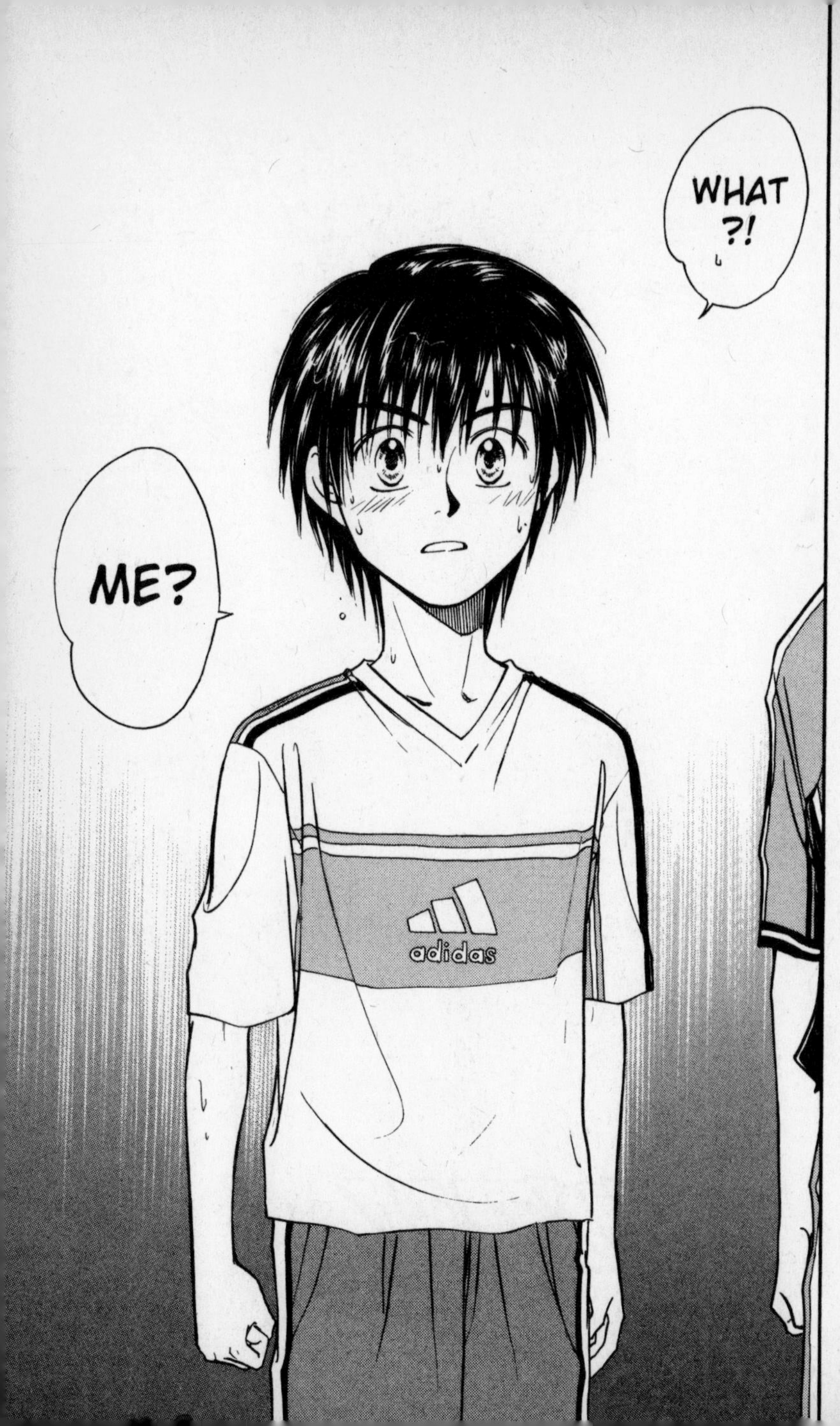
WHAT ?!
ME?
adidas

WHISTLE!™

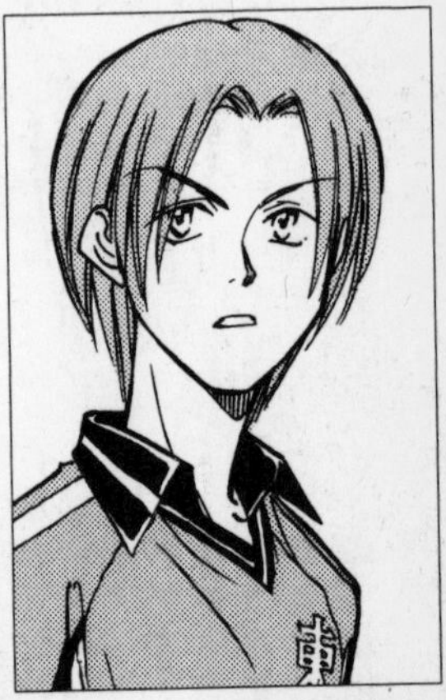

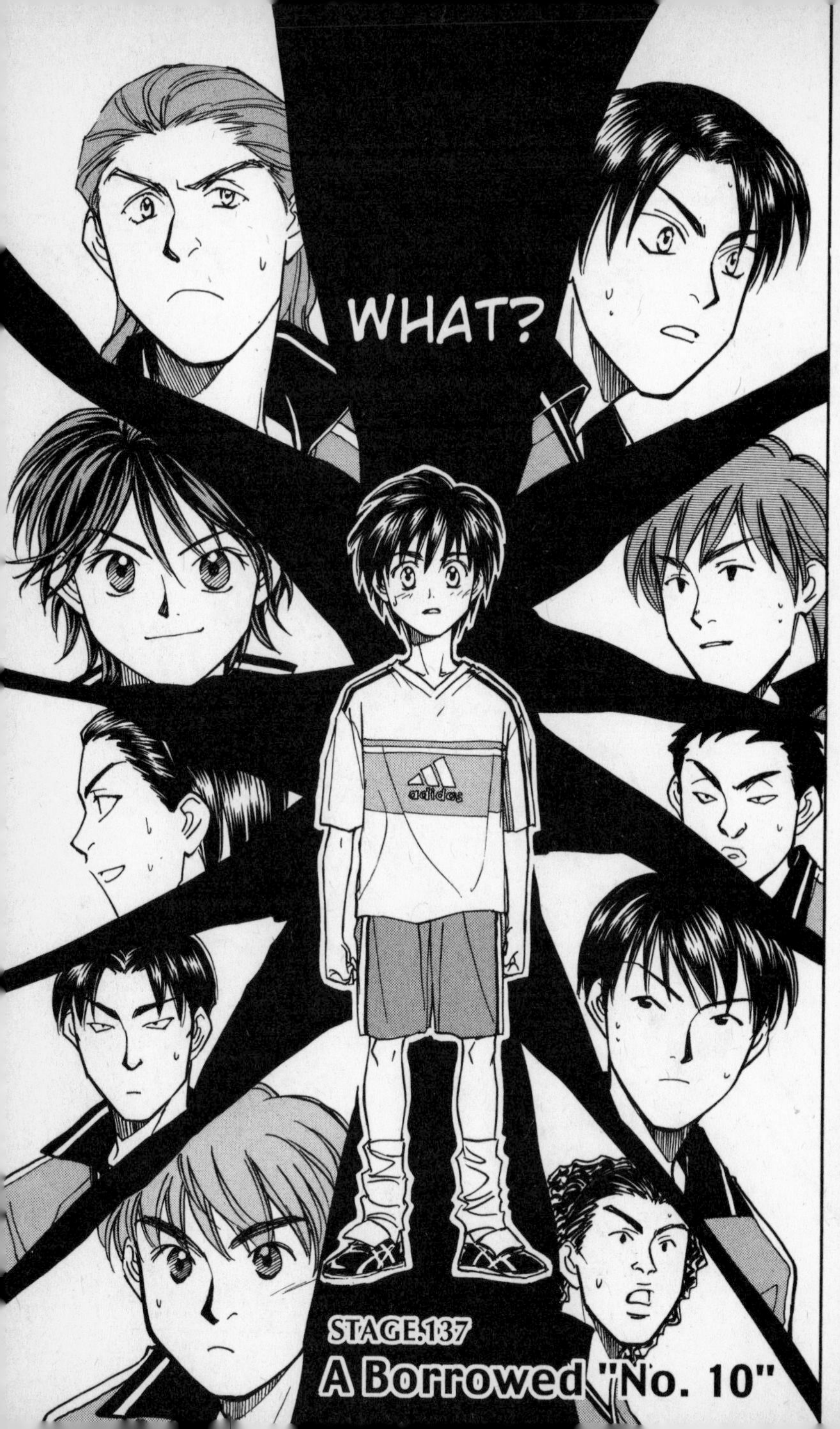
WHAT?
adidas
STAGE.137
A Borrowed "No. 10"

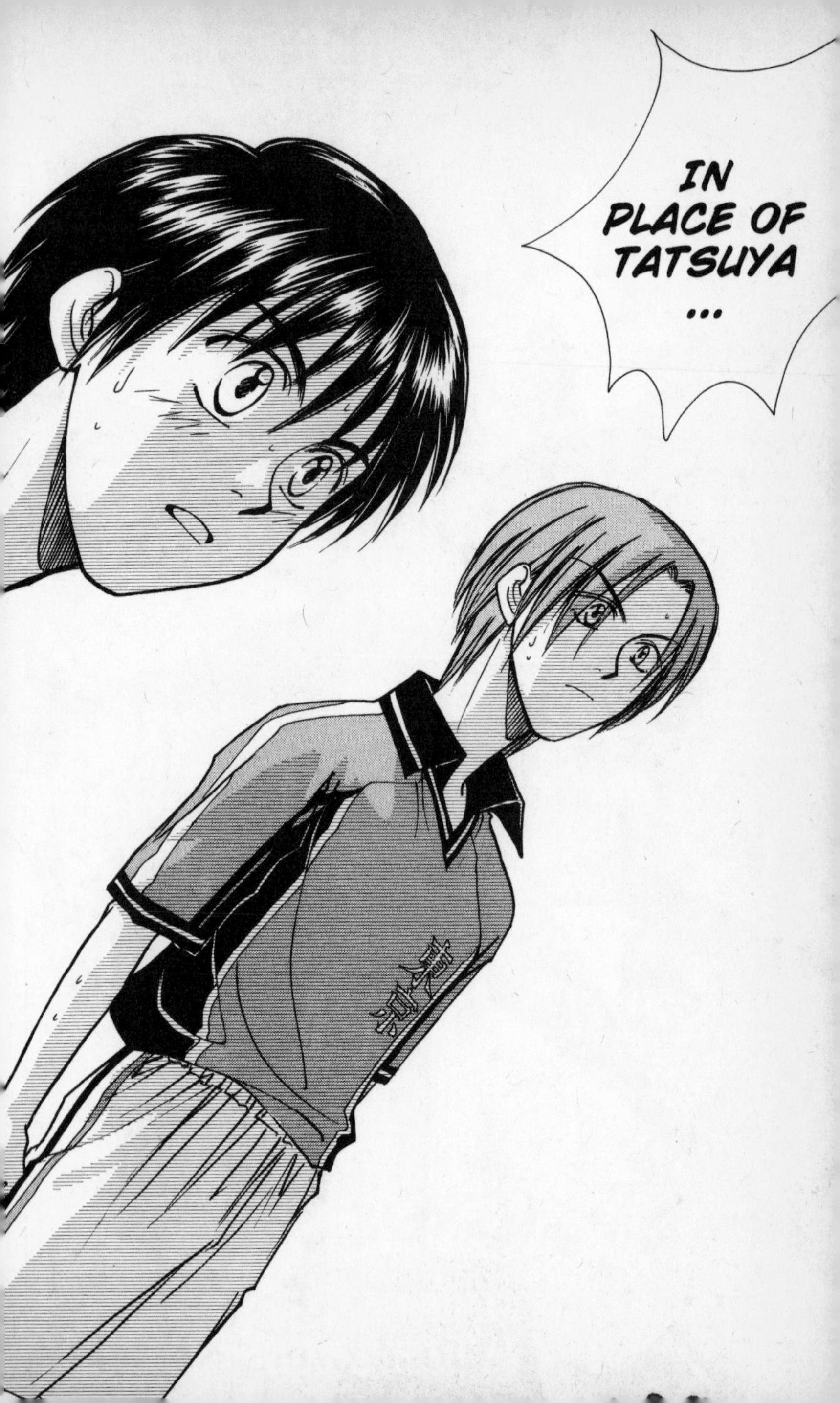
IN PLACE OF TATSUYA ...

STAGE.137
A Borrowed "No. 10"

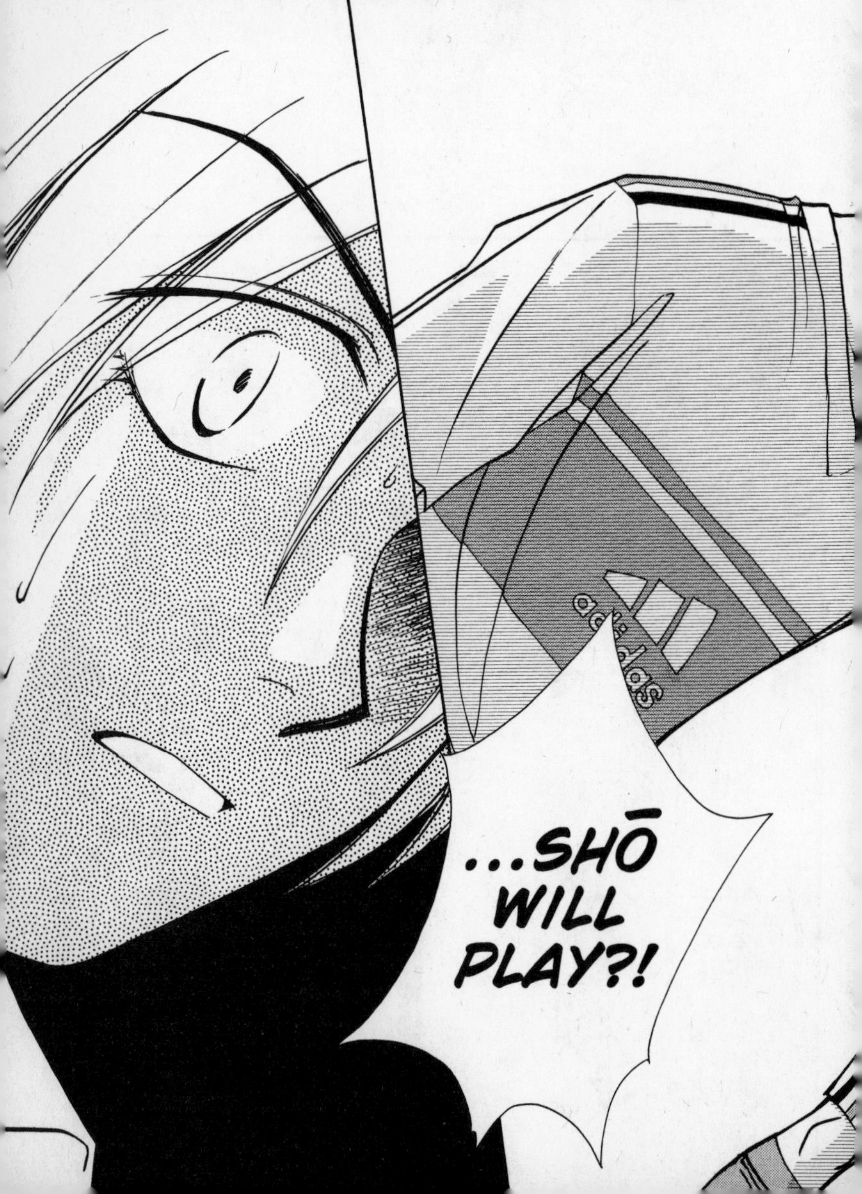

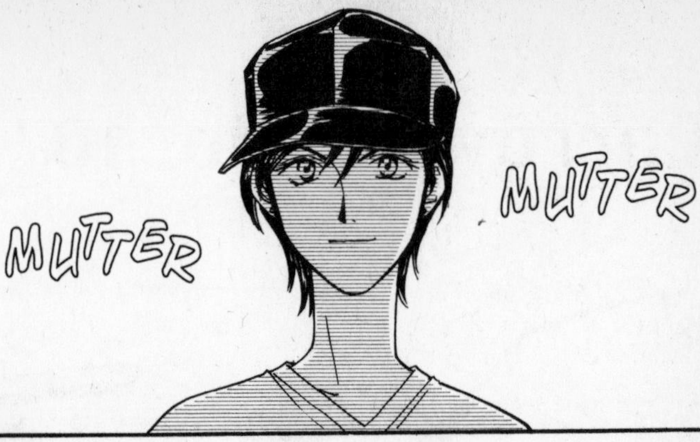
MUTTER
MUTTER

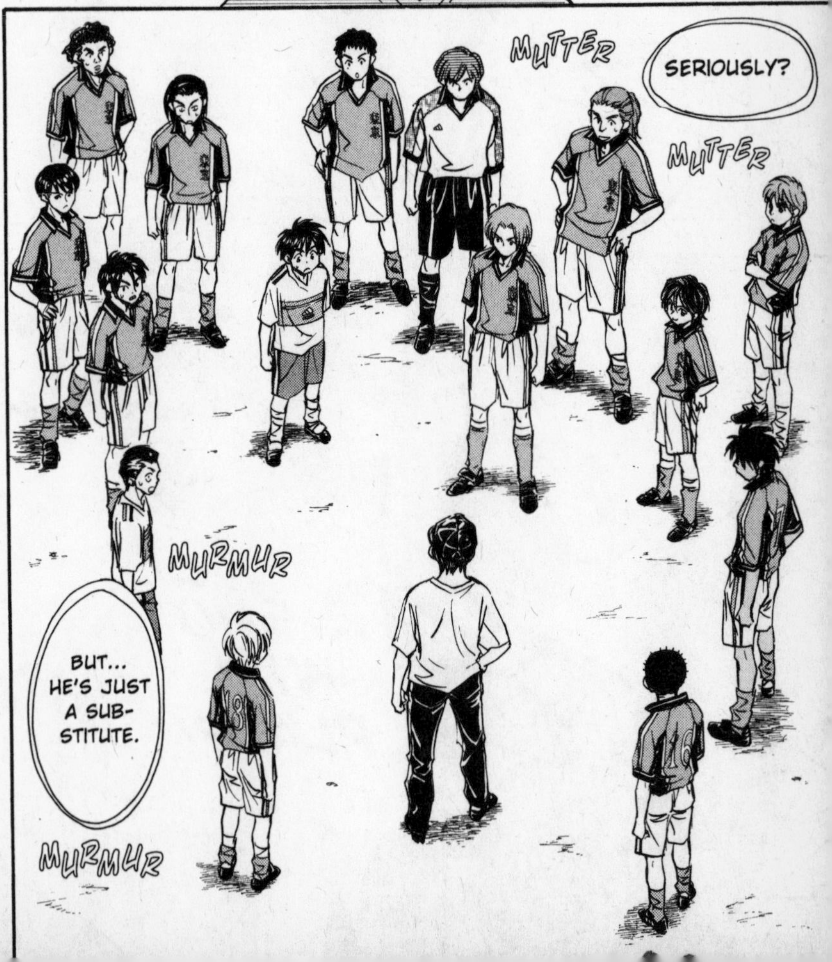
MUTTER
SERIOUSLY?
MUTTER
MURMUR
BUT... HE'S JUST A SUB-STITUTE.
MURMUR

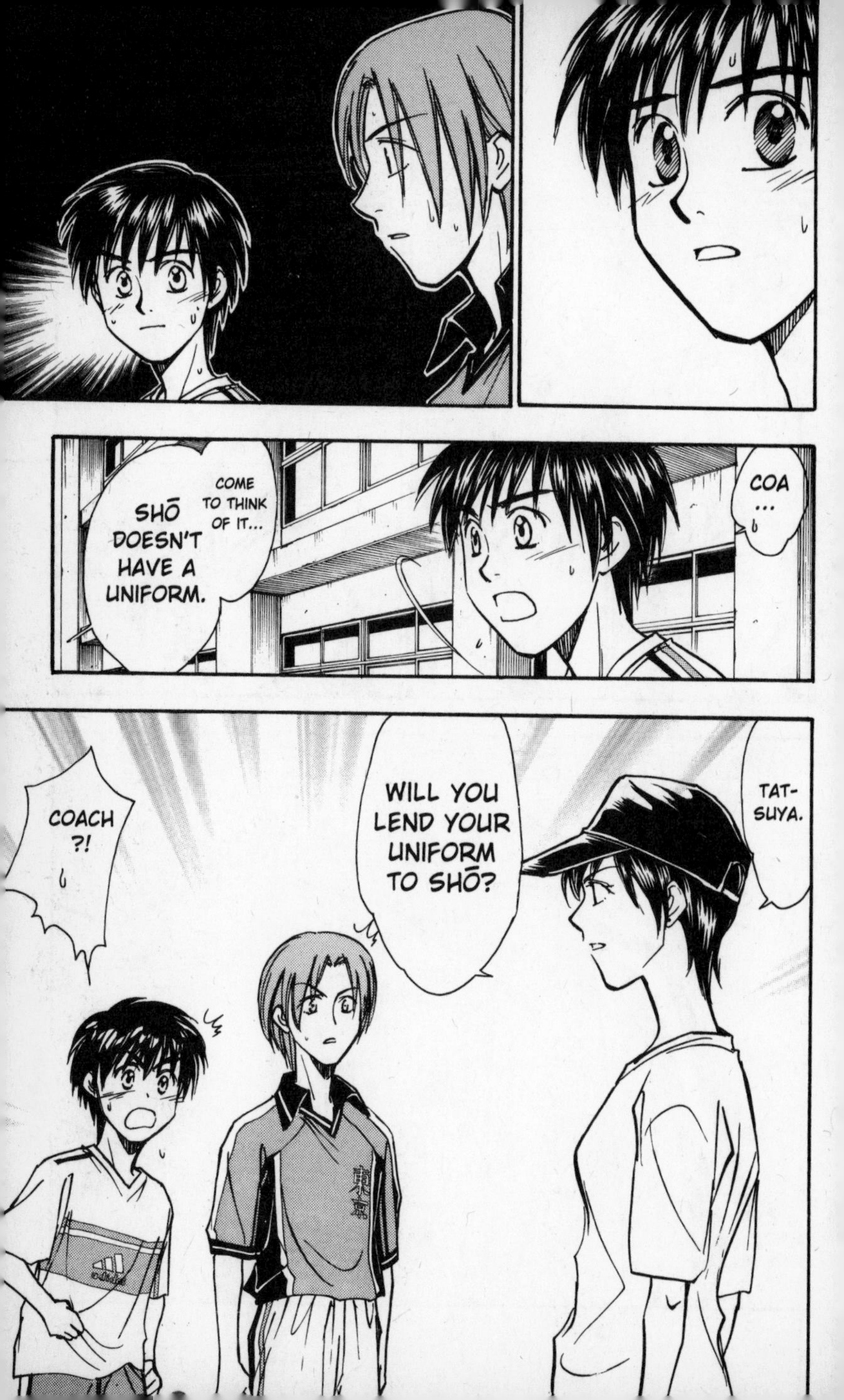
COA...
COME TO THINK OF IT...
SHŌ DOESN'T HAVE A UNIFORM.
TAT-SUYA.
WILL YOU LEND YOUR UNIFORM TO SHŌ?
COACH?!

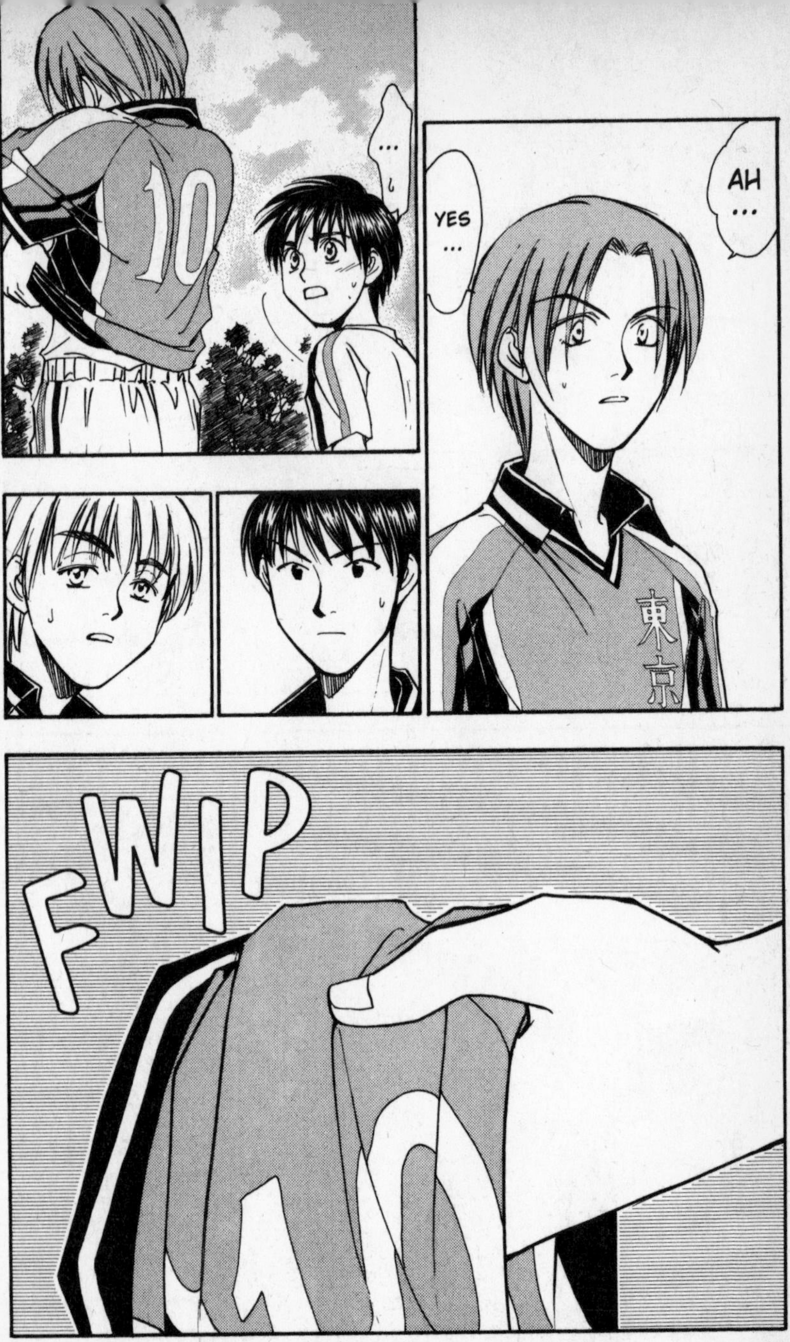
AH ...
YES ...
...
FWIP

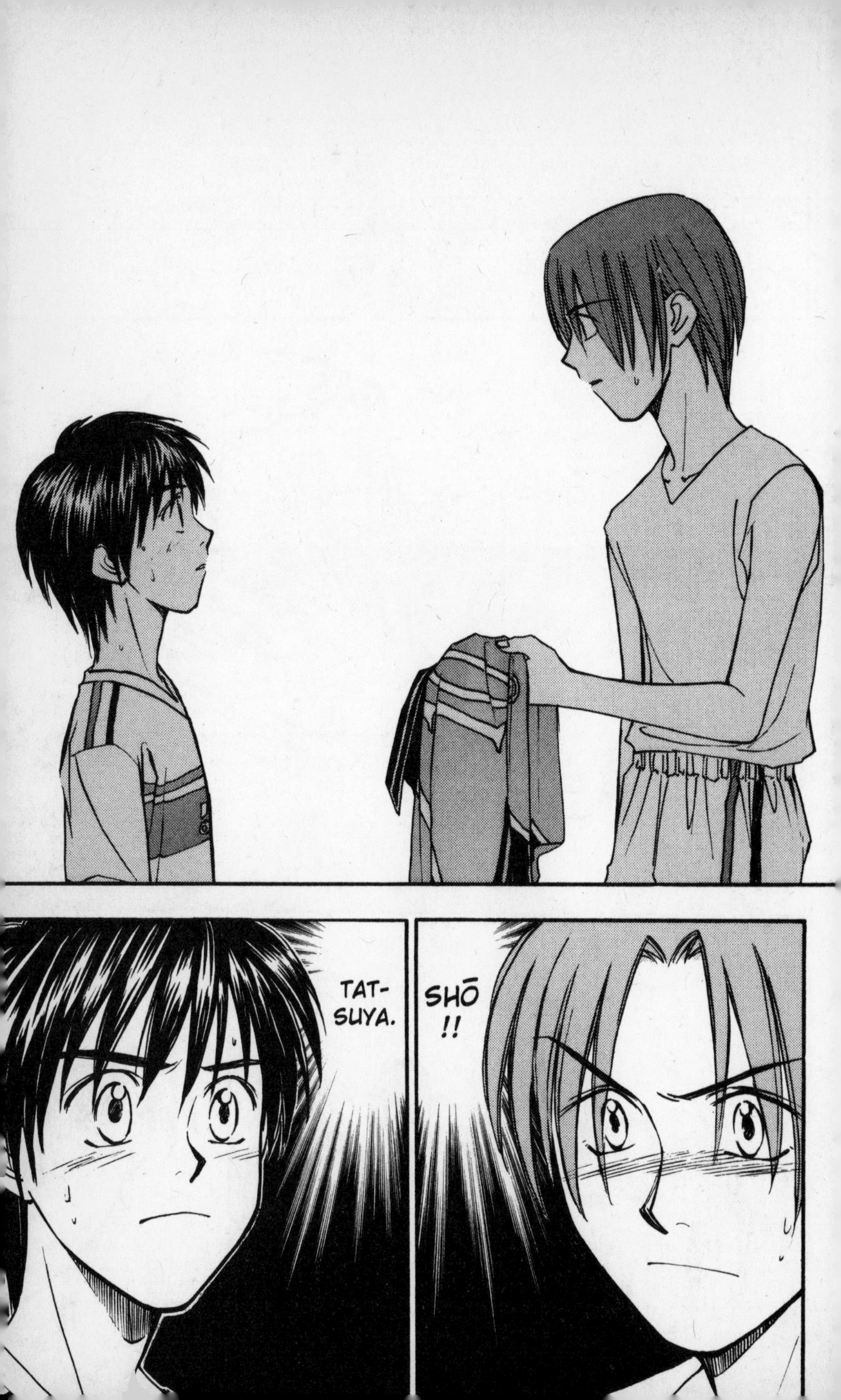
SHŌ !!
TAT-SUYA.

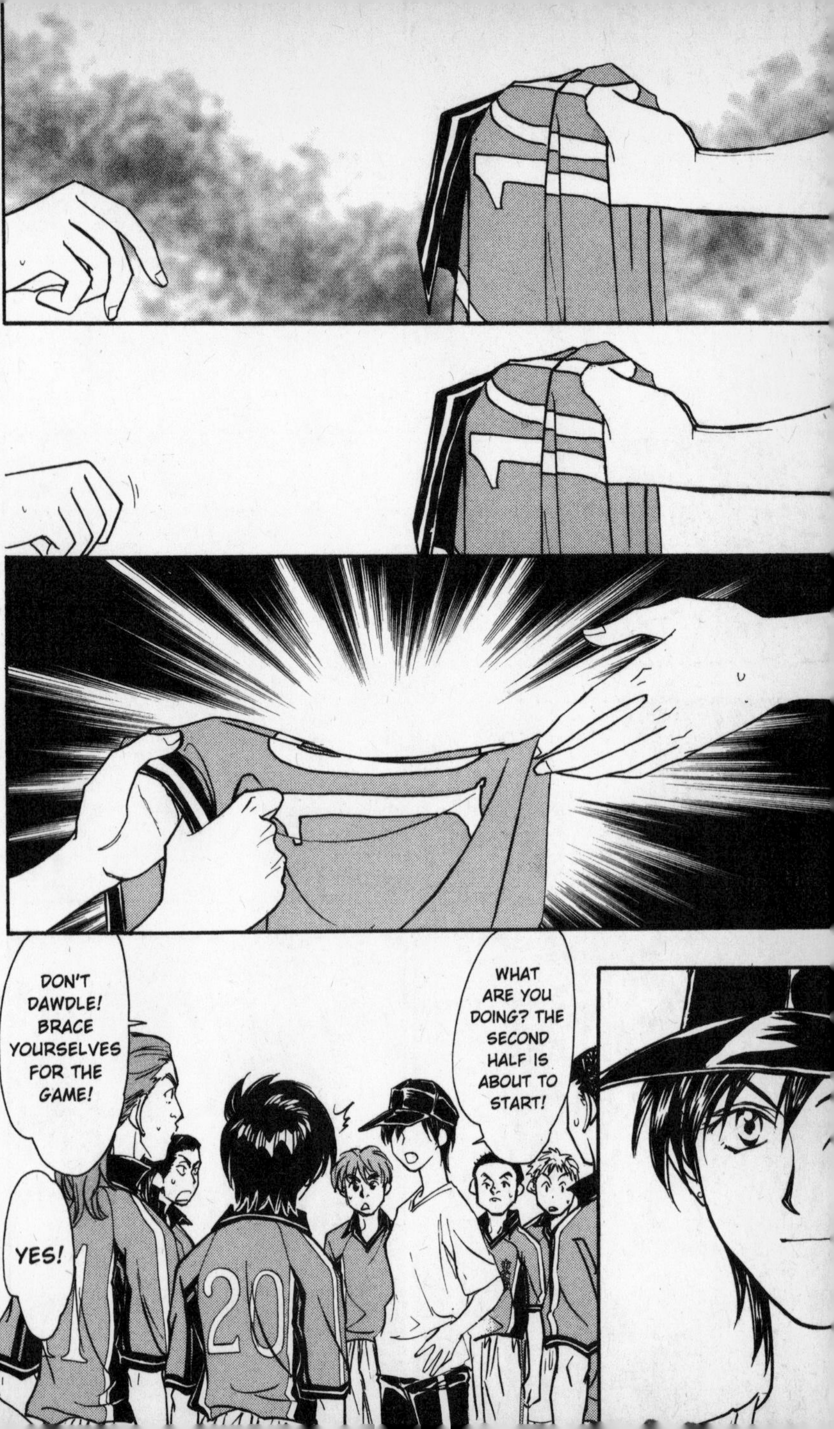
WHAT ARE YOU DOING? THE SECOND HALF IS ABOUT TO START!
DON'T DAWDLE! BRACE YOURSELVES FOR THE GAME!
YES!

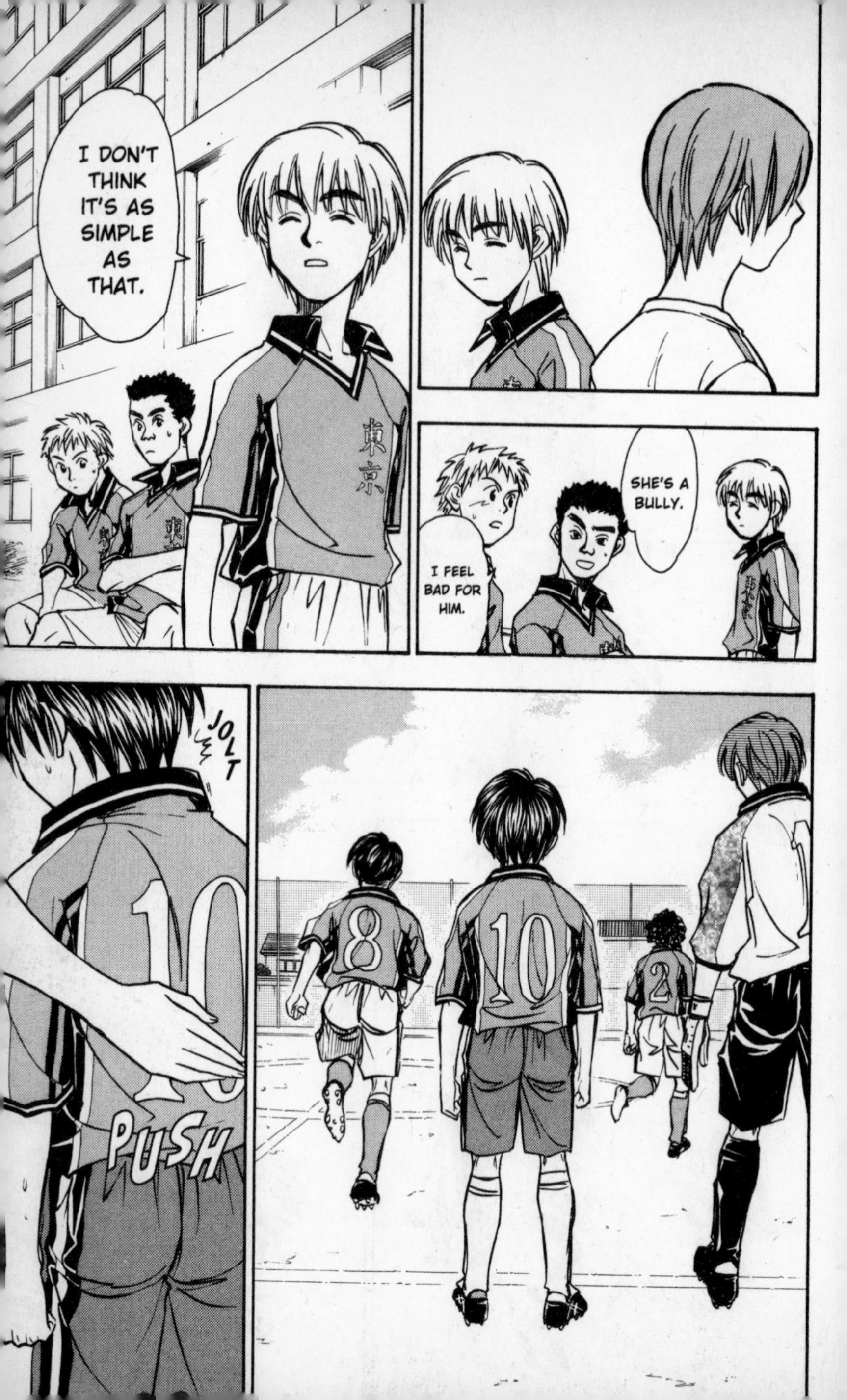
SHE'S A BULLY.
I FEEL BAD FOR HIM.
I DON'T THINK IT'S AS SIMPLE AS THAT.
JOLT
PUSH

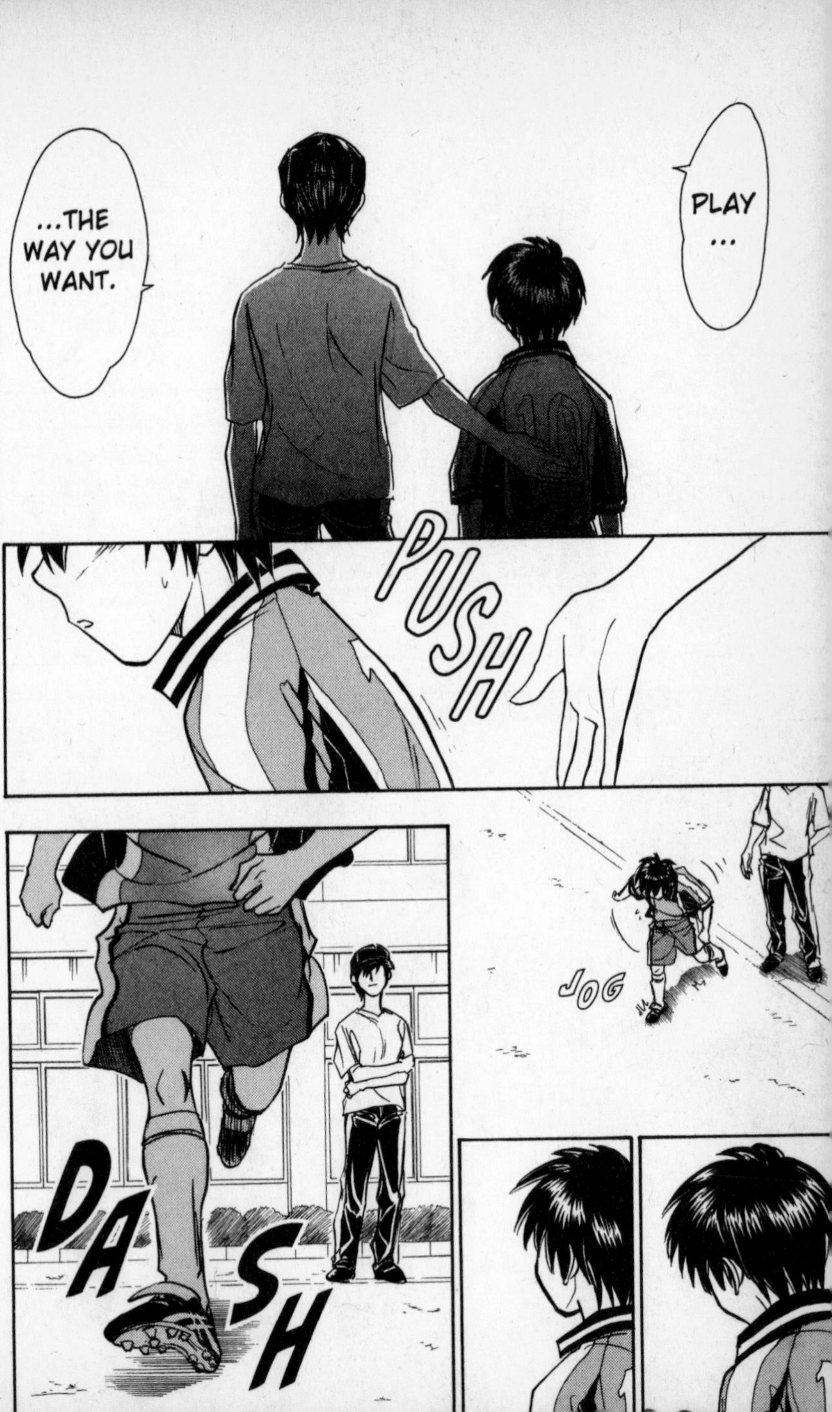
PLAY ...
...THE WAY YOU WANT.
PUSH
JOG
DASH

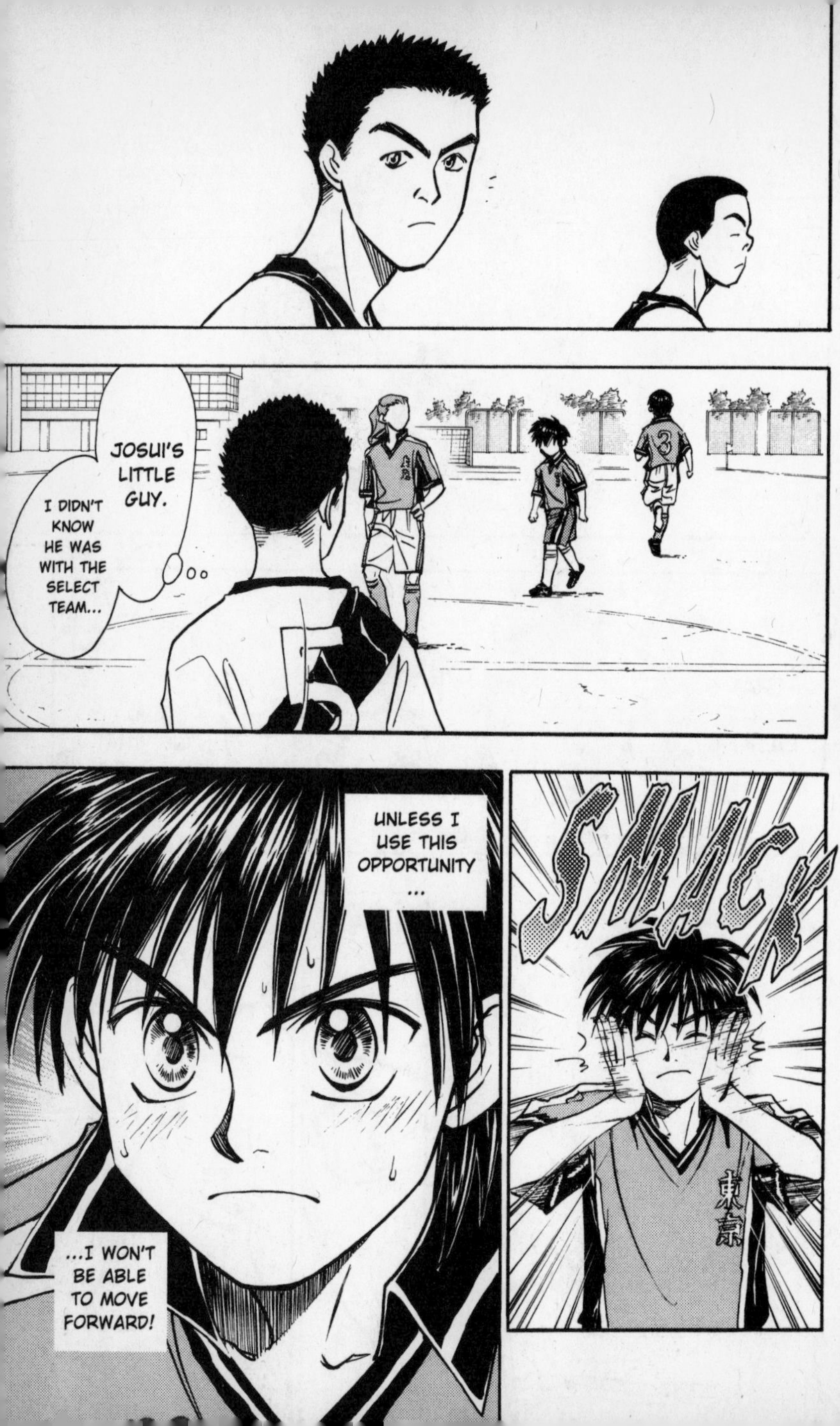
JOSUI'S LITTLE GUY.
I DIDN'T KNOW HE WAS WITH THE SELECT TEAM...
SMACK
UNLESS I USE THIS OPPORTUNITY ...
...I WON'T BE ABLE TO MOVE FORWARD!

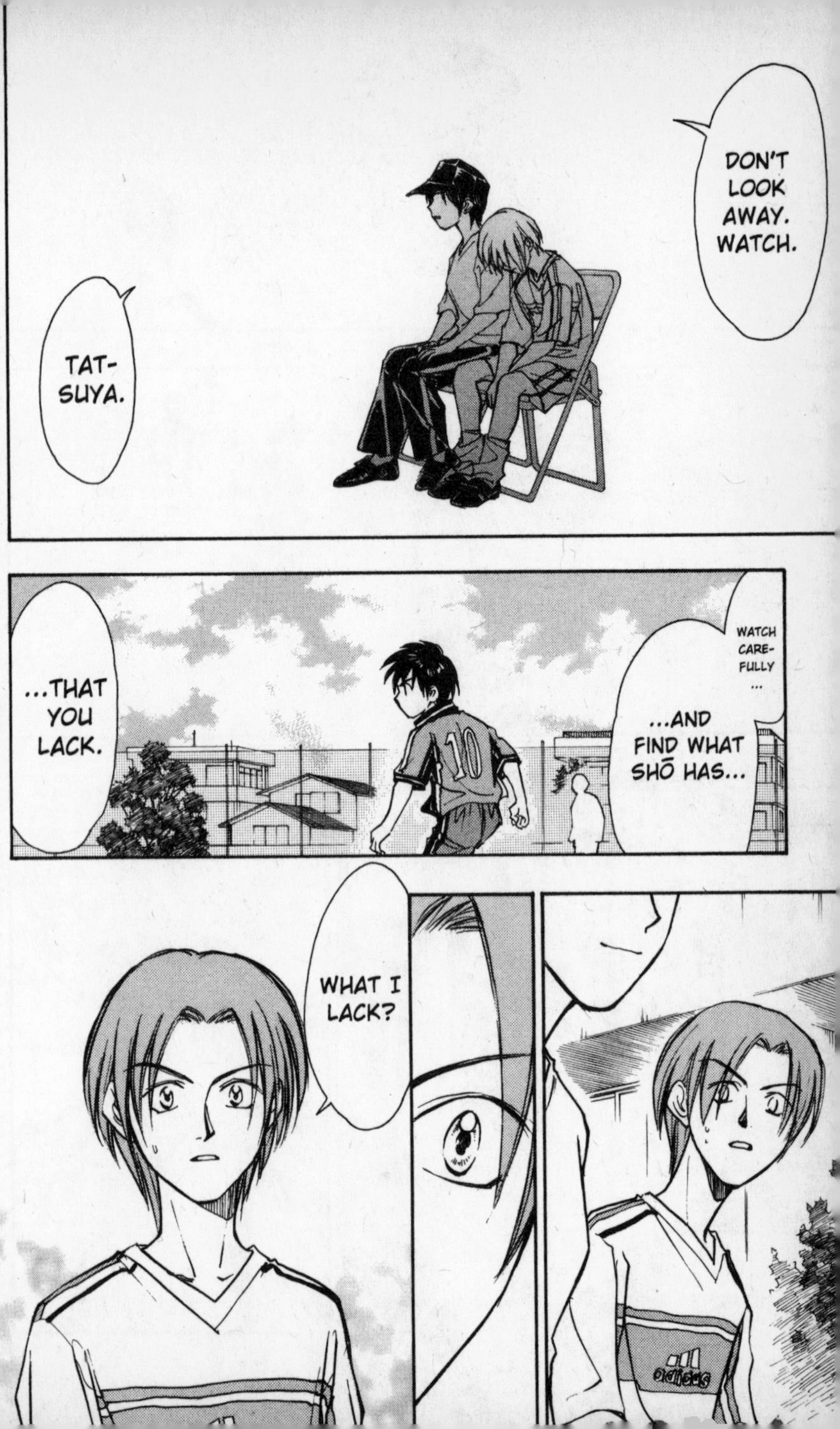
DON'T LOOK AWAY. WATCH.
TAT-SUYA.
WATCH CARE-FULLY...
...AND FIND WHAT SHŌ HAS...
...THAT YOU LACK.
WHAT I LACK?

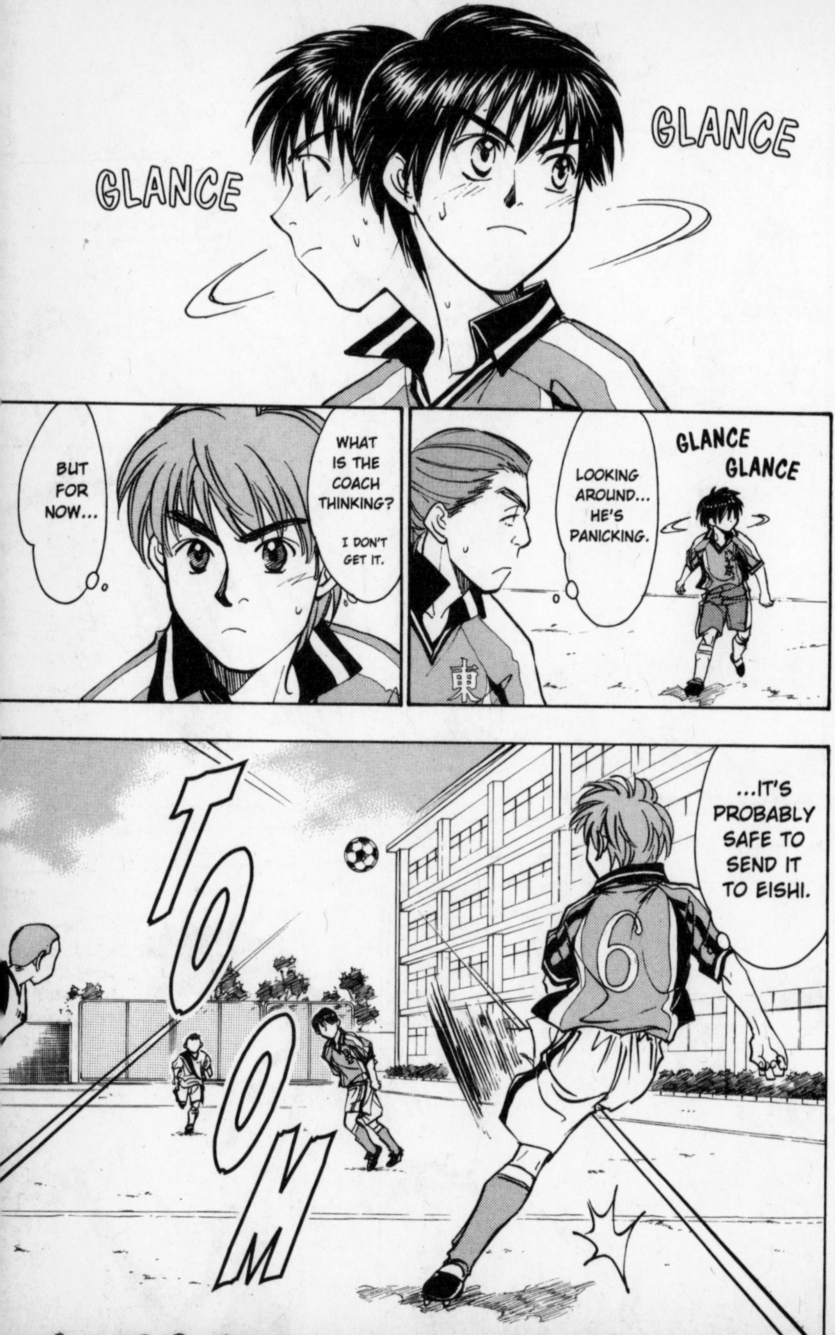
GLANCE
GLANCE
GLANCE
GLANCE
LOOKING AROUND... HE'S PANICKING.
WHAT IS THE COACH THINKING?
I DON'T GET IT.
BUT FOR NOW...
...IT'S PROBABLY SAFE TO SEND IT TO EISHI.
TOOOM

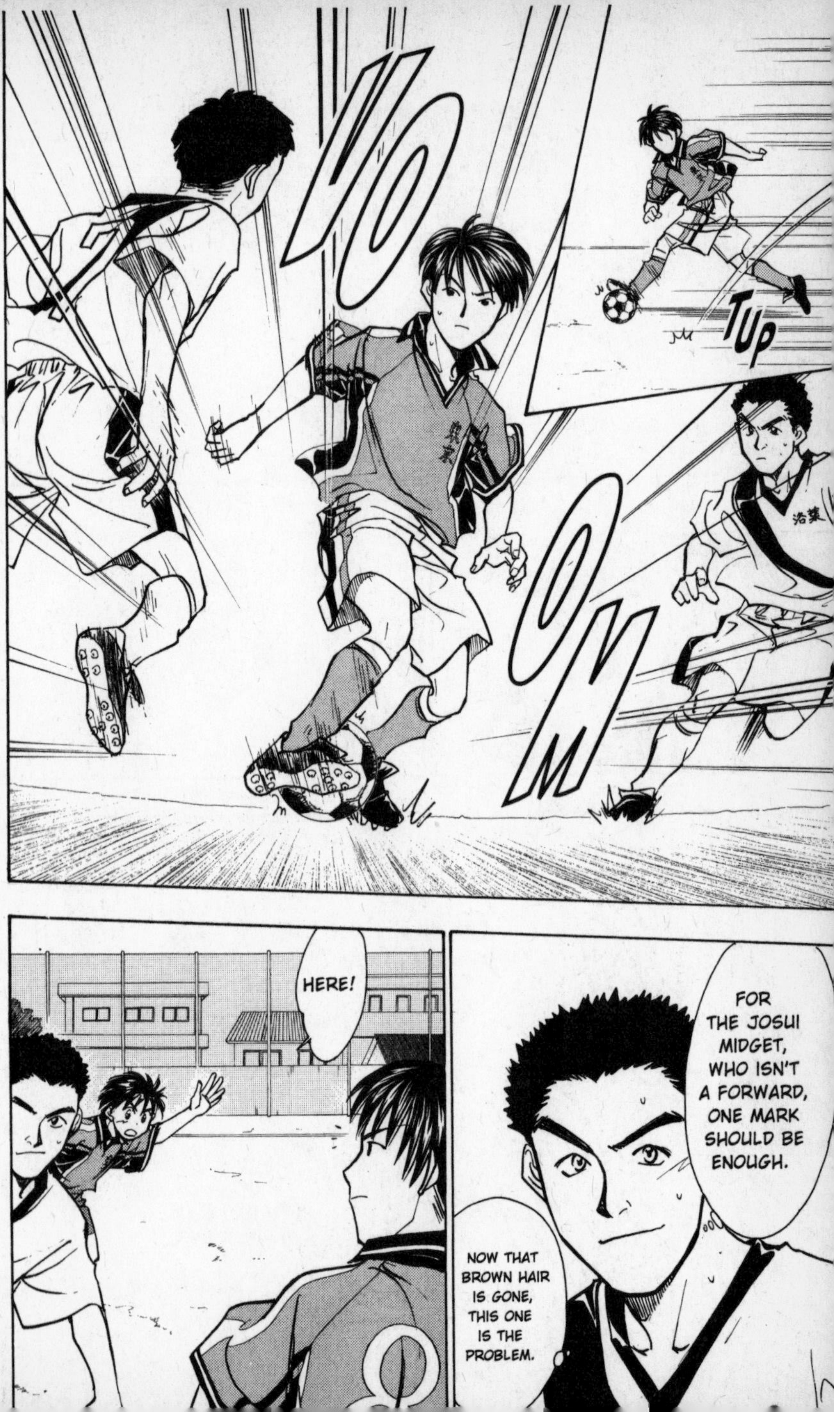
TUP
FOR THE JOSUI MIDGET, WHO ISN'T A FORWARD, ONE MARK SHOULD BE ENOUGH.
NOW THAT BROWN HAIR IS GONE, THIS ONE IS THE PROBLEM.
HERE!

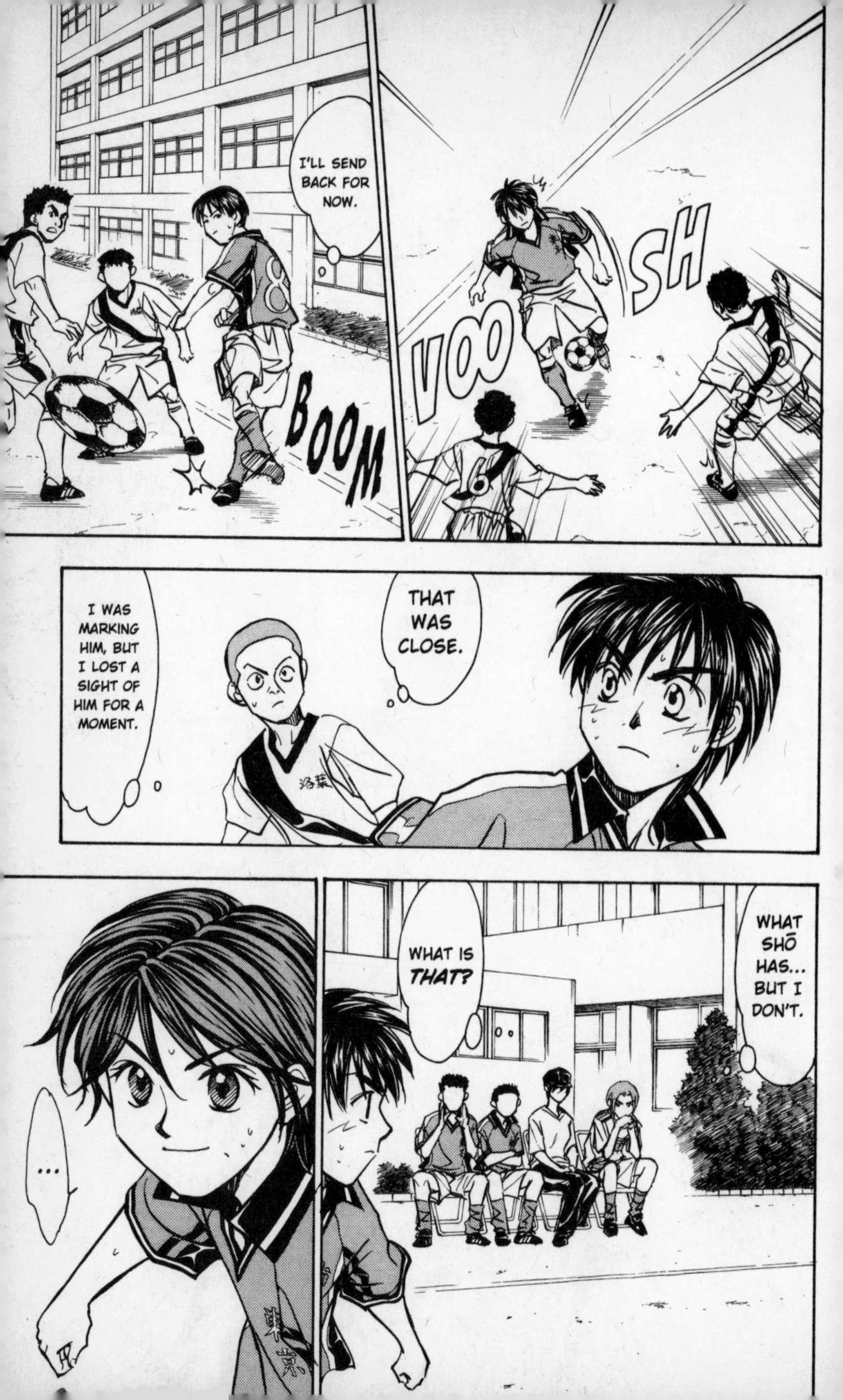
VOOSH
I'LL SEND BACK FOR NOW.
BOOM
THAT WAS CLOSE.
I WAS MARKING HIM, BUT I LOST A SIGHT OF HIM FOR A MOMENT.
WHAT SHŌ HAS... BUT I DON'T.
WHAT IS *THAT?*
...

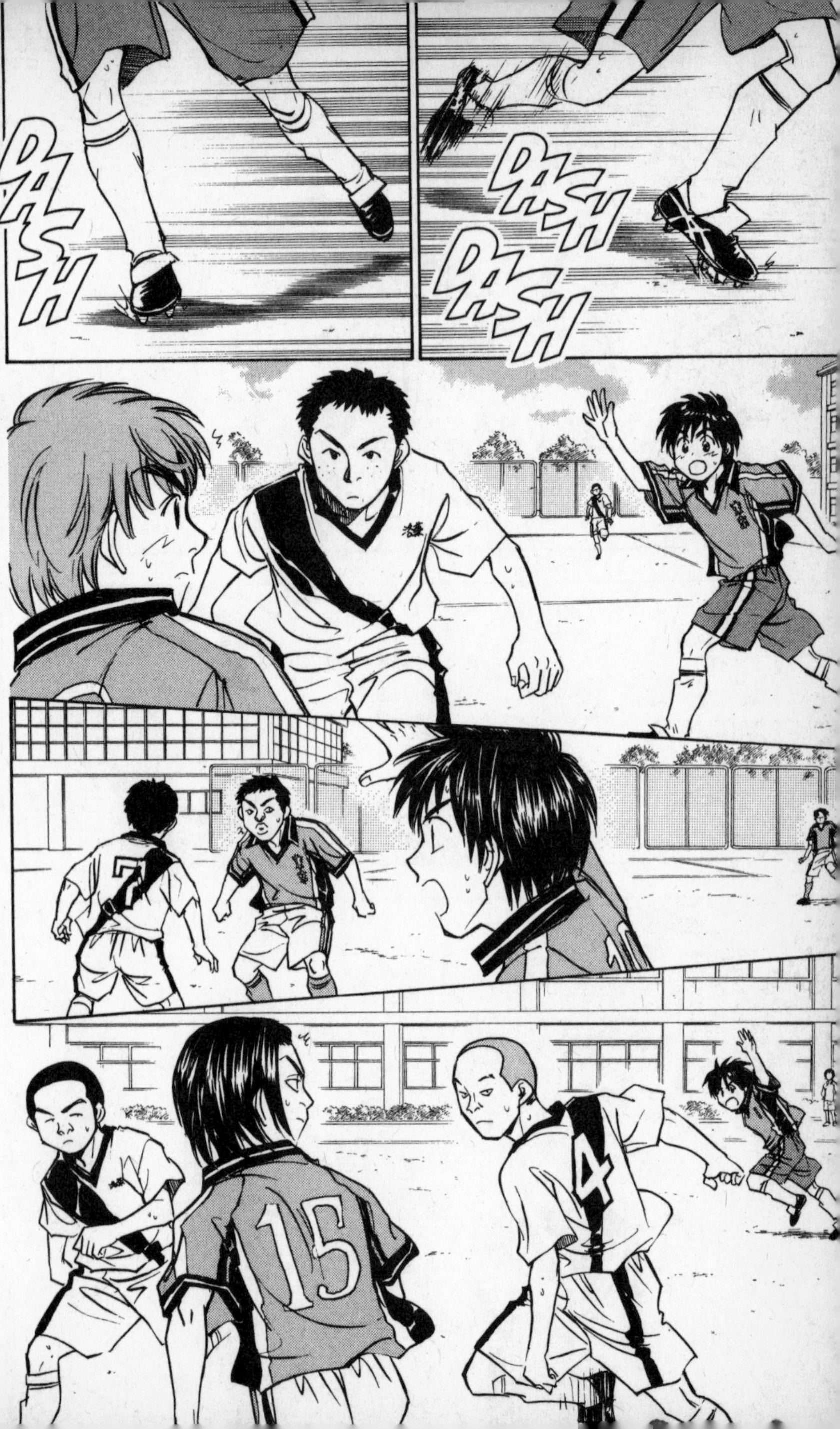
DASH
DASH
DASH

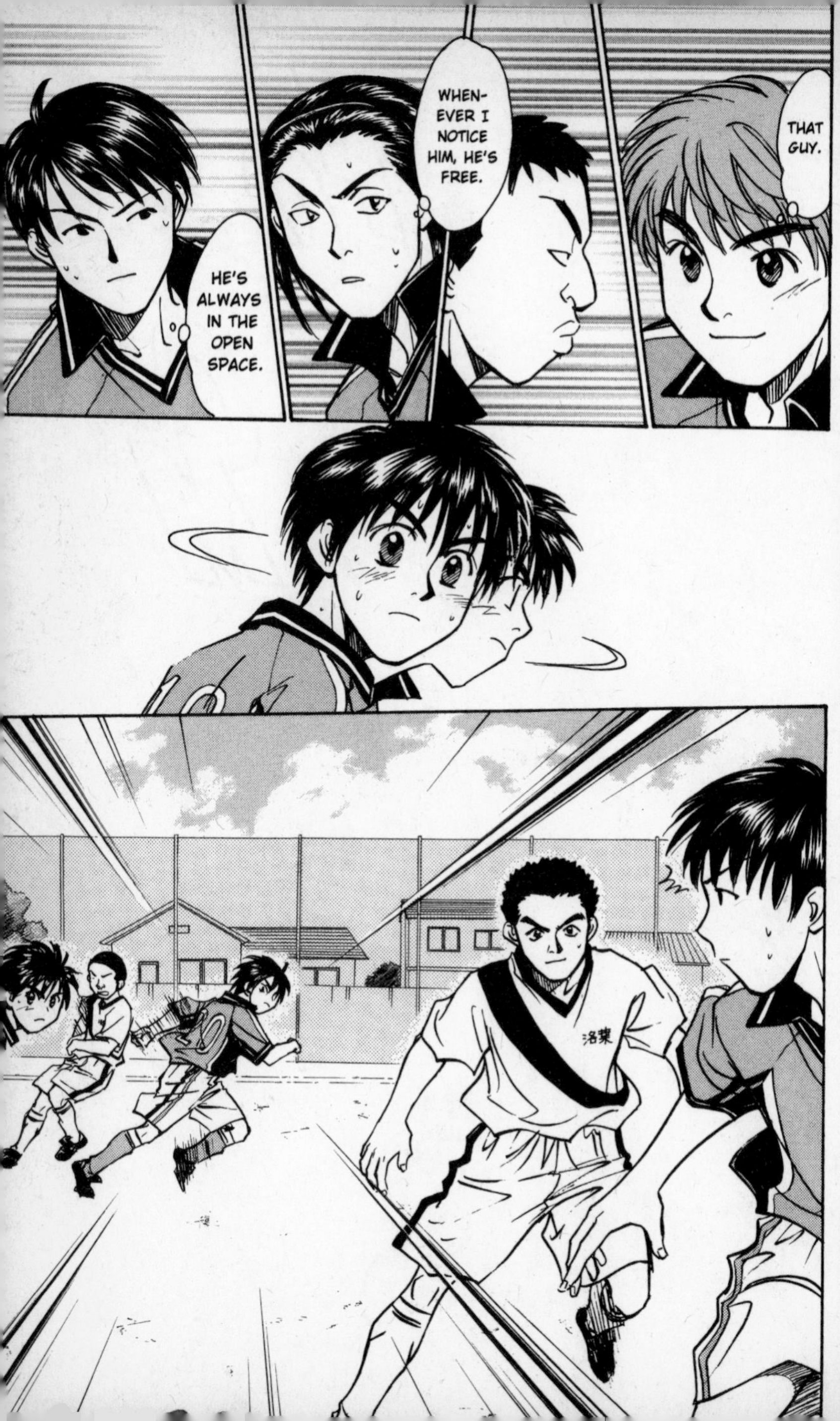
THAT GUY.
WHEN-EVER I NOTICE HIM, HE'S FREE.
HE'S ALWAYS IN THE OPEN SPACE.
洛葉

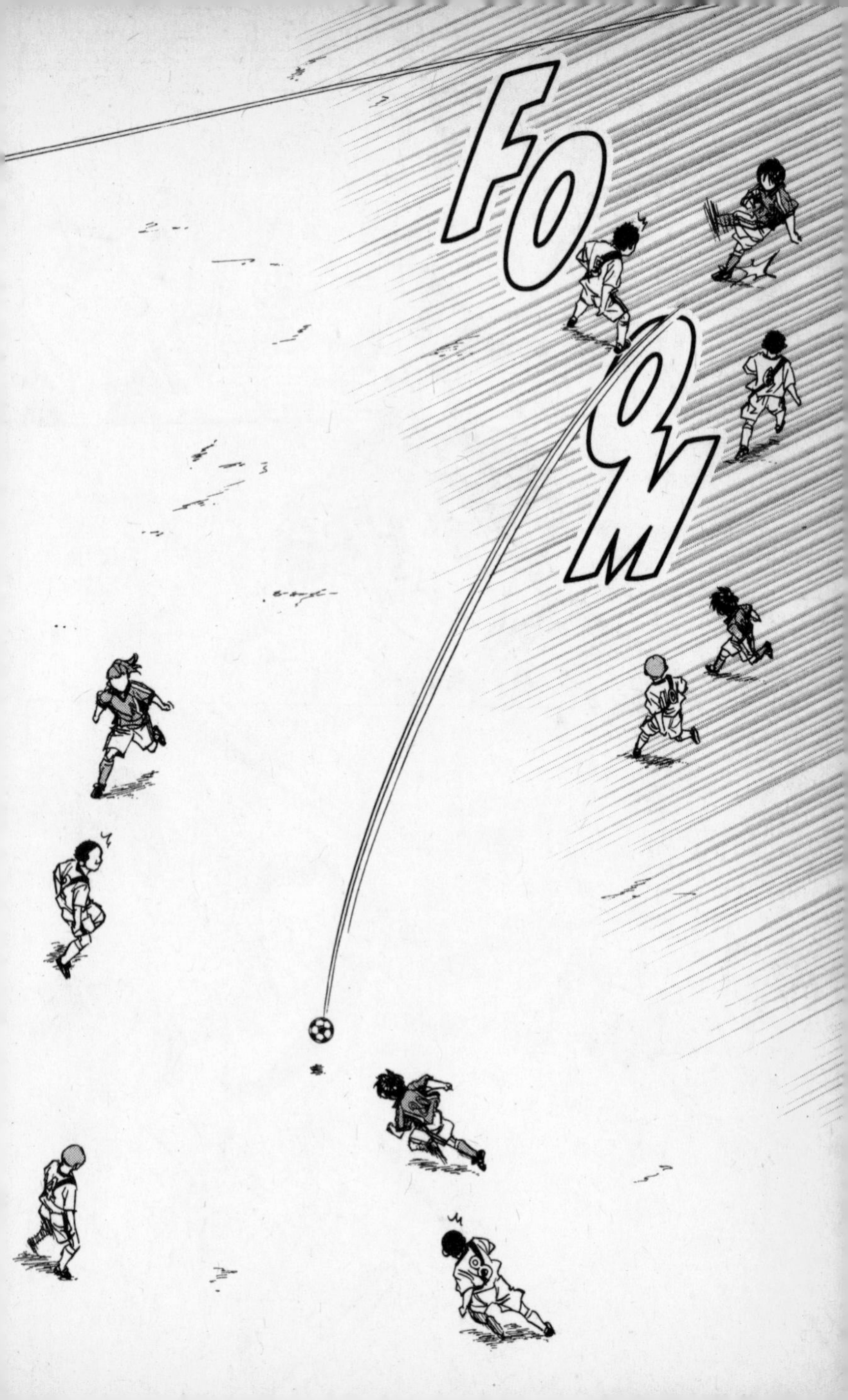
FOOM

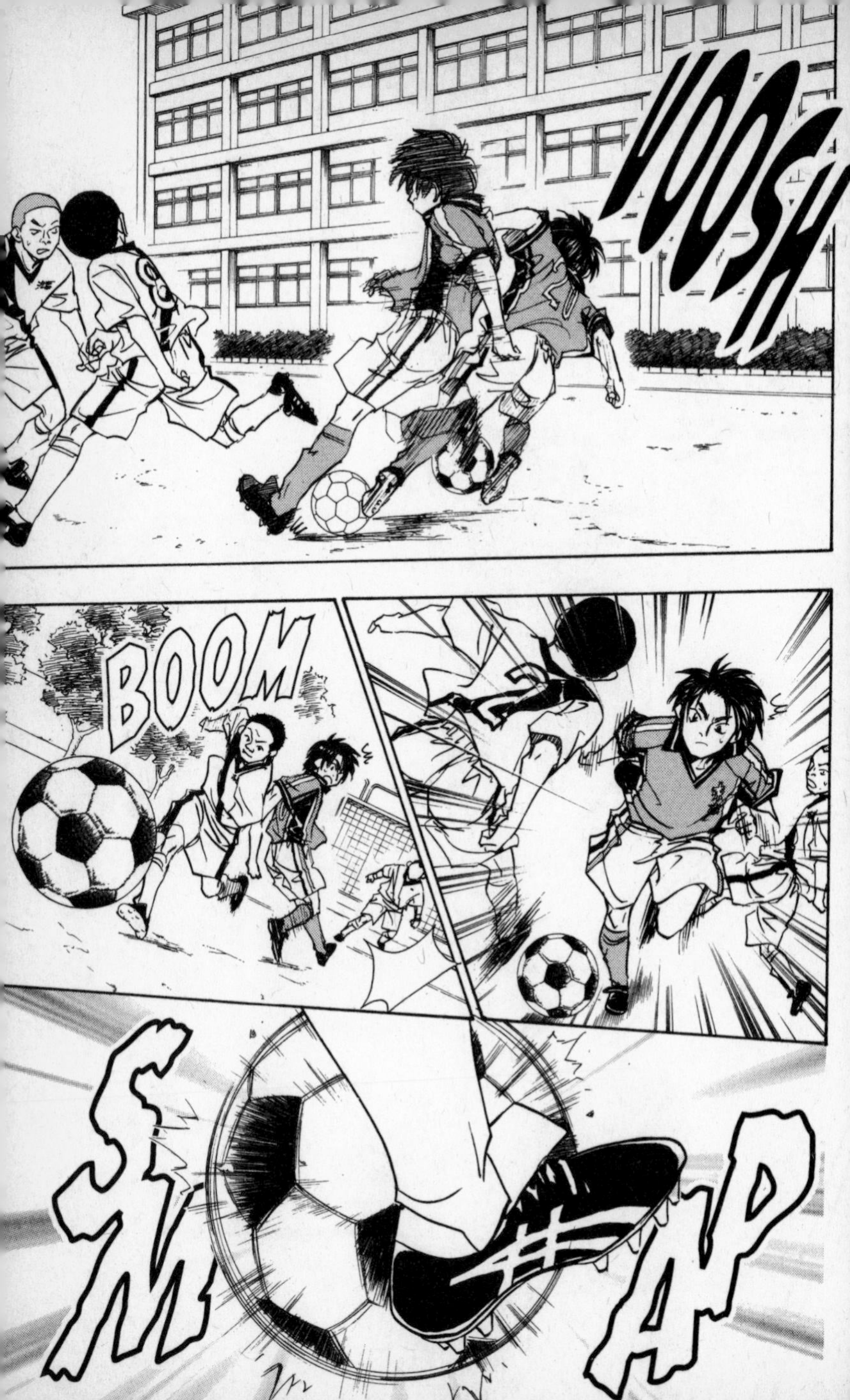
VOOSH
BOOM
SMAP

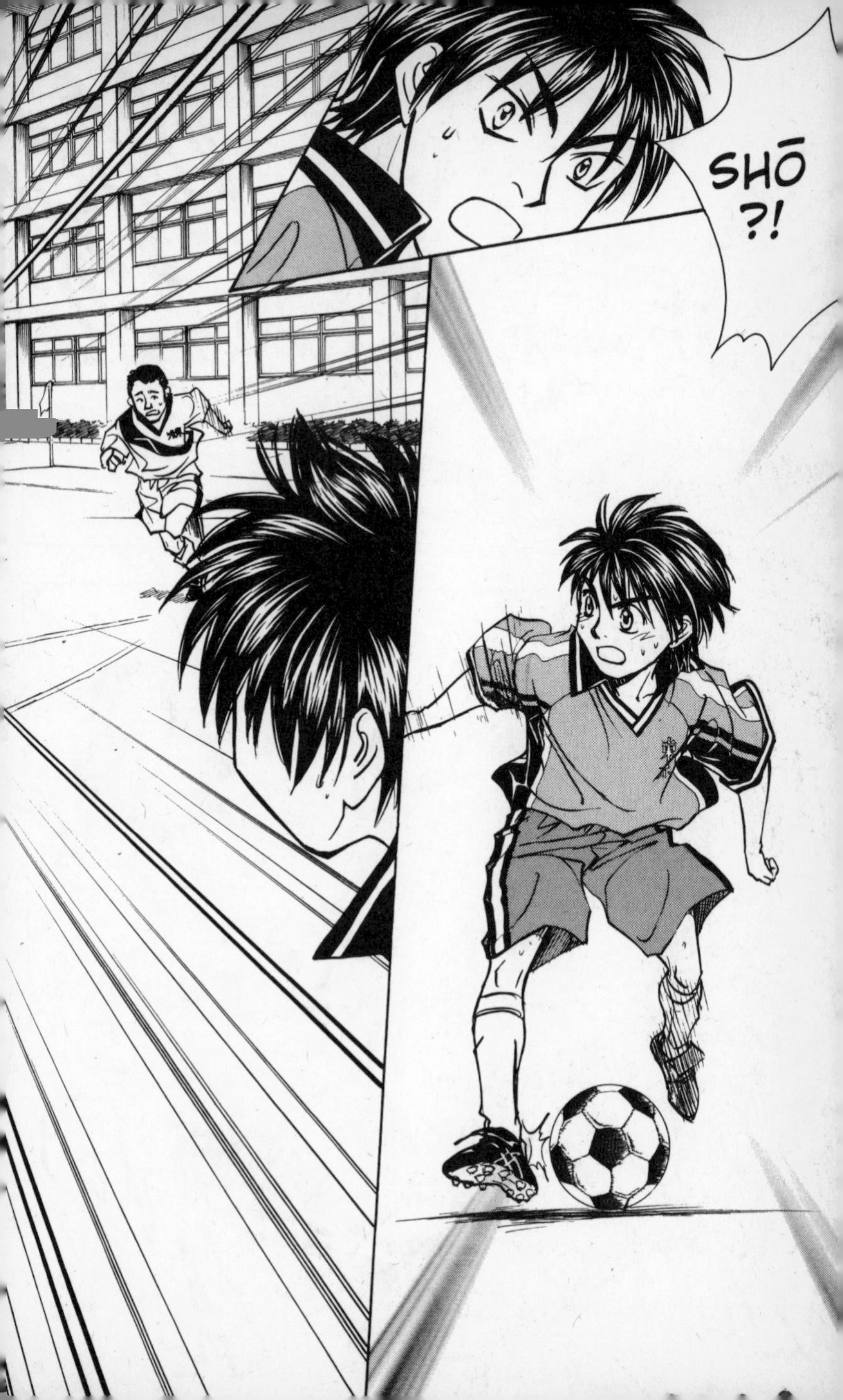
SHŌ ?!

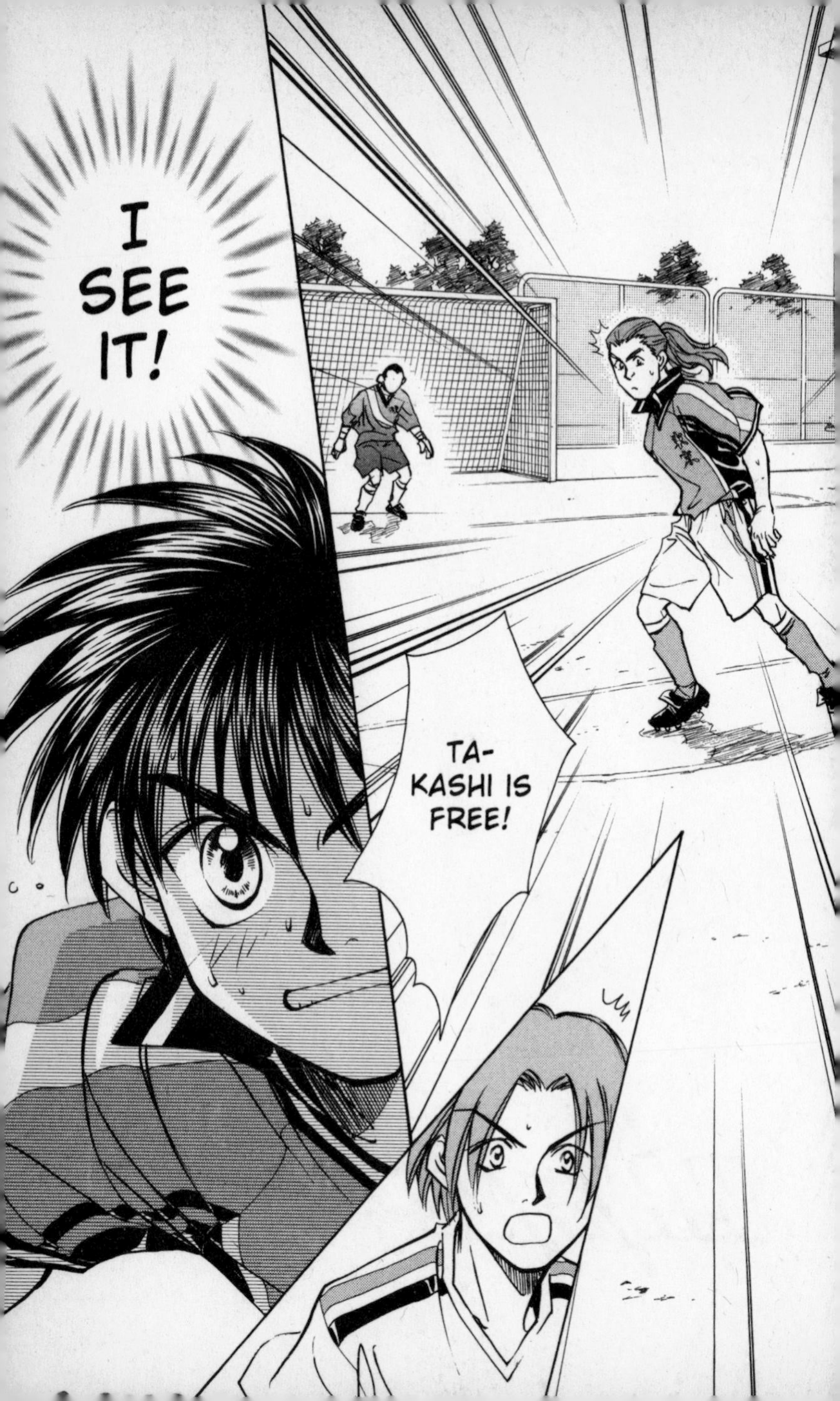
TA-
KASHI IS
FREE!
I
SEE
IT!

WHISTLE!™

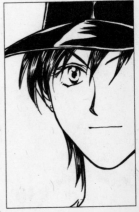

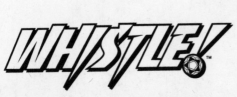

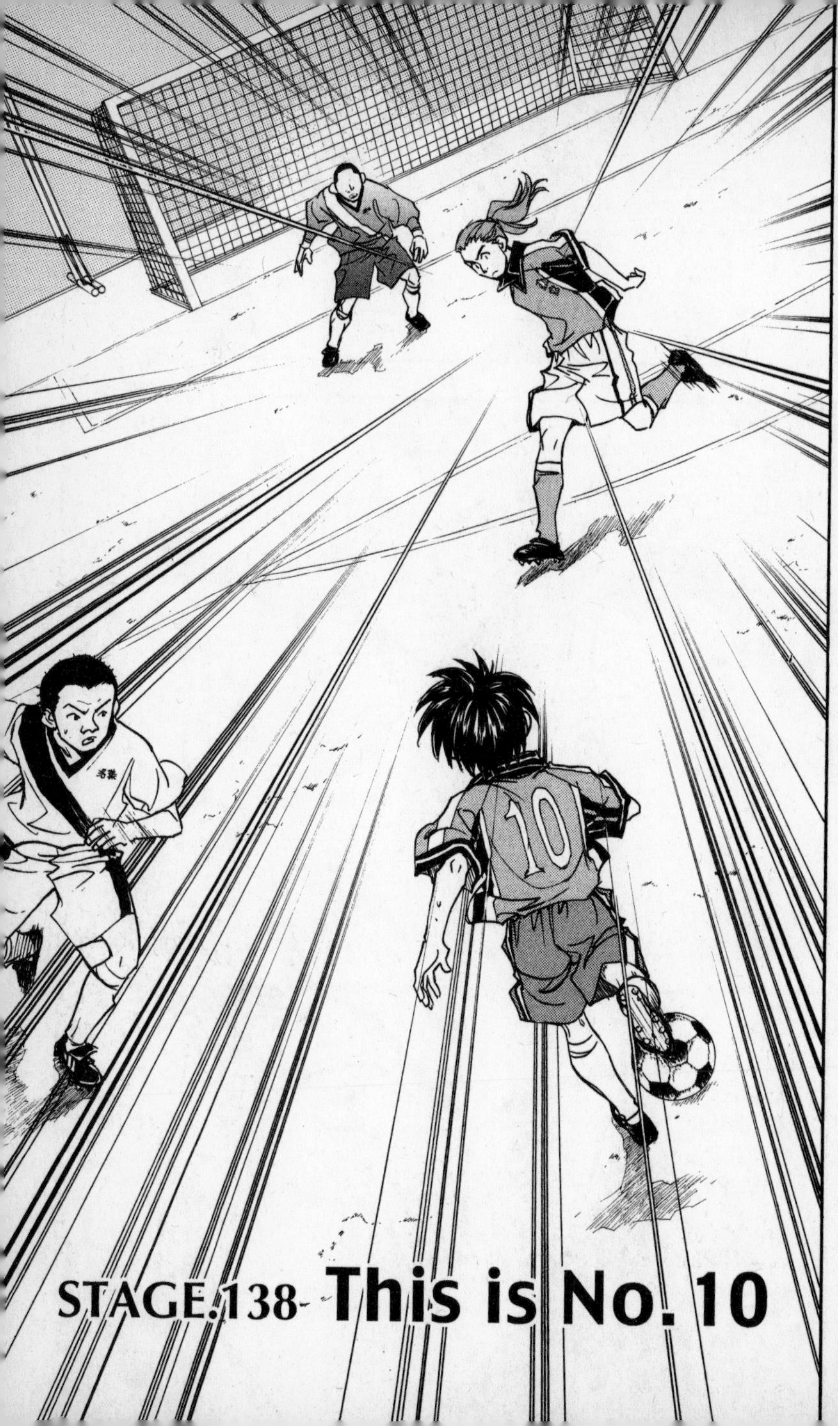

STAGE.138 This is No. 10

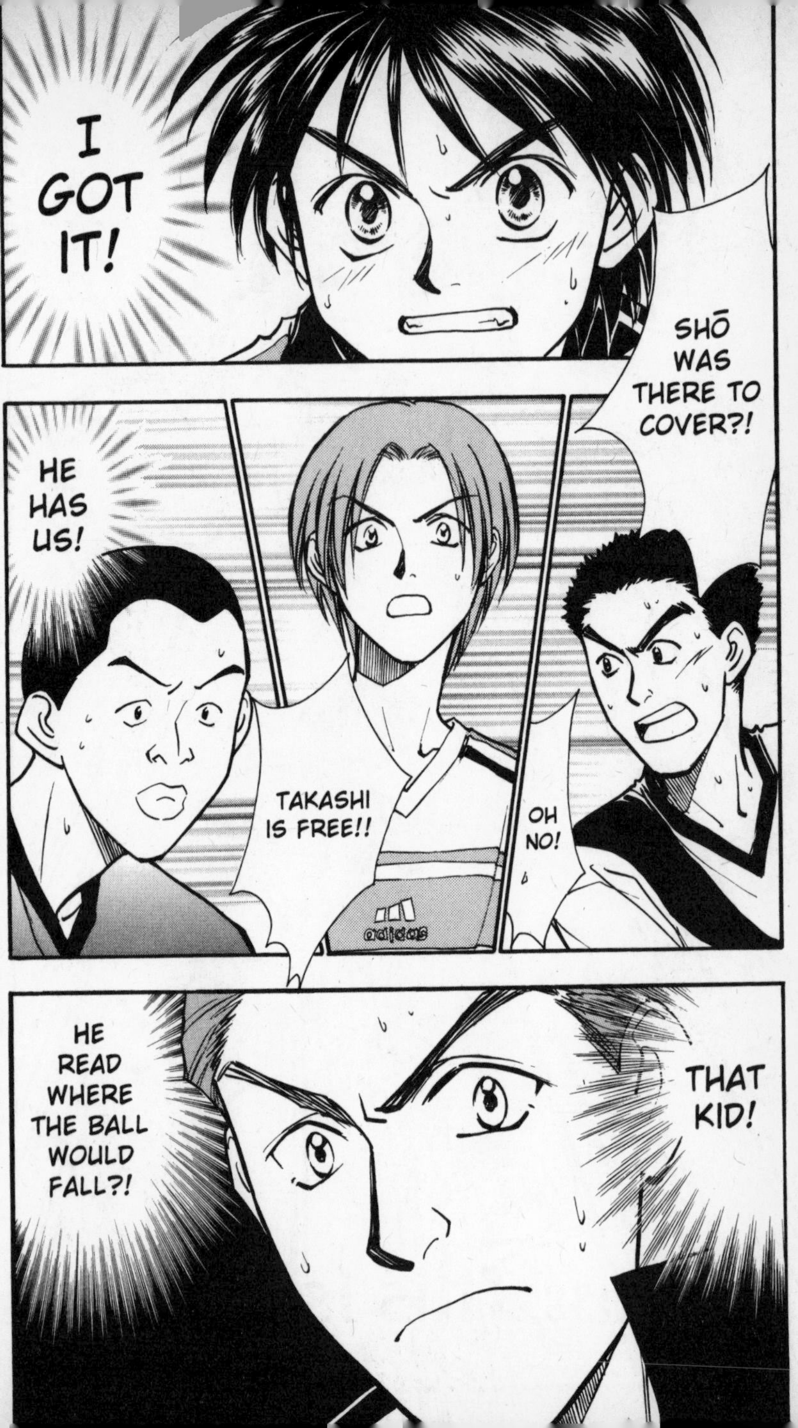
I GOT IT!
SHŌ WAS THERE TO COVER?!
OH NO!
TAKASHI IS FREE!!
HE HAS US!
THAT KID!
HE READ WHERE THE BALL WOULD FALL?!

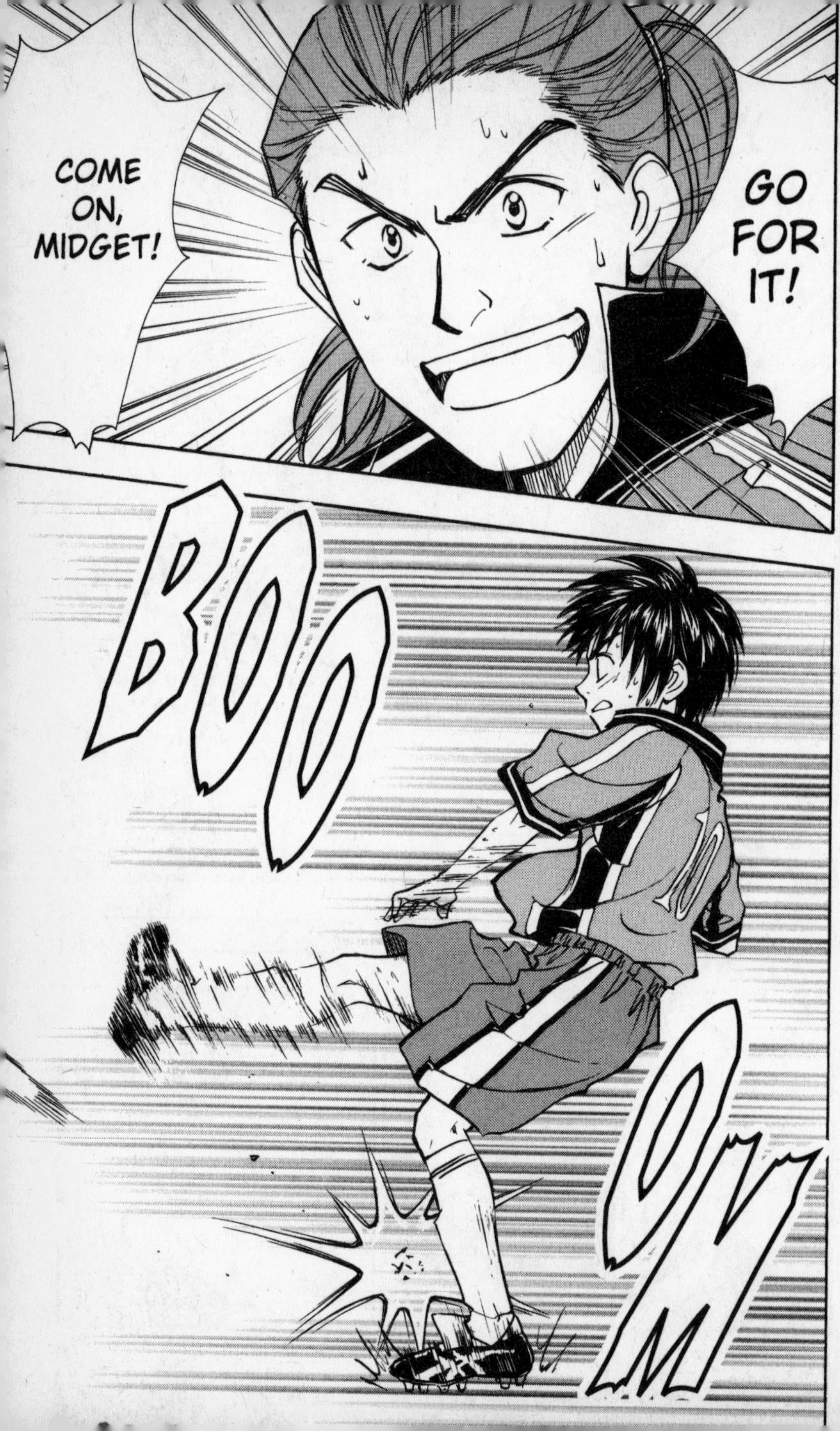
GO FOR IT!
COME ON, MIDGET!
BOOOOM

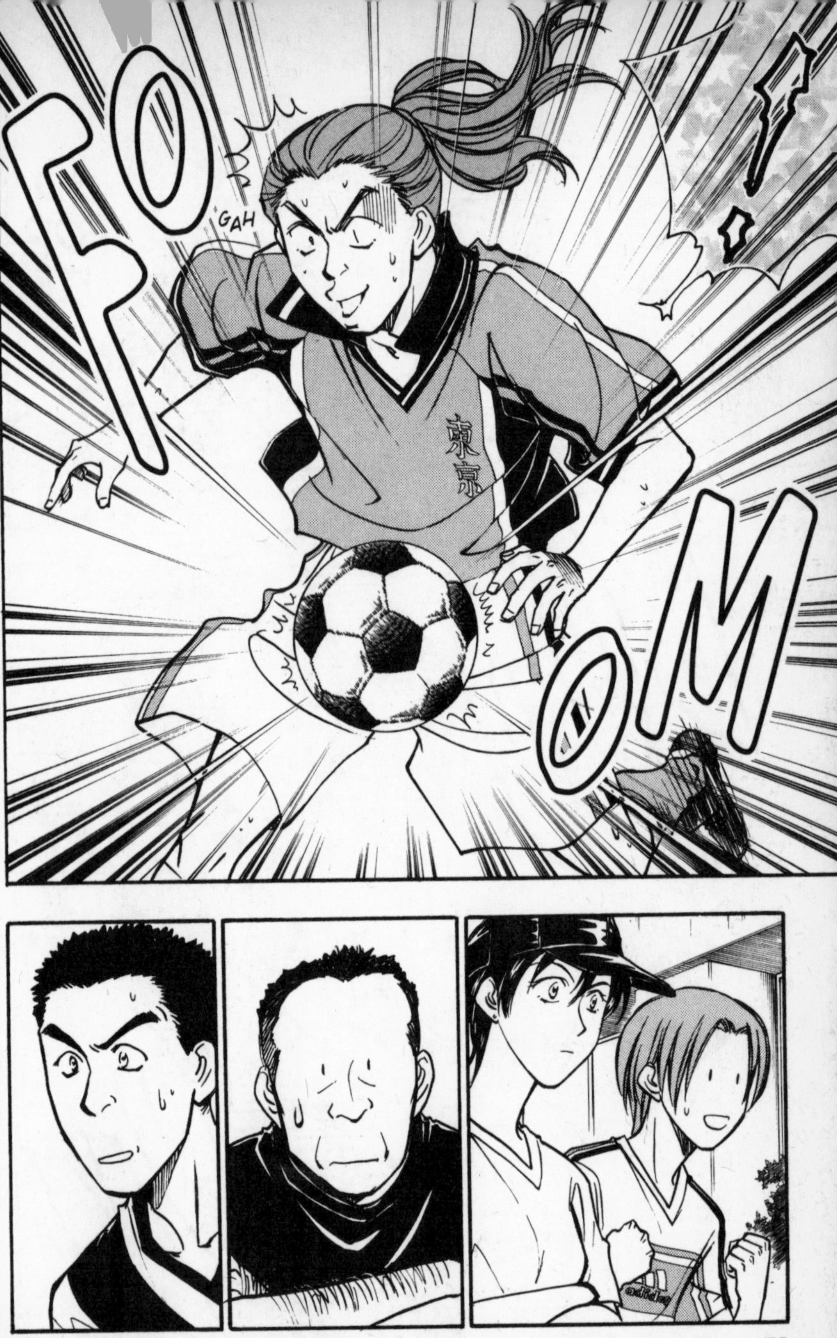

VROOM
GAH

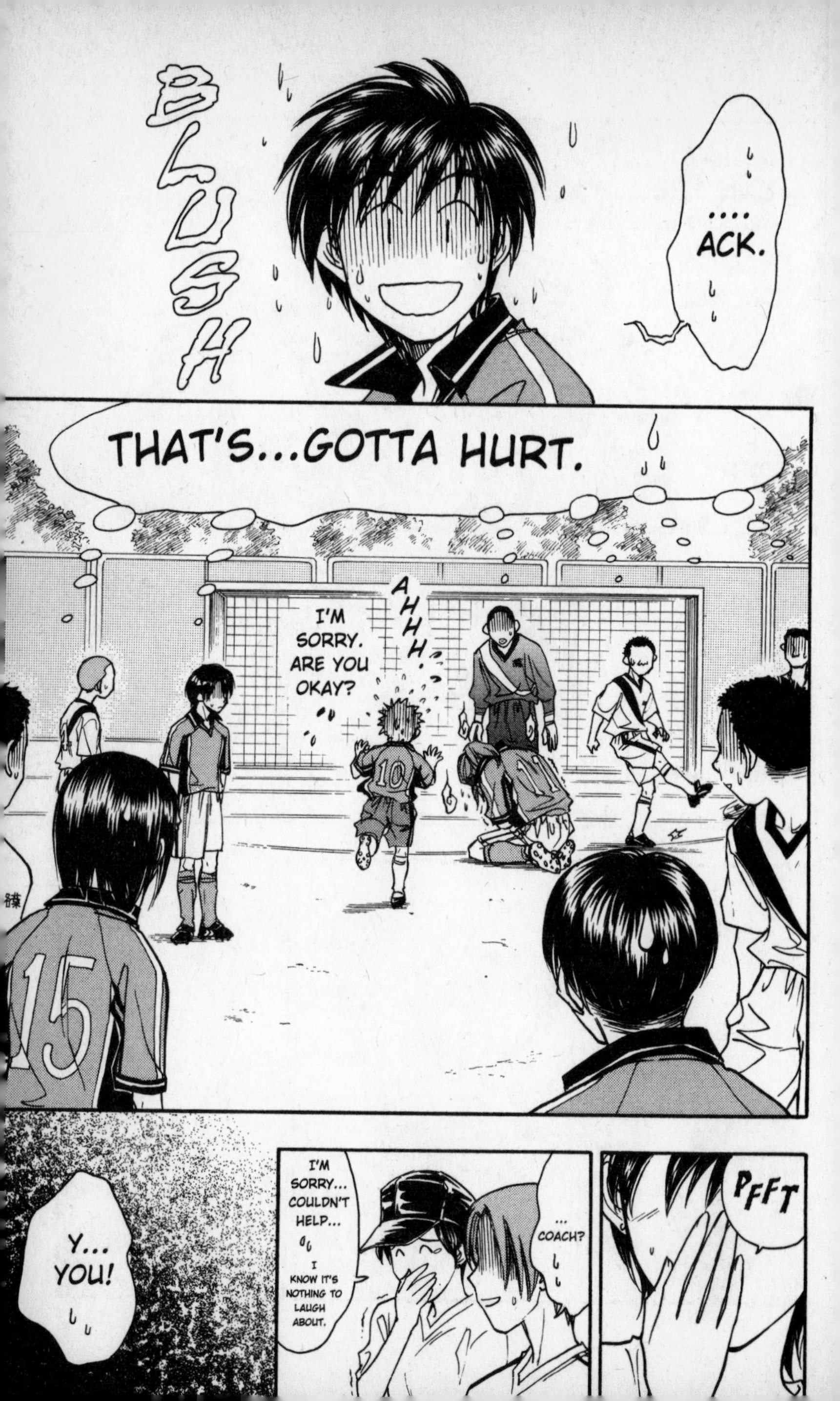
.... ACK.
BLUSH
THAT'S...GOTTA HURT.
AHHH
I'M SORRY. ARE YOU OKAY?
PFFT
... COACH?
I'M SORRY... COULDN'T HELP...
I KNOW IT'S NOTHING TO LAUGH ABOUT.
Y... YOU!

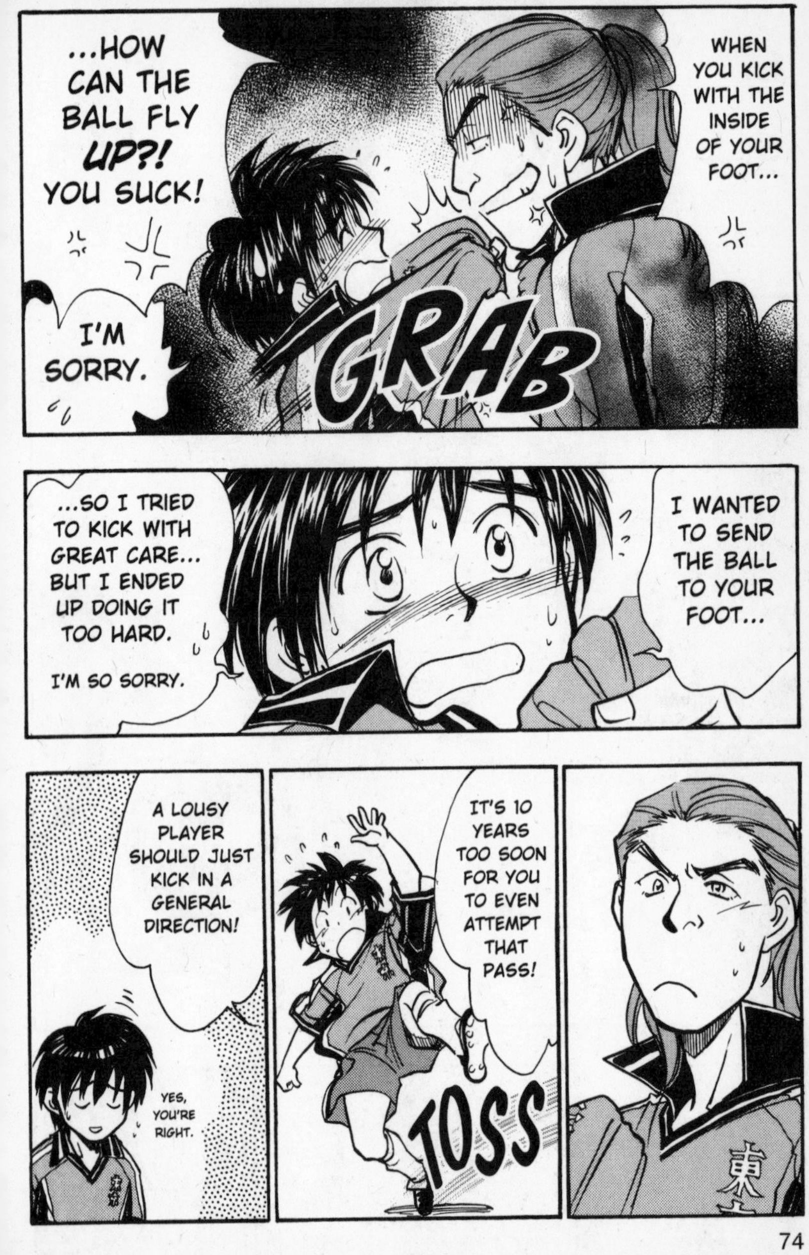
WHEN YOU KICK WITH THE INSIDE OF YOUR FOOT...
...HOW CAN THE BALL FLY UP?! YOU SUCK!
GRAB
I'M SORRY.
I WANTED TO SEND THE BALL TO YOUR FOOT...
...SO I TRIED TO KICK WITH GREAT CARE... BUT I ENDED UP DOING IT TOO HARD.
I'M SO SORRY.
IT'S 10 YEARS TOO SOON FOR YOU TO EVEN ATTEMPT THAT PASS!
TOSS
A LOUSY PLAYER SHOULD JUST KICK IN A GENERAL DIRECTION!
YES, YOU'RE RIGHT.

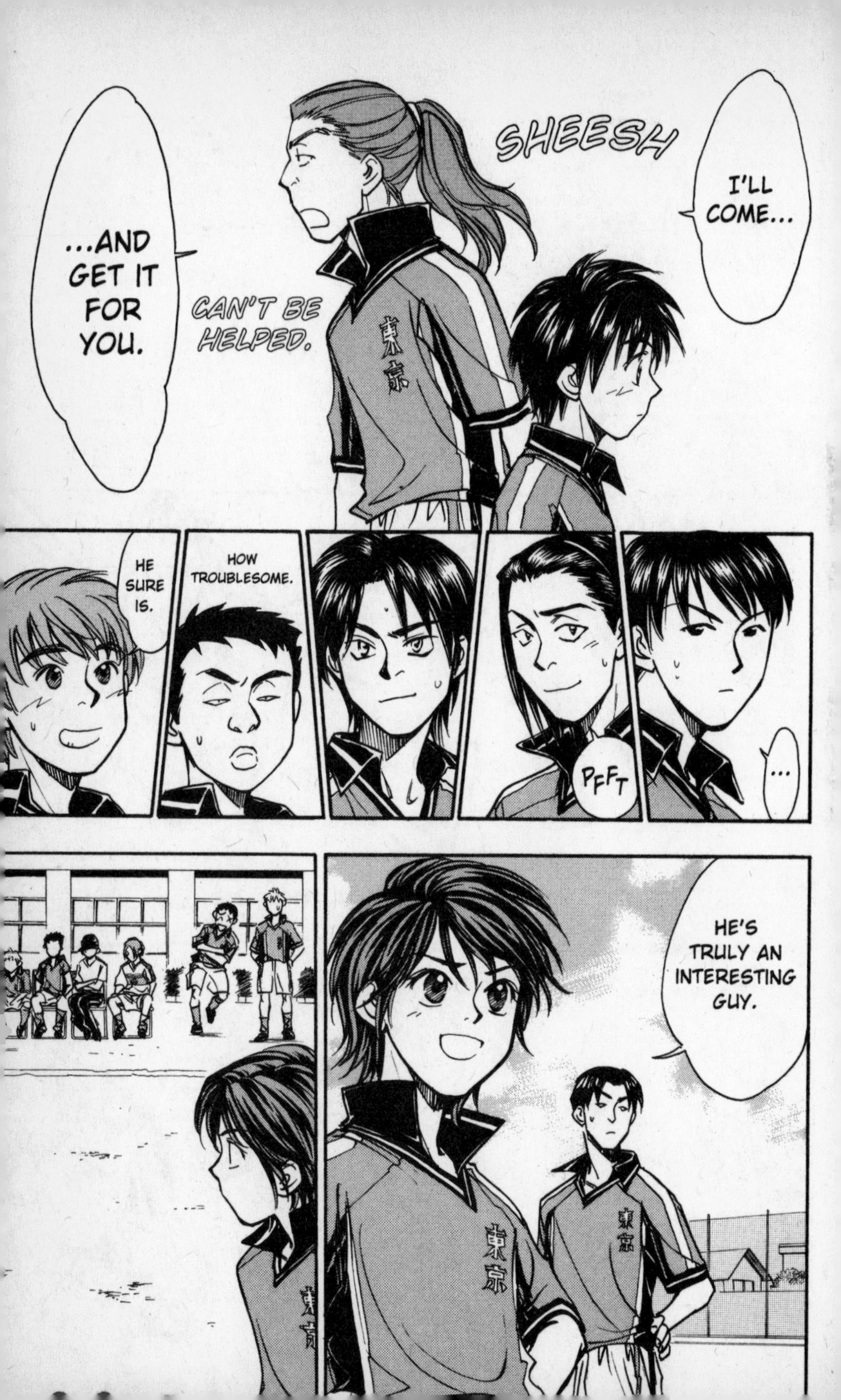
I'LL COME...
SHEESH
...AND GET IT FOR YOU.
CAN'T BE HELPED.
...
PFFT
HOW TROUBLESOME.
HE SURE IS.
HE'S TRULY AN INTERESTING GUY.

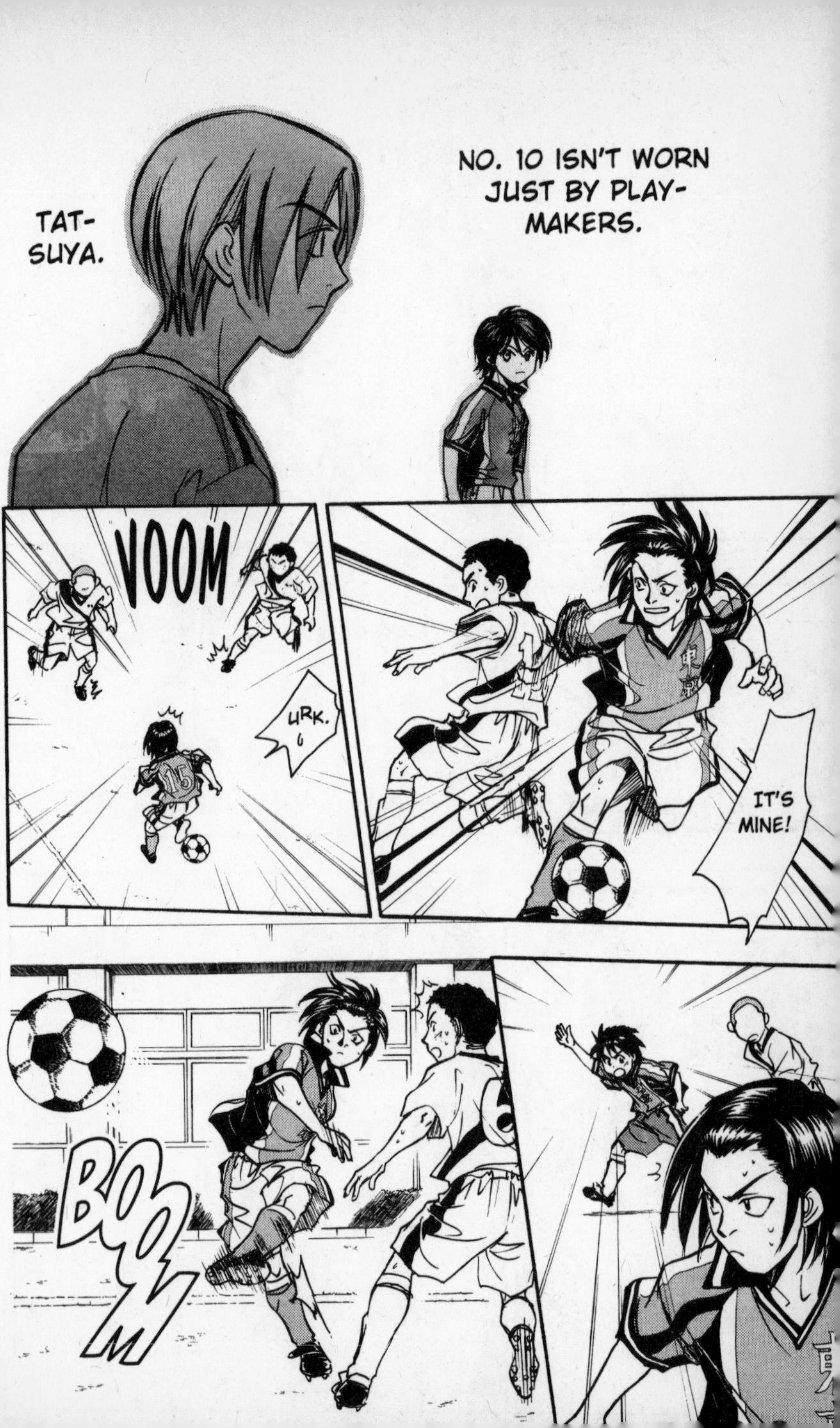
NO. 10 ISN'T WORN JUST BY PLAY-MAKERS.
TAT-SUYA.
IT'S MINE!
VOOM
URK.
BOOOM

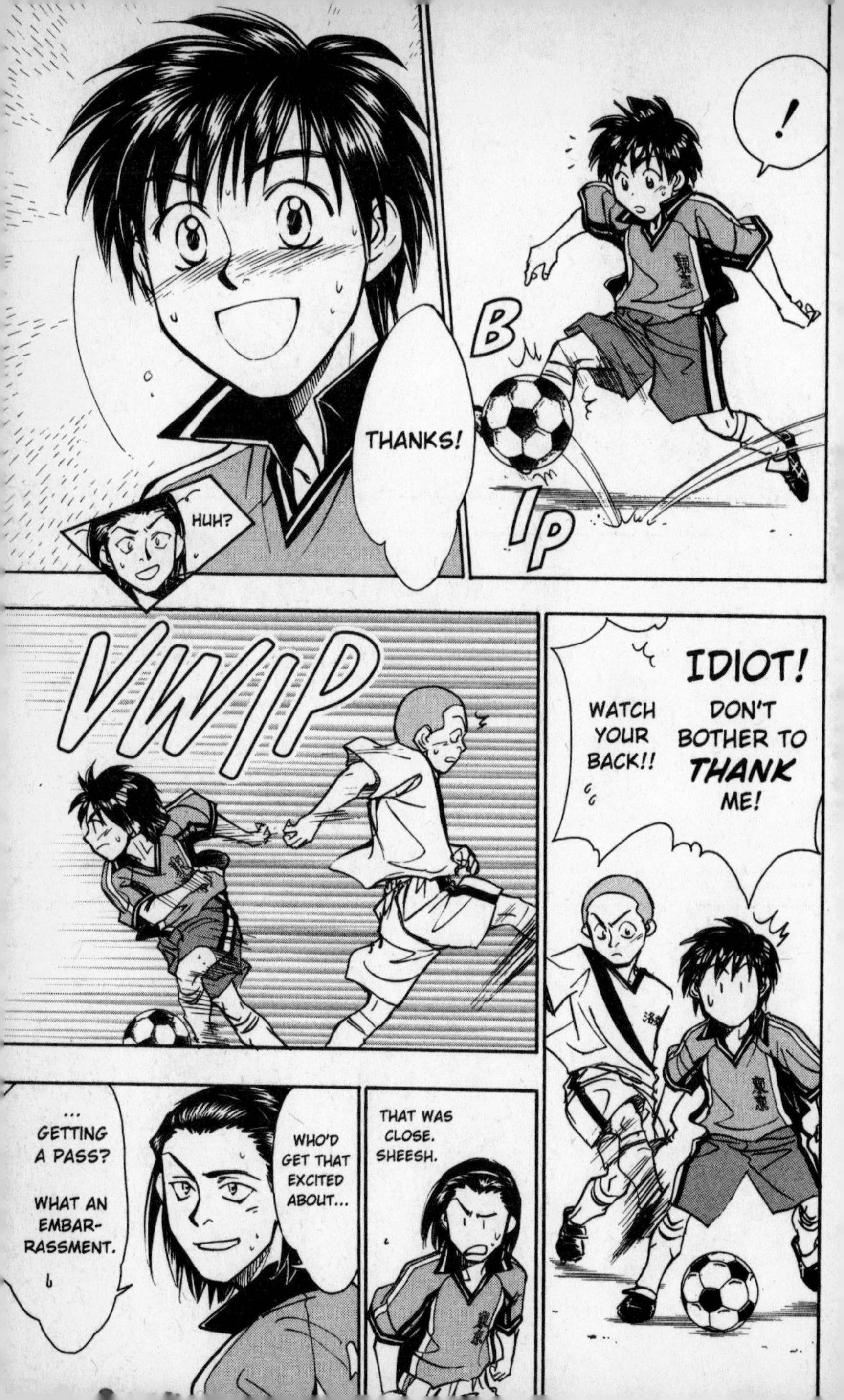
!
BIP
THANKS!
HUH?
IDIOT! DON'T BOTHER TO THANK ME!
WATCH YOUR BACK!!
VWIP
THAT WAS CLOSE. SHEESH.
WHO'D GET THAT EXCITED ABOUT...
... GETTING A PASS?
WHAT AN EMBARRASSMENT.

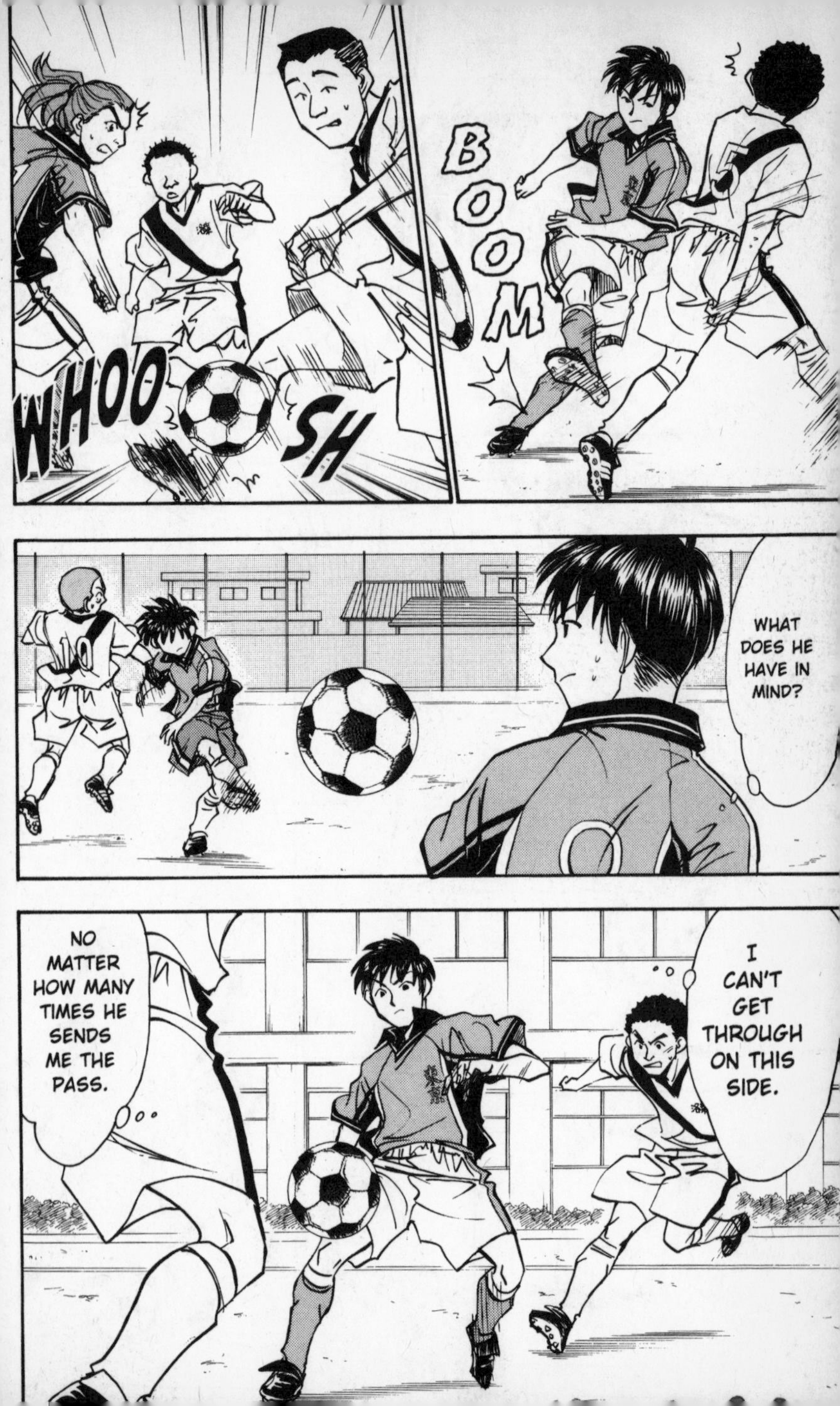
BOOM
WHOOSH
WHAT DOES HE HAVE IN MIND?
I CAN'T GET THROUGH ON THIS SIDE.
NO MATTER HOW MANY TIMES HE SENDS ME THE PASS.

READ THIS WAY

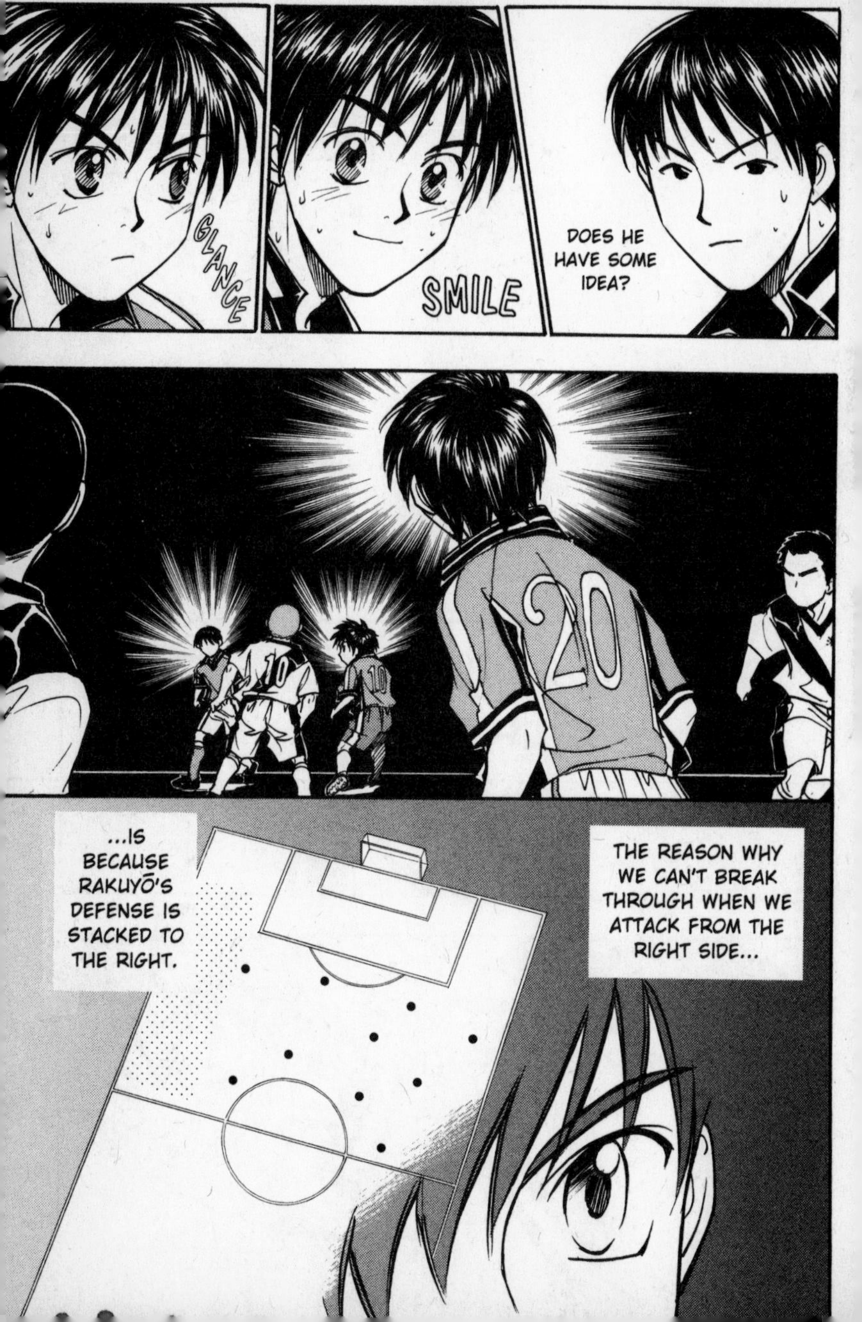
DOES HE HAVE SOME IDEA?
SMILE
GLANCE
THE REASON WHY WE CAN'T BREAK THROUGH WHEN WE ATTACK FROM THE RIGHT SIDE...
...IS BECAUSE RAKUYŌ'S DEFENSE IS STACKED TO THE RIGHT.

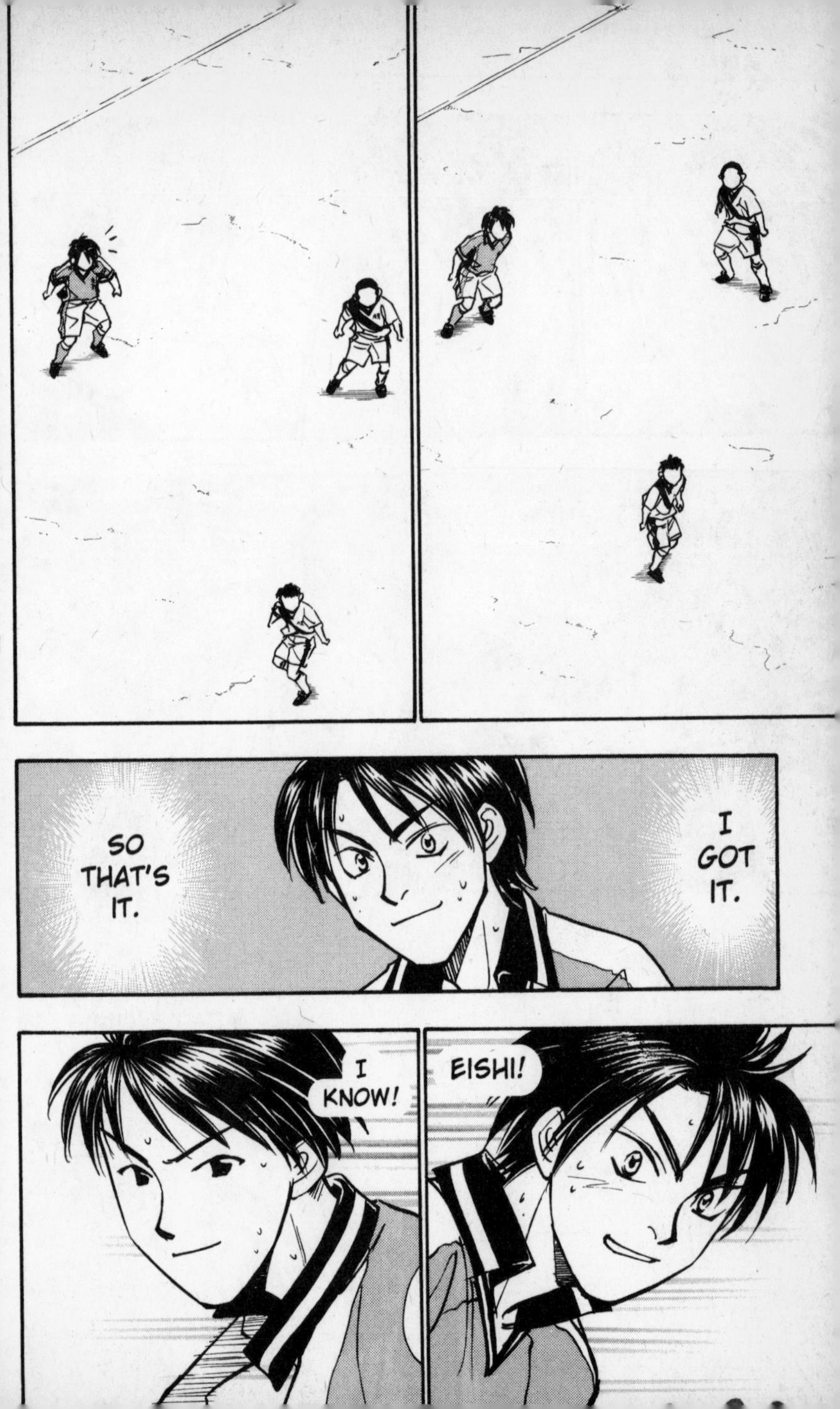
I GOT IT.
SO THAT'S IT.
EISHI!
I KNOW!

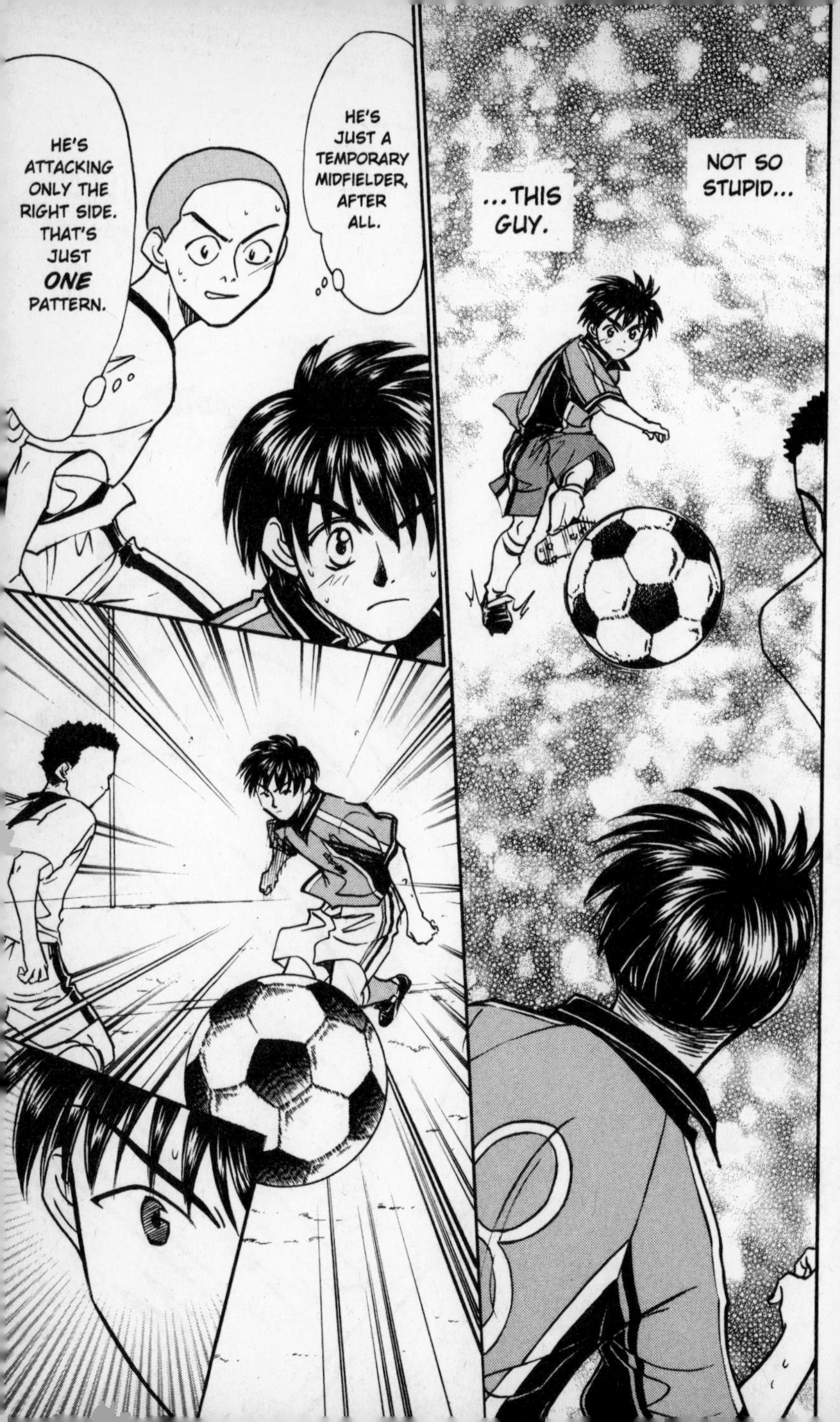
NOT SO STUPID...
...THIS GUY.
HE'S JUST A TEMPORARY MIDFIELDER, AFTER ALL.
HE'S ATTACKING ONLY THE RIGHT SIDE. THAT'S JUST **ONE** PATTERN.

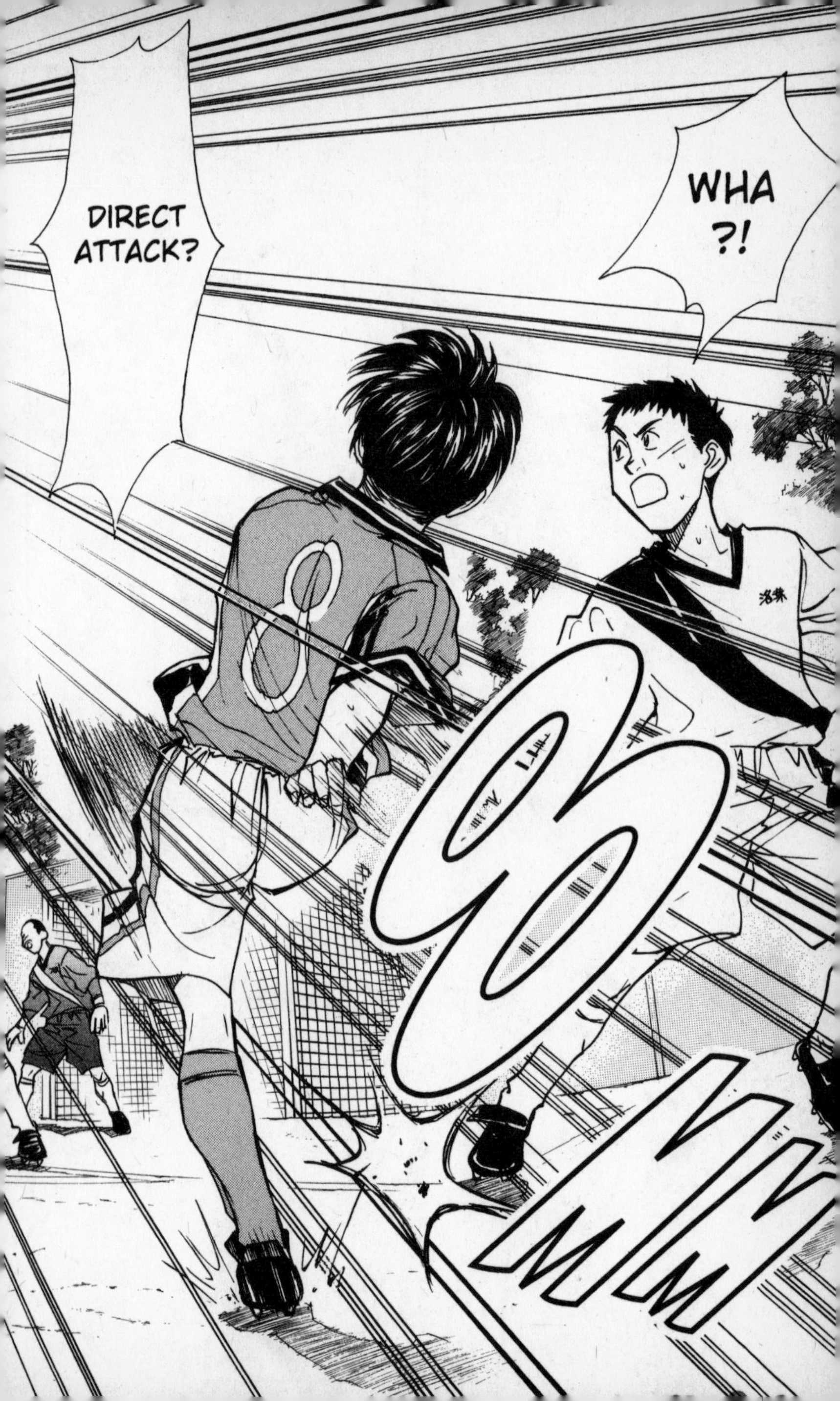
WHA ?!
DIRECT ATTACK?

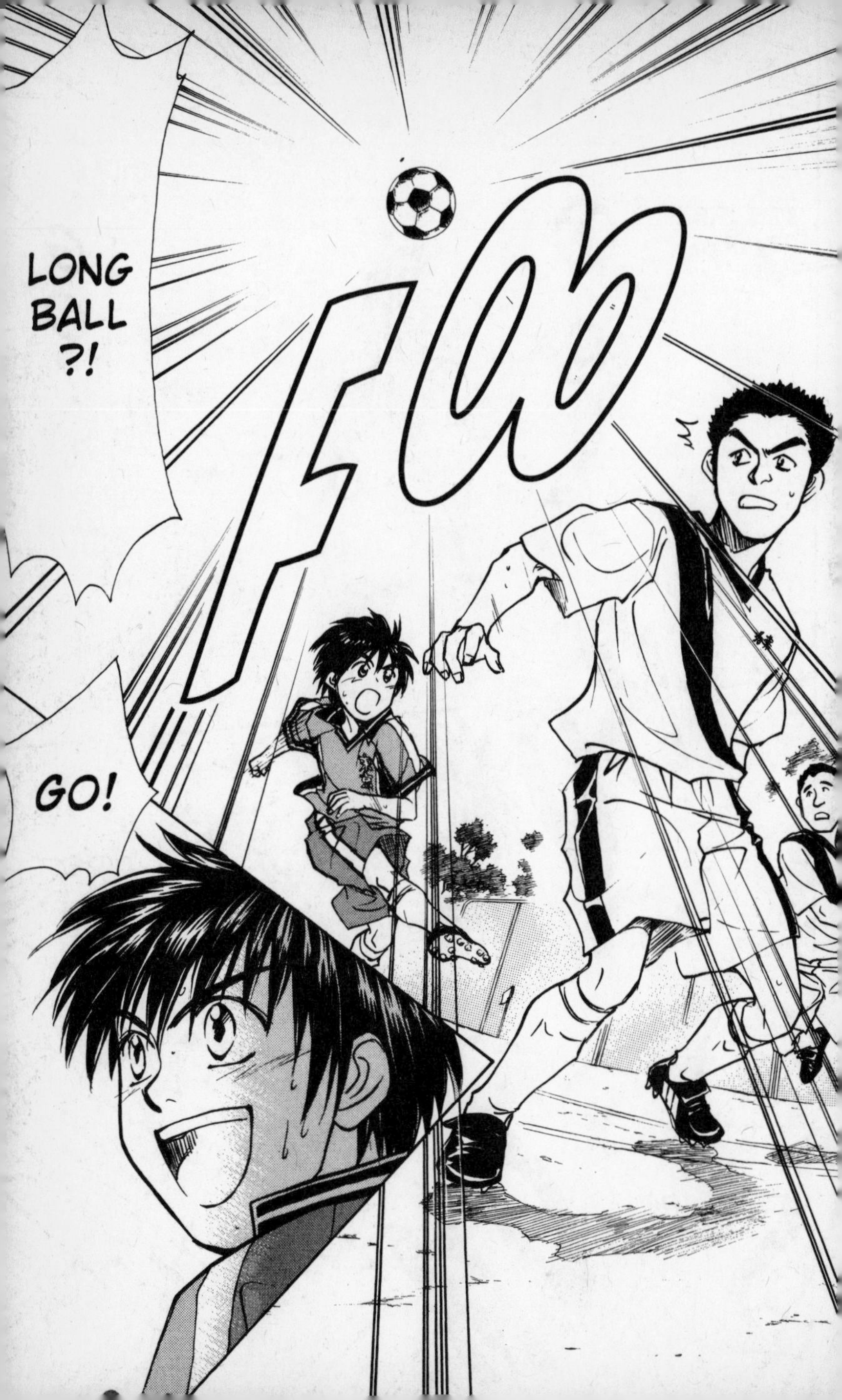
FOO
LONG BALL ?!
GO!

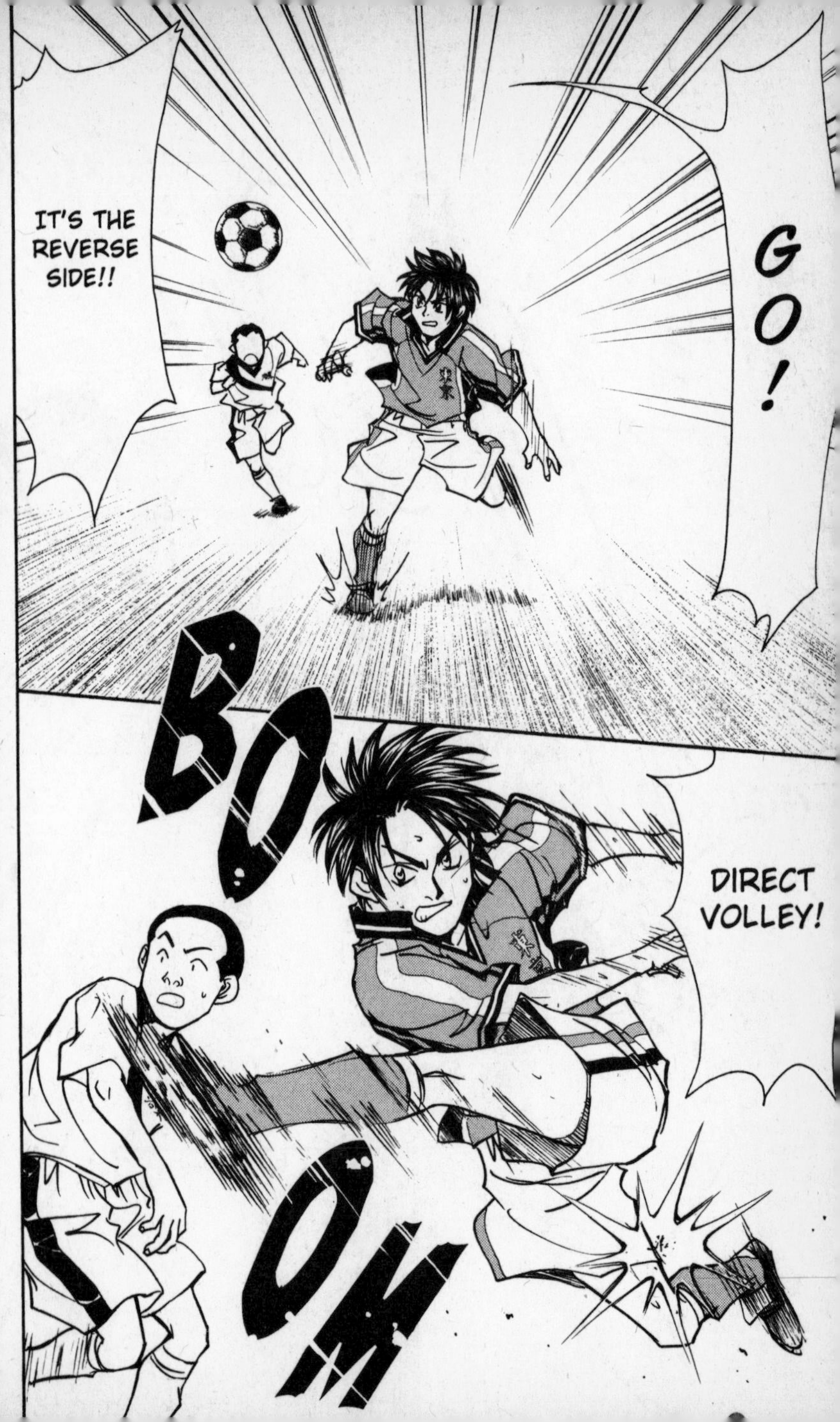
GO!
IT'S THE REVERSE SIDE!!
DIRECT VOLLEY!
BOOM

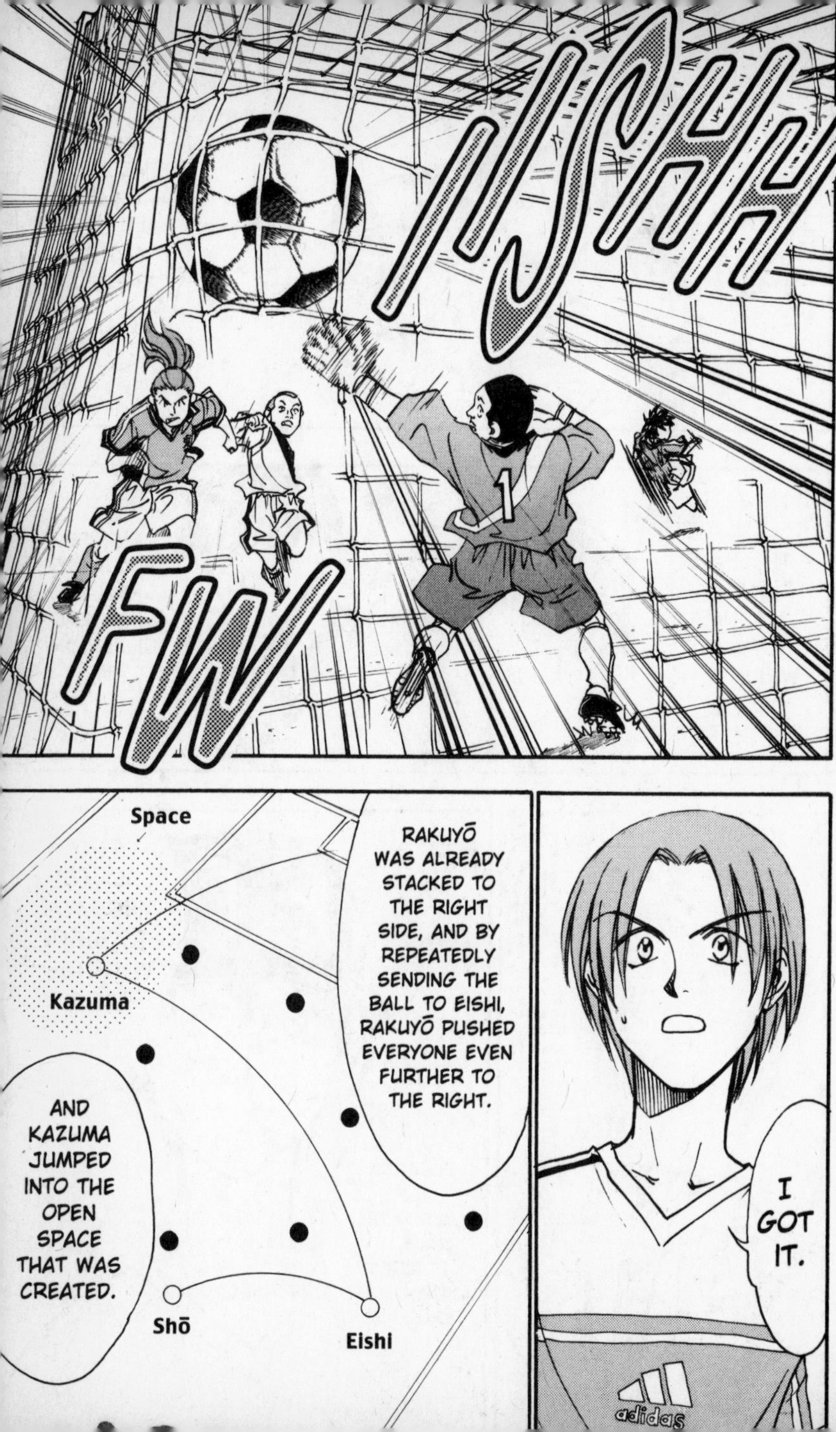
WSHH
FW
I GOT IT.
RAKUYŌ WAS ALREADY STACKED TO THE RIGHT SIDE, AND BY REPEATEDLY SENDING THE BALL TO EISHI, RAKUYŌ PUSHED EVERYONE EVEN FURTHER TO THE RIGHT.
Space
Kazuma
Shō
Eishi
AND KAZUMA JUMPED INTO THE OPEN SPACE THAT WAS CREATED.

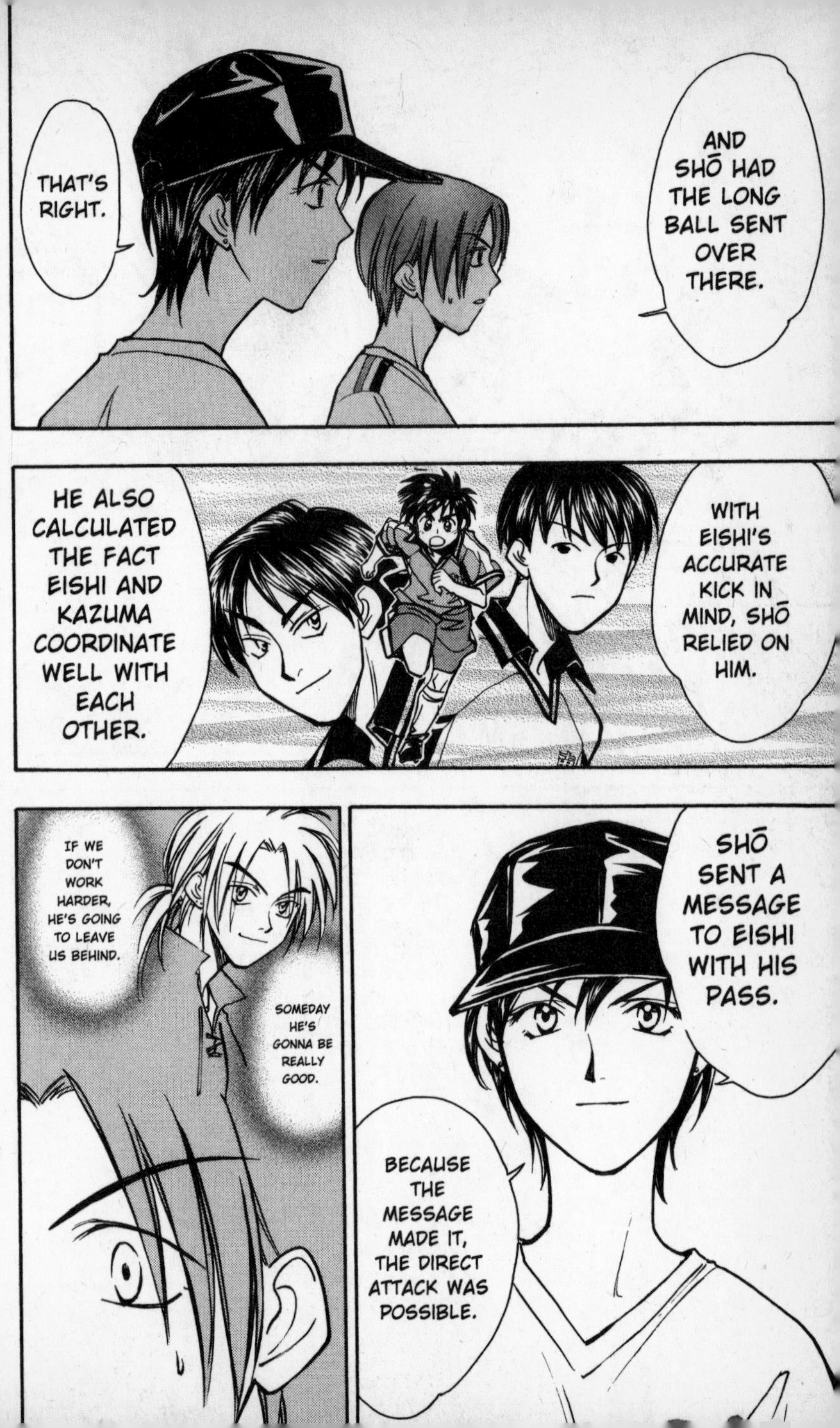
AND SHŌ HAD THE LONG BALL SENT OVER THERE.
THAT'S RIGHT.
WITH EISHI'S ACCURATE KICK IN MIND, SHŌ RELIED ON HIM.
HE ALSO CALCULATED THE FACT EISHI AND KAZUMA COORDINATE WELL WITH EACH OTHER.
SHŌ SENT A MESSAGE TO EISHI WITH HIS PASS.
BECAUSE THE MESSAGE MADE IT, THE DIRECT ATTACK WAS POSSIBLE.
IF WE DON'T WORK HARDER, HE'S GOING TO LEAVE US BEHIND.
SOMEDAY HE'S GONNA BE REALLY GOOD.

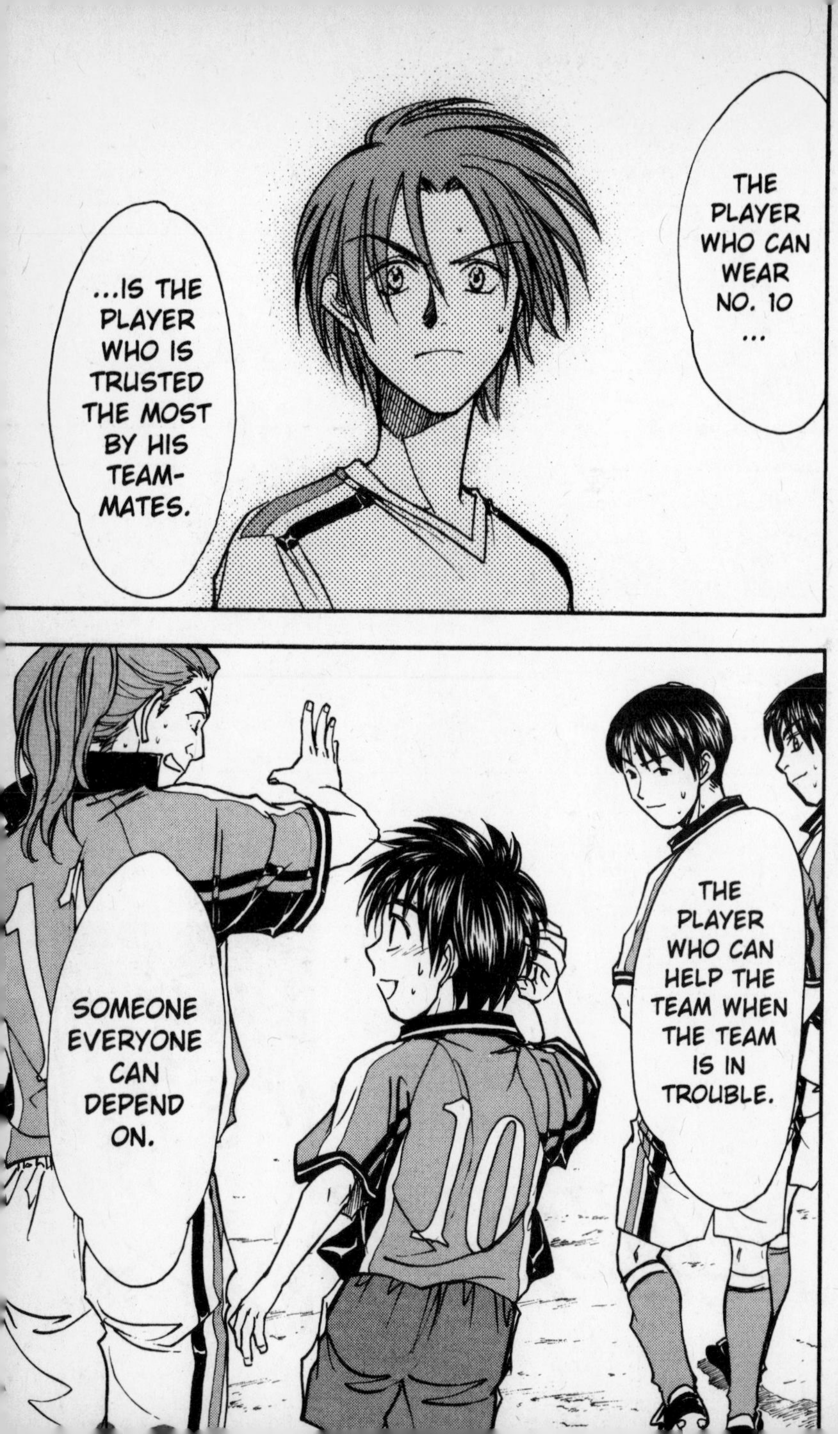
THE PLAYER WHO CAN WEAR NO. 10 ...
...IS THE PLAYER WHO IS TRUSTED THE MOST BY HIS TEAM-MATES.
THE PLAYER WHO CAN HELP THE TEAM WHEN THE TEAM IS IN TROUBLE.
SOMEONE EVERYONE CAN DEPEND ON.

SMILE

WHISTLE!™

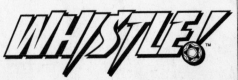

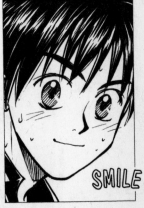

STAGE.139
The Talent of the Man Beside You

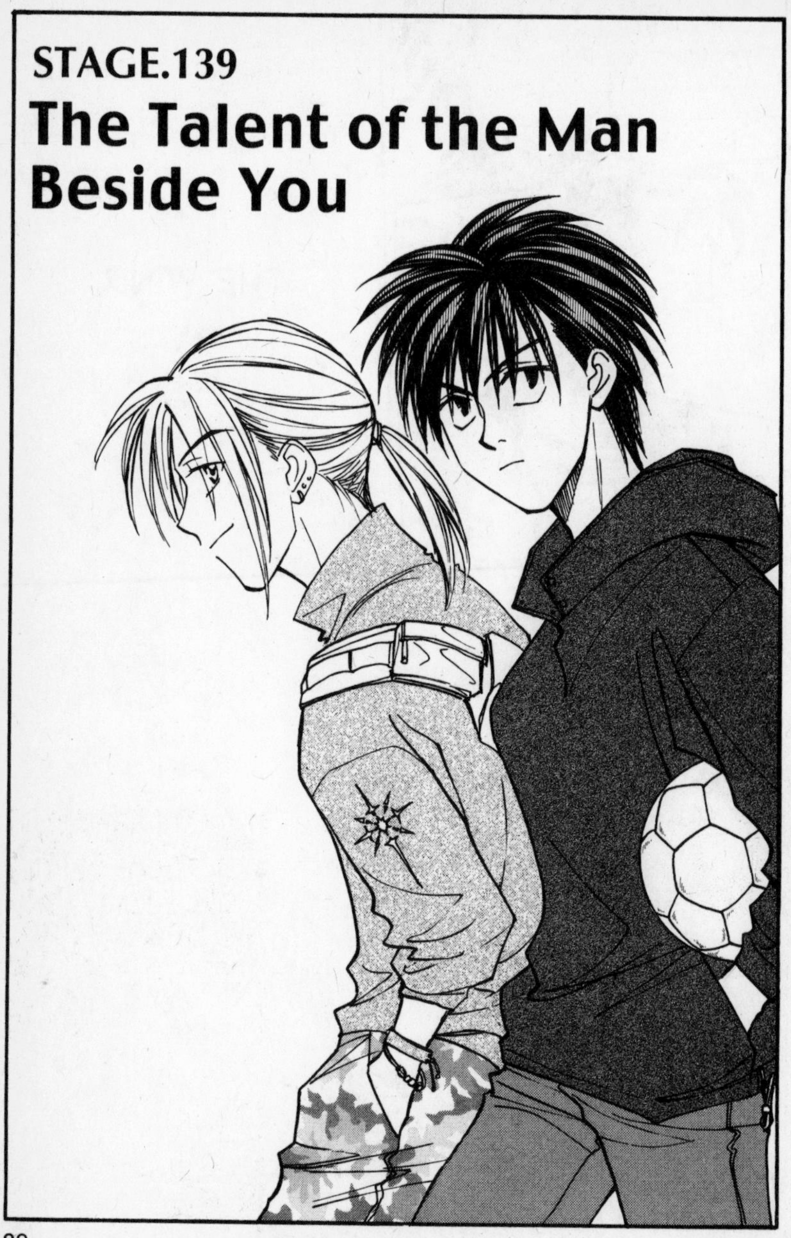

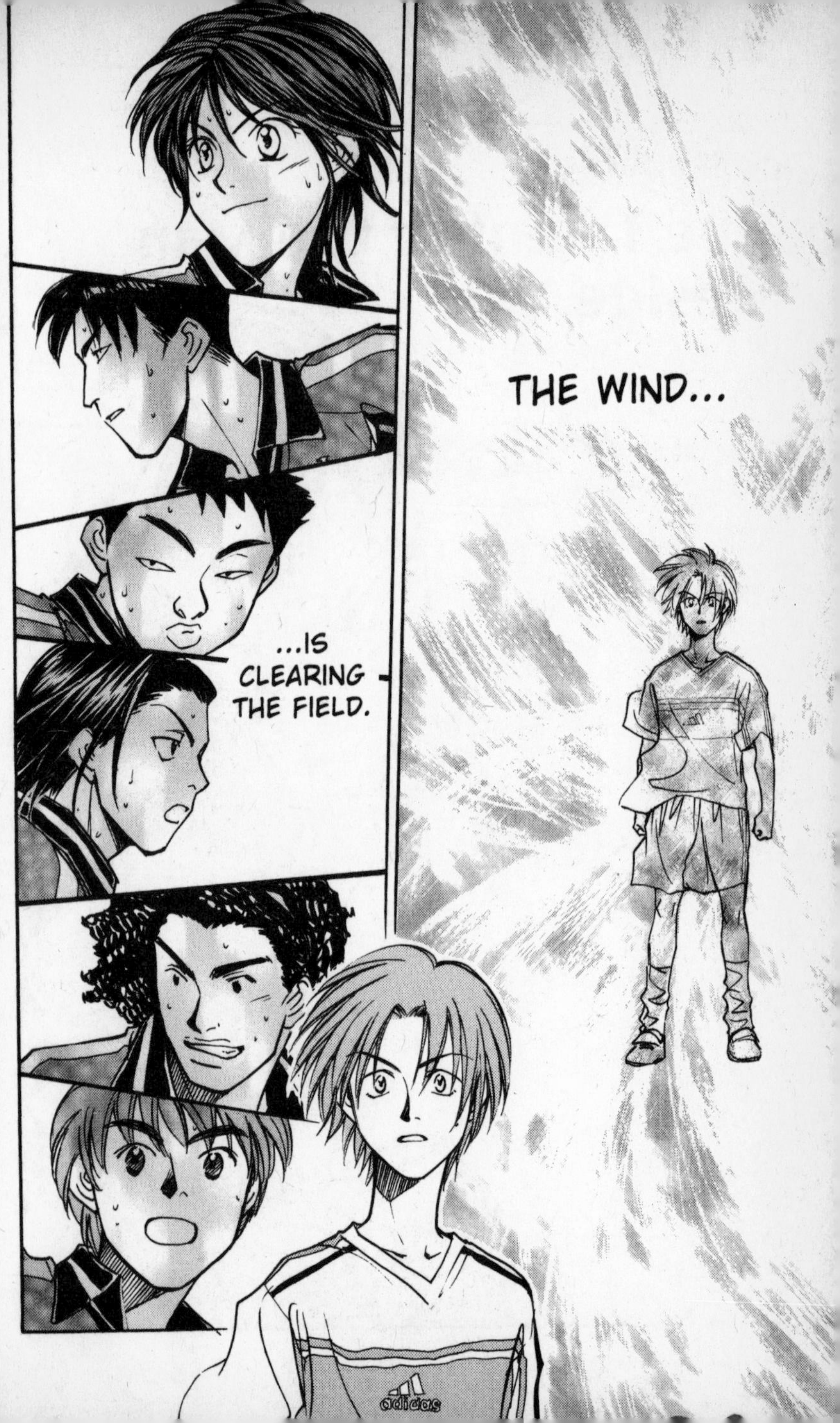
THE WIND...
...IS CLEARING THE FIELD.

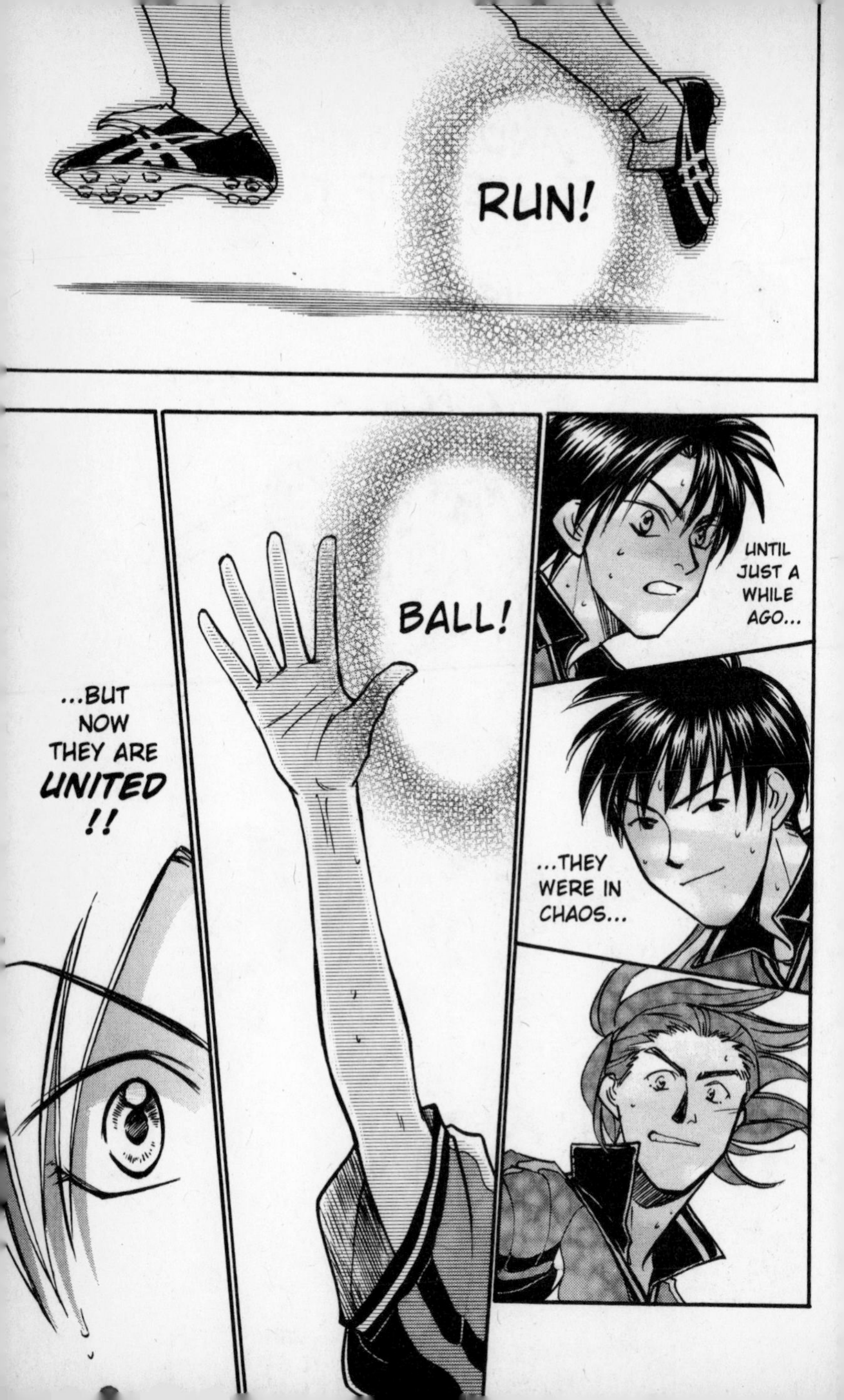
RUN!
UNTIL JUST A WHILE AGO...
...THEY WERE IN CHAOS...
BALL!
...BUT NOW THEY ARE UNITED!!

AND AT THE CENTER OF IT...

...IS SHŌ!!

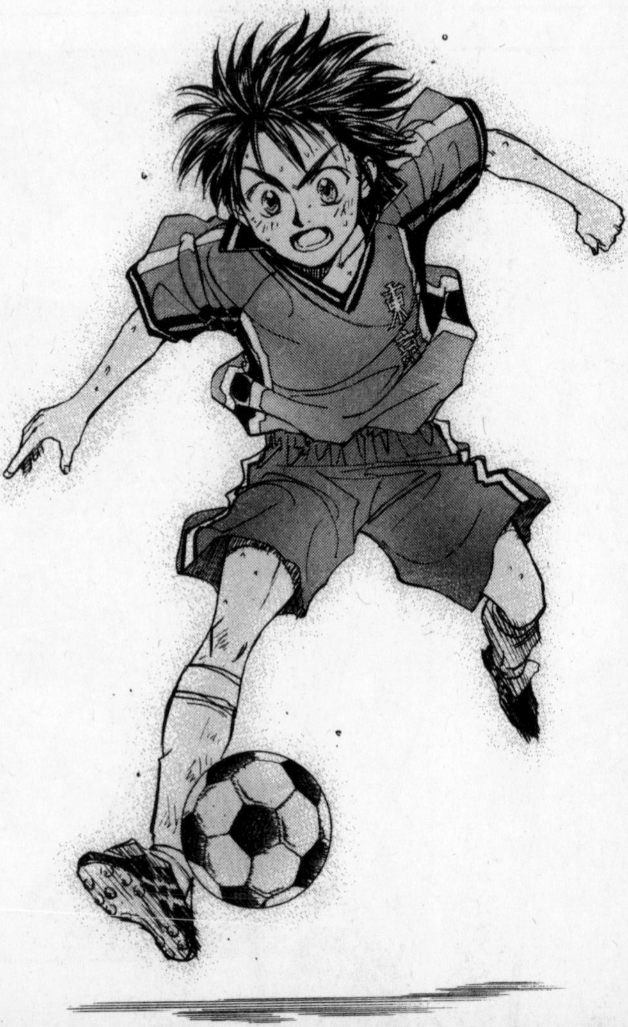

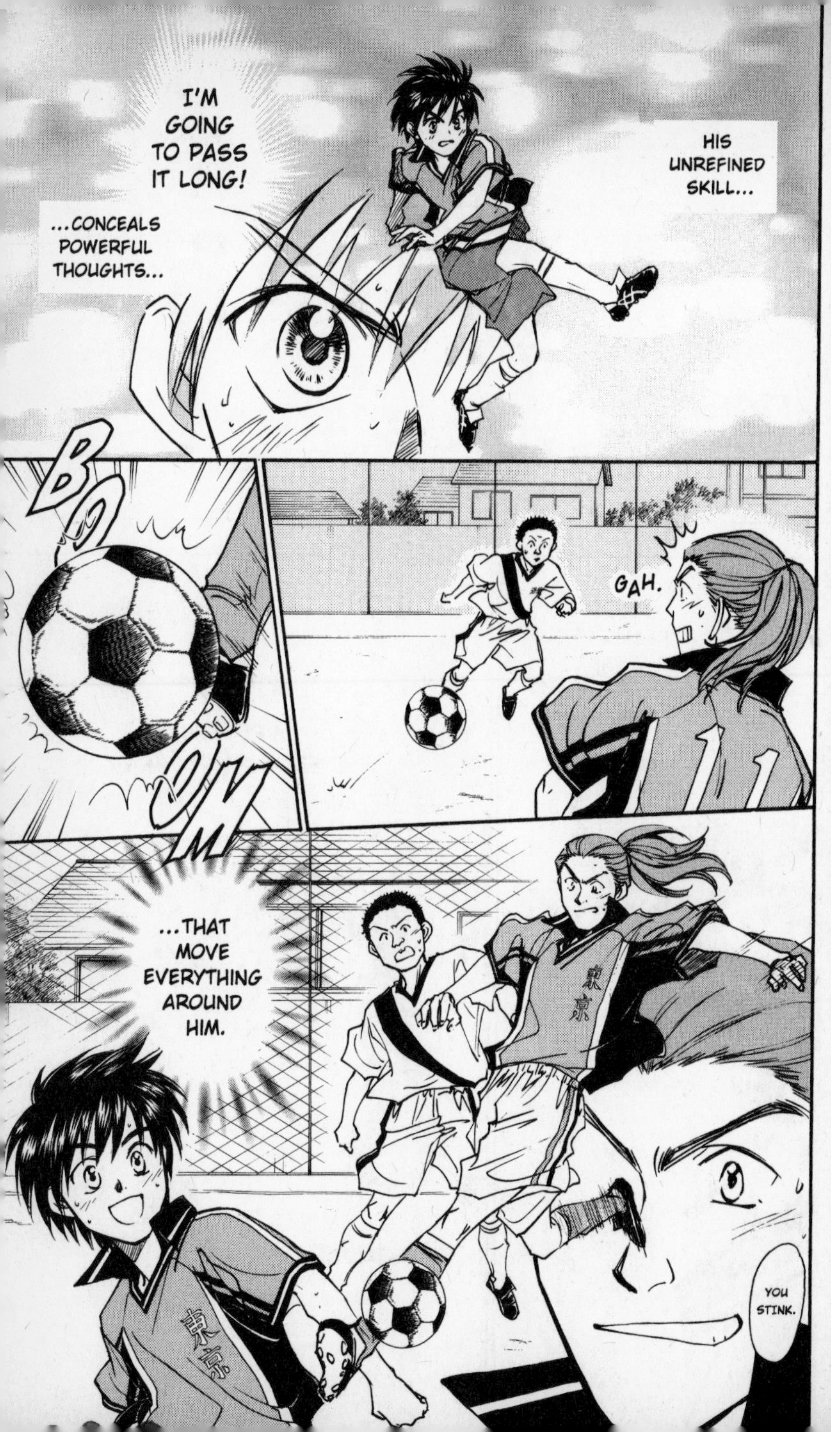
HIS UNREFINED SKILL...
I'M GOING TO PASS IT LONG!
...CONCEALS POWERFUL THOUGHTS...
GAH.
BOOM
...THAT MOVE EVERYTHING AROUND HIM.
YOU STINK.

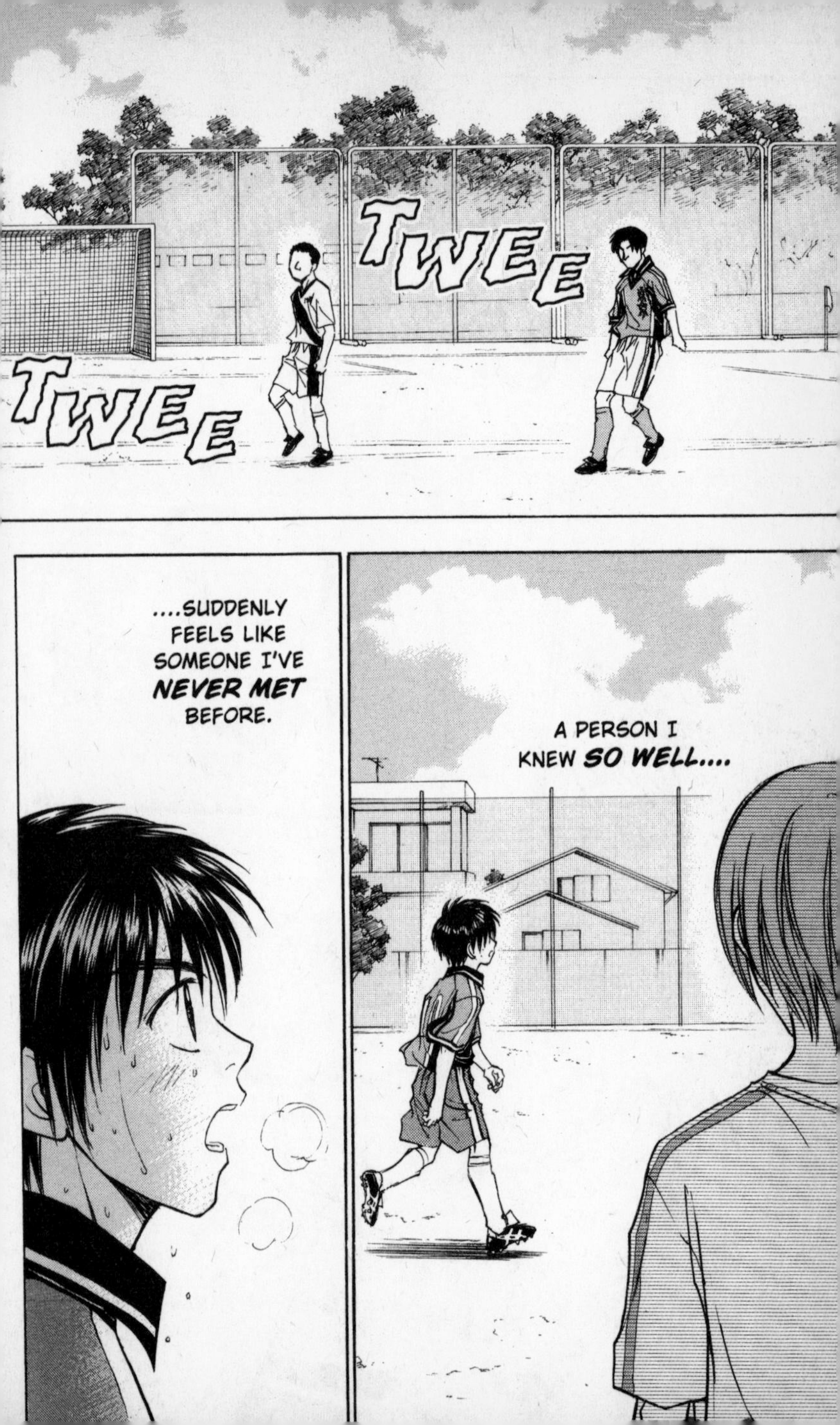
TWEE
TWEE
A PERSON I KNEW SO WELL....
....SUDDENLY FEELS LIKE SOMEONE I'VE NEVER MET BEFORE.

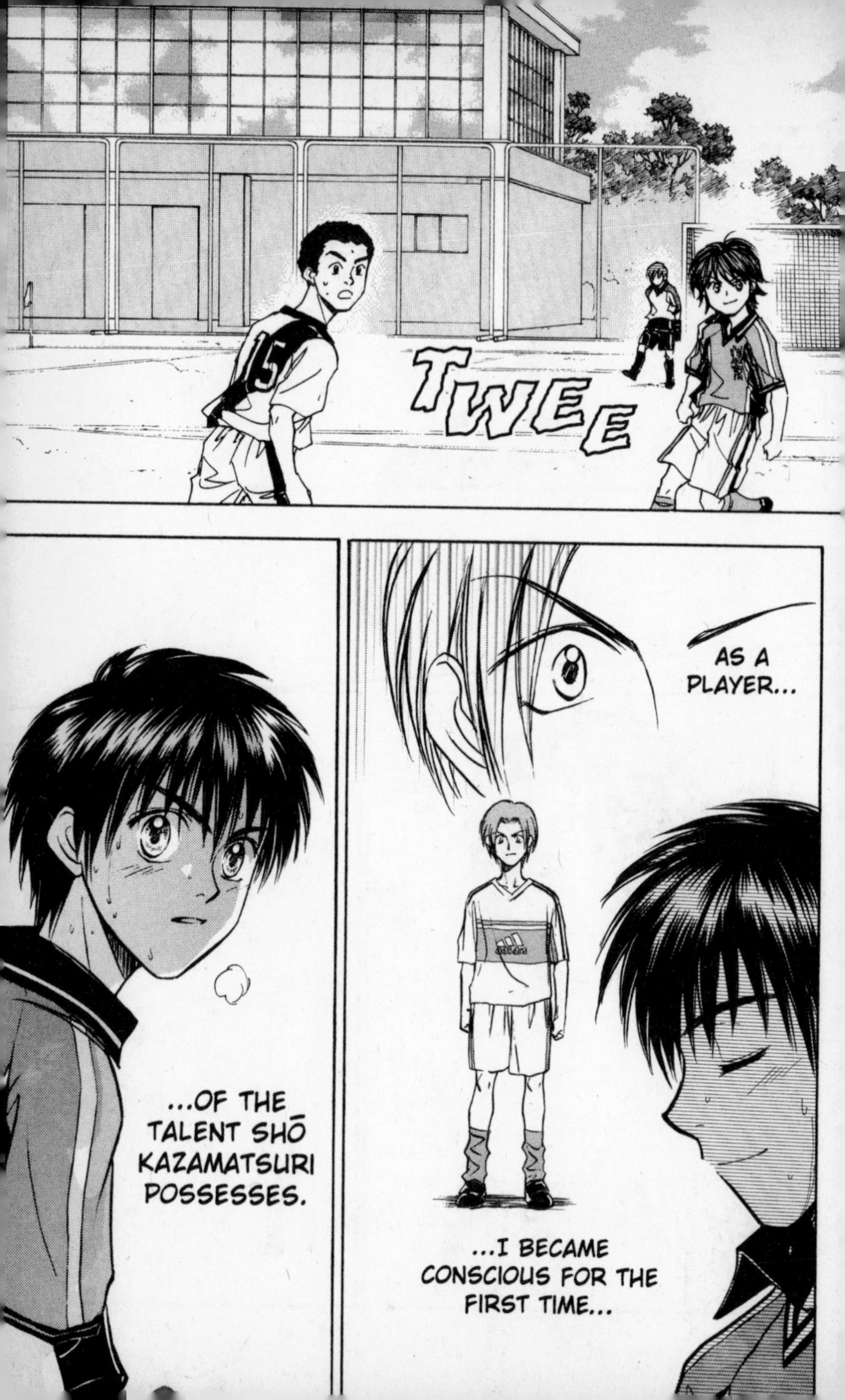
TWEE
AS A PLAYER...
...I BECAME CONSCIOUS FOR THE FIRST TIME...
...OF THE TALENT SHŌ KAZAMATSURI POSSESSES.

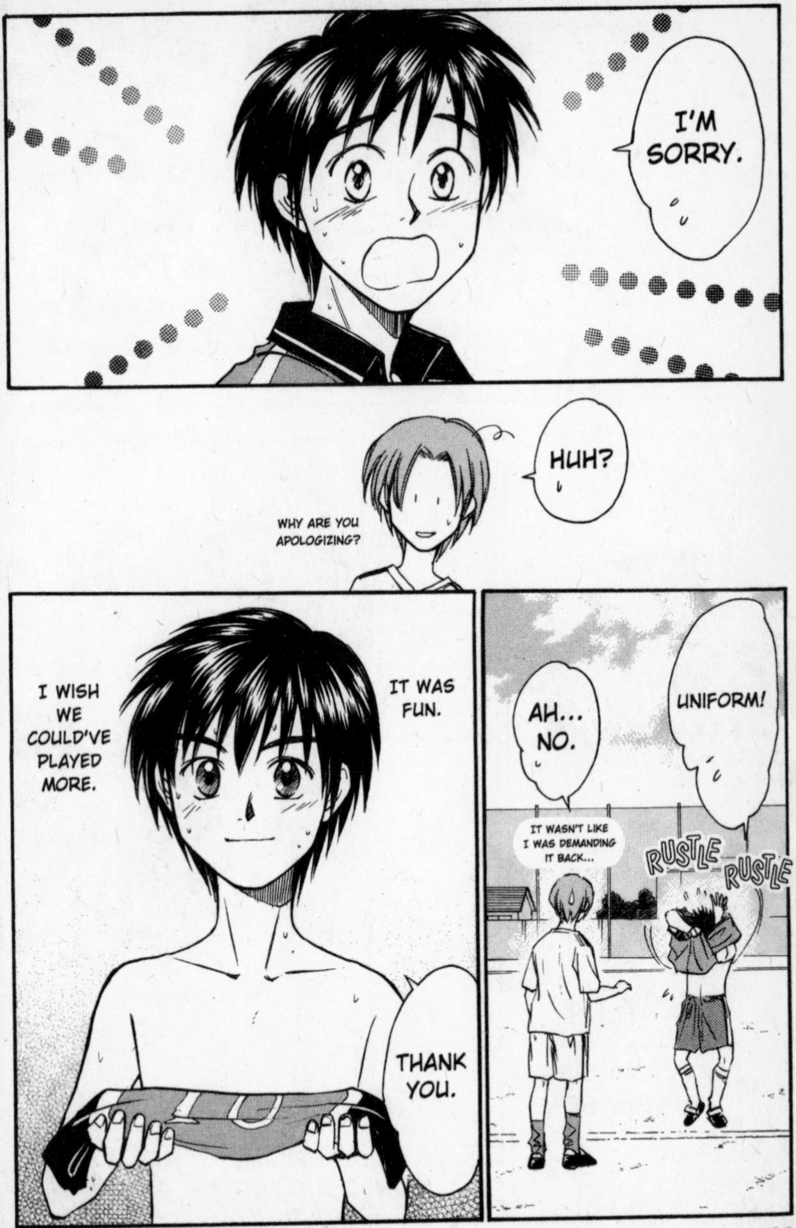
I'M SORRY.
HUH?
WHY ARE YOU APOLOGIZING?
UNIFORM!
AH... NO.
IT WASN'T LIKE I WAS DEMANDING IT BACK...
RUSTLE RUSTLE
IT WAS FUN.
I WISH WE COULD'VE PLAYED MORE.
THANK YOU.

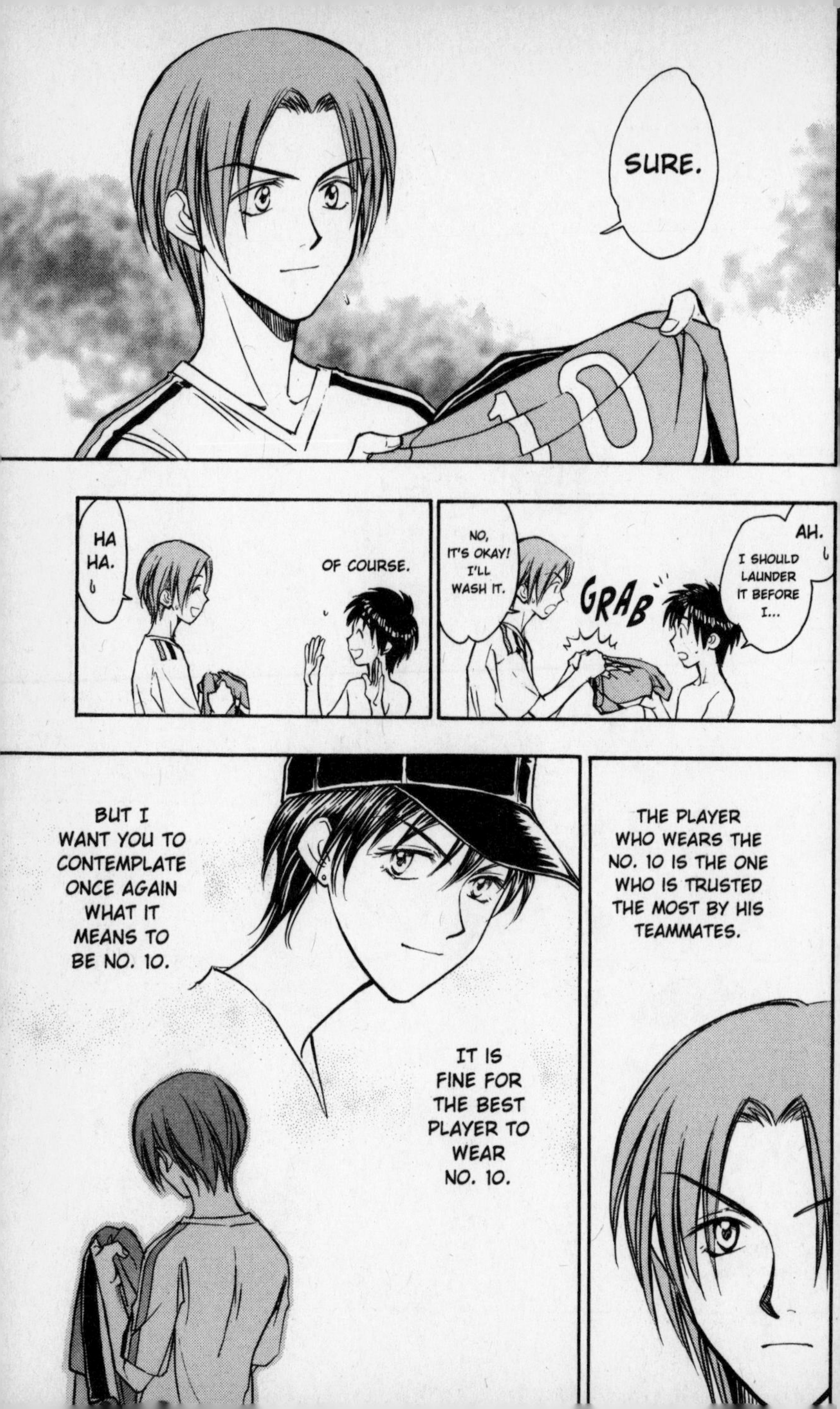
SURE.
AH. I SHOULD LAUNDER IT BEFORE I...
GRAB
NO, IT'S OKAY! I'LL WASH IT.
OF COURSE.
HA HA.
THE PLAYER WHO WEARS THE NO. 10 IS THE ONE WHO IS TRUSTED THE MOST BY HIS TEAMMATES.
BUT I WANT YOU TO CONTEMPLATE ONCE AGAIN WHAT IT MEANS TO BE NO. 10.
IT IS FINE FOR THE BEST PLAYER TO WEAR NO. 10.

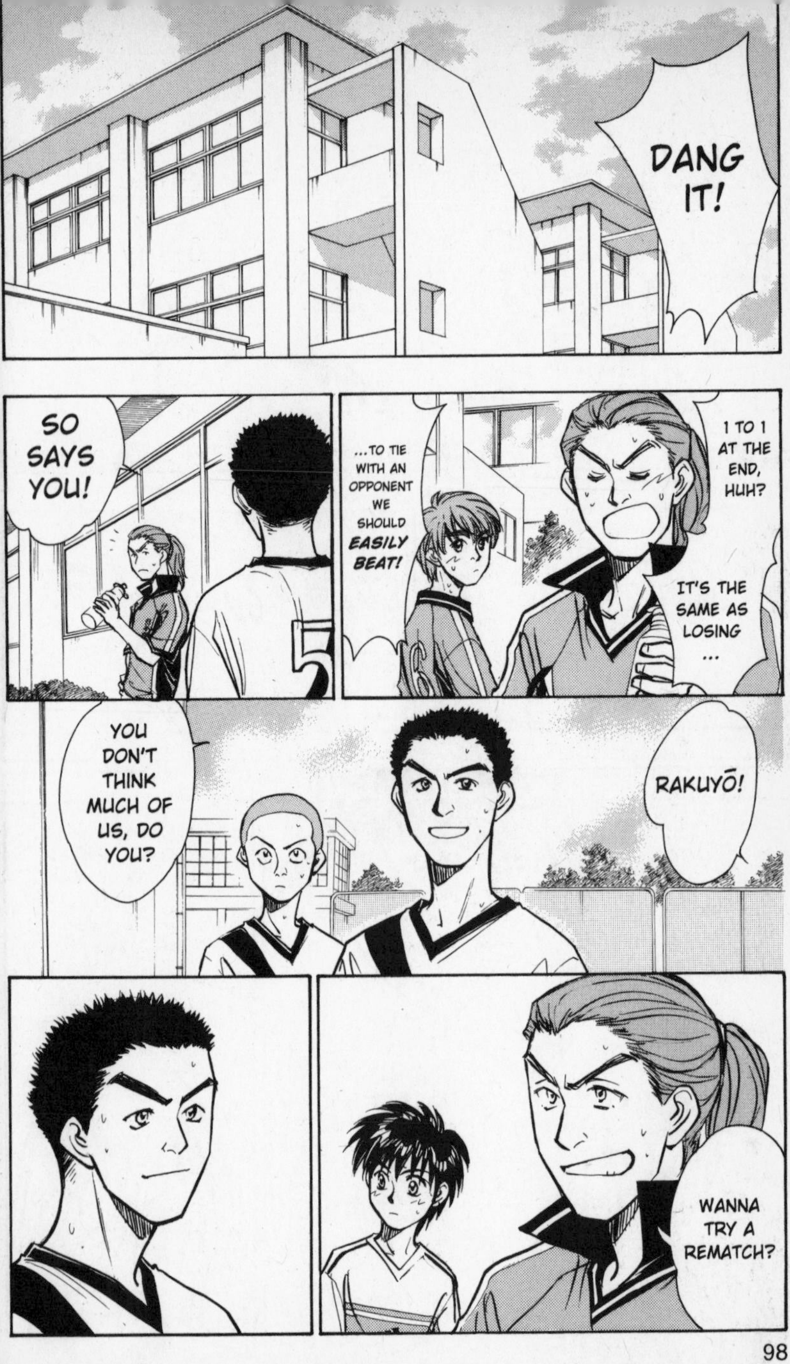
DANG IT!
1 TO 1 AT THE END, HUH?
IT'S THE SAME AS LOSING ...
...TO TIE WITH AN OPPONENT WE SHOULD *EASILY BEAT!*
SO SAYS YOU!
RAKUYŌ!
YOU DON'T THINK MUCH OF US, DO YOU?
WANNA TRY A REMATCH?

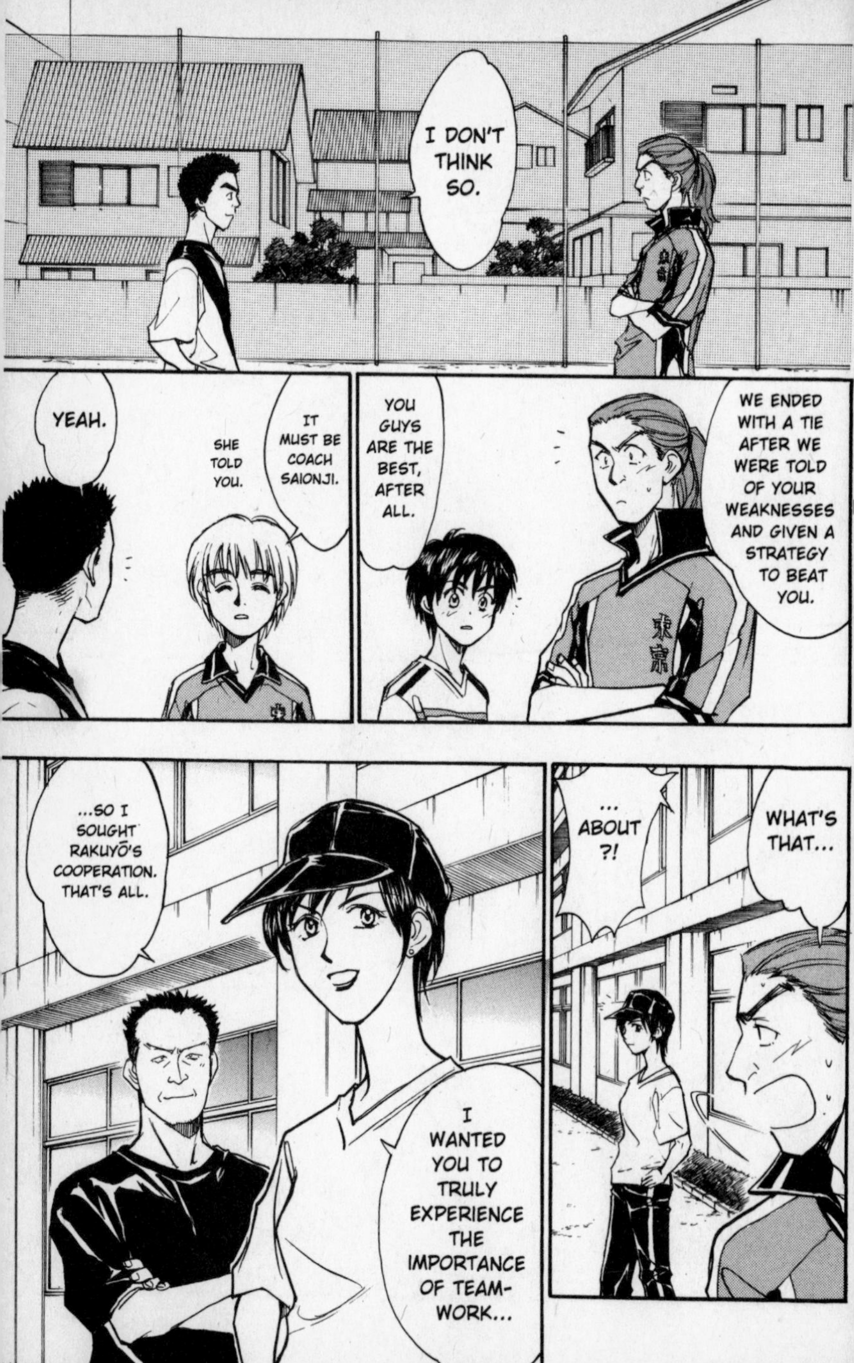

I DON'T THINK SO.
WE ENDED WITH A TIE AFTER WE WERE TOLD OF YOUR WEAKNESSES AND GIVEN A STRATEGY TO BEAT YOU.
YOU GUYS ARE THE BEST, AFTER ALL.
IT MUST BE COACH SAIONJI.
SHE TOLD YOU.
YEAH.
WHAT'S THAT...
... ABOUT ?!
I WANTED YOU TO TRULY EXPERIENCE THE IMPORTANCE OF TEAM-WORK...
...SO I SOUGHT RAKUYŌ'S COOPERATION. THAT'S ALL.

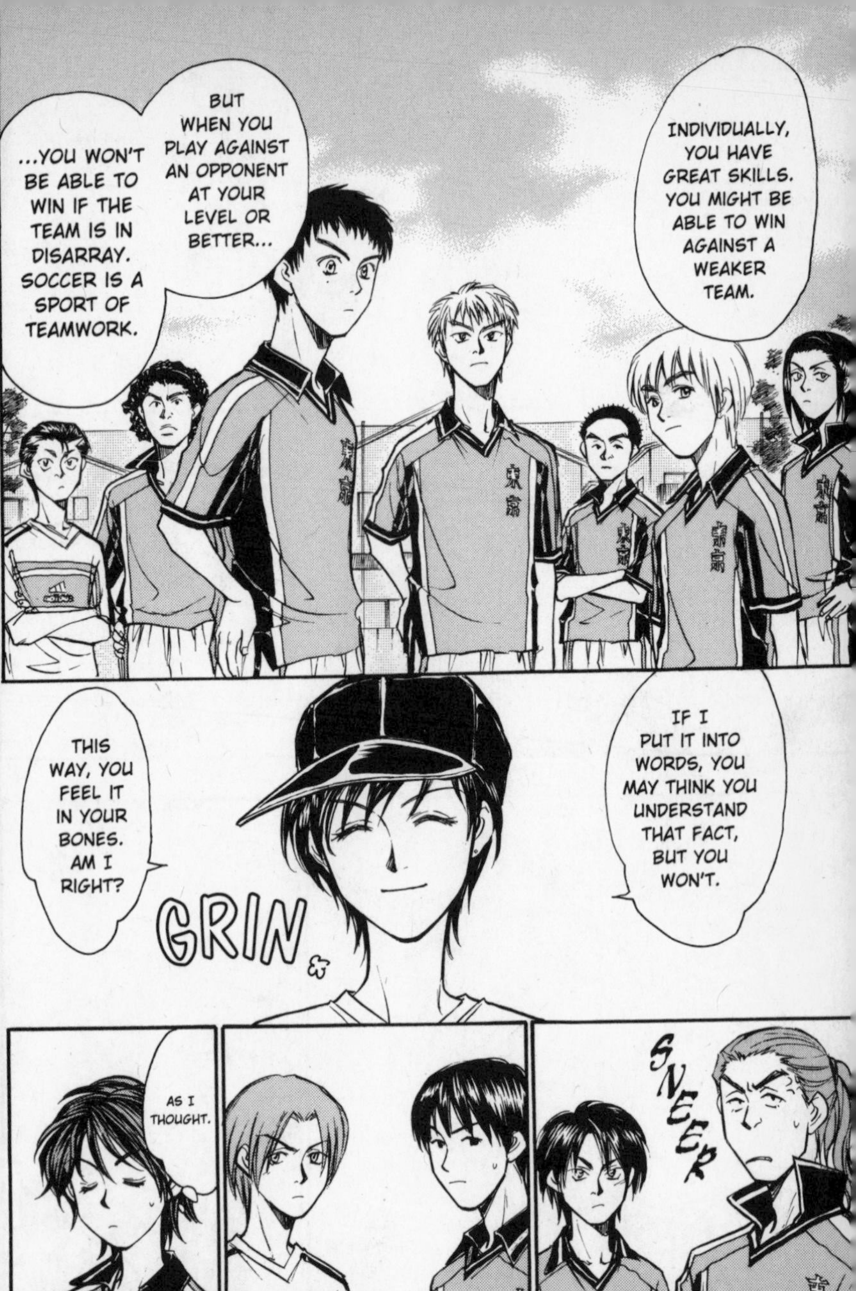
INDIVIDUALLY, YOU HAVE GREAT SKILLS. YOU MIGHT BE ABLE TO WIN AGAINST A WEAKER TEAM.
BUT WHEN YOU PLAY AGAINST AN OPPONENT AT YOUR LEVEL OR BETTER...
...YOU WON'T BE ABLE TO WIN IF THE TEAM IS IN DISARRAY. SOCCER IS A SPORT OF TEAMWORK.
IF I PUT IT INTO WORDS, YOU MAY THINK YOU UNDERSTAND THAT FACT, BUT YOU WON'T.
THIS WAY, YOU FEEL IT IN YOUR BONES. AM I RIGHT?
GRIN
SNEER
AS I THOUGHT.

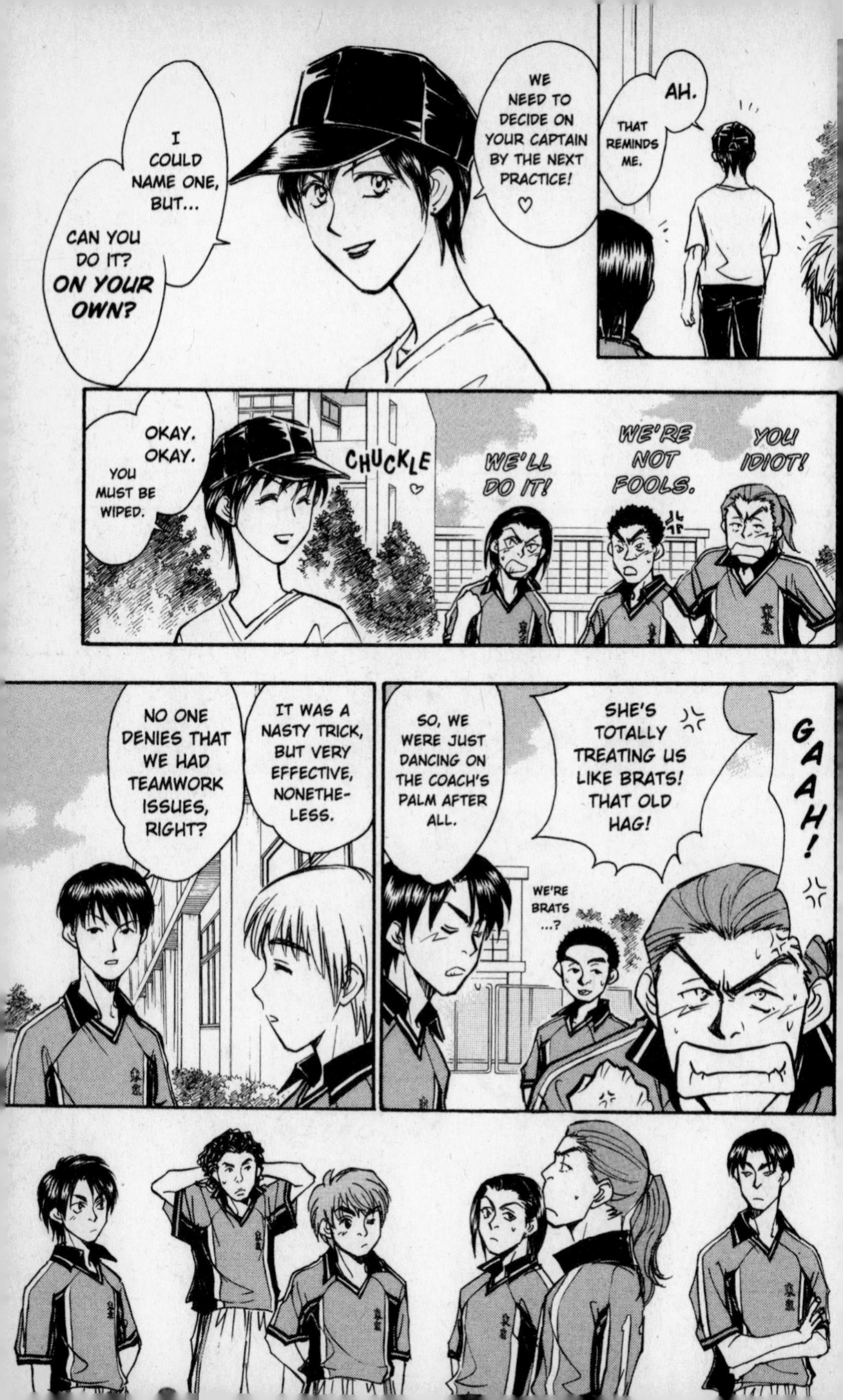

AH.
THAT REMINDS ME.
WE NEED TO DECIDE ON YOUR CAPTAIN BY THE NEXT PRACTICE! ♡
I COULD NAME ONE, BUT...
CAN YOU DO IT? ON YOUR OWN?
YOU IDIOT!
WE'RE NOT FOOLS.
WE'LL DO IT!
CHUCKLE ♡
OKAY. OKAY.
YOU MUST BE WIPED.
GAAH!
SHE'S TOTALLY TREATING US LIKE BRATS! THAT OLD HAG!
SO, WE WERE JUST DANCING ON THE COACH'S PALM AFTER ALL.
WE'RE BRATS ...?
IT WAS A NASTY TRICK, BUT VERY EFFECTIVE, NONETHELESS.
NO ONE DENIES THAT WE HAD TEAMWORK ISSUES, RIGHT?

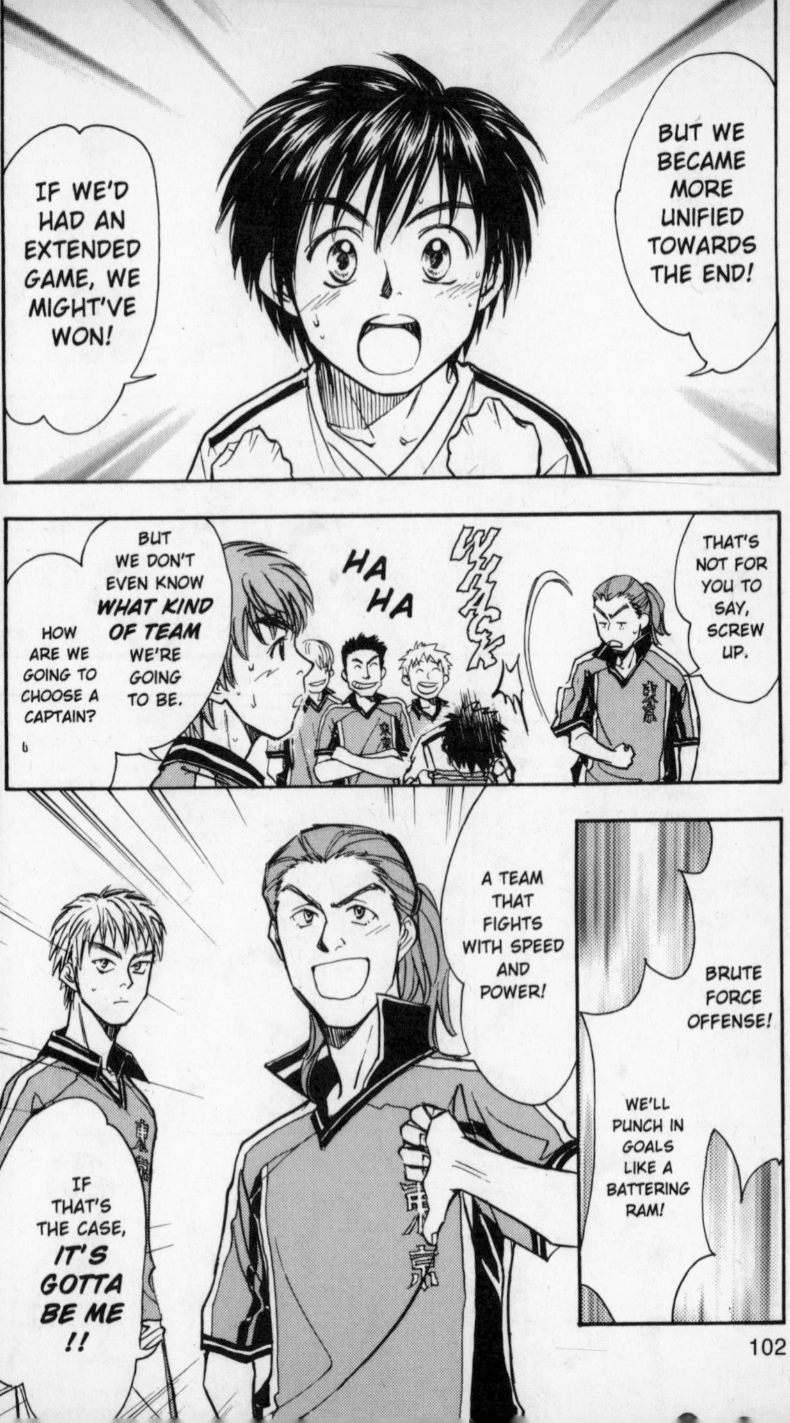
BUT WE BECAME MORE UNIFIED TOWARDS THE END!
IF WE'D HAD AN EXTENDED GAME, WE MIGHT'VE WON!
THAT'S NOT FOR YOU TO SAY, SCREW UP.
WHACK
HA HA
BUT WE DON'T EVEN KNOW WHAT KIND OF TEAM WE'RE GOING TO BE.
HOW ARE WE GOING TO CHOOSE A CAPTAIN?
BRUTE FORCE OFFENSE!
WE'LL PUNCH IN GOALS LIKE A BATTERING RAM!
A TEAM THAT FIGHTS WITH SPEED AND POWER!
IF THAT'S THE CASE, IT'S GOTTA BE ME!!

READ THIS WAY

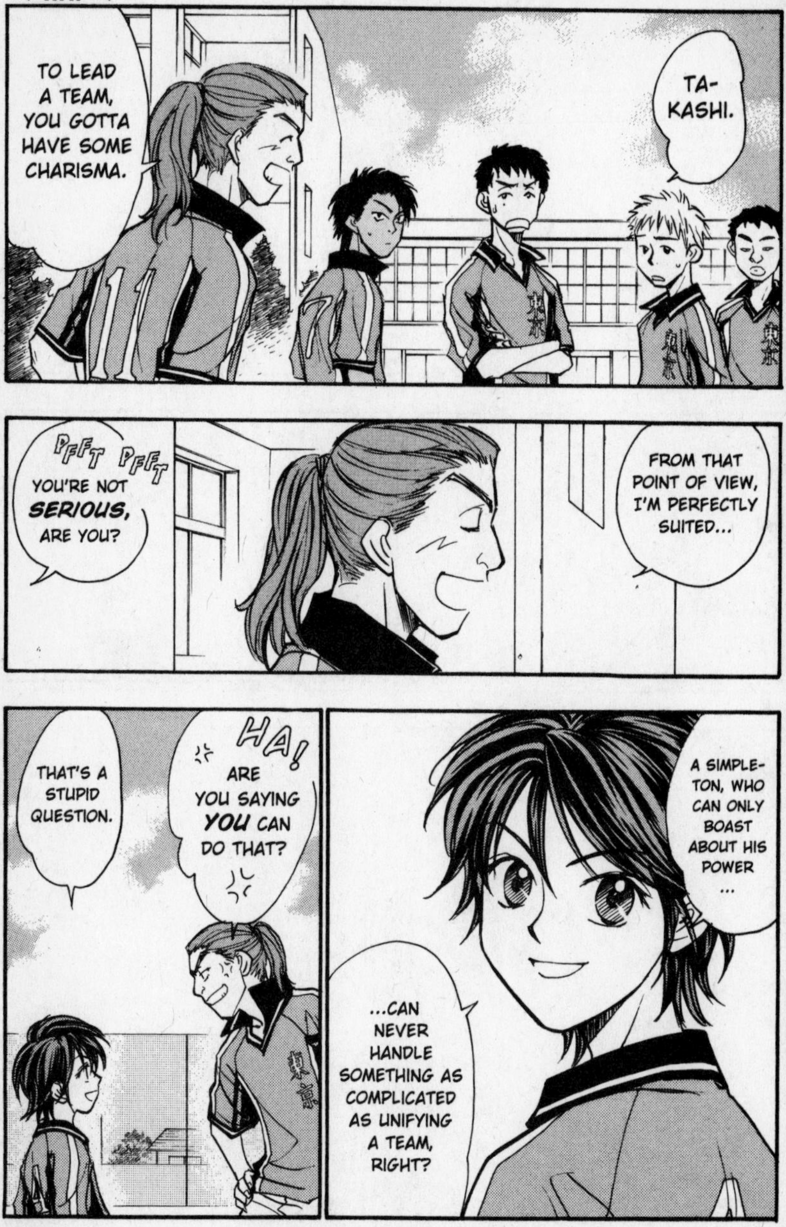

TA-KASHI.
TO LEAD A TEAM, YOU GOTTA HAVE SOME CHARISMA.
FROM THAT POINT OF VIEW, I'M PERFECTLY SUITED...
PFFT PFFT
YOU'RE NOT SERIOUS, ARE YOU?
A SIMPLETON, WHO CAN ONLY BOAST ABOUT HIS POWER...
...CAN NEVER HANDLE SOMETHING AS COMPLICATED AS UNIFYING A TEAM, RIGHT?
HA!
ARE YOU SAYING YOU CAN DO THAT?
THAT'S A STUPID QUESTION.

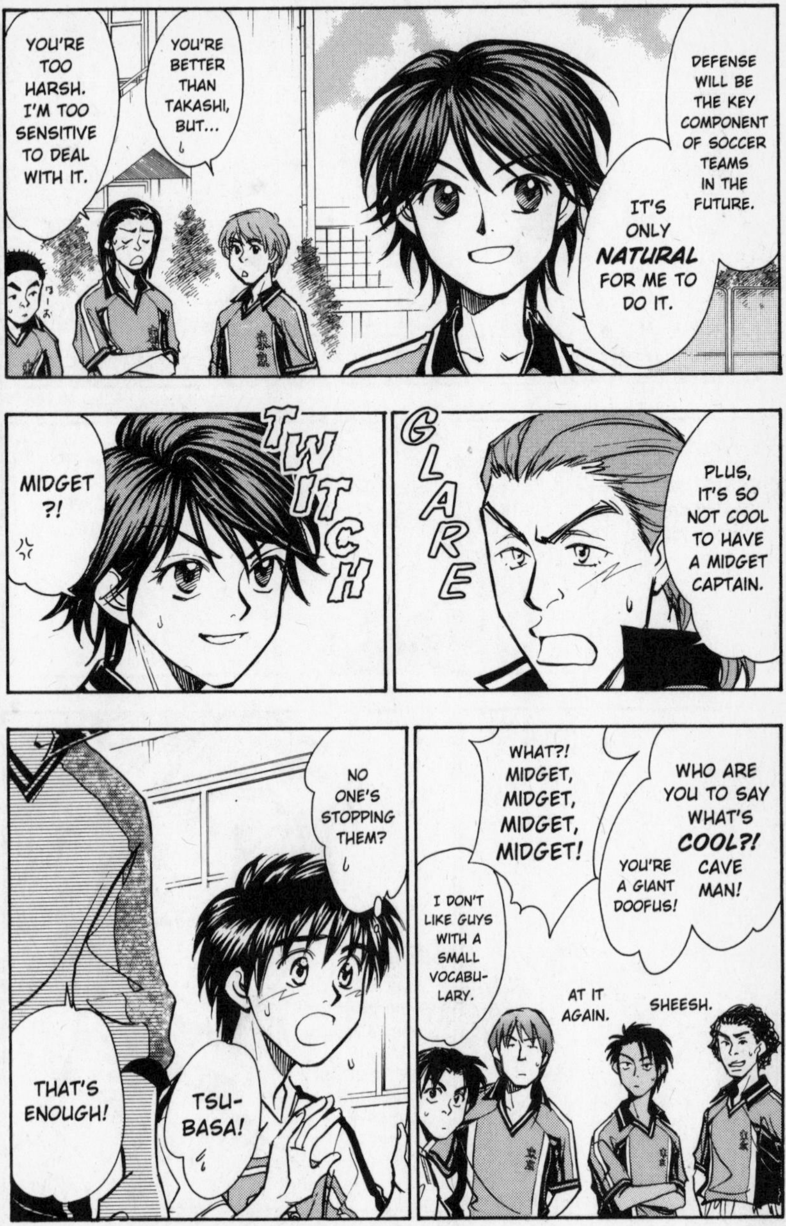
DEFENSE WILL BE THE KEY COMPONENT OF SOCCER TEAMS IN THE FUTURE.
IT'S ONLY **NATURAL** FOR ME TO DO IT.
YOU'RE BETTER THAN TAKASHI, BUT...
YOU'RE TOO HARSH. I'M TOO SENSITIVE TO DEAL WITH IT.
GLARE
PLUS, IT'S SO NOT COOL TO HAVE A MIDGET CAPTAIN.
TWITCH
MIDGET?!
WHO ARE YOU TO SAY WHAT'S **COOL?!** CAVE MAN!
WHAT?! MIDGET, MIDGET, MIDGET, MIDGET!
YOU'RE A GIANT DOOFUS!
I DON'T LIKE GUYS WITH A SMALL VOCABULARY.
SHEESH.
AT IT AGAIN.
NO ONE'S STOPPING THEM?
TSU-BASA!
THAT'S ENOUGH!

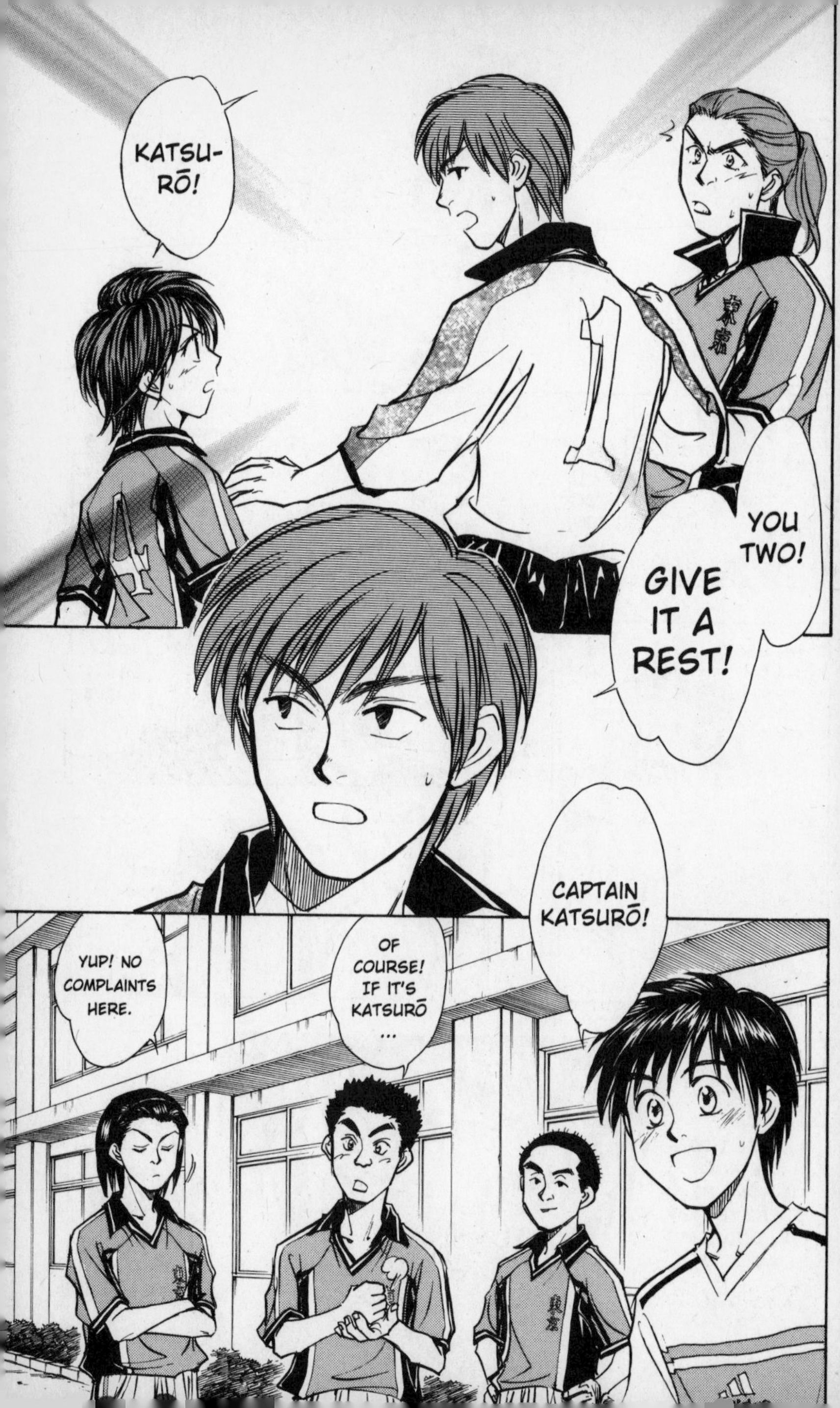
KATSU-RŌ!
YOU TWO!
GIVE IT A REST!
CAPTAIN KATSURŌ!
OF COURSE! IF IT'S KATSURŌ ...
YUP! NO COMPLAINTS HERE.

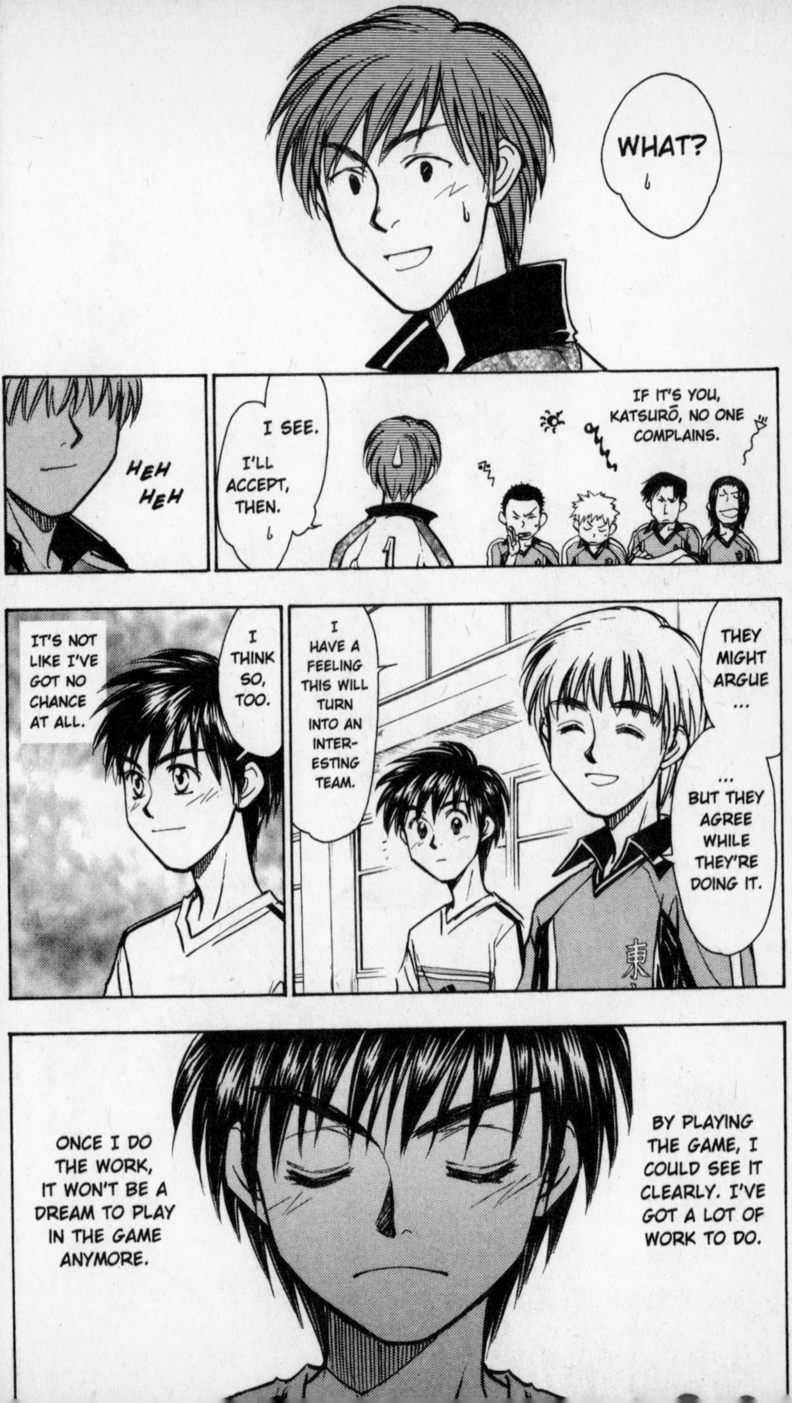
WHAT?
IF IT'S YOU, KATSURŌ, NO ONE COMPLAINS.
I SEE.
I'LL ACCEPT, THEN.
HEH HEH
THEY MIGHT ARGUE ...
... BUT THEY AGREE WHILE THEY'RE DOING IT.
I HAVE A FEELING THIS WILL TURN INTO AN INTERESTING TEAM.
I THINK SO, TOO.
IT'S NOT LIKE I'VE GOT NO CHANCE AT ALL.
BY PLAYING THE GAME, I COULD SEE IT CLEARLY. I'VE GOT A LOT OF WORK TO DO.
ONCE I DO THE WORK, IT WON'T BE A DREAM TO PLAY IN THE GAME ANYMORE.

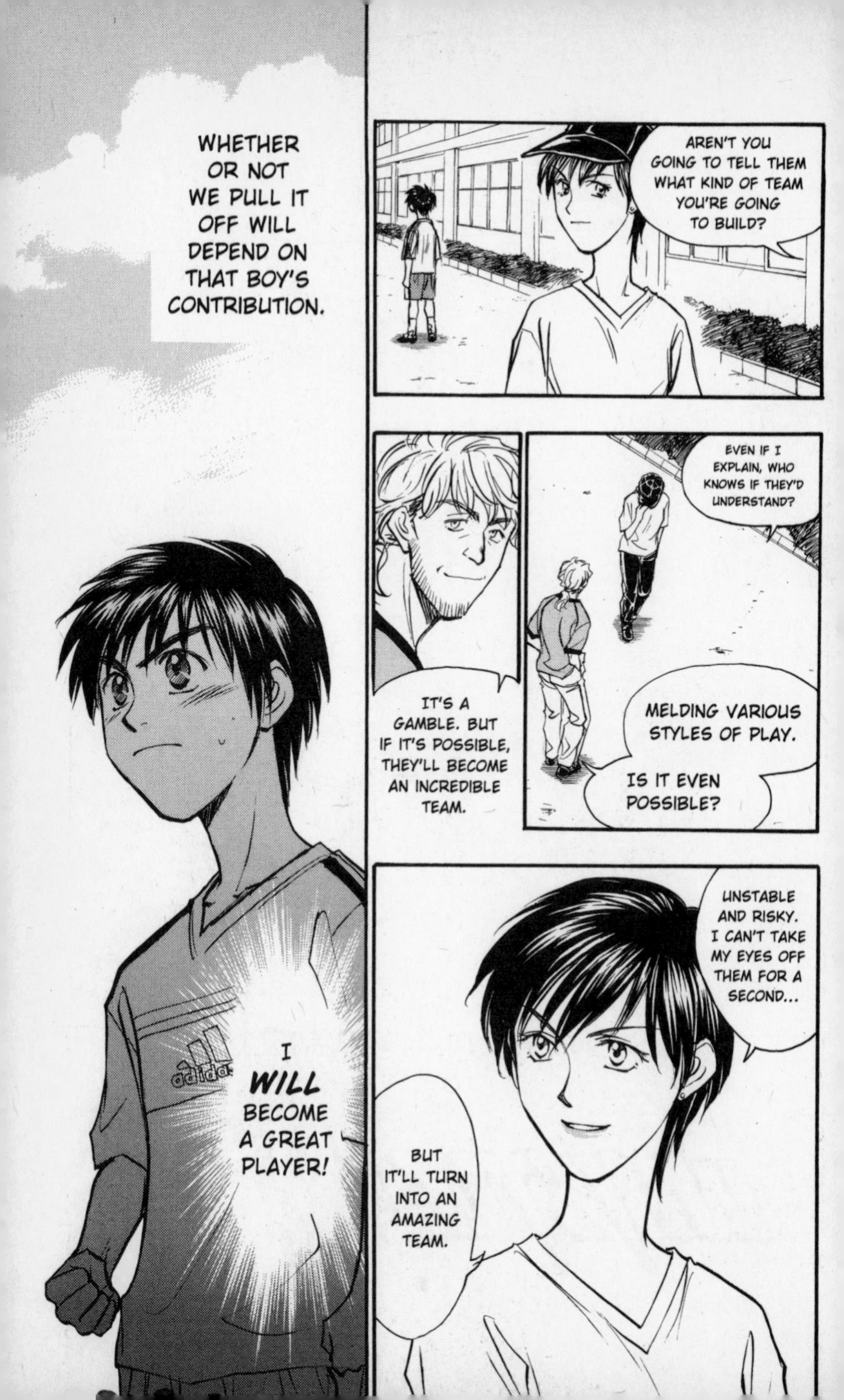
AREN'T YOU GOING TO TELL THEM WHAT KIND OF TEAM YOU'RE GOING TO BUILD?
EVEN IF I EXPLAIN, WHO KNOWS IF THEY'D UNDERSTAND?
MELDING VARIOUS STYLES OF PLAY.
IS IT EVEN POSSIBLE?
IT'S A GAMBLE. BUT IF IT'S POSSIBLE, THEY'LL BECOME AN INCREDIBLE TEAM.
UNSTABLE AND RISKY. I CAN'T TAKE MY EYES OFF THEM FOR A SECOND...
BUT IT'LL TURN INTO AN AMAZING TEAM.
WHETHER OR NOT WE PULL IT OFF WILL DEPEND ON THAT BOY'S CONTRIBUTION.
I ***WILL*** BECOME A GREAT PLAYER!

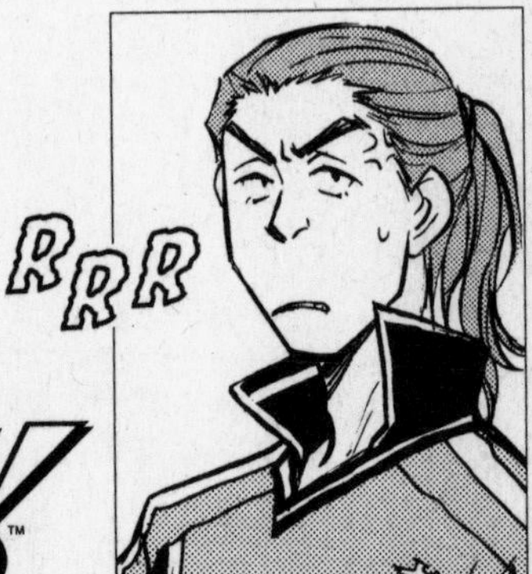
RRR

WHISTLE!™

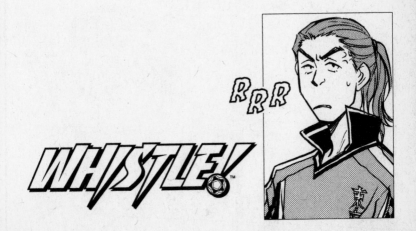

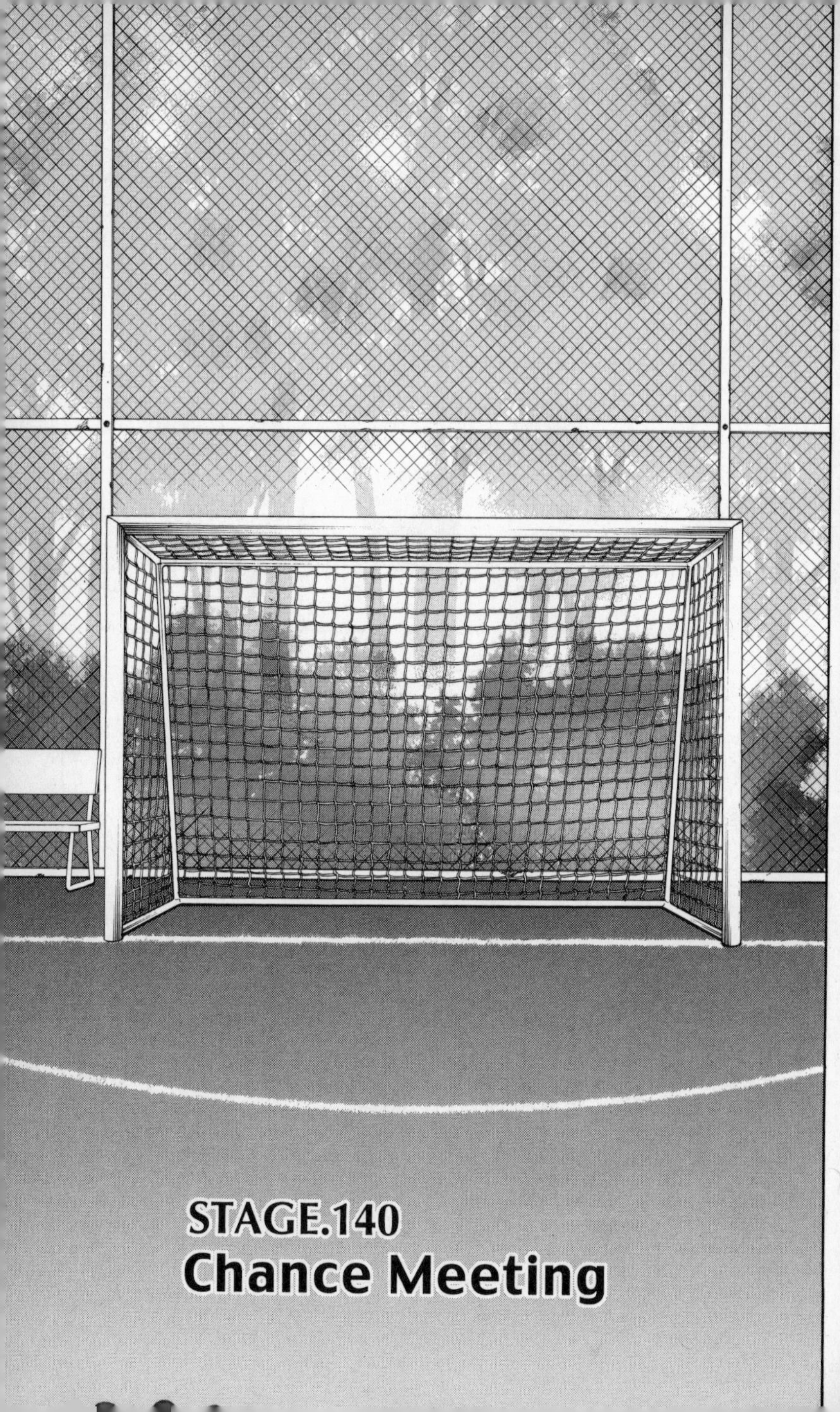
STAGE.140
Chance Meeting

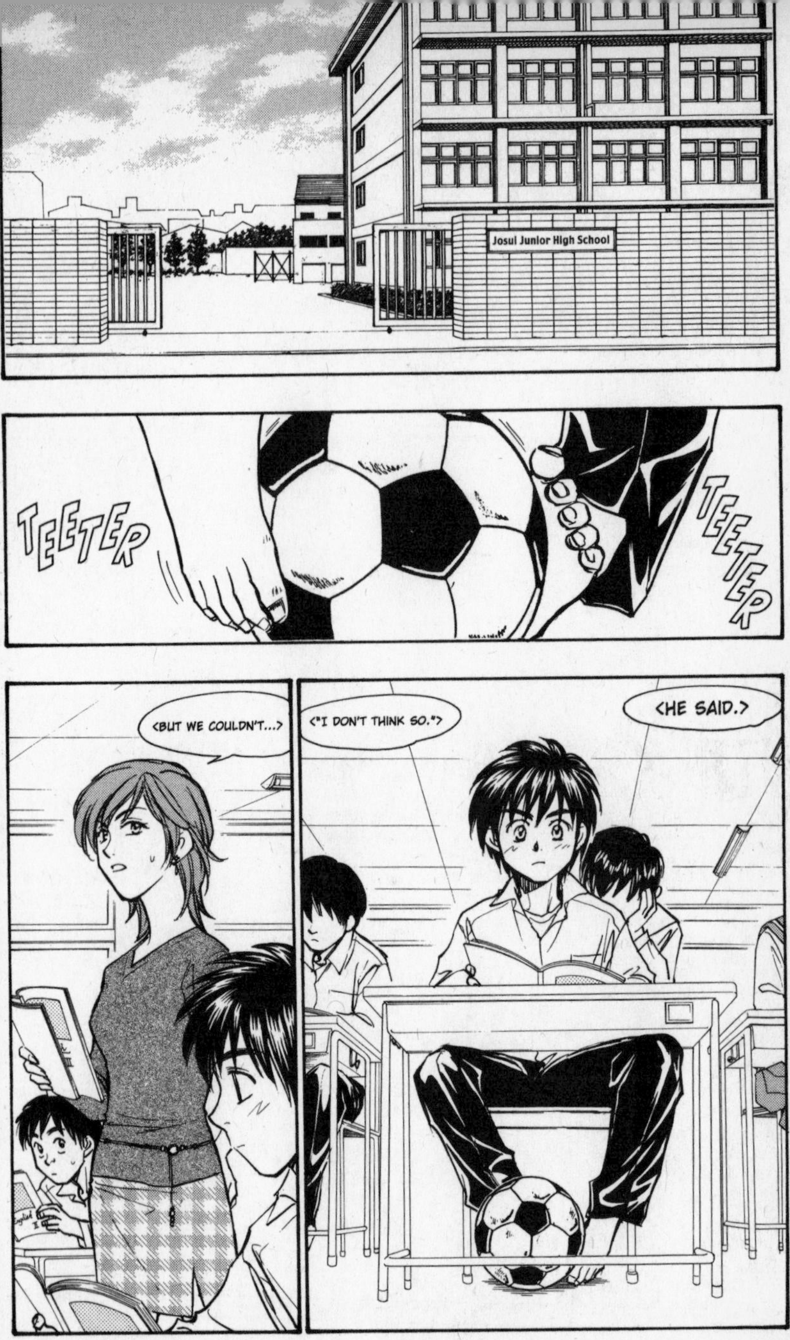
Josui Junior High School
TEETER
TEETER
<HE SAID.>
<"I DON'T THINK SO.">
<BUT WE COULDN'T...>

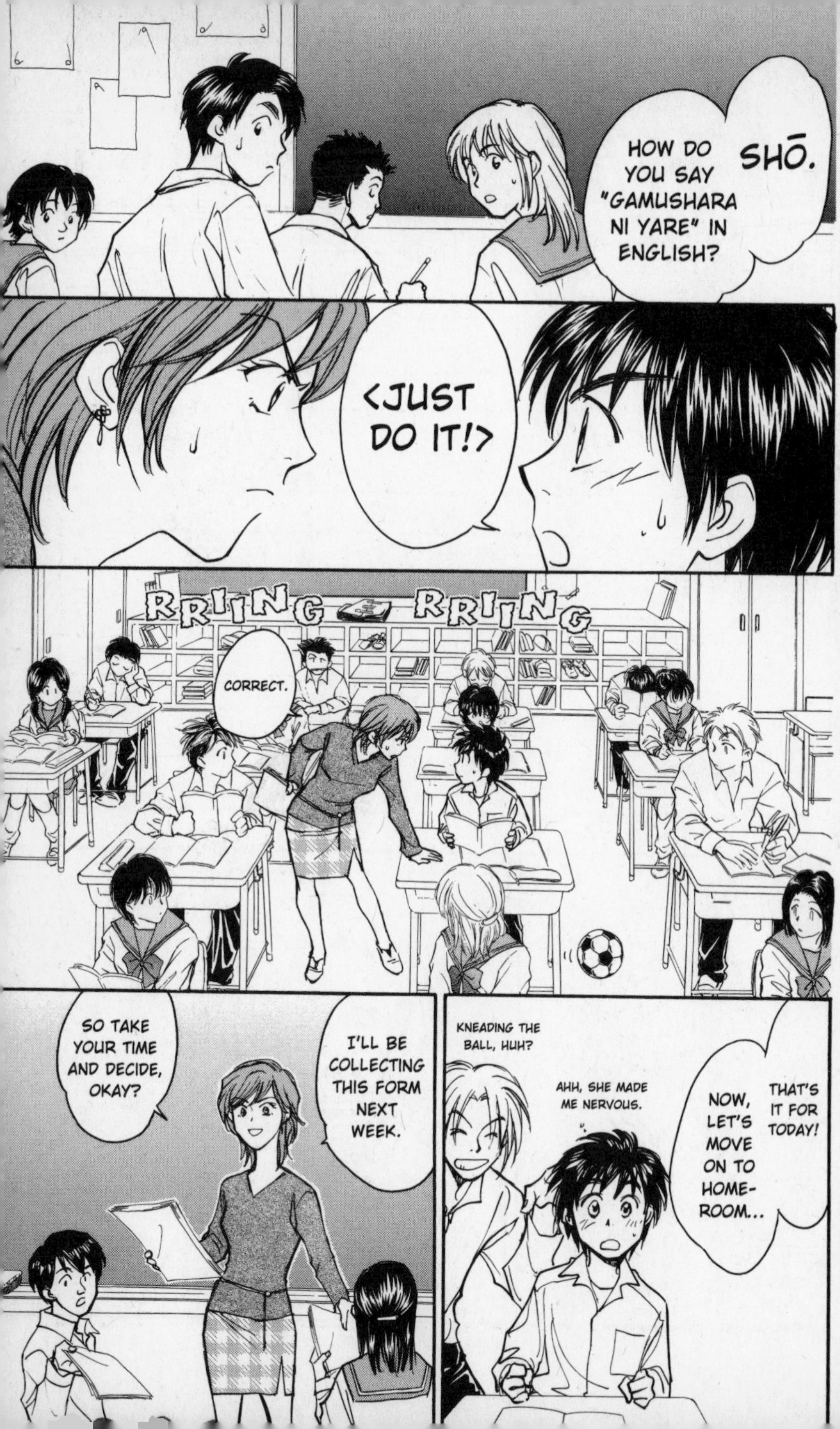
SHŌ.
HOW DO YOU SAY "GAMUSHARA NI YARE" IN ENGLISH?
<JUST DO IT!>
RRIING RRIING
CORRECT.
THAT'S IT FOR TODAY!
NOW, LET'S MOVE ON TO HOME-ROOM...
KNEADING THE BALL, HUH?
AHH, SHE MADE ME NERVOUS.
I'LL BE COLLECTING THIS FORM NEXT WEEK.
SO TAKE YOUR TIME AND DECIDE, OKAY?

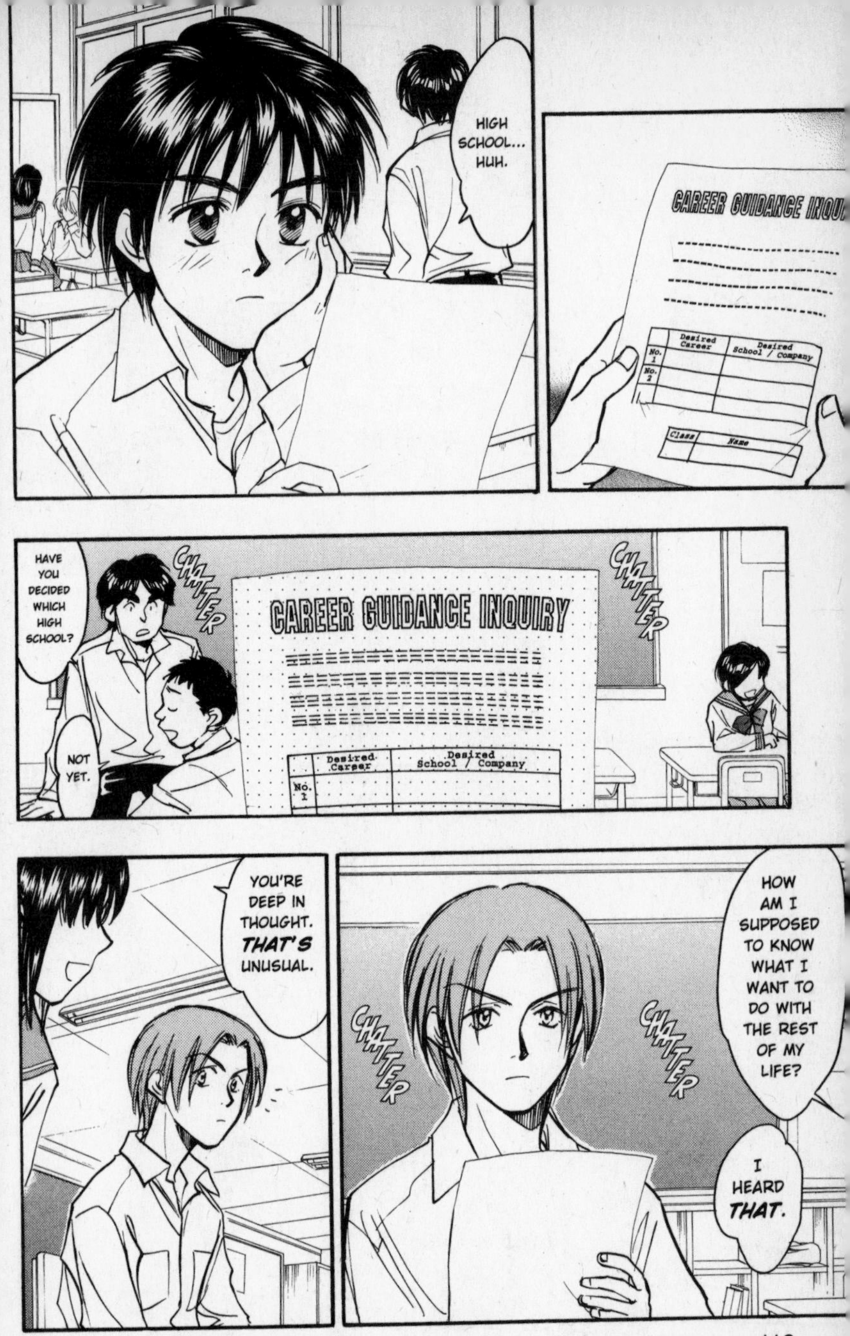
CAREER GUIDANCE
Desired Career
Desired School / Company
No. 1
No. 2
Class
Name
HIGH SCHOOL... HUH.
CHATTER
CAREER GUIDANCE INQUIRY
Desired Career
Desired School / Company
No. 1
CHATTER
HAVE YOU DECIDED WHICH HIGH SCHOOL?
NOT YET.
HOW AM I SUPPOSED TO KNOW WHAT I WANT TO DO WITH THE REST OF MY LIFE?
CHATTER
CHATTER
I HEARD THAT.
YOU'RE DEEP IN THOUGHT. THAT'S UNUSUAL.

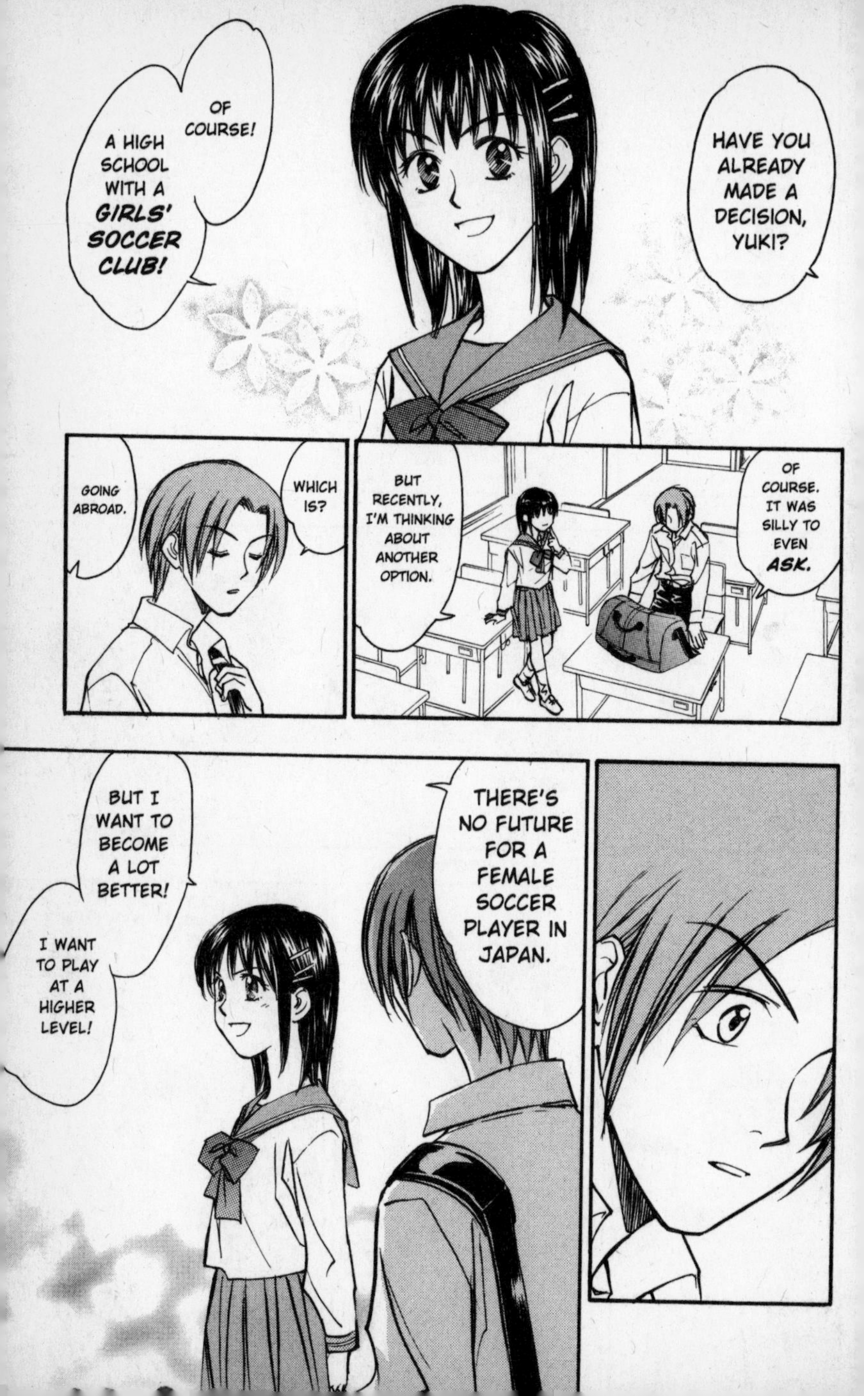
HAVE YOU ALREADY MADE A DECISION, YUKI?
OF COURSE!
A HIGH SCHOOL WITH A **GIRLS' SOCCER CLUB!**
OF COURSE. IT WAS SILLY TO EVEN **ASK.**
BUT RECENTLY, I'M THINKING ABOUT ANOTHER OPTION.
WHICH IS?
GOING ABROAD.
THERE'S NO FUTURE FOR A FEMALE SOCCER PLAYER IN JAPAN.
BUT I WANT TO BECOME A LOT BETTER!
I WANT TO PLAY AT A HIGHER LEVEL!

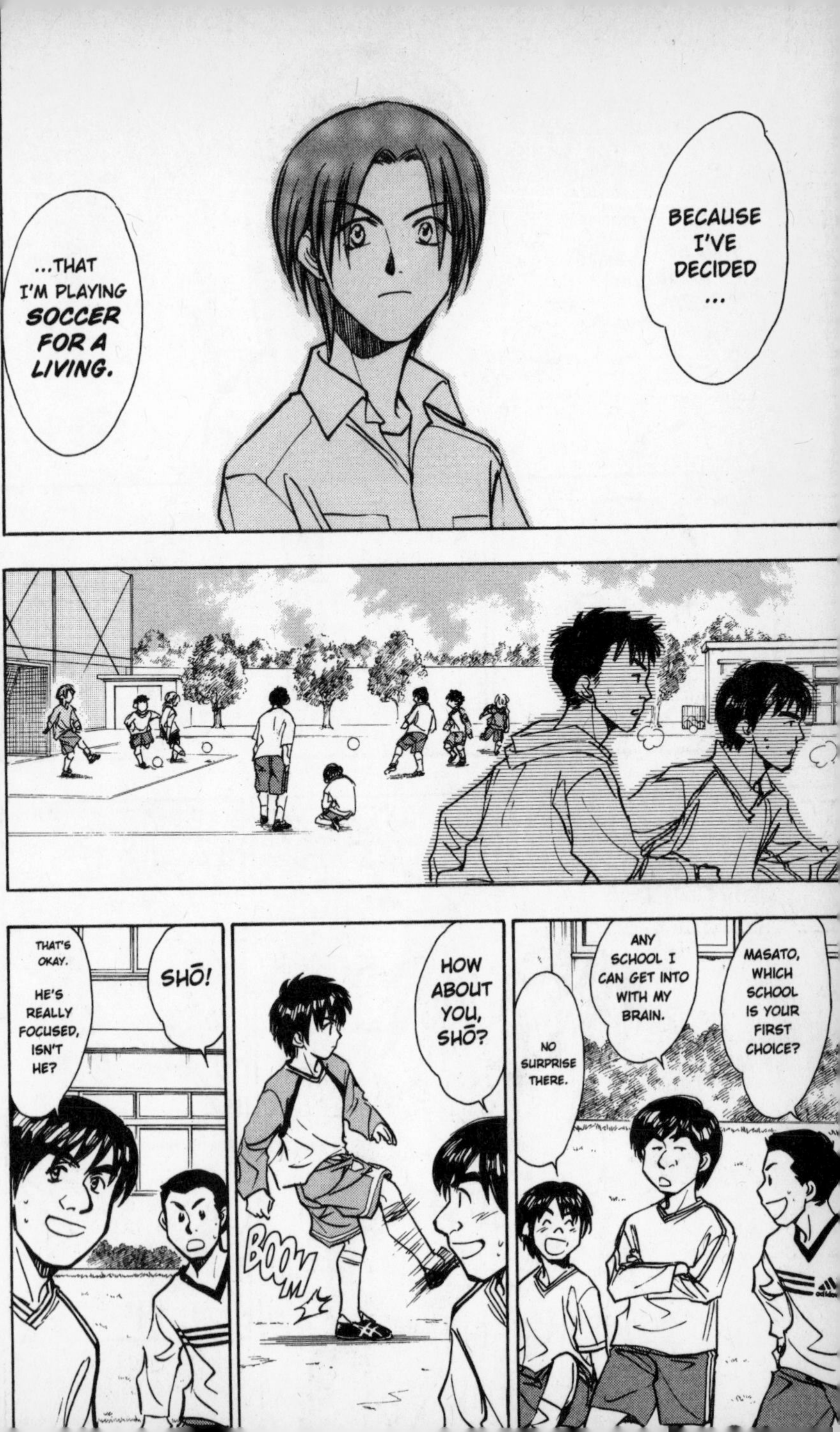
BECAUSE I'VE DECIDED ...
...THAT I'M PLAYING SOCCER FOR A LIVING.
MASATO, WHICH SCHOOL IS YOUR FIRST CHOICE?
ANY SCHOOL I CAN GET INTO WITH MY BRAIN.
NO SURPRISE THERE.
HOW ABOUT YOU, SHŌ?
BOOM
SHŌ!
THAT'S OKAY. HE'S REALLY FOCUSED, ISN'T HE?

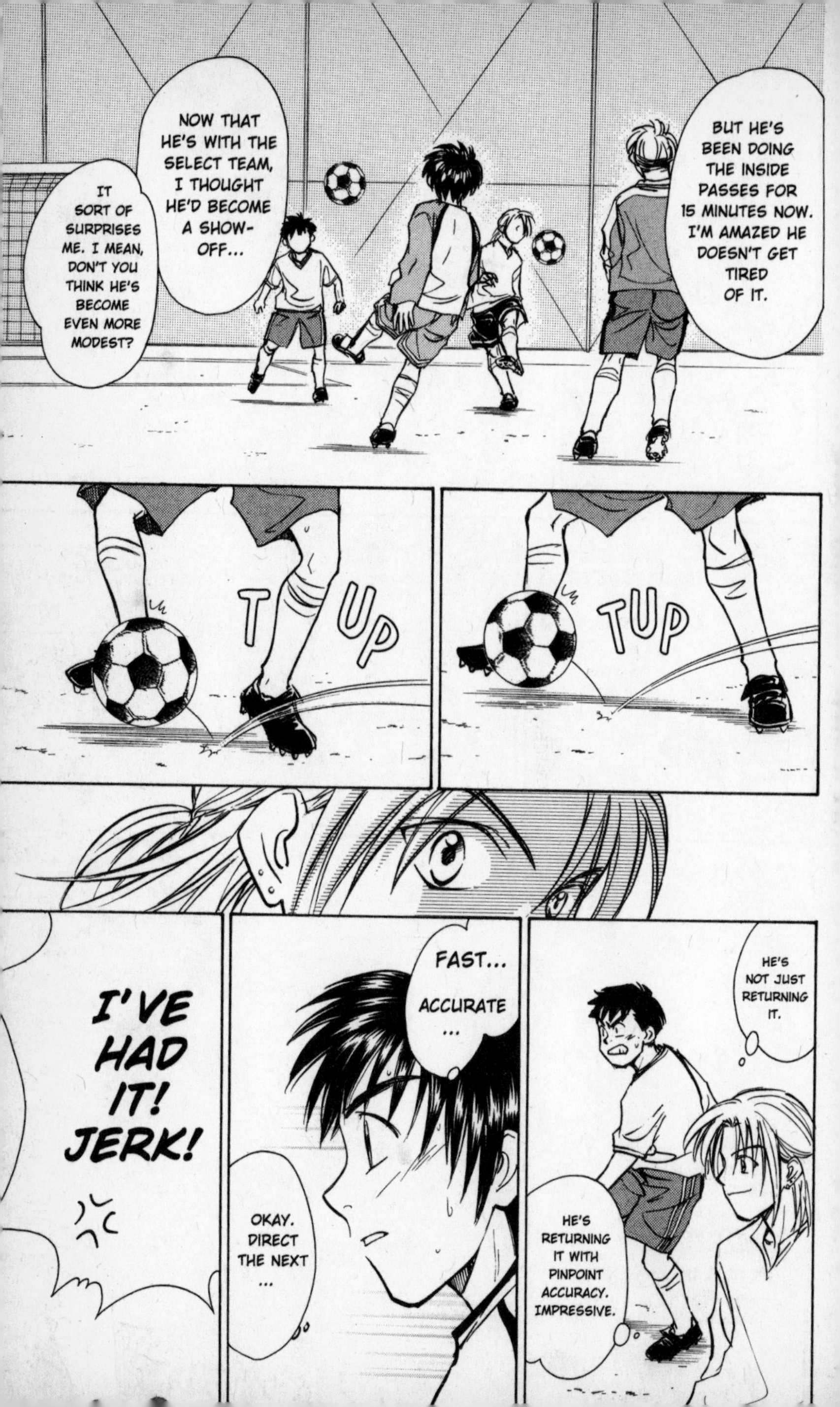
BUT HE'S BEEN DOING THE INSIDE PASSES FOR 15 MINUTES NOW. I'M AMAZED HE DOESN'T GET TIRED OF IT.
NOW THAT HE'S WITH THE SELECT TEAM, I THOUGHT HE'D BECOME A SHOW-OFF...
IT SORT OF SURPRISES ME. I MEAN, DON'T YOU THINK HE'S BECOME EVEN MORE MODEST?
TUP
T UP
HE'S NOT JUST RETURNING IT.
HE'S RETURNING IT WITH PINPOINT ACCURACY. IMPRESSIVE.
FAST... ACCURATE ...
OKAY. DIRECT THE NEXT ...
I'VE HAD IT! JERK!

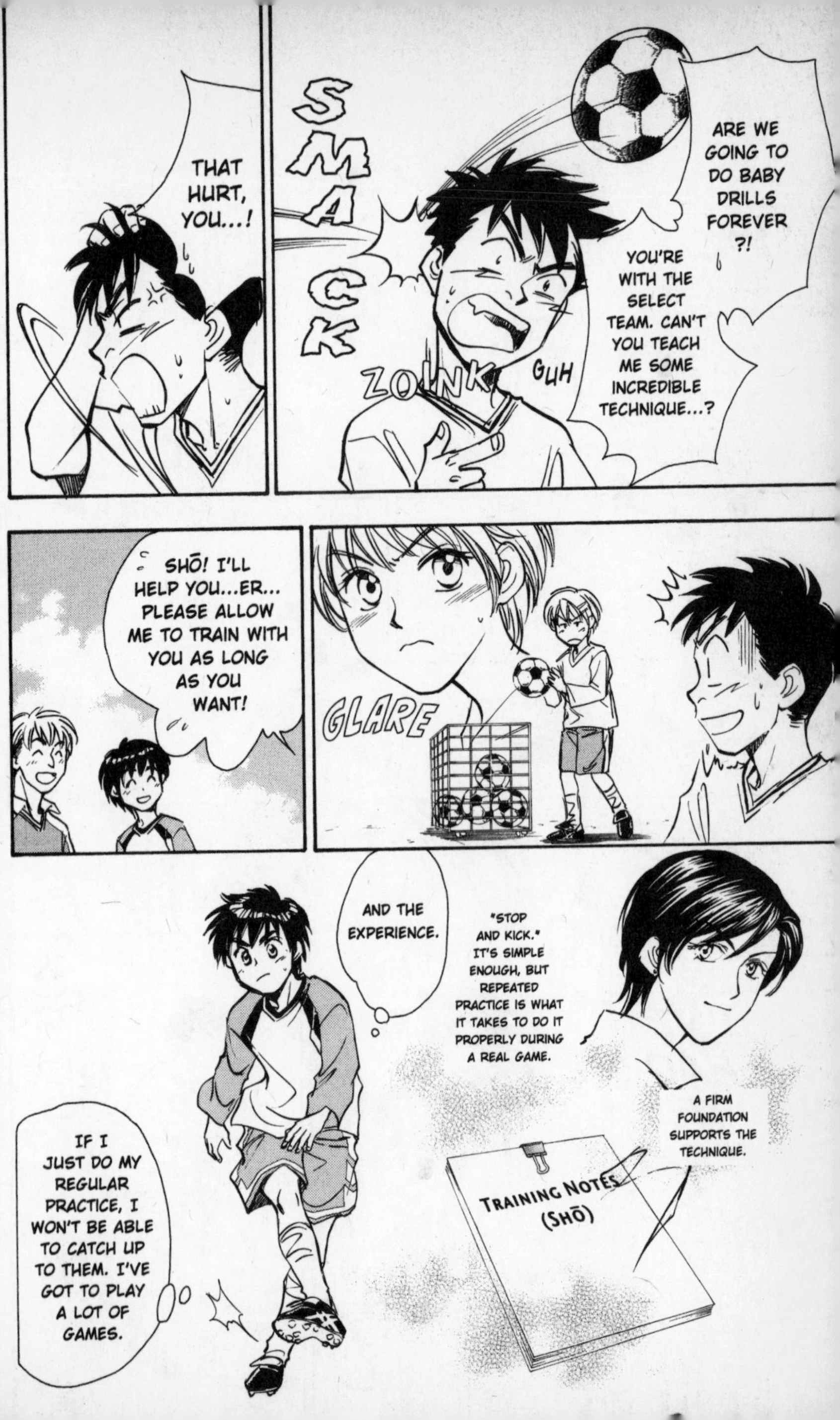
ARE WE GOING TO DO BABY DRILLS FOREVER?!
YOU'RE WITH THE SELECT TEAM. CAN'T YOU TEACH ME SOME INCREDIBLE TECHNIQUE...?
SMACK
GUH
ZOINK
THAT HURT, YOU...!
GLARE
SHŌ! I'LL HELP YOU...ER... PLEASE ALLOW ME TO TRAIN WITH YOU AS LONG AS YOU WANT!
A FIRM FOUNDATION SUPPORTS THE TECHNIQUE.
TRAINING NOTES (SHŌ)
"STOP AND KICK." IT'S SIMPLE ENOUGH, BUT REPEATED PRACTICE IS WHAT IT TAKES TO DO IT PROPERLY DURING A REAL GAME.
AND THE EXPERIENCE.
IF I JUST DO MY REGULAR PRACTICE, I WON'T BE ABLE TO CATCH UP TO THEM. I'VE GOT TO PLAY A LOT OF GAMES.

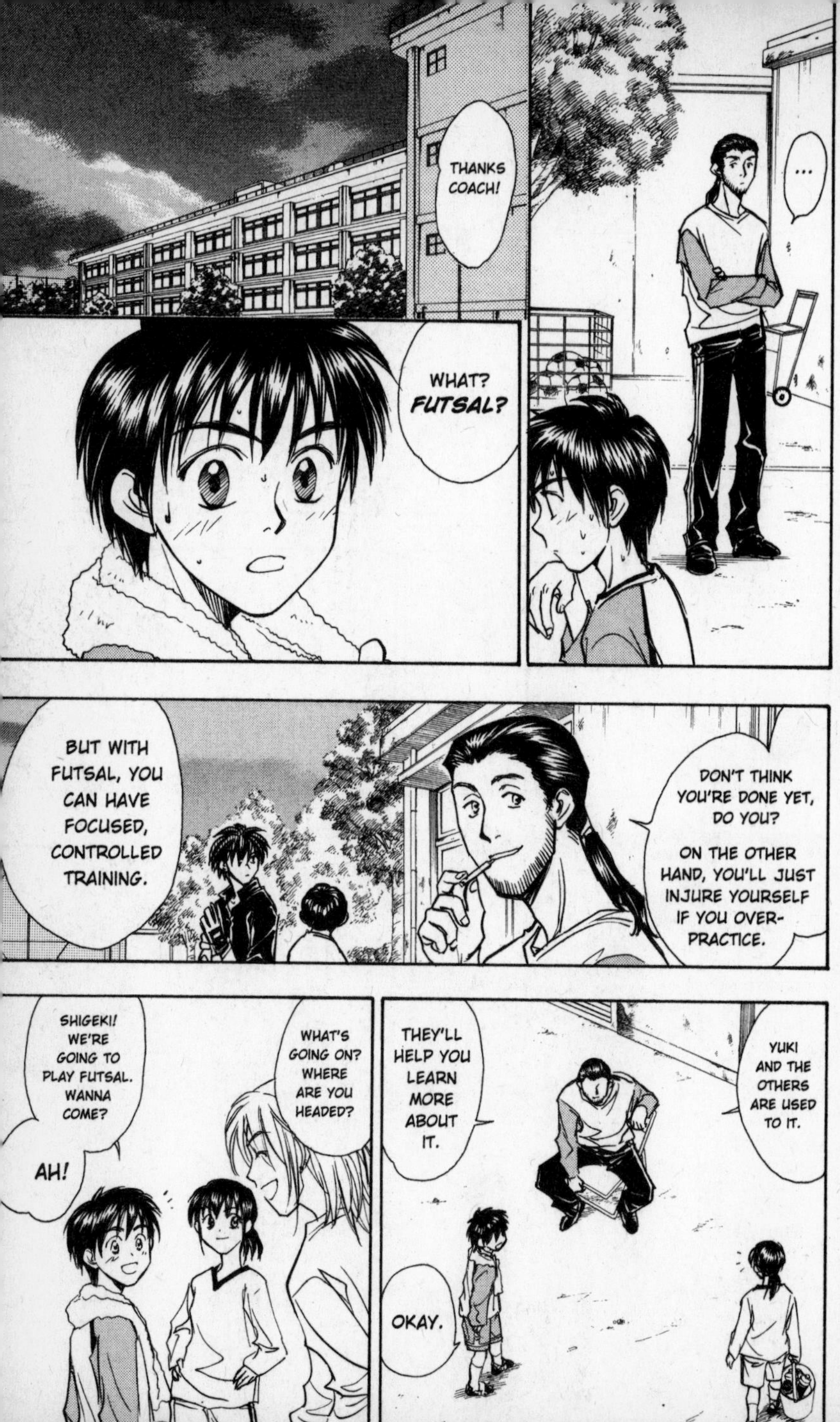
...
THANKS COACH!
WHAT? *FUTSAL?*
DON'T THINK YOU'RE DONE YET, DO YOU?
ON THE OTHER HAND, YOU'LL JUST INJURE YOURSELF IF YOU OVER-PRACTICE.
BUT WITH FUTSAL, YOU CAN HAVE FOCUSED, CONTROLLED TRAINING.
YUKI AND THE OTHERS ARE USED TO IT.
THEY'LL HELP YOU LEARN MORE ABOUT IT.
OKAY.
WHAT'S GOING ON? WHERE ARE YOU HEADED?
SHIGEKI! WE'RE GOING TO PLAY FUTSAL. WANNA COME?
AH!

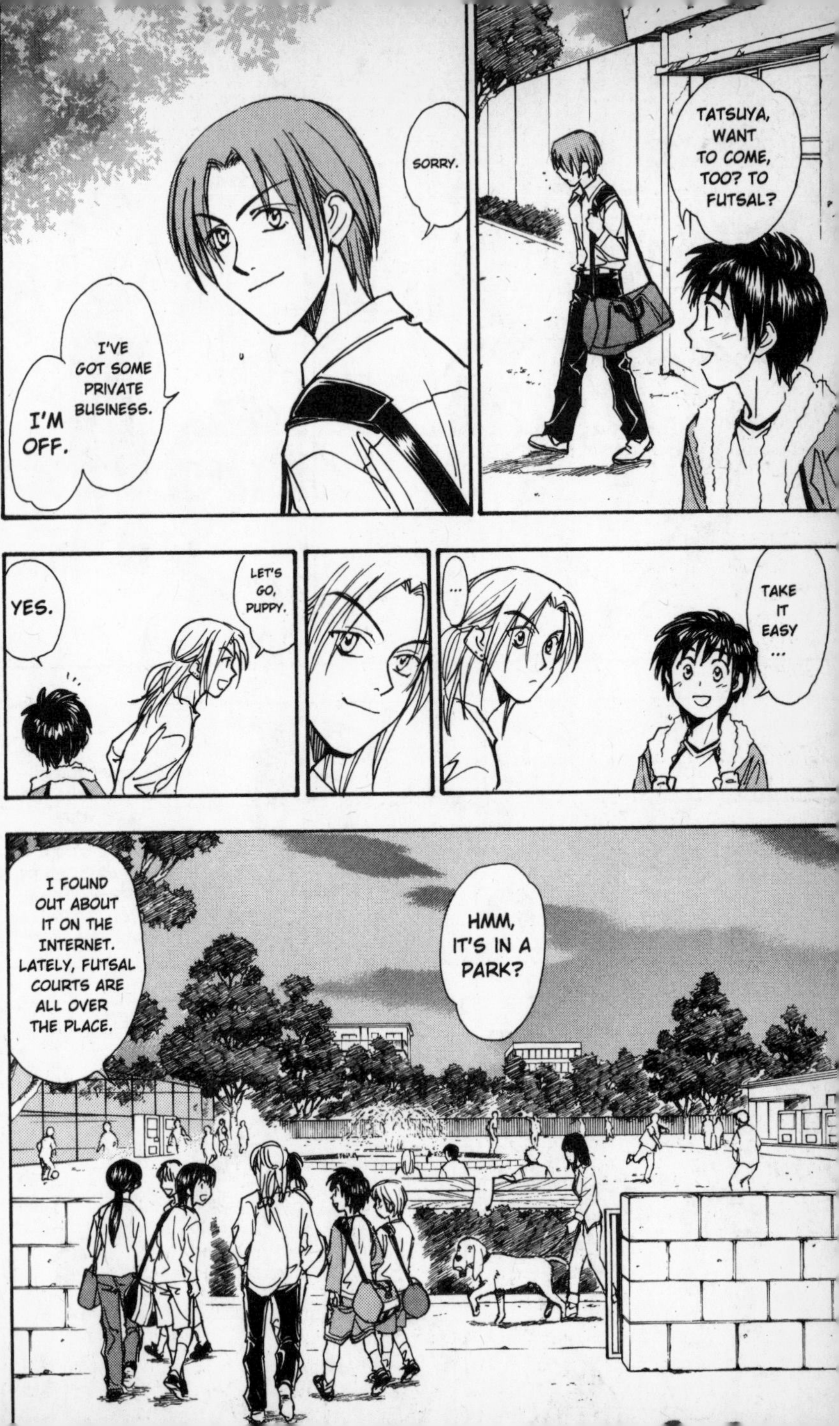
TATSUYA, WANT TO COME, TOO? TO FUTSAL?
SORRY.
I'VE GOT SOME PRIVATE BUSINESS.
I'M OFF.
TAKE IT EASY ...
...
LET'S GO, PUPPY.
YES.
HMM, IT'S IN A PARK?
I FOUND OUT ABOUT IT ON THE INTERNET. LATELY, FUTSAL COURTS ARE ALL OVER THE PLACE.

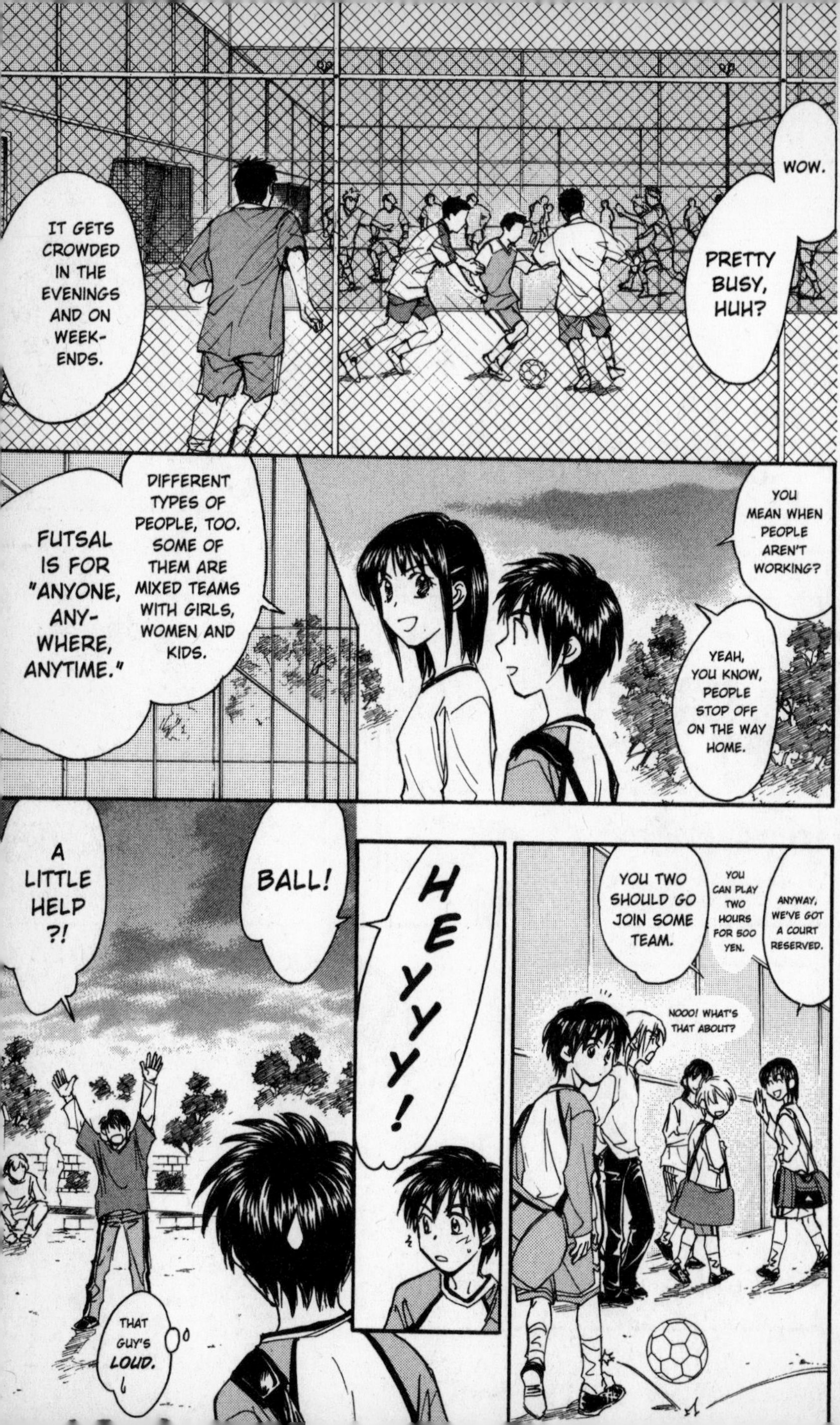
WOW.
PRETTY BUSY, HUH?
IT GETS CROWDED IN THE EVENINGS AND ON WEEK-ENDS.
YOU MEAN WHEN PEOPLE AREN'T WORKING?
YEAH, YOU KNOW, PEOPLE STOP OFF ON THE WAY HOME.
DIFFERENT TYPES OF PEOPLE, TOO. SOME OF THEM ARE MIXED TEAMS WITH GIRLS, WOMEN AND KIDS.
FUTSAL IS FOR "ANYONE, ANY-WHERE, ANYTIME."
ANYWAY, WE'VE GOT A COURT RESERVED.
YOU CAN PLAY TWO HOURS FOR 500 YEN.
YOU TWO SHOULD GO JOIN SOME TEAM.
NOOO! WHAT'S THAT ABOUT?
HEYYY!
BALL!
A LITTLE HELP ?!
THAT GUY'S LOUD.

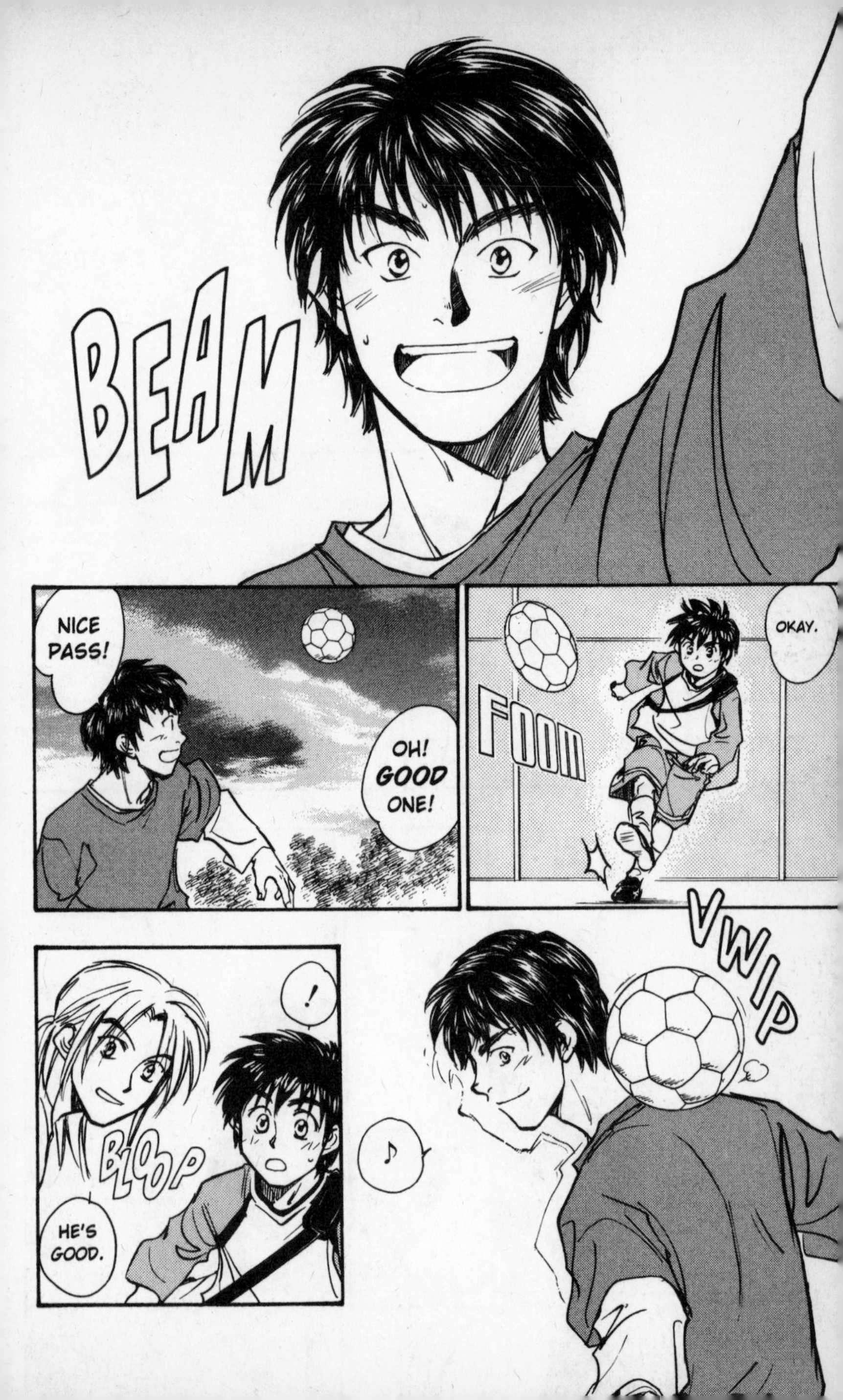
BEAM
OKAY.
FOOM
NICE PASS!
OH! GOOD ONE!
VWIP
♪
!
BLOOP
HE'S GOOD.

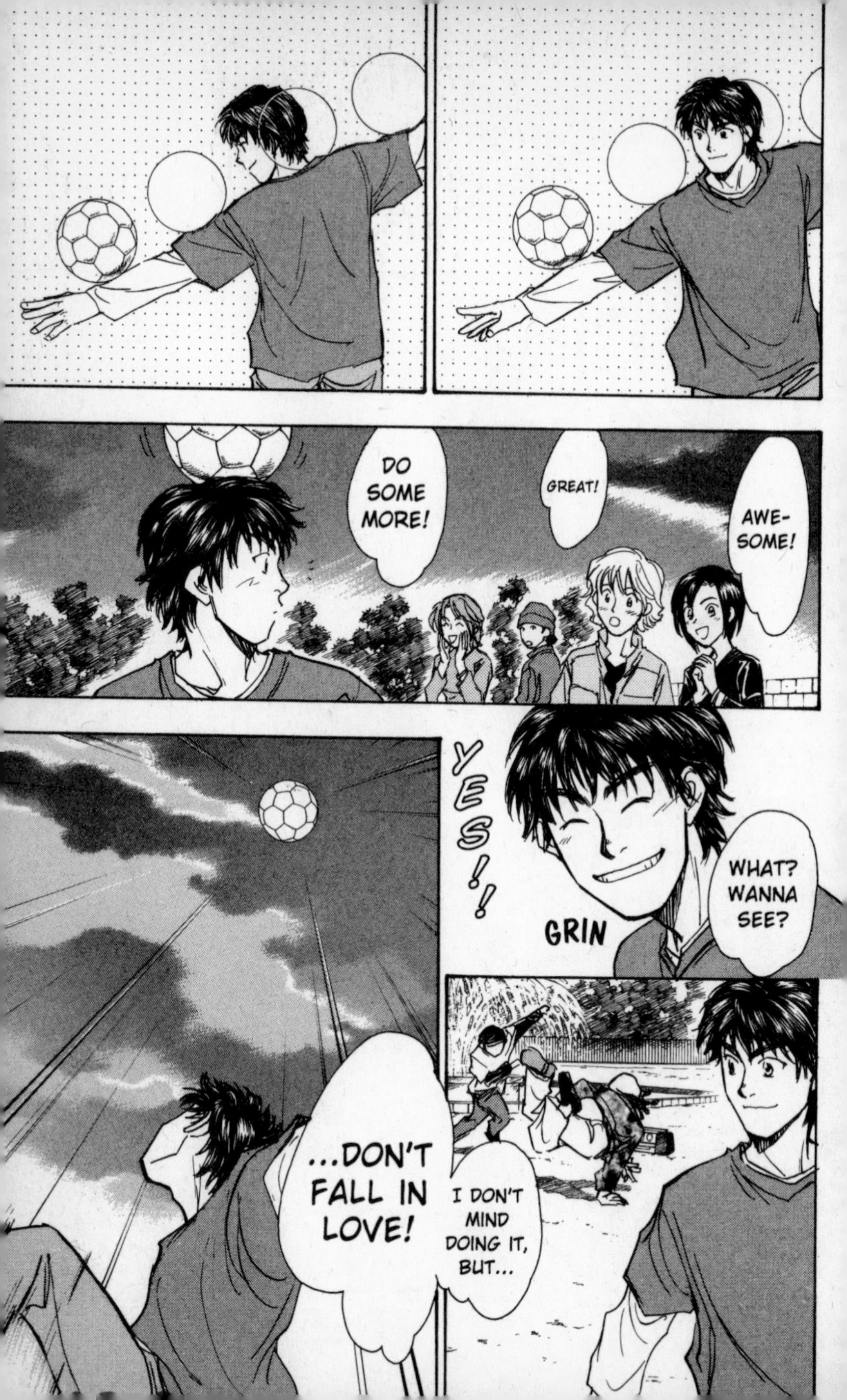
AWE-SOME!
GREAT!
DO SOME MORE!
WHAT? WANNA SEE?
YES!!
GRIN
I DON'T MIND DOING IT, BUT...
...DON'T FALL IN LOVE!

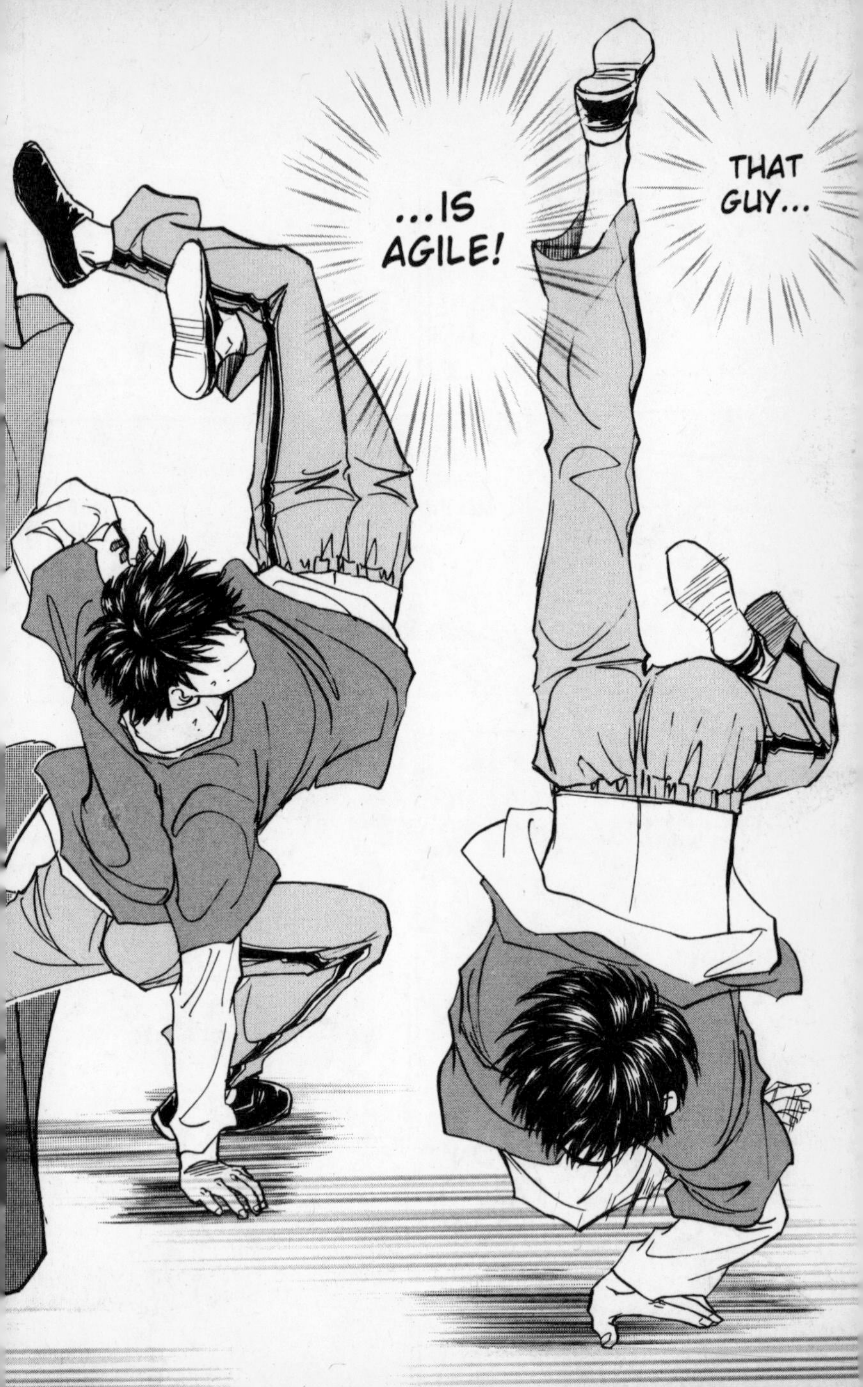
THAT GUY...
...IS AGILE!

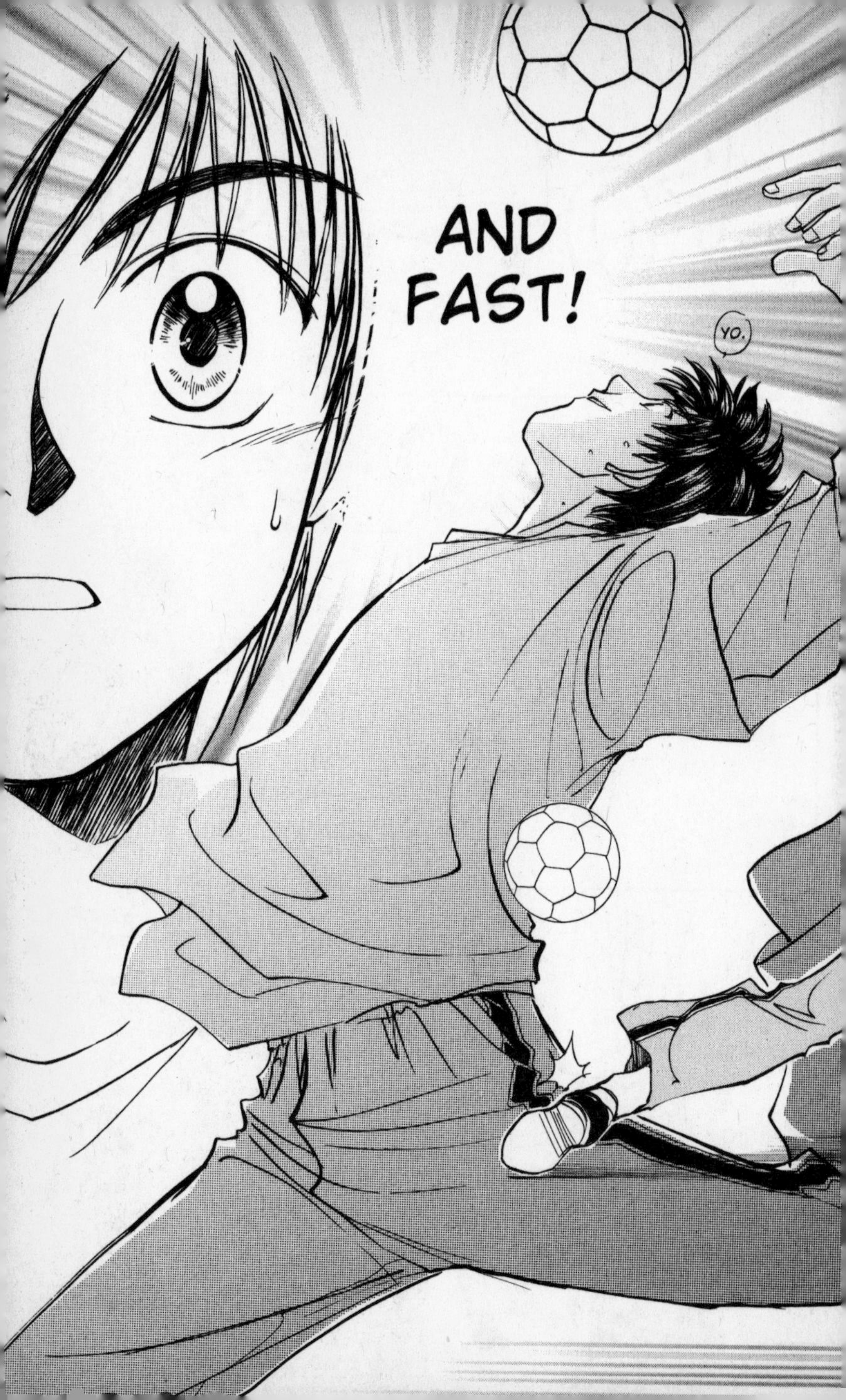
AND FAST!
YO.

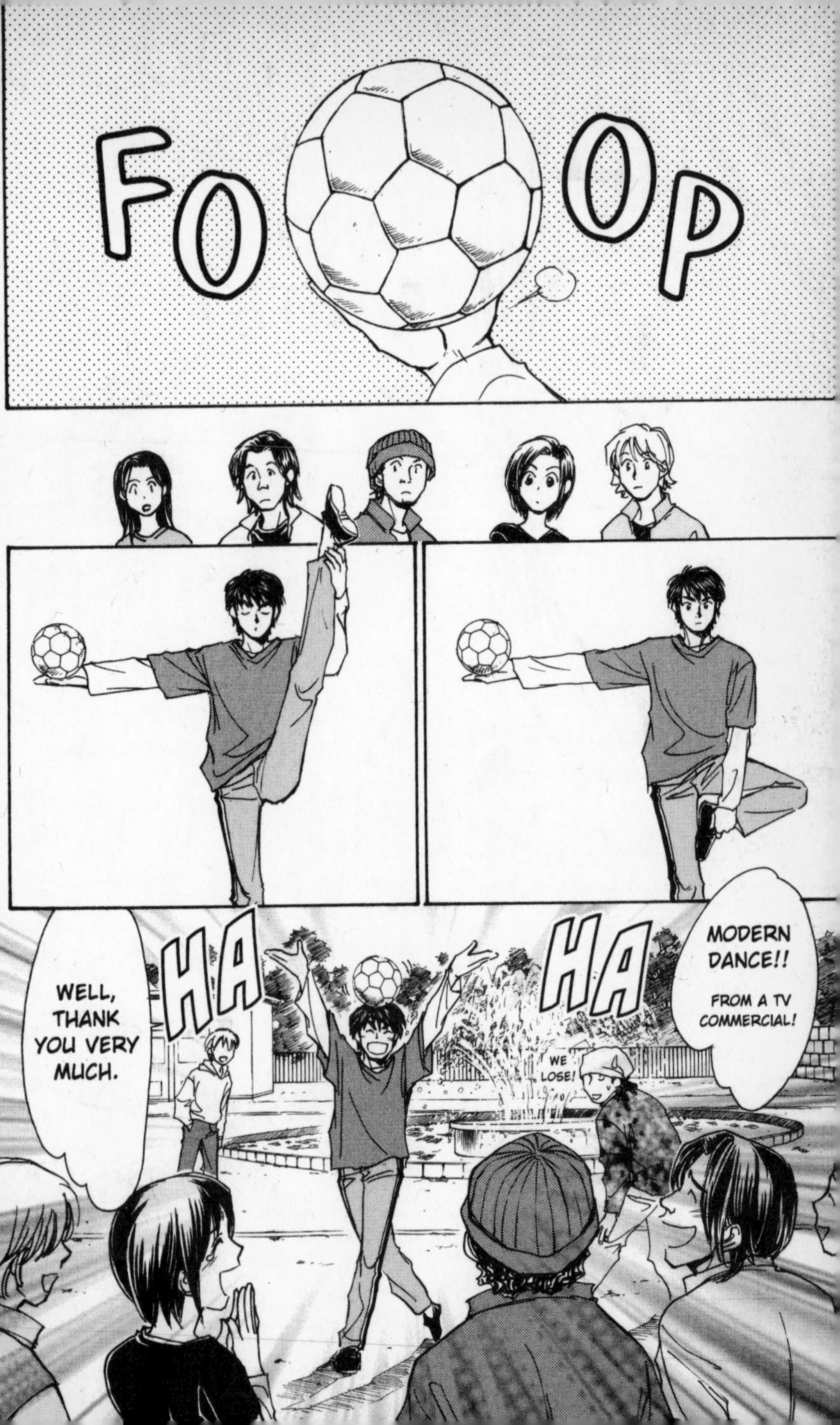
FO OP
MODERN DANCE!!
FROM A TV COMMERCIAL!
HA
WE LOSE!
HA
WELL, THANK YOU VERY MUCH.

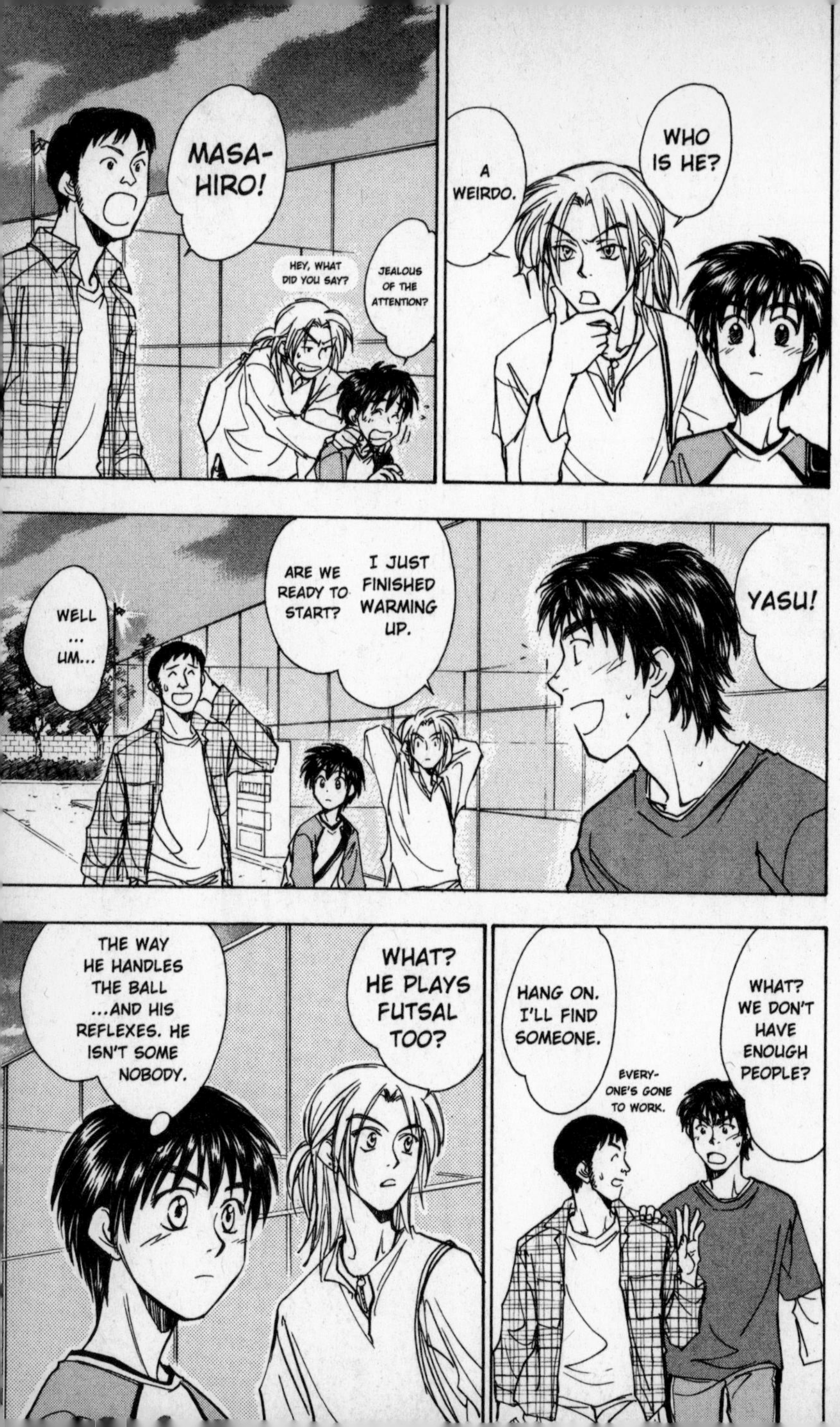
WHO IS HE?
A WEIRDO.
MASA-HIRO!
JEALOUS OF THE ATTENTION?
HEY, WHAT DID YOU SAY?
YASU!
I JUST FINISHED WARMING UP.
ARE WE READY TO START?
WELL ... UM...
WHAT? WE DON'T HAVE ENOUGH PEOPLE?
EVERY-ONE'S GONE TO WORK.
HANG ON. I'LL FIND SOMEONE.
WHAT? HE PLAYS FUTSAL TOO?
THE WAY HE HANDLES THE BALL ...AND HIS REFLEXES. HE ISN'T SOME NOBODY.

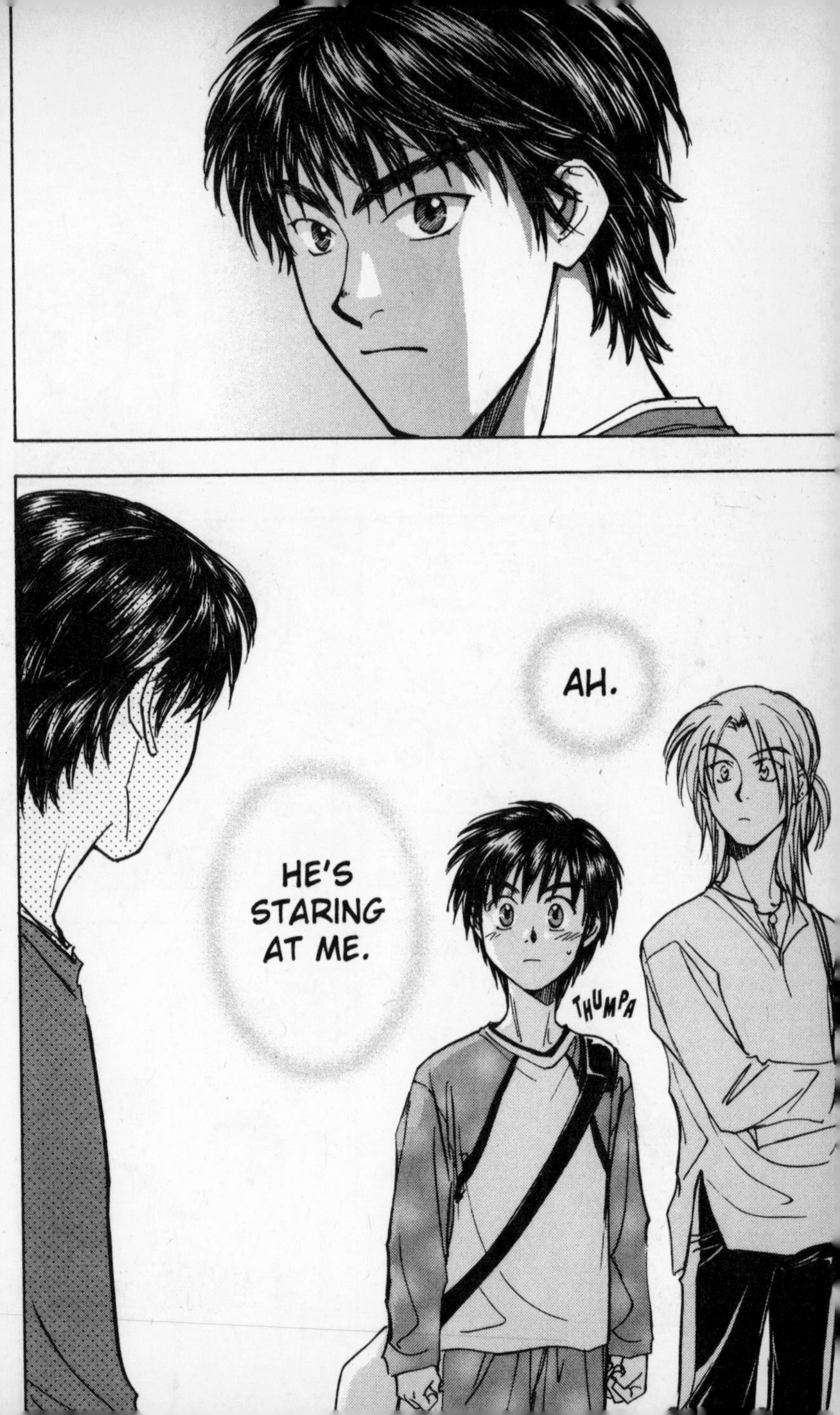
AH.
HE'S STARING AT ME.
THUMPA

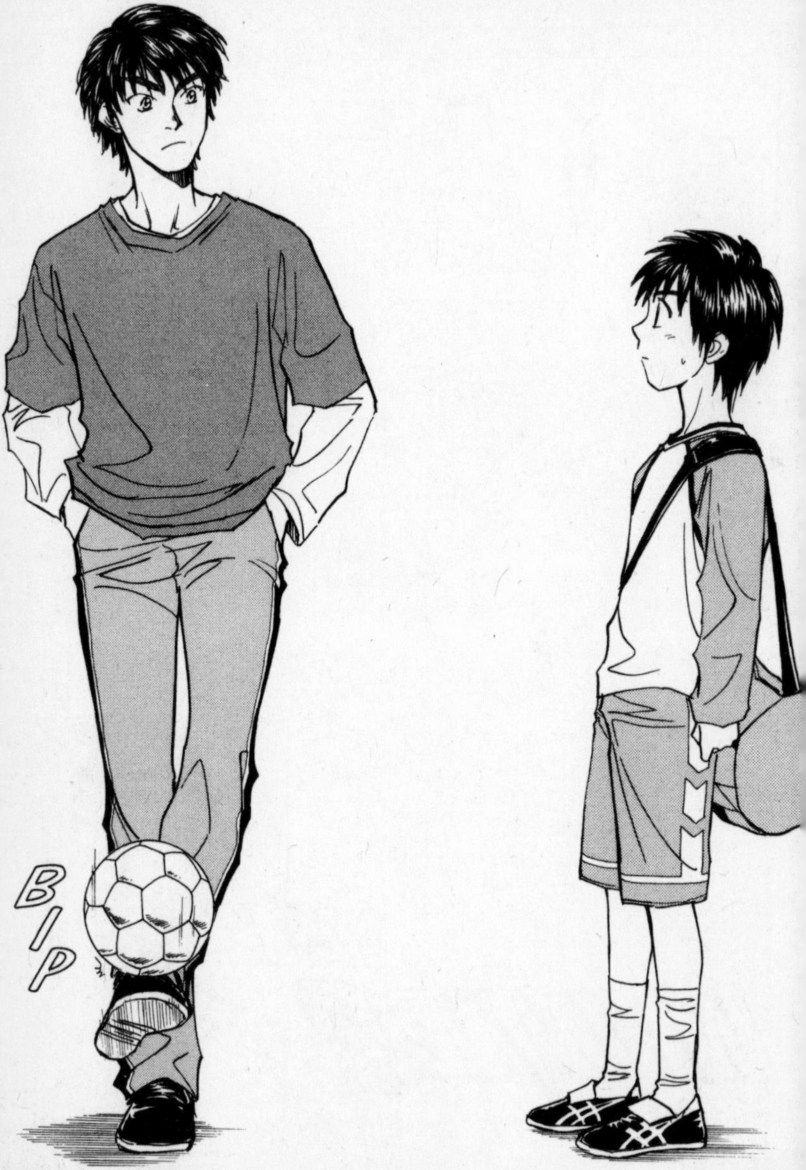
BIP

IT'S HARD TO
TELL IF KAORU'S
EYES ARE OPEN
OR CLOSED.

GOMI

WHISTLE!?

ASSISTANT: K HAMMER

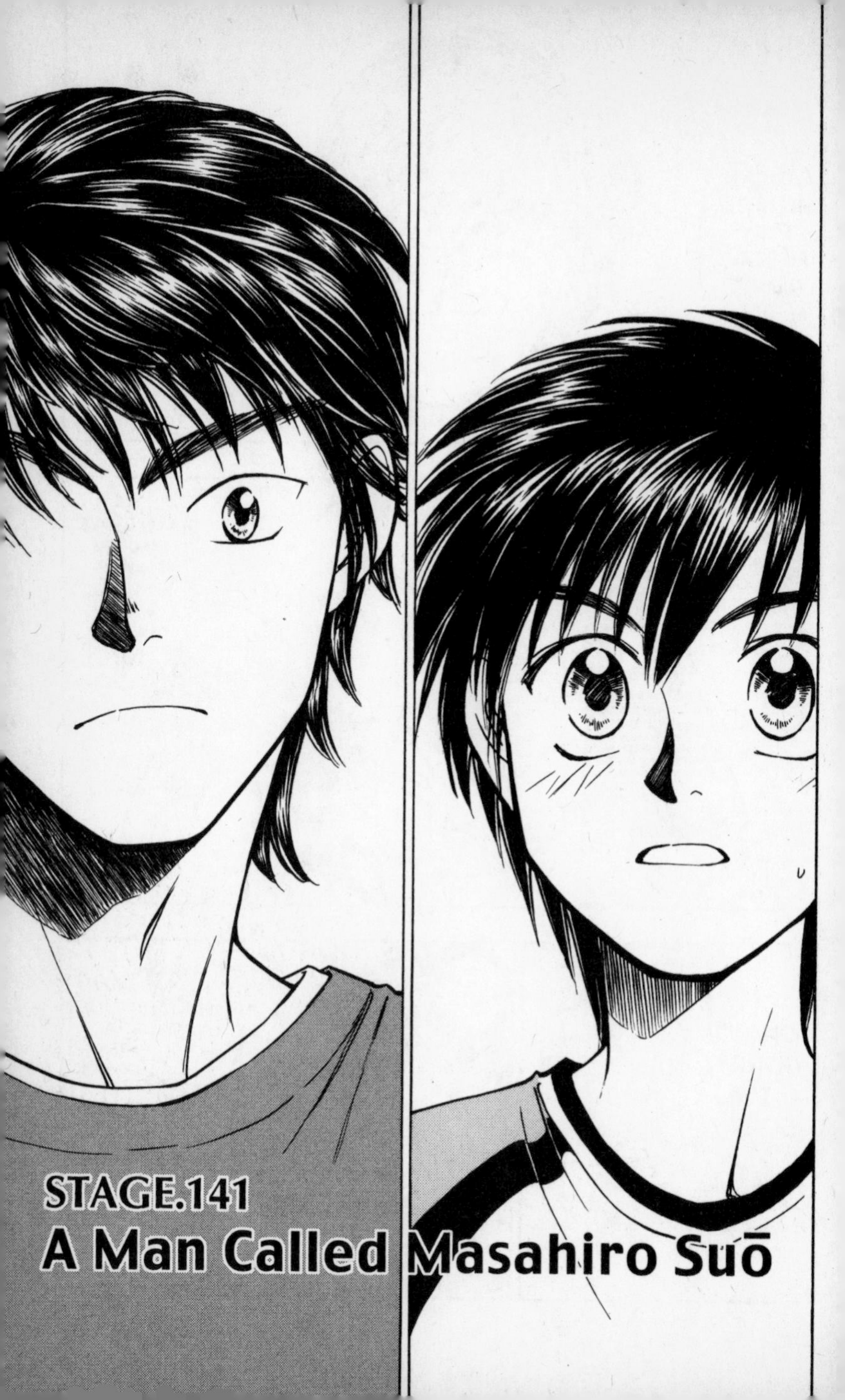
STAGE.141
A Man Called Masahiro Suō

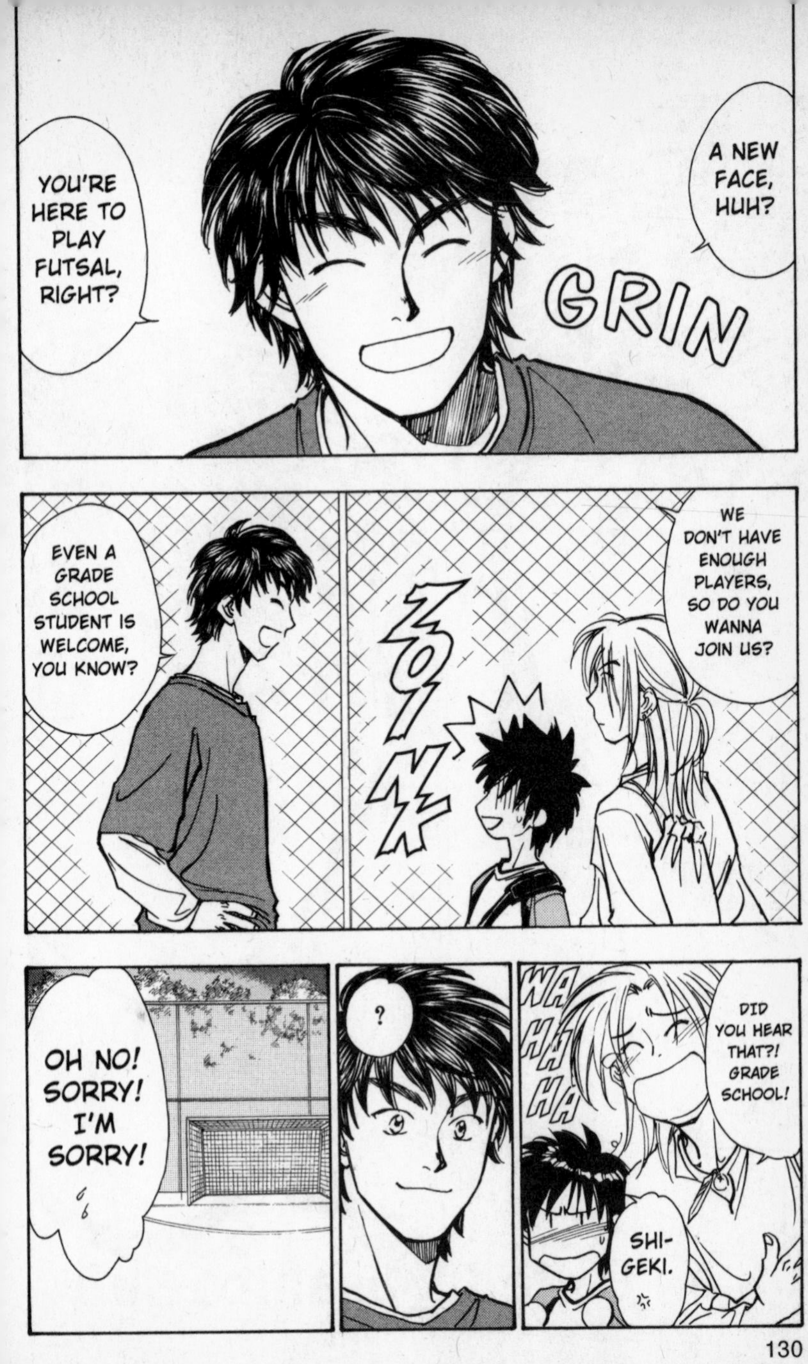
A NEW FACE, HUH?
GRIN
YOU'RE HERE TO PLAY FUTSAL, RIGHT?
WE DON'T HAVE ENOUGH PLAYERS, SO DO YOU WANNA JOIN US?
ZOINK
EVEN A GRADE SCHOOL STUDENT IS WELCOME, YOU KNOW?
WAHAHAHA
DID YOU HEAR THAT?! GRADE SCHOOL!
SHI-GEKI.
?
OH NO! SORRY! I'M SORRY!

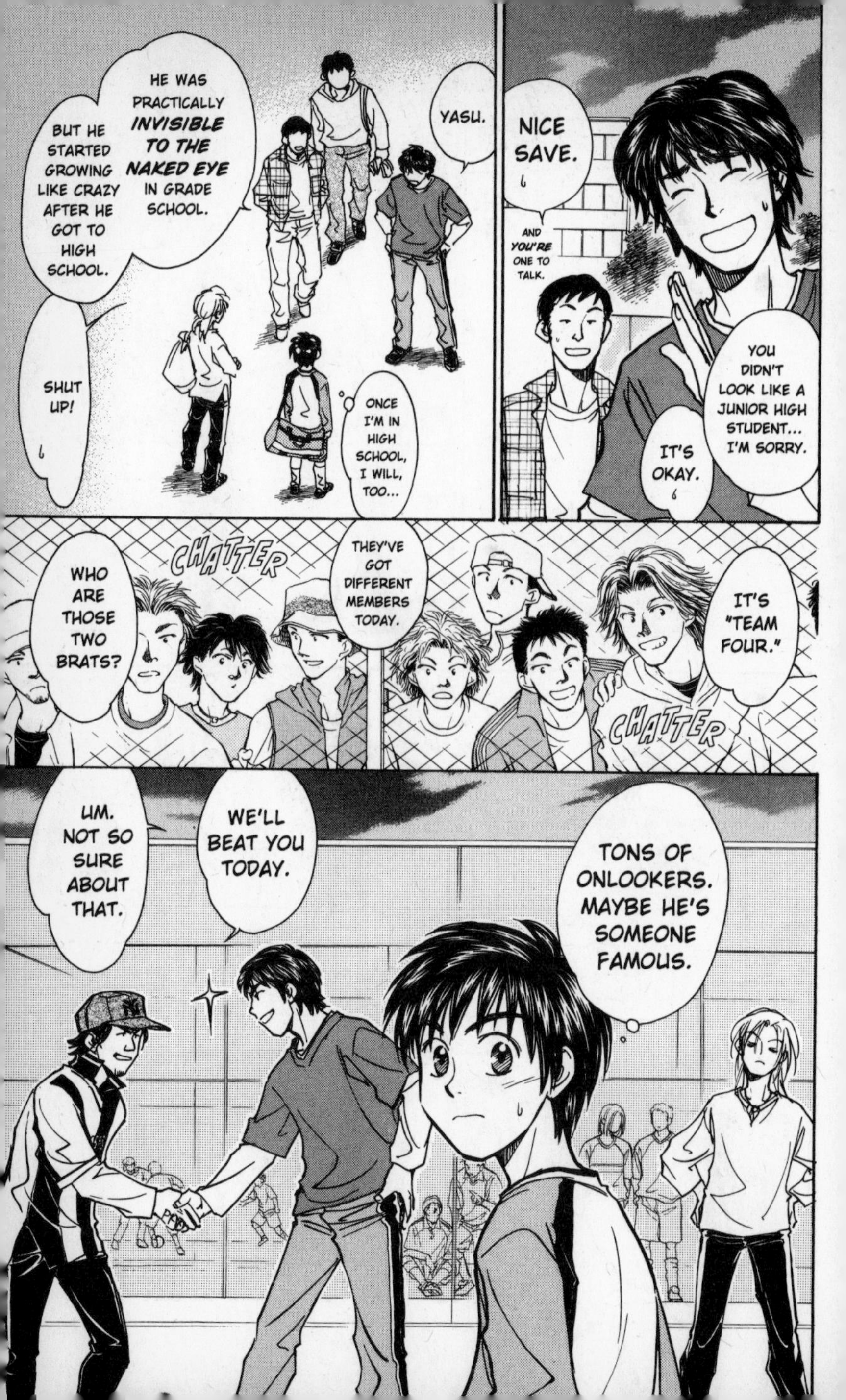
NICE SAVE.
AND YOU'RE ONE TO TALK.
YOU DIDN'T LOOK LIKE A JUNIOR HIGH STUDENT... I'M SORRY.
IT'S OKAY.
YASU.
HE WAS PRACTICALLY INVISIBLE TO THE NAKED EYE IN GRADE SCHOOL.
BUT HE STARTED GROWING LIKE CRAZY AFTER HE GOT TO HIGH SCHOOL.
SHUT UP!
ONCE I'M IN HIGH SCHOOL, I WILL, TOO...
IT'S "TEAM FOUR."
CHATTER
THEY'VE GOT DIFFERENT MEMBERS TODAY.
CHATTER
WHO ARE THOSE TWO BRATS?
TONS OF ONLOOKERS. MAYBE HE'S SOMEONE FAMOUS.
WE'LL BEAT YOU TODAY.
UM. NOT SO SURE ABOUT THAT.

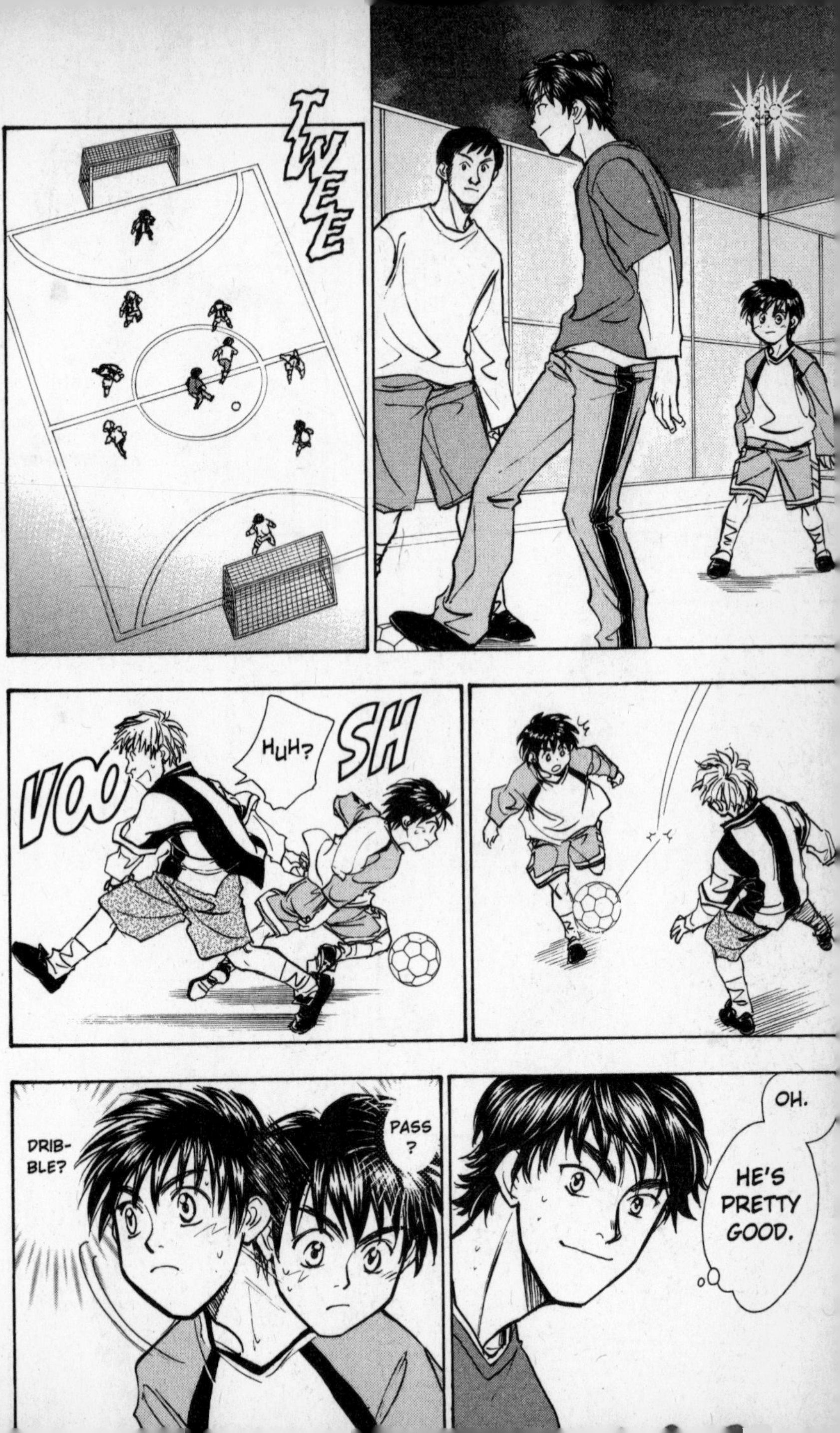
TWEE
SH
HUH?
VOO
OH.
HE'S PRETTY GOOD.
PASS?
DRIB-BLE?

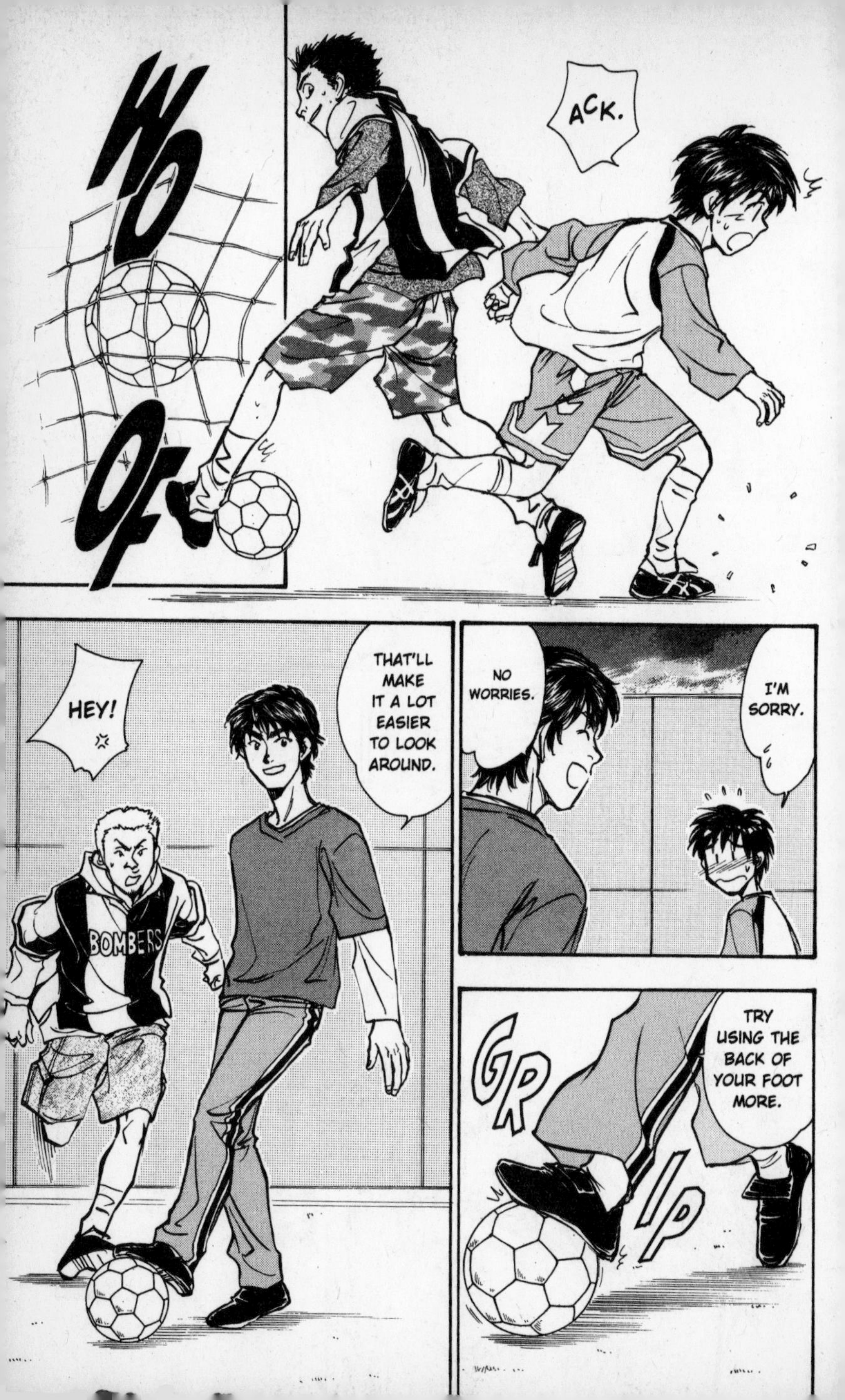
ACK.
WOOF
I'M SORRY.
NO WORRIES.
TRY USING THE BACK OF YOUR FOOT MORE.
GRIP
THAT'LL MAKE IT A LOT EASIER TO LOOK AROUND.
HEY!
BOMBERS

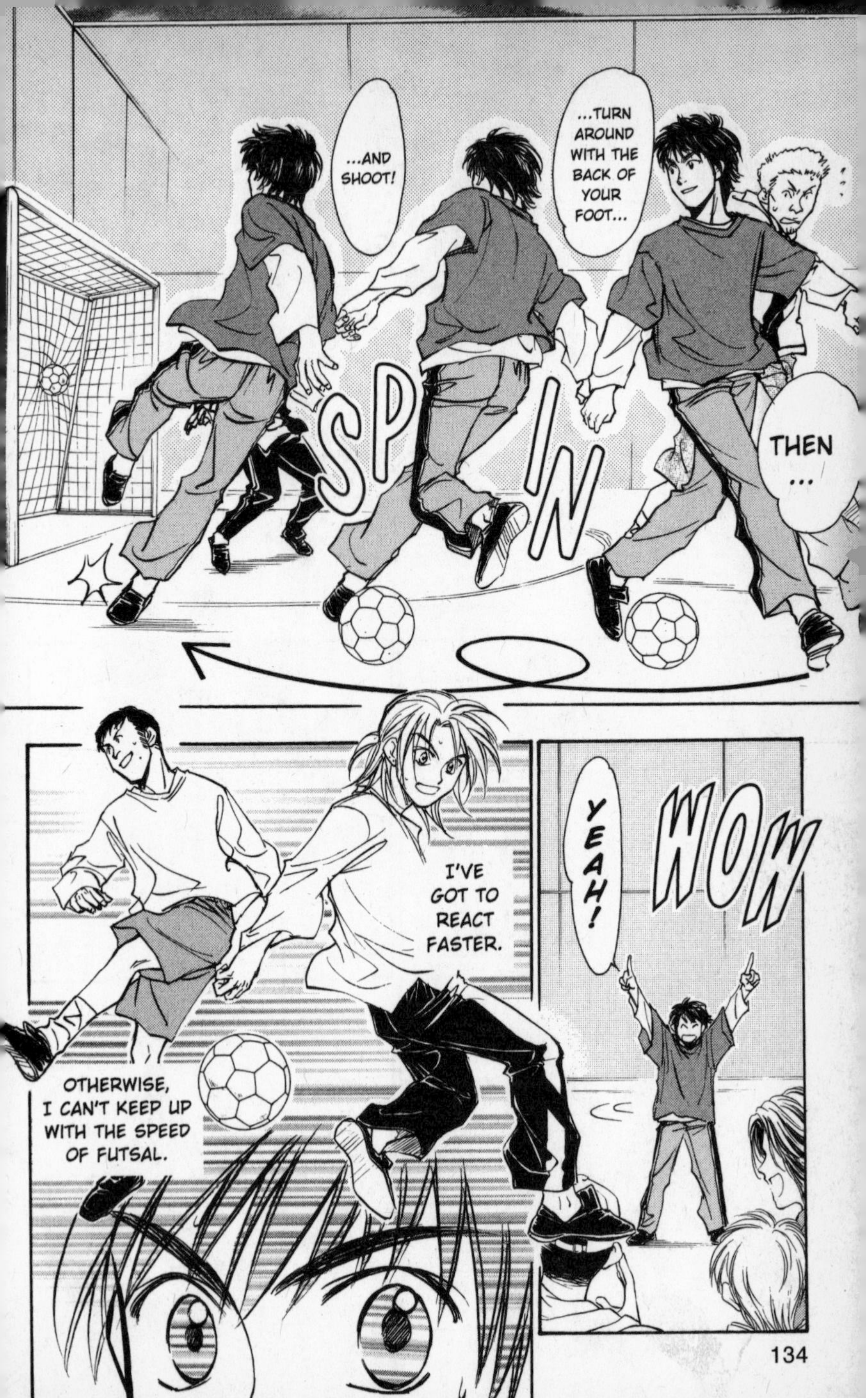
THEN...
...TURN AROUND WITH THE BACK OF YOUR FOOT...
SPIN
...AND SHOOT!
WOW
YEAH!
I'VE GOT TO REACT FASTER.
OTHERWISE, I CAN'T KEEP UP WITH THE SPEED OF FUTSAL.

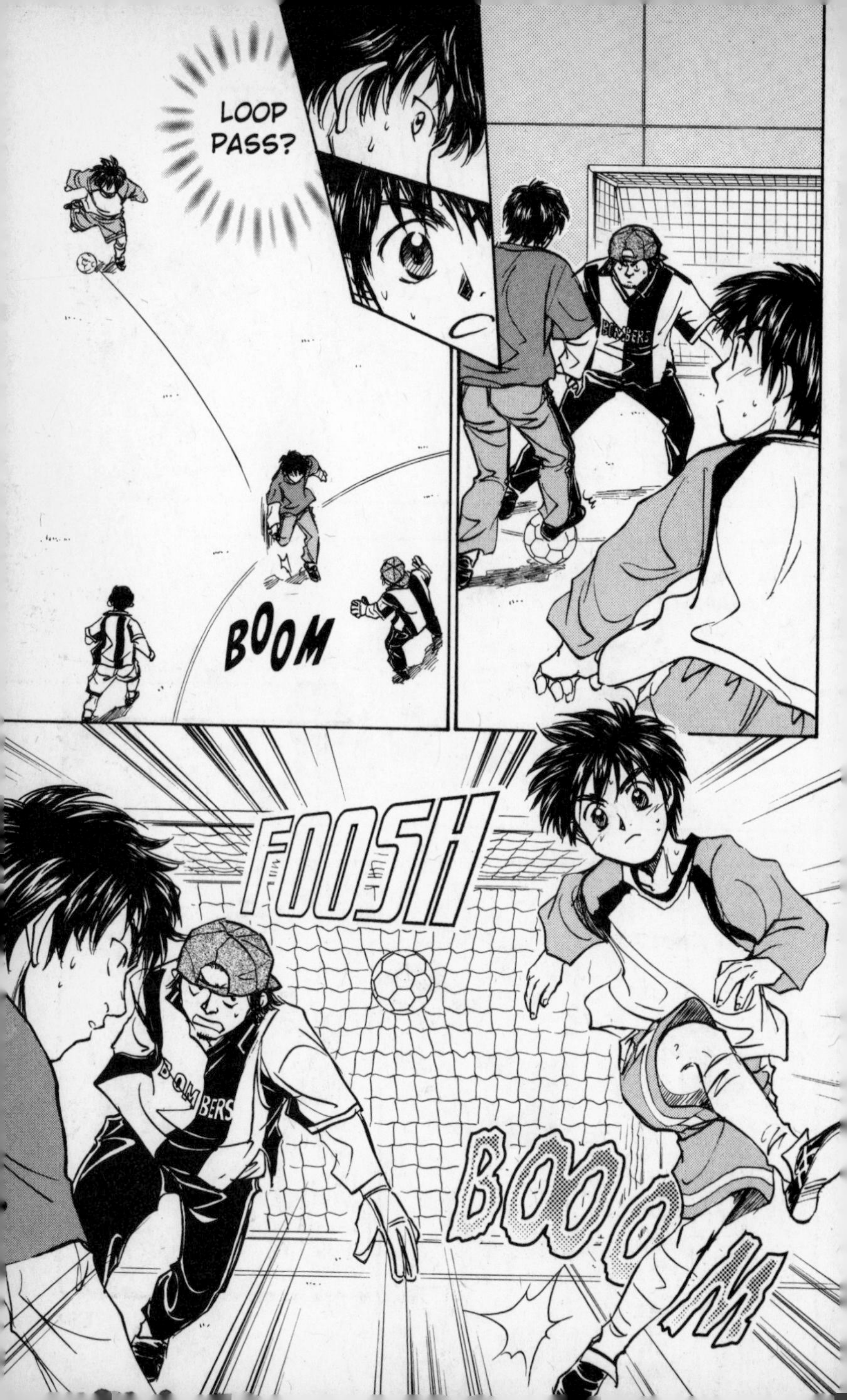

LOOP PASS?
BOOM
FOOSH
BOOOOM

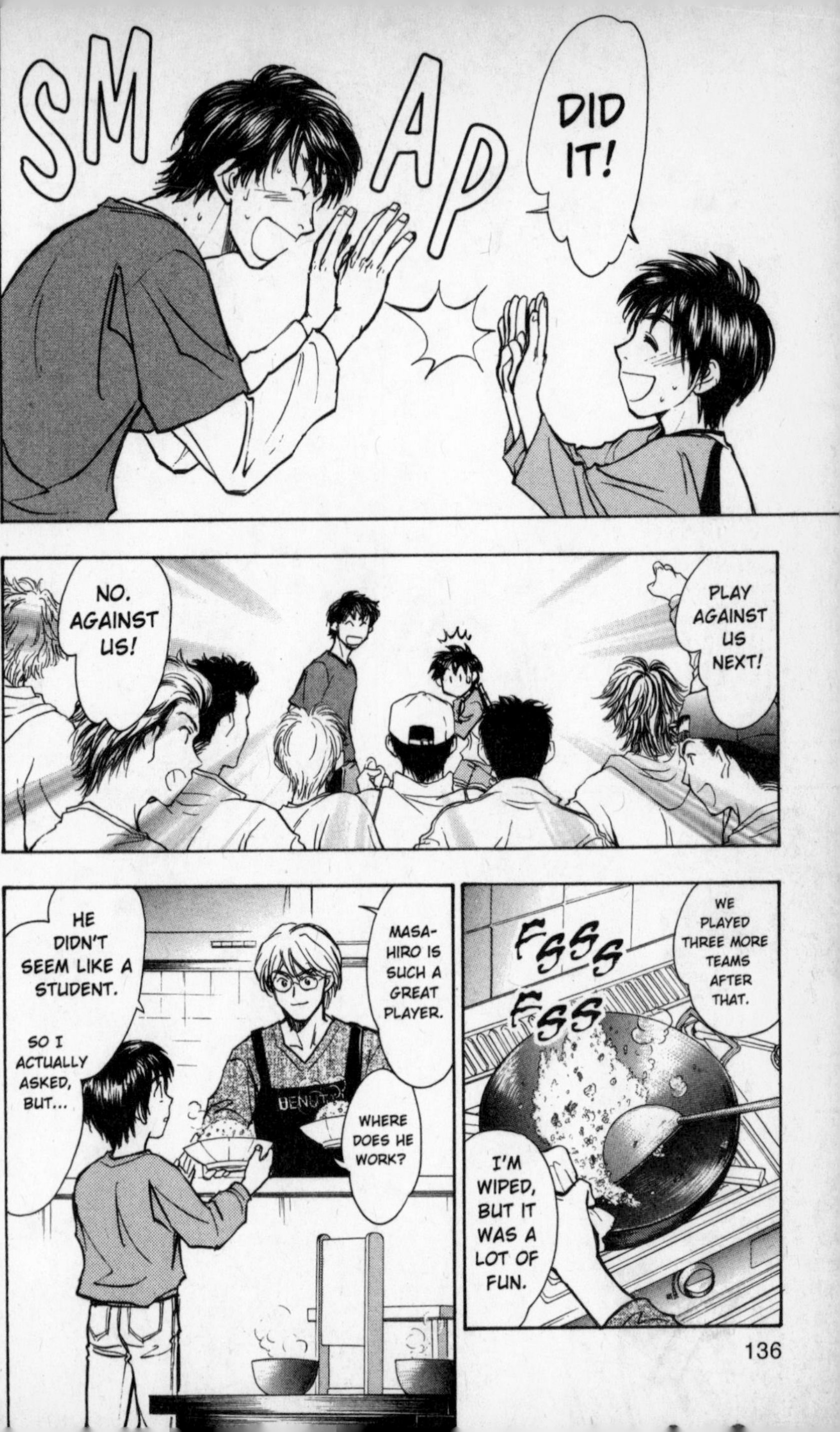
SMAP
DID IT!
PLAY AGAINST US NEXT!
NO. AGAINST US!
WE PLAYED THREE MORE TEAMS AFTER THAT.
FSSS FSS
I'M WIPED, BUT IT WAS A LOT OF FUN.
MASA-HIRO IS SUCH A GREAT PLAYER.
HE DIDN'T SEEM LIKE A STUDENT.
WHERE DOES HE WORK?
SO I ACTUALLY ASKED, BUT...

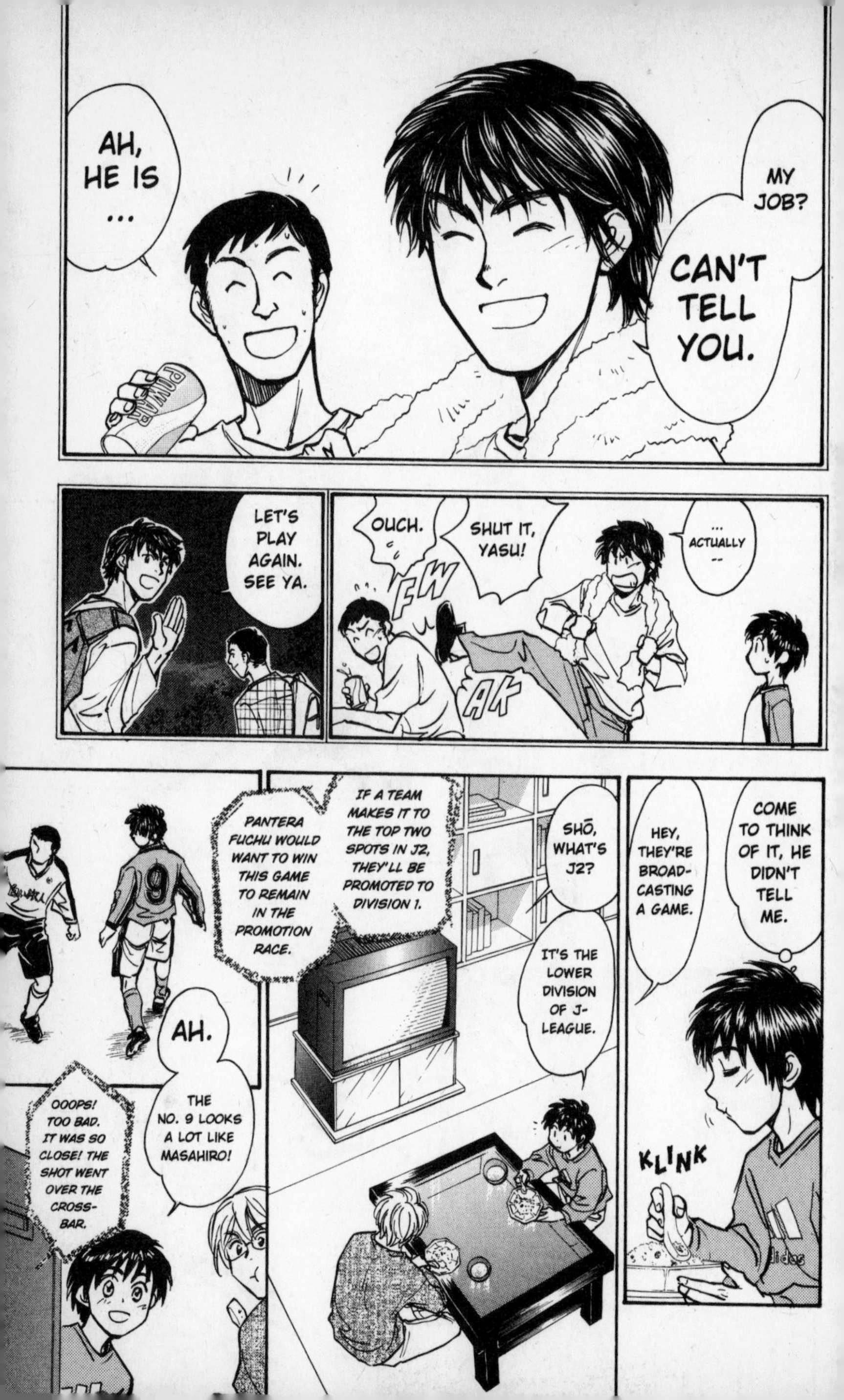
MY JOB?
CAN'T TELL YOU.
AH, HE IS ...
... ACTUALLY --
SHUT IT, YASU!
OUCH.
FWAK
LET'S PLAY AGAIN. SEE YA.
COME TO THINK OF IT, HE DIDN'T TELL ME.
HEY, THEY'RE BROAD-CASTING A GAME.
KLINK
SHŌ, WHAT'S J2?
IT'S THE LOWER DIVISION OF J-LEAGUE.
IF A TEAM MAKES IT TO THE TOP TWO SPOTS IN J2, THEY'LL BE PROMOTED TO DIVISION 1.
PANTERA FUCHU WOULD WANT TO WIN THIS GAME TO REMAIN IN THE PROMOTION RACE.
AH.
THE NO. 9 LOOKS A LOT LIKE MASAHIRO!
OOOPS! TOO BAD. IT WAS SO CLOSE! THE SHOT WENT OVER THE CROSS-BAR.

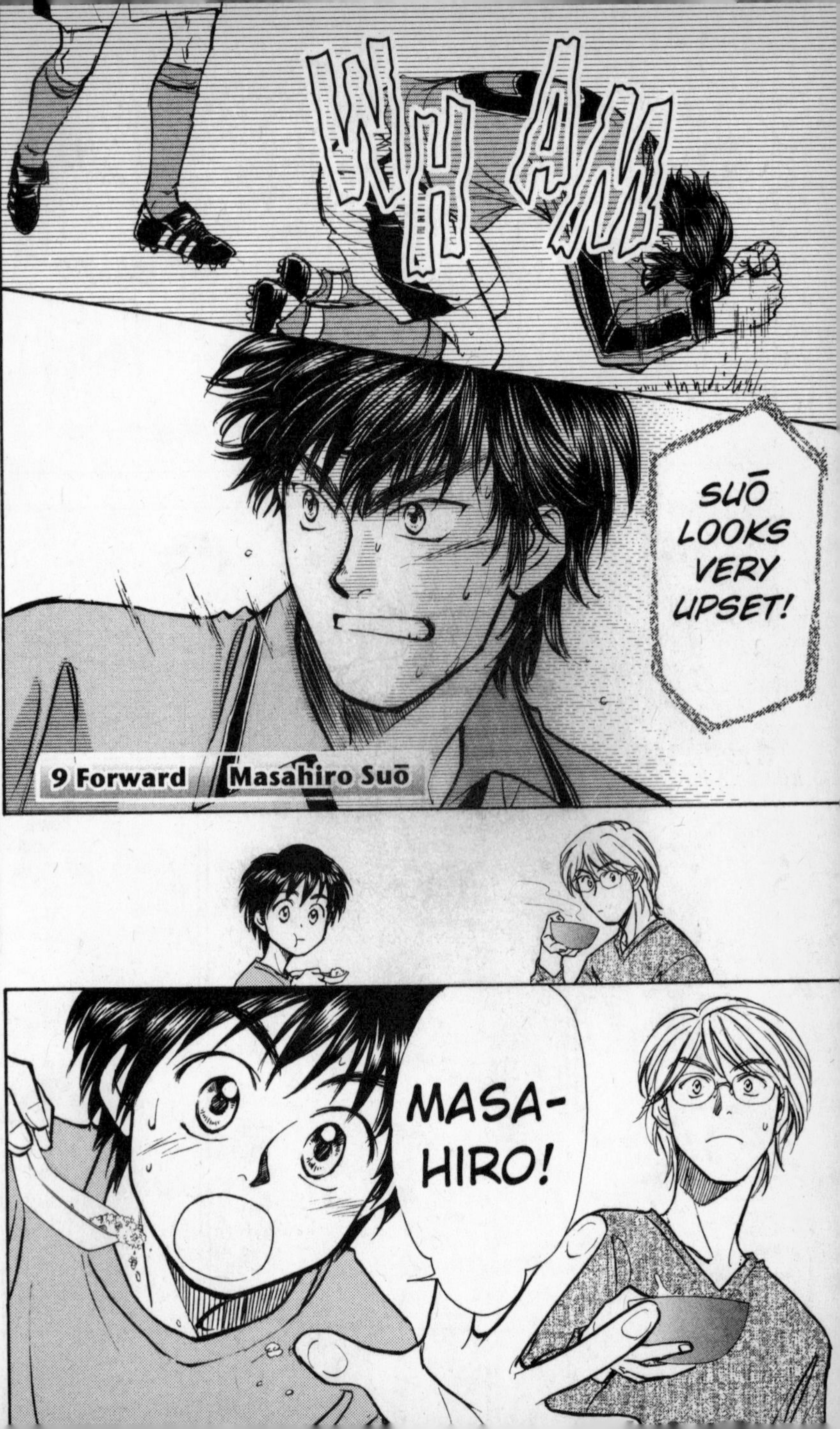
WHAM
SUŌ LOOKS VERY UPSET!
9 Forward
Masahiro Suō
MASA-HIRO!

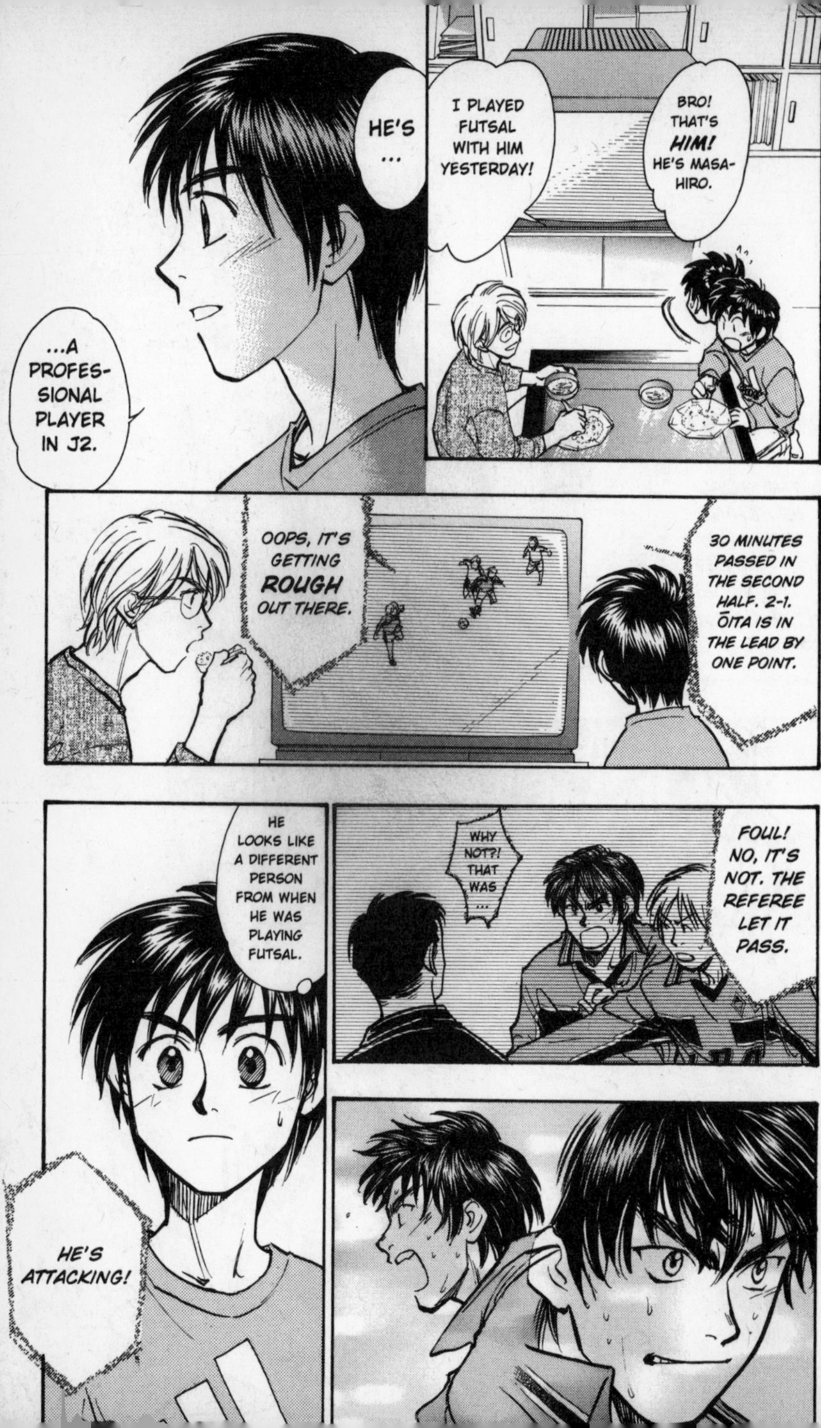
BRO! THAT'S **HIM!** HE'S MASA-HIRO.
I PLAYED FUTSAL WITH HIM YESTERDAY!
HE'S ...
...A PROFES-SIONAL PLAYER IN J2.
30 MINUTES PASSED IN THE SECOND HALF. 2-1. ŌITA IS IN THE LEAD BY ONE POINT.
OOPS, IT'S GETTING **ROUGH** OUT THERE.
FOUL! NO, IT'S NOT. THE REFEREE LET IT PASS.
WHY NOT?! THAT WAS ...
HE LOOKS LIKE A DIFFERENT PERSON FROM WHEN HE WAS PLAYING FUTSAL.
HE'S ATTACKING!

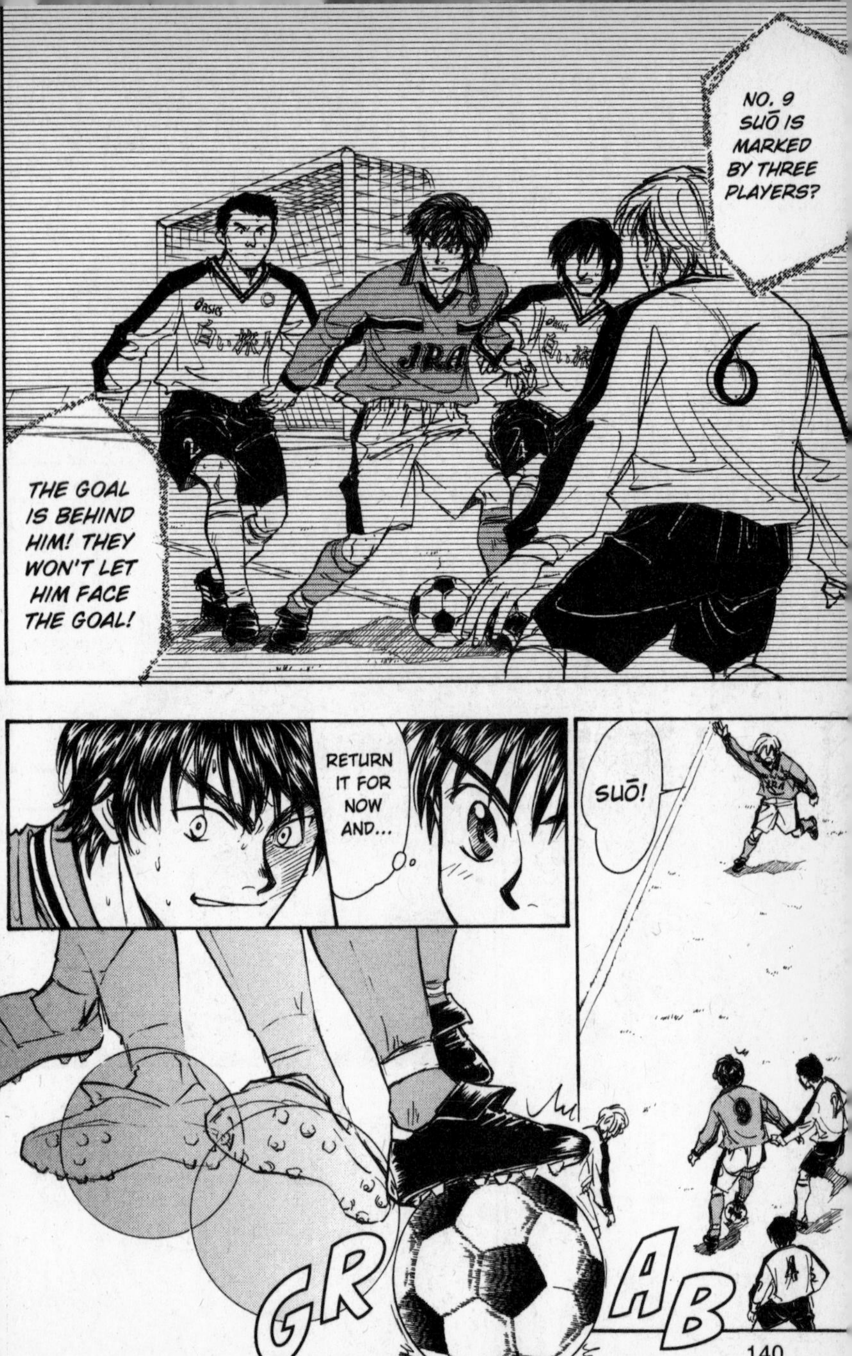
NO. 9 SUŌ IS MARKED BY THREE PLAYERS?
THE GOAL IS BEHIND HIM! THEY WON'T LET HIM FACE THE GOAL!
SUŌ!
RETURN IT FOR NOW AND...
GRAB

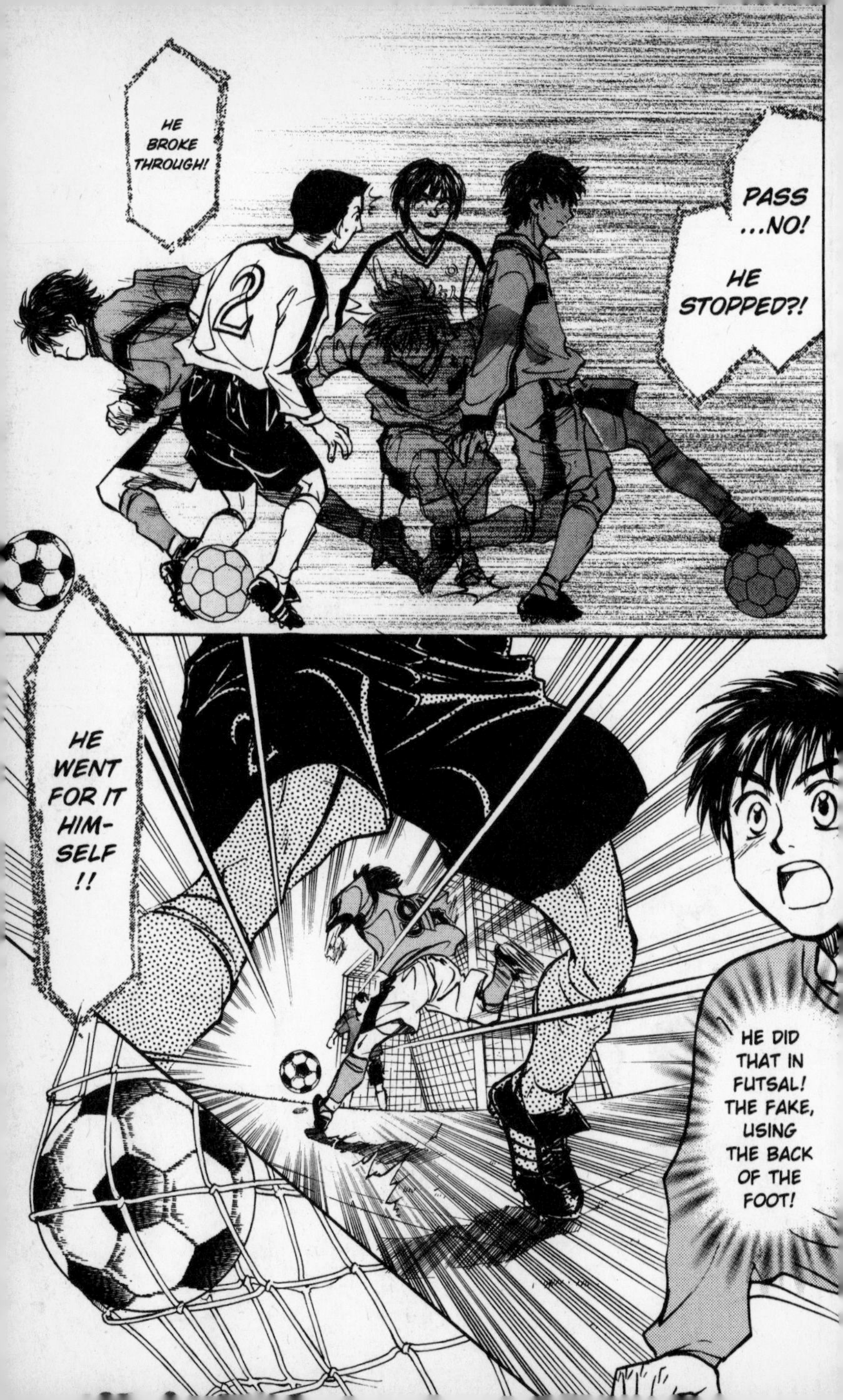
PASS ...NO! HE STOPPED?!
HE BROKE THROUGH!
HE DID THAT IN FUTSAL! THE FAKE, USING THE BACK OF THE FOOT!
HE WENT FOR IT HIM-SELF !!

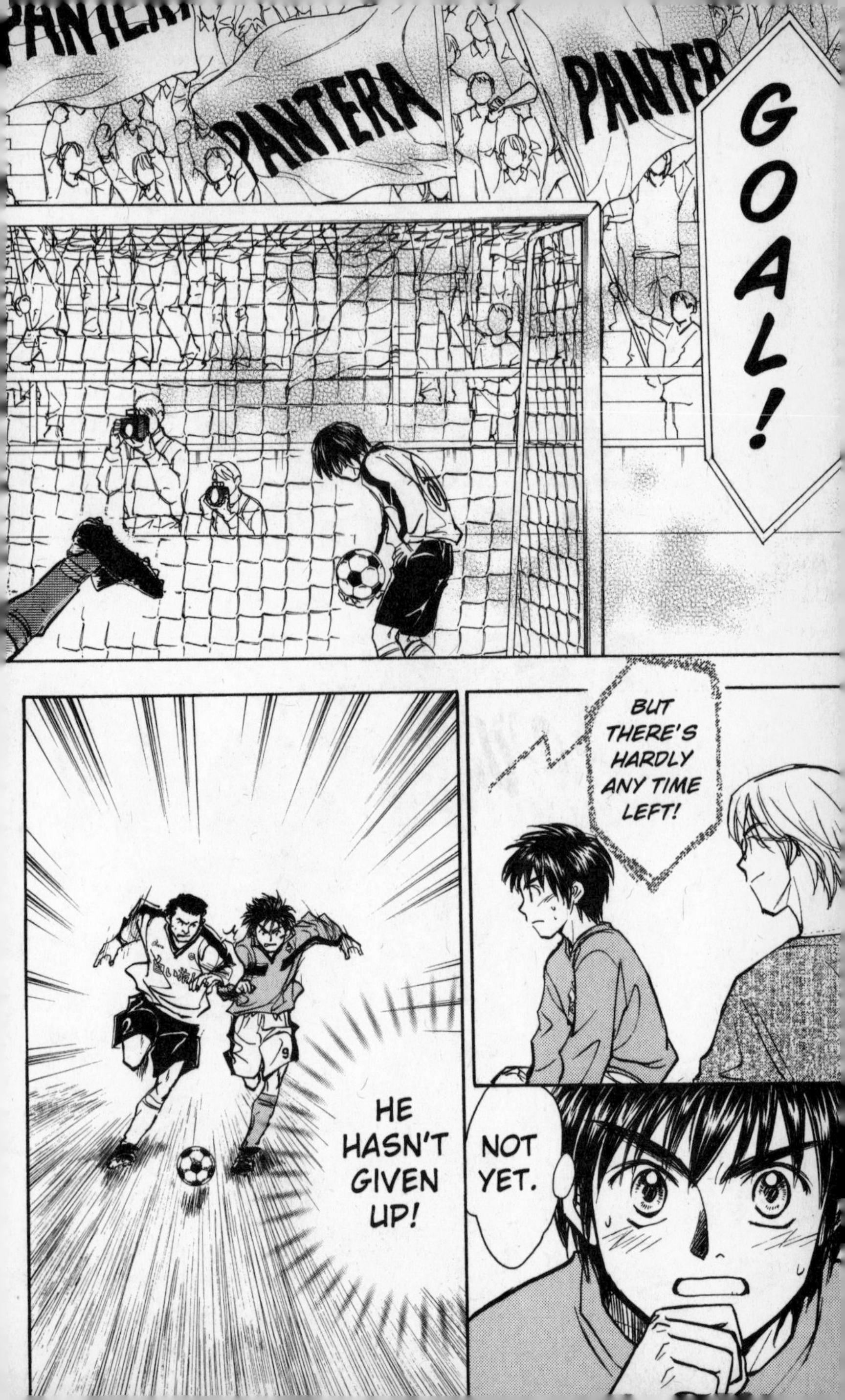
GOAL!
PANTER
PANTERA
BUT THERE'S HARDLY ANY TIME LEFT!
NOT YET.
HE HASN'T GIVEN UP!

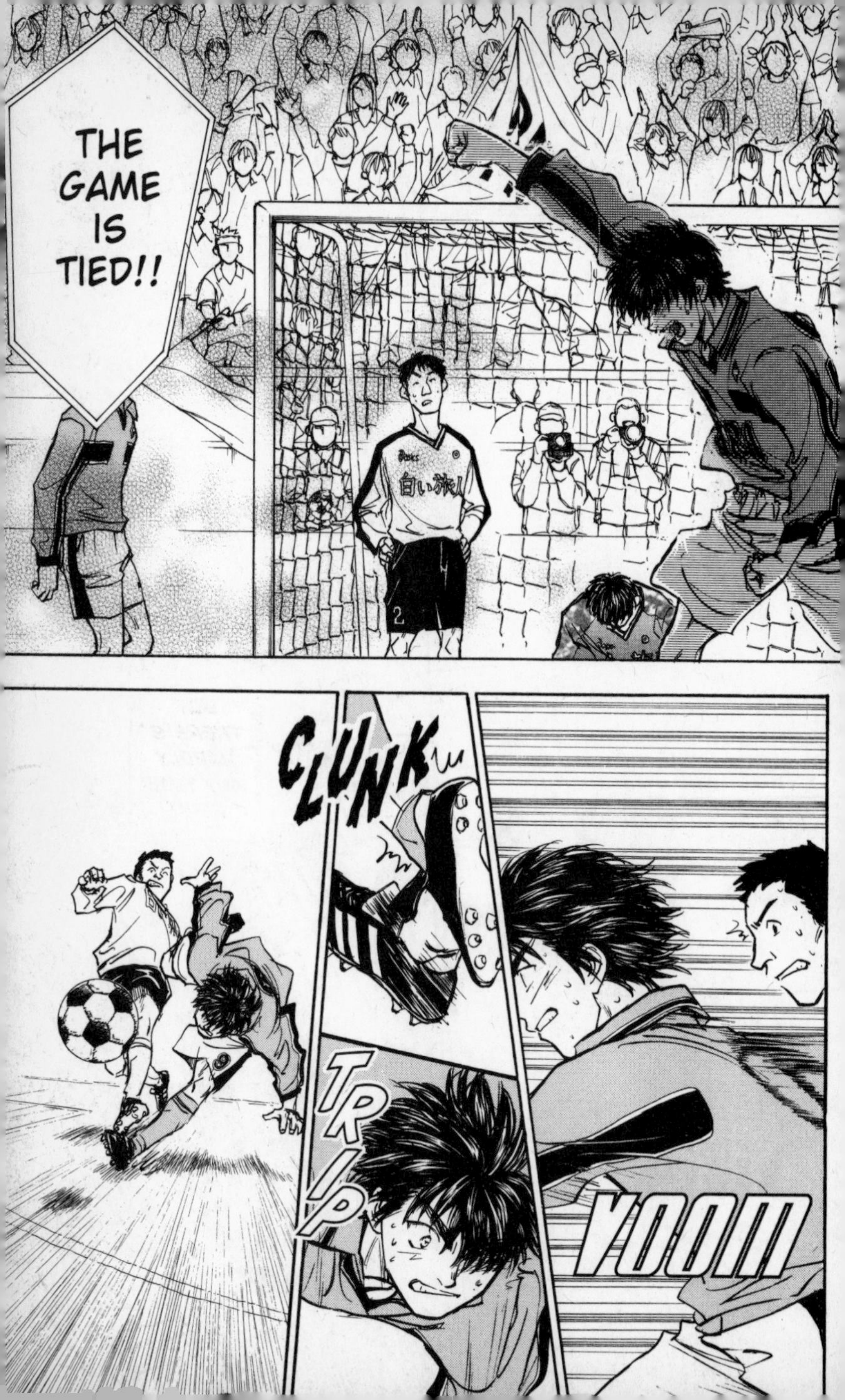
THE GAME IS TIED!!
白い旅人
VOOM
CLUNK
TRIP

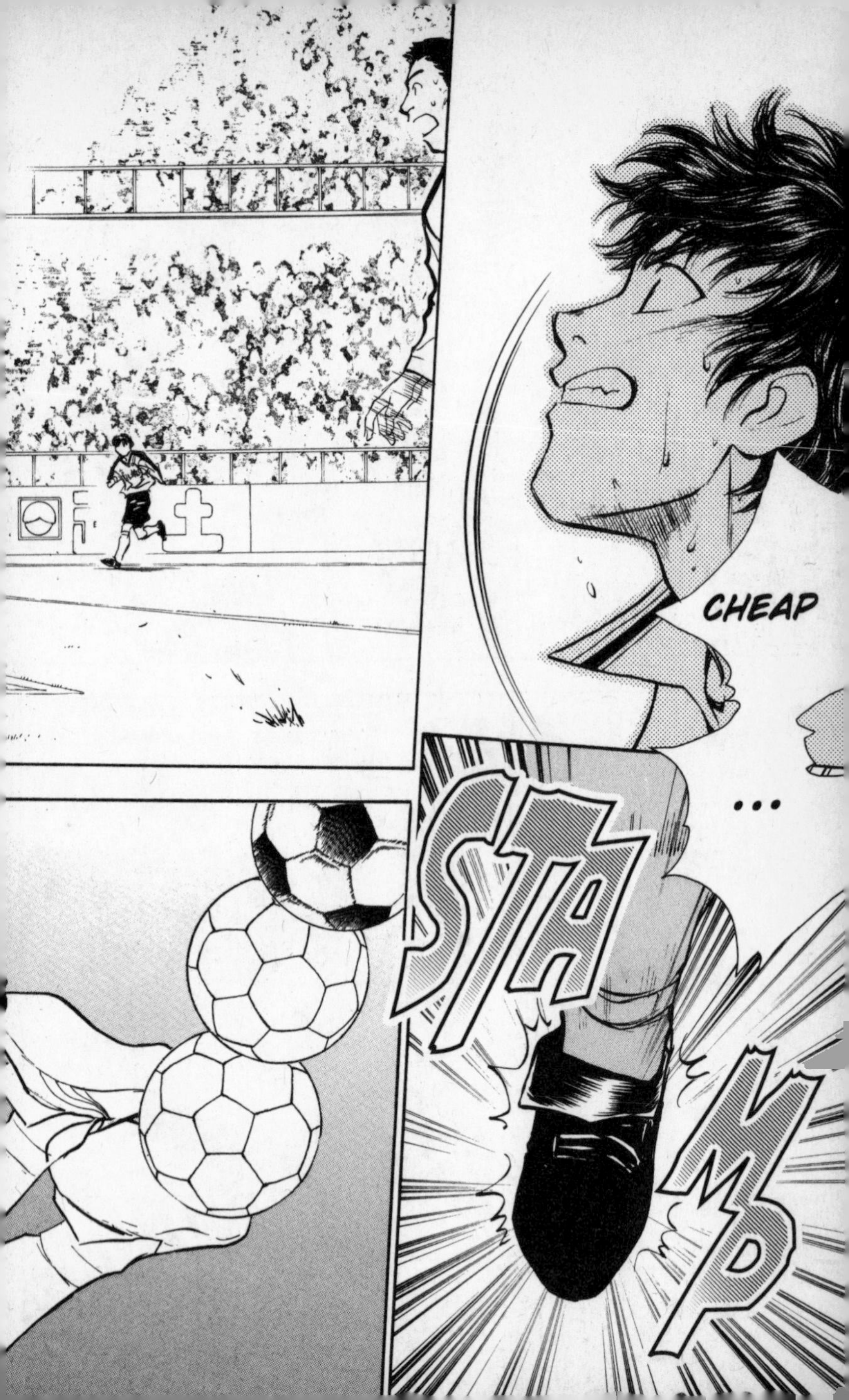
CHEAP
...
STAMP

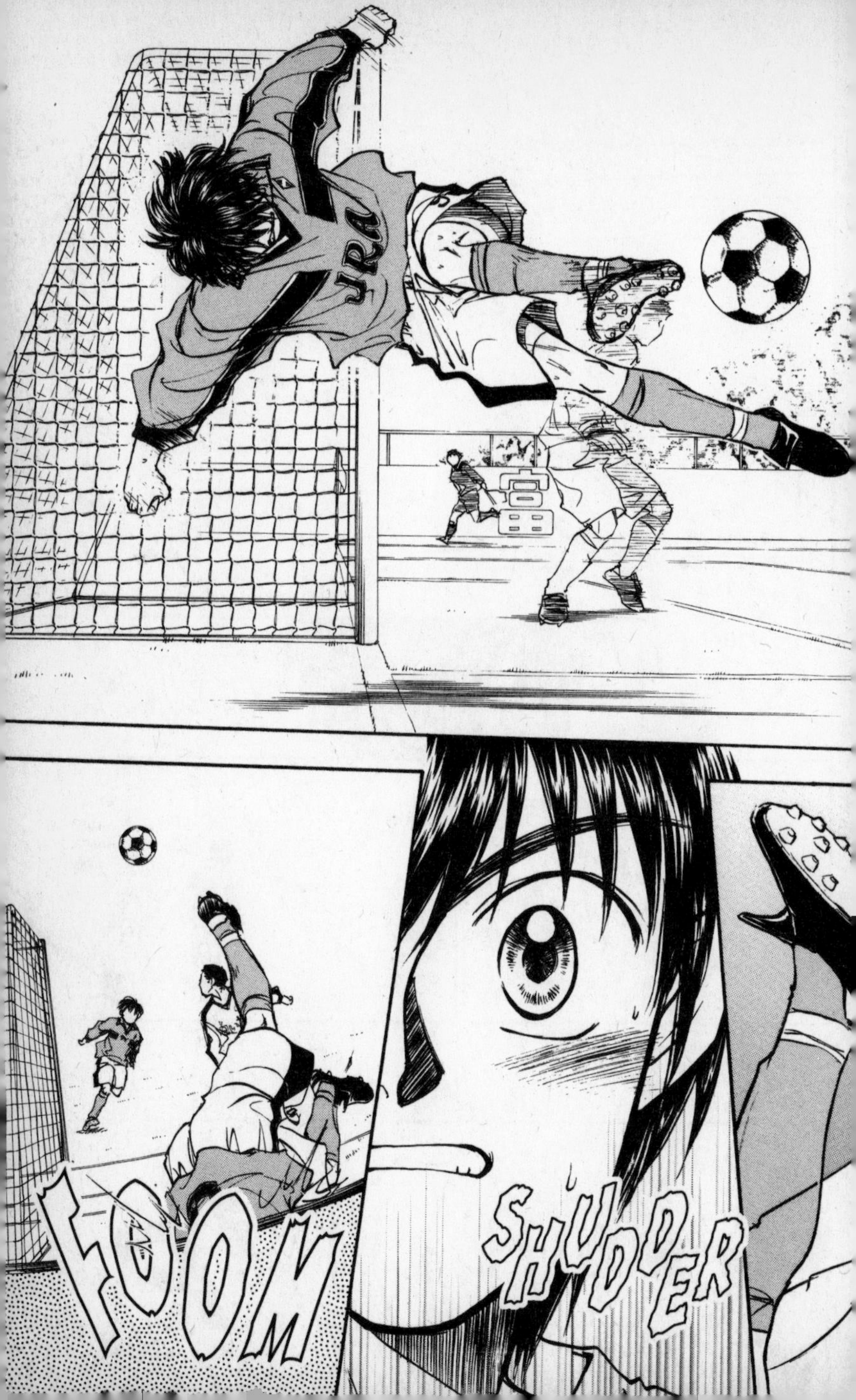
SHUDDER
FOOM

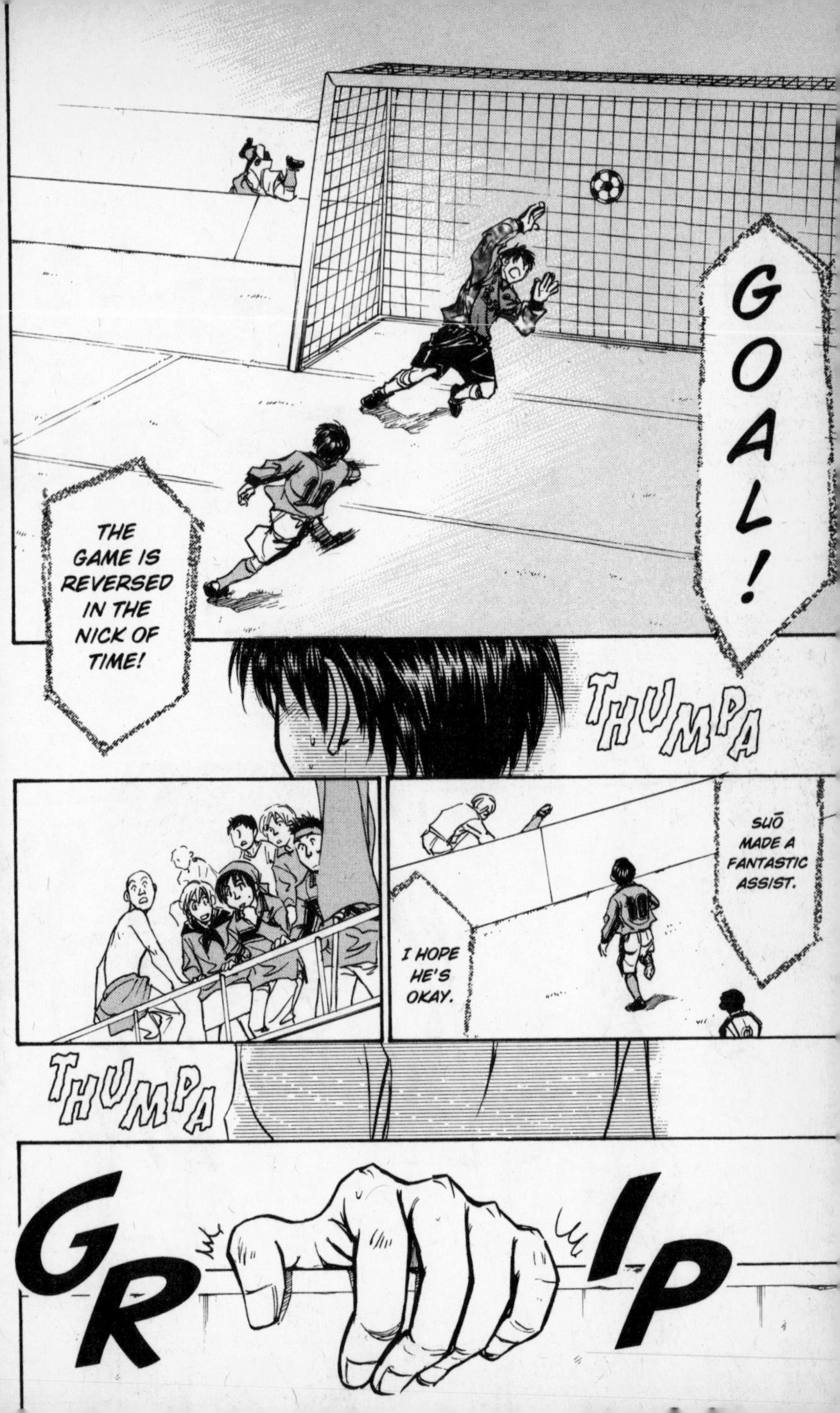
GOAL!
THE GAME IS REVERSED IN THE NICK OF TIME!
THUMPA
SUŌ MADE A FANTASTIC ASSIST.
I HOPE HE'S OKAY.
THUMPA
GRIP

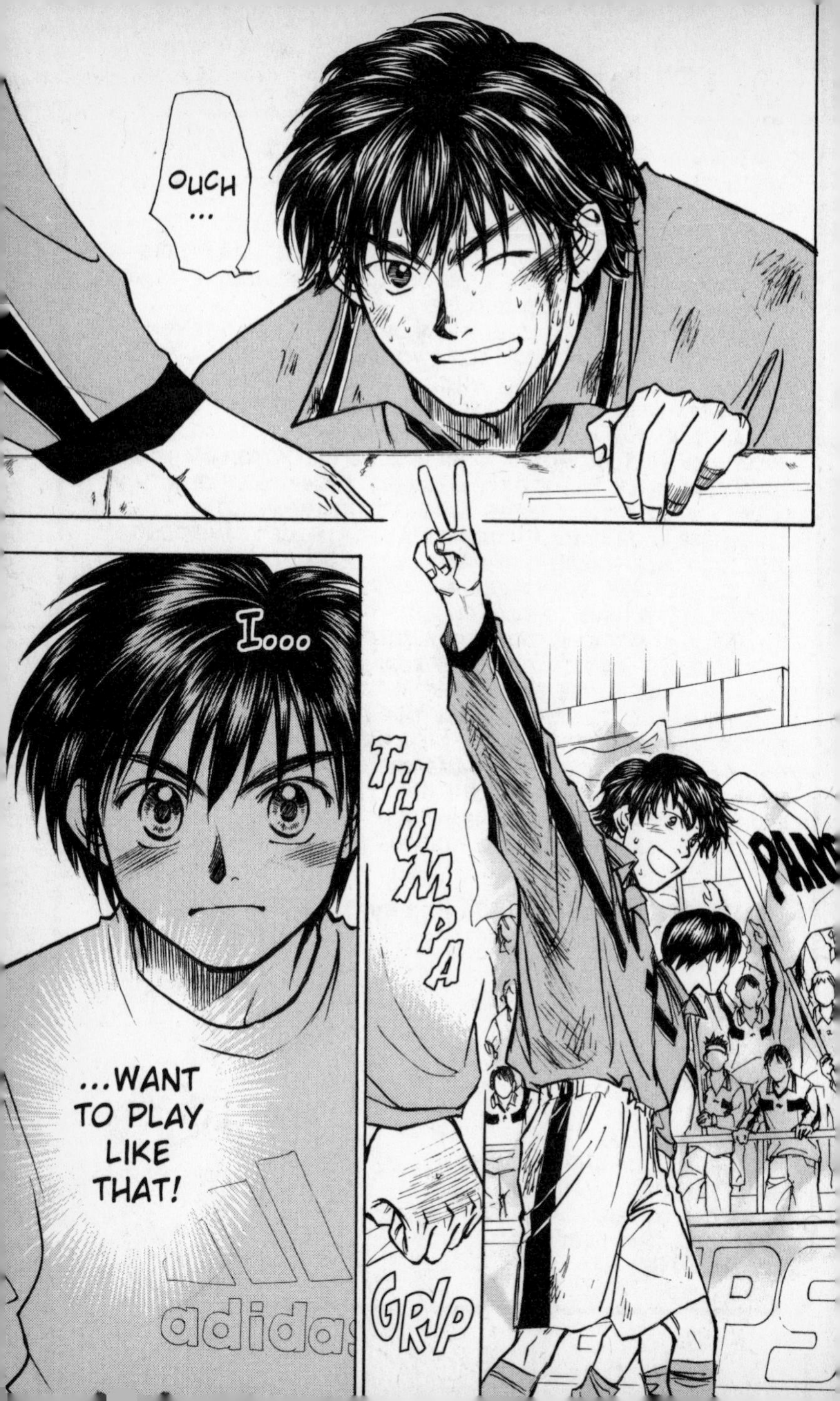
OUCH ...
PAN
THUMPA
GRIP
I...
...WANT TO PLAY LIKE THAT!

●J2●

J-LEAGUE STARTED IN 1993 WITH 10 TEAMS. AFTER THAT, THE TOP TWO TEAMS OF THE JFL (WHICH IS THE CURRENT J2) THAT QUALIFIED TO JOIN J1 WERE PROMOTED TO J LEAGUE EACH YEAR.

AS A RESULT, BY THE YEAR 1998, THE J-LEAGUE HAD MUSHROOMED TO 18 TEAMS. SO, IN 1999, J-LEAGUE WAS DIVIDED INTO DIVISION 1 AND DIVISION 2, AS J1 AND J2, AND RESTARTED WITH 16 TEAMS IN J1 AND 10 TEAMS IN J2.

AND STARTING IN 1999, THEY BEGAN AUTOMATICALLY SWAPPING THE BOTTOM TWO OF J1 WITH THE TOP TWO OF J2. IN ADDITION, EVEN IF THE TEAM BELONGED TO JFL, WHICH IS BELOW J2, IF THE TEAM PERFORMED WELL AND SATISFIED THE CONDITIONS FOR JOINING J-LEAGUE, IT WAS ALLOWED TO BE PROMOTED TO J2. MITO HOLLYHOCK WAS PROMOTED TO J2 IN 2000 AND YOKOHAMA FC IN 2001. CURRENTLY, IN 2001, THE J-LEAGUE CONSISTS OF J1 WITH 16 TEAMS AND J2 WITH 12 TEAMS, MAKING 28 TEAMS IN TOTAL.

PLAYERS IN J2 HAVE A ROUGH TIME OF IT. SOME TEAMS DON'T OWN THE PLACE WHERE THEY PRACTICE NOR DO THEY HAVE THEIR OWN CLUBHOUSES. EVEN THOUGH THEY'RE PROFESSIONAL TEAMS, SOME PLAYERS HAVE TO TAKE ON PART-TIME JOBS TO SUPPORT THEMSELVES. NOT ONLY THAT, THEY MUST ENDURE FOUR LONG TOURNAMENTS IN WHICH THEY PLAY AGAINST EVERY TEAM, WHICH ADDS UP TO 44 GAMES EVERY YEAR.

COMPARED TO J1, J2 MUST FACE THIS LONG, HARSH, LEAGUE BATTLE. DESPITE THE HARDSHIP, THEIR DREAMS ARE AS STRONG AS THAT OF PLAYERS IN J1. THE TEAMS ARE CHERISHED BY THE LOCAL FANS AND LOVED BY FANS OF THE SPORT THROUGHOUT JAPAN. IF AND WHEN J2 HOLDS A GAME IN YOUR NEIGHBORHOOD, PLEASE GO WATCH THE PLAYERS WHO ARE WORKING HARD TO JOIN J1.

—— **Tatsuya Watanabe (Winning Run)**

(AUTHOR'S VOICE)
IN REALITY, J1 AND J2 DID NOT BEGIN THEIR AUTOMATIC SWAPPING IN 1998. HOWEVER, FOR DRAMATIZATION PURPOSES, THAT FACT HAS BEEN CHANGED.

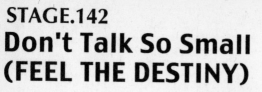

STAGE.142

Don't Talk So Small (FEEL THE DESTINY)

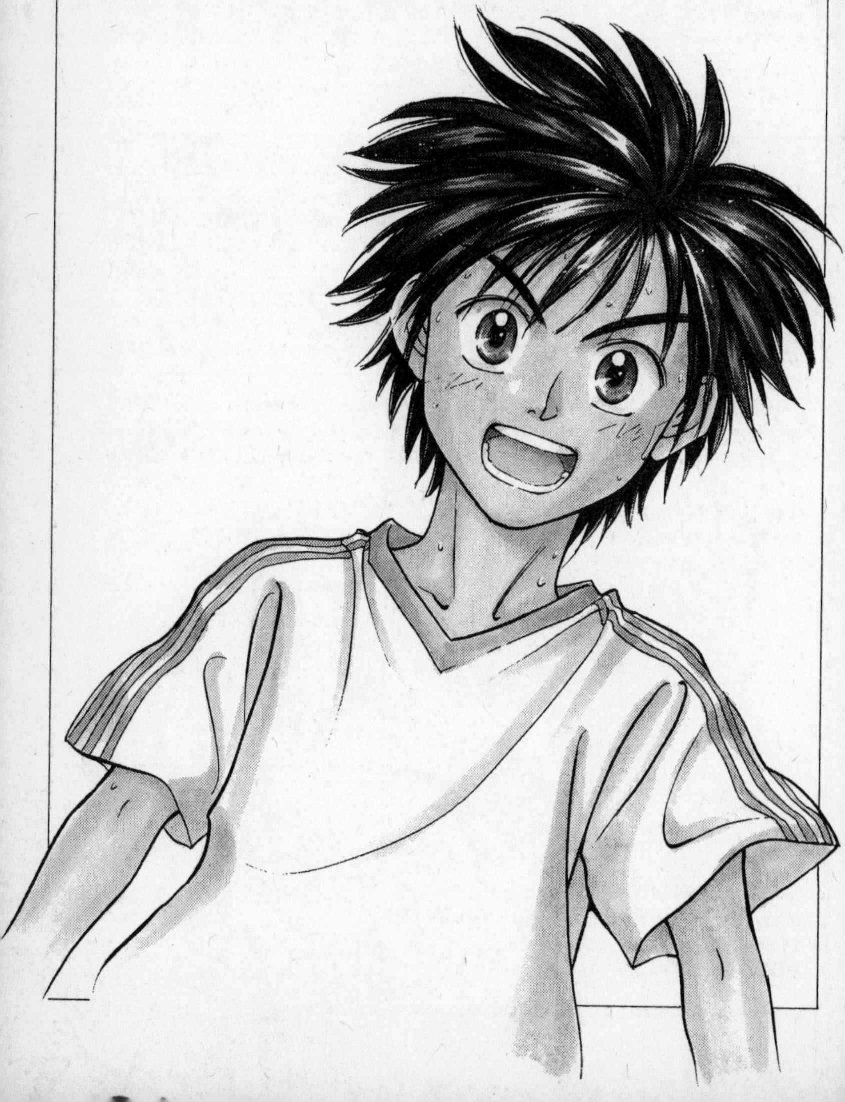

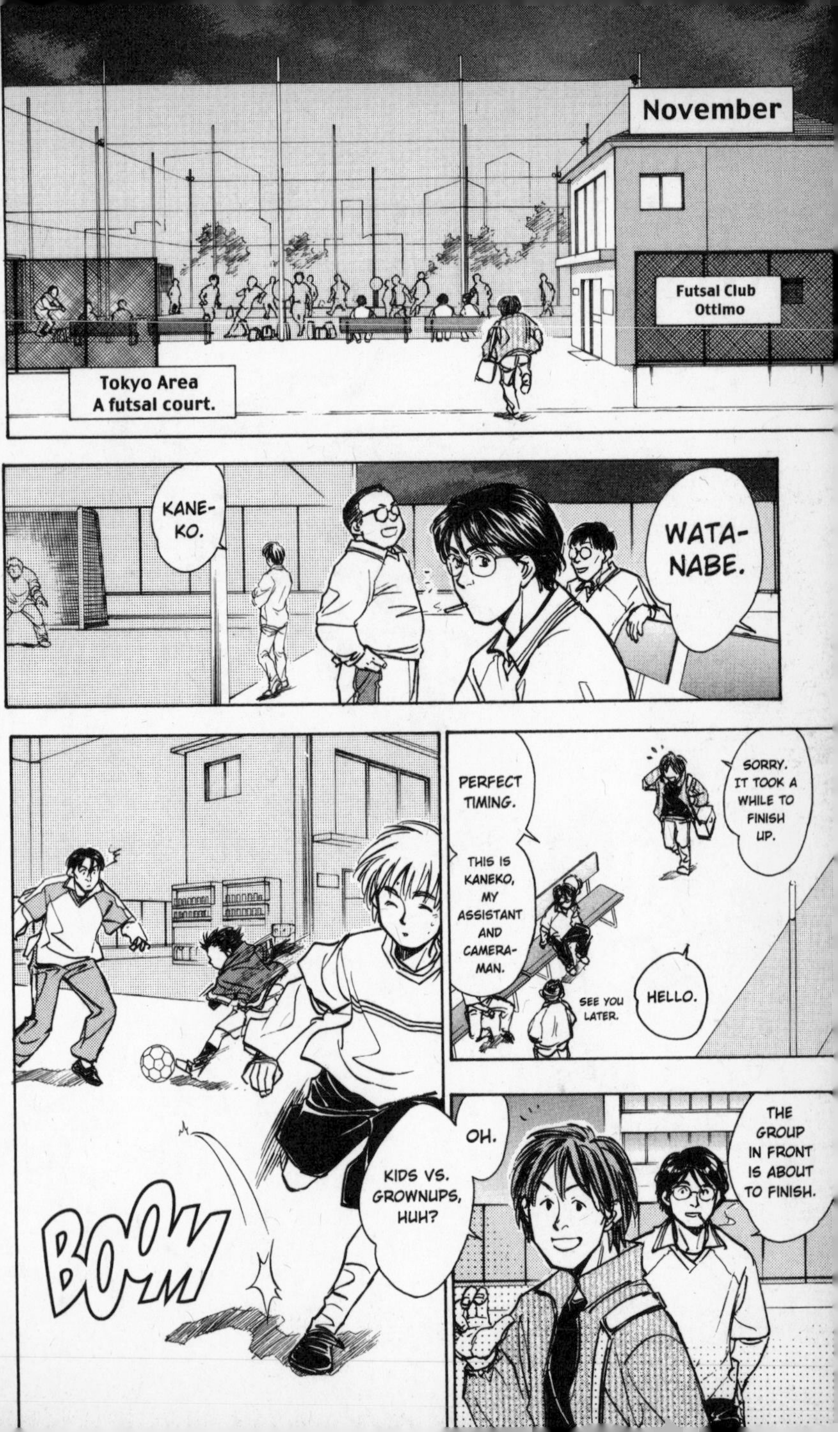

November
Futsal Club Ottimo
Tokyo Area A futsal court.
WATA-NABE.
KANE-KO.
SORRY. IT TOOK A WHILE TO FINISH UP.
PERFECT TIMING.
THIS IS KANEKO, MY ASSISTANT AND CAMERA-MAN.
HELLO.
SEE YOU LATER.
THE GROUP IN FRONT IS ABOUT TO FINISH.
OH.
KIDS VS. GROWNUPS, HUH?
BOOM

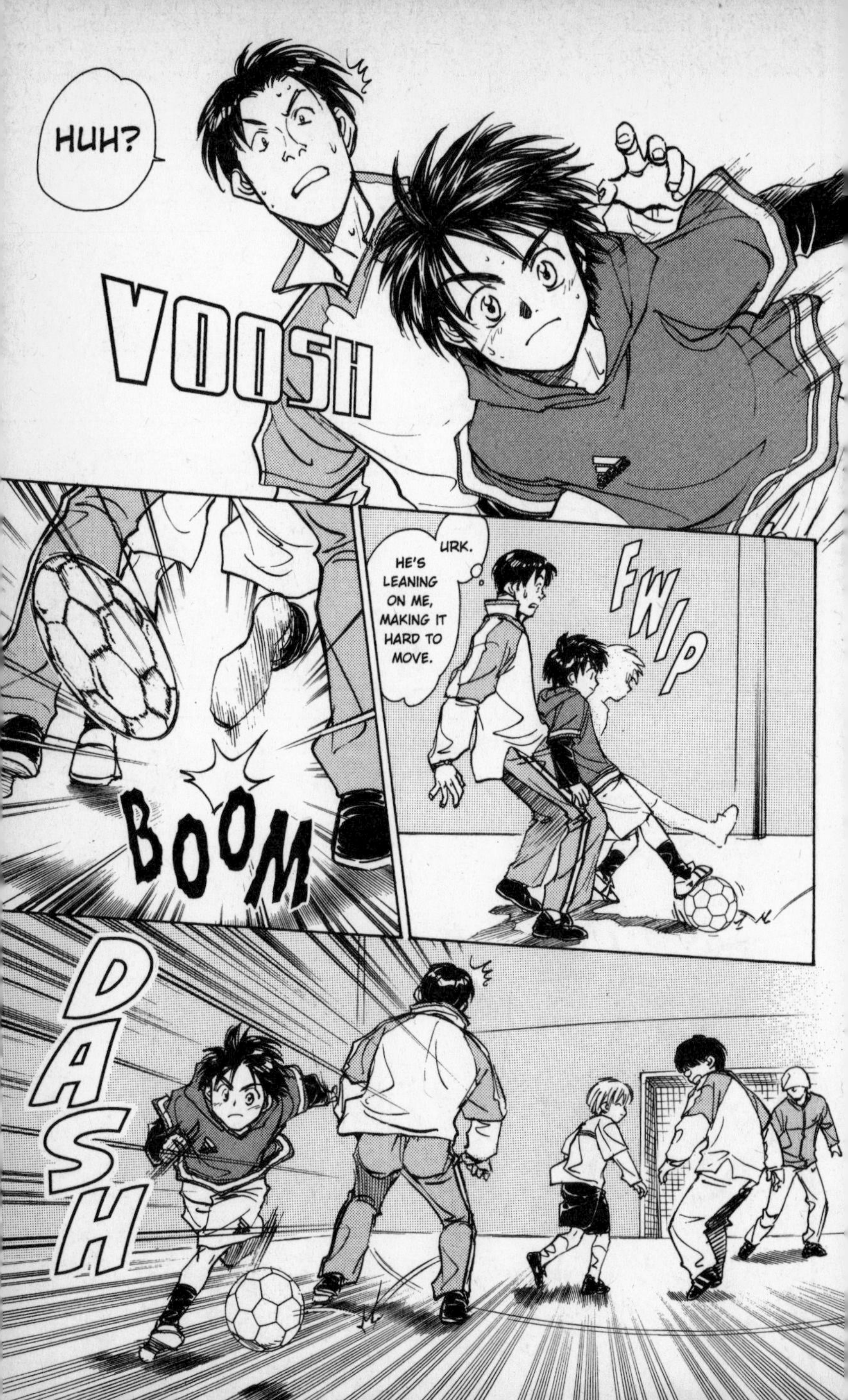
HUH?
VOOSH
URK.
HE'S LEANING ON ME, MAKING IT HARD TO MOVE.
FWIP
BOOM
DASH

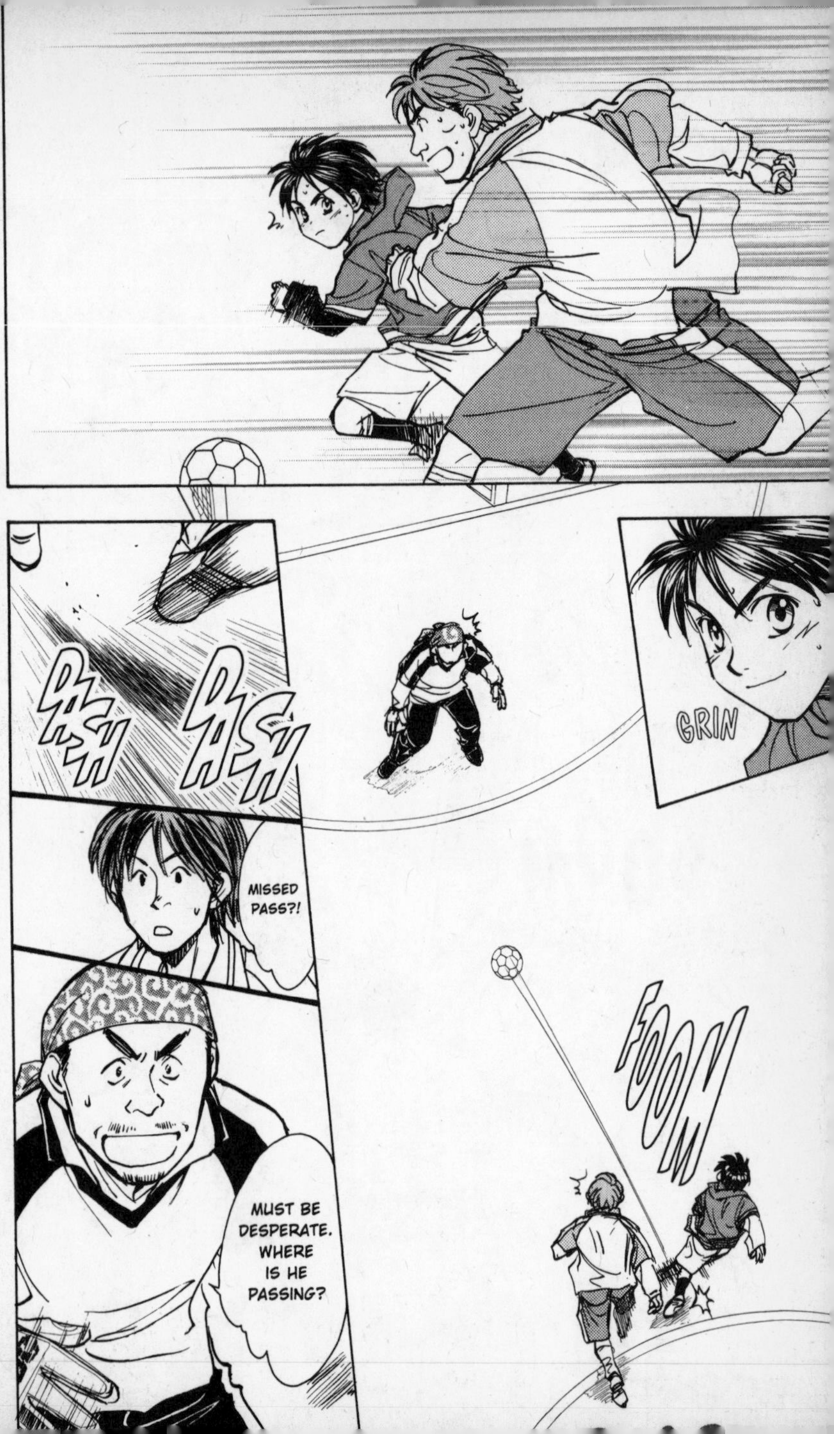
GRIN
FOOM
BASH
BASH
MISSED PASS?!
MUST BE DESPERATE. WHERE IS HE PASSING?

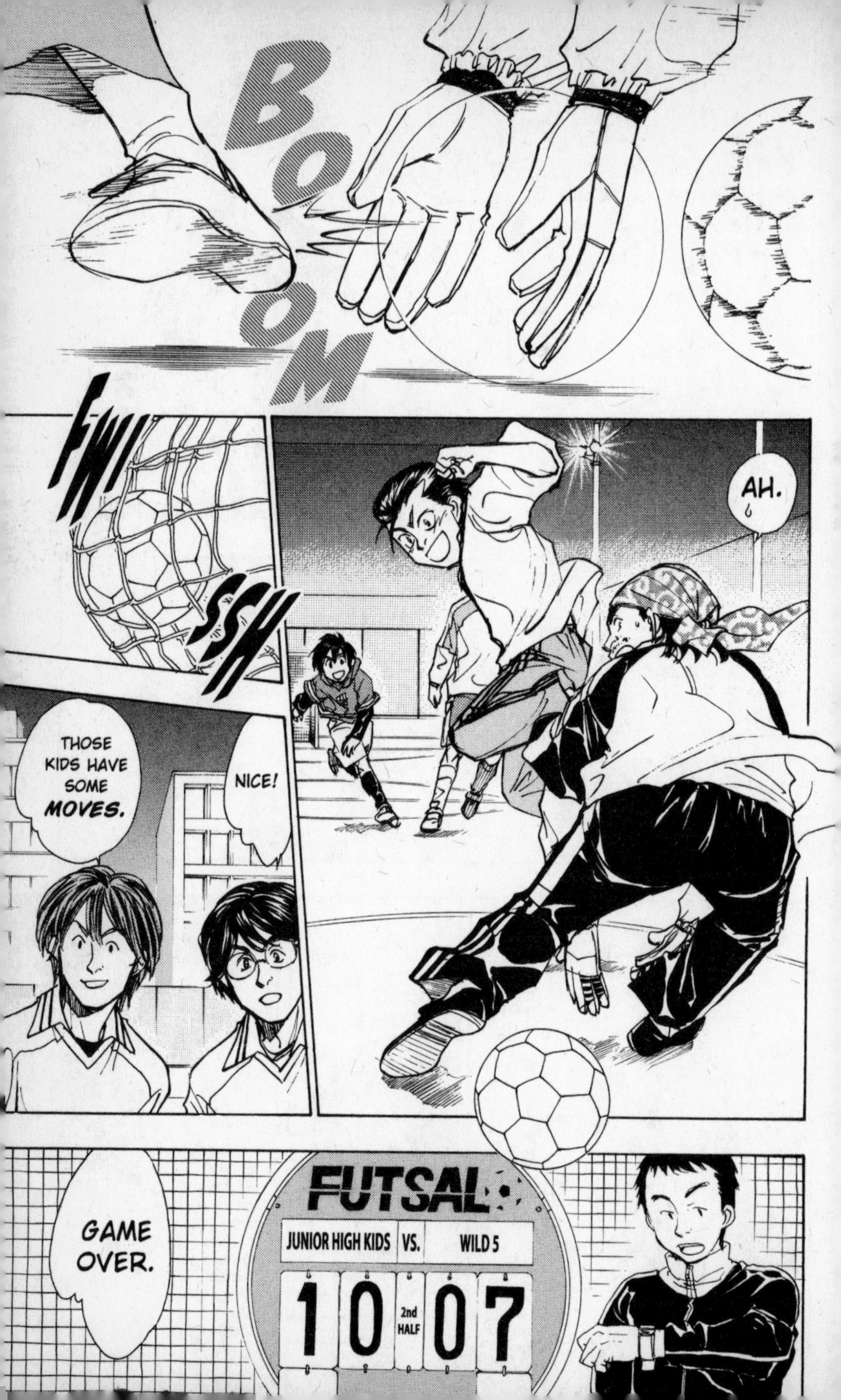
BOOM
AH.
FWISSH
NICE!
THOSE KIDS HAVE SOME MOVES.
FUTSAL
JUNIOR HIGH KIDS
VS.
WILD 5
10
2nd HALF
07
GAME OVER.

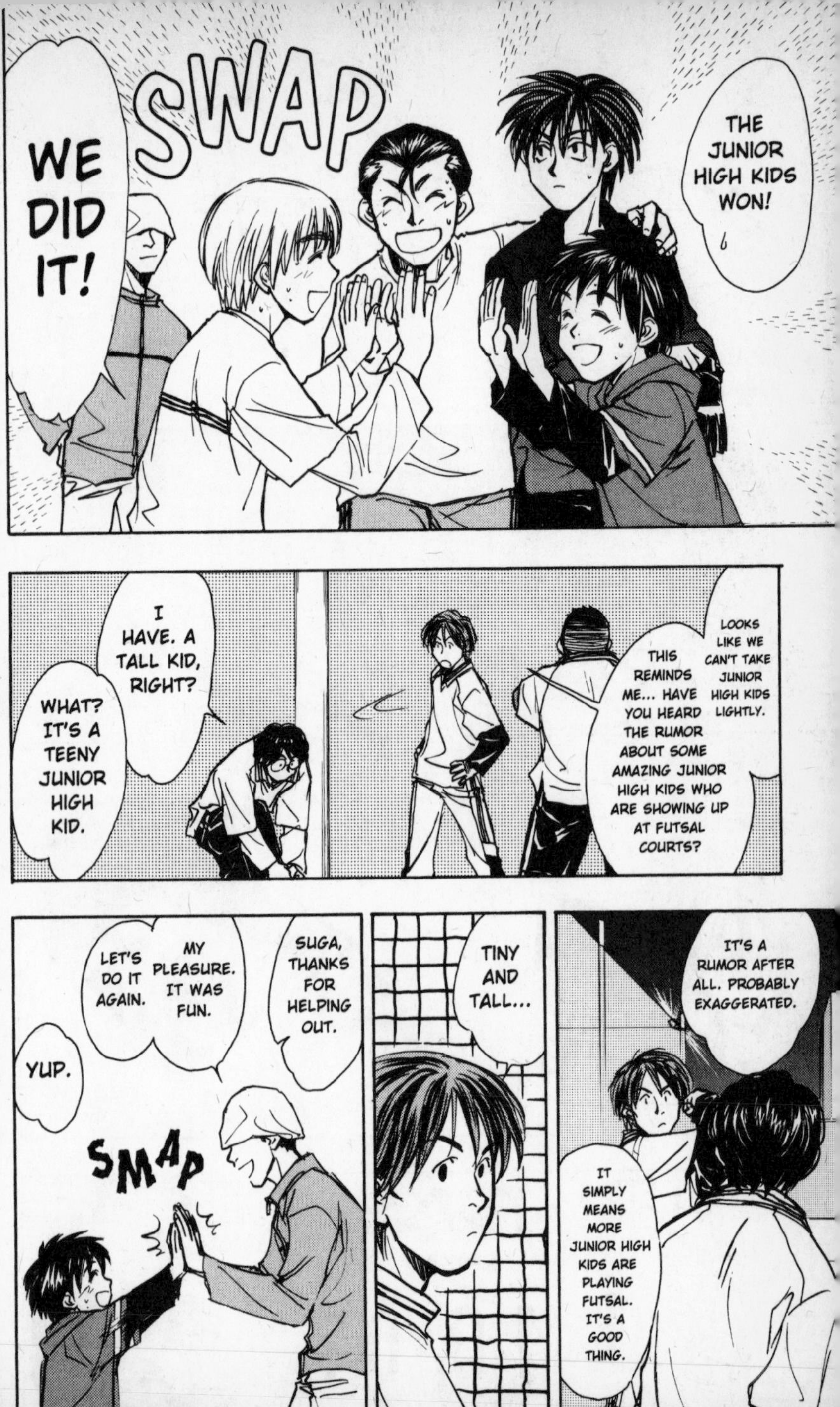
THE JUNIOR HIGH KIDS WON!
SWAP
WE DID IT!
LOOKS LIKE WE CAN'T TAKE JUNIOR HIGH KIDS LIGHTLY.
THIS REMINDS ME... HAVE YOU HEARD THE RUMOR ABOUT SOME AMAZING JUNIOR HIGH KIDS WHO ARE SHOWING UP AT FUTSAL COURTS?
I HAVE. A TALL KID, RIGHT?
WHAT? IT'S A TEENY JUNIOR HIGH KID.
IT'S A RUMOR AFTER ALL. PROBABLY EXAGGERATED.
IT SIMPLY MEANS MORE JUNIOR HIGH KIDS ARE PLAYING FUTSAL. IT'S A GOOD THING.
TINY AND TALL...
SUGA, THANKS FOR HELPING OUT.
MY PLEASURE. IT WAS FUN.
LET'S DO IT AGAIN.
YUP.
SMAP

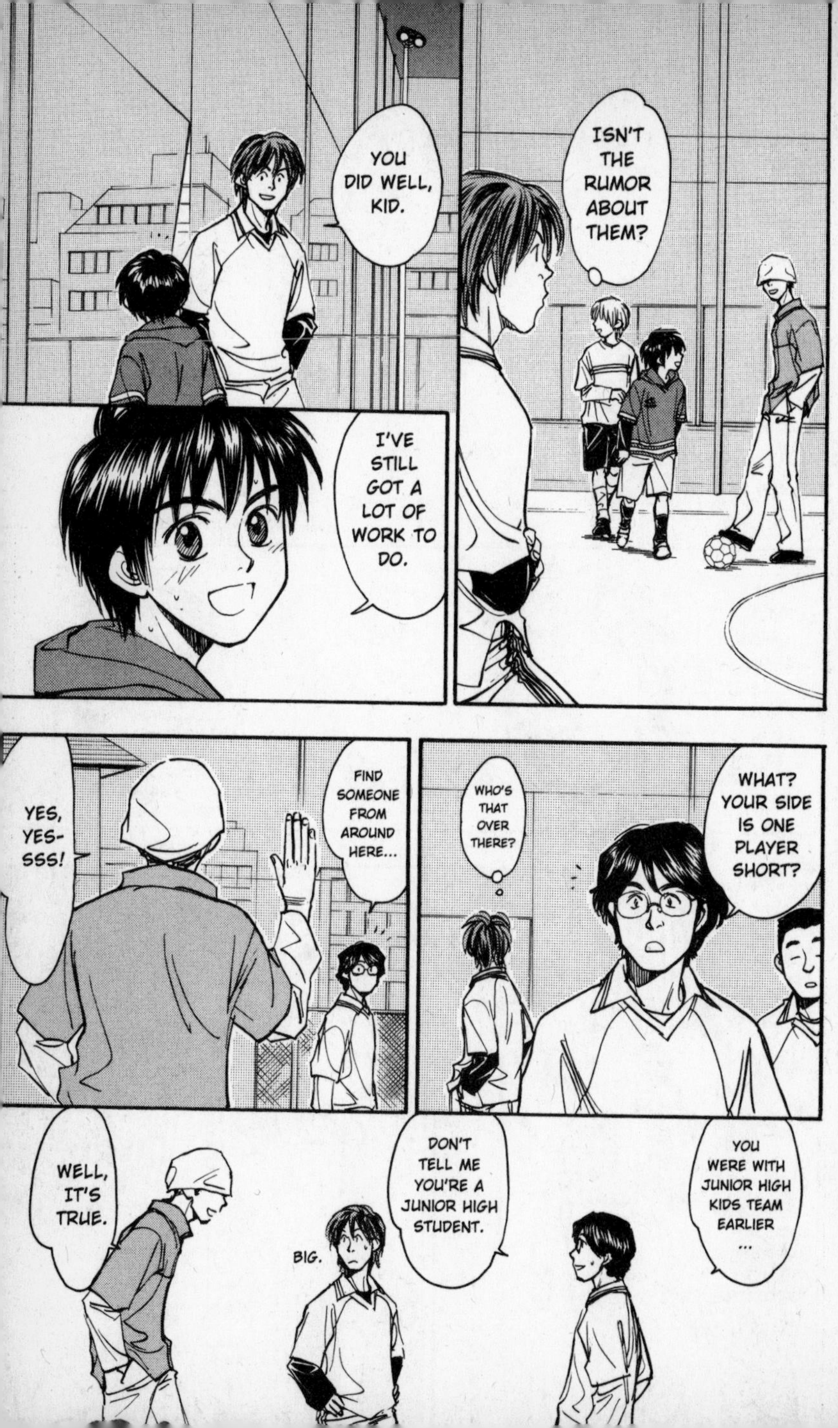
ISN'T THE RUMOR ABOUT THEM?
YOU DID WELL, KID.
I'VE STILL GOT A LOT OF WORK TO DO.
WHAT? YOUR SIDE IS ONE PLAYER SHORT?
WHO'S THAT OVER THERE?
FIND SOMEONE FROM AROUND HERE...
YES, YES-SSS!
YOU WERE WITH JUNIOR HIGH KIDS TEAM EARLIER ...
DON'T TELL ME YOU'RE A JUNIOR HIGH STUDENT.
BIG.
WELL, IT'S TRUE.

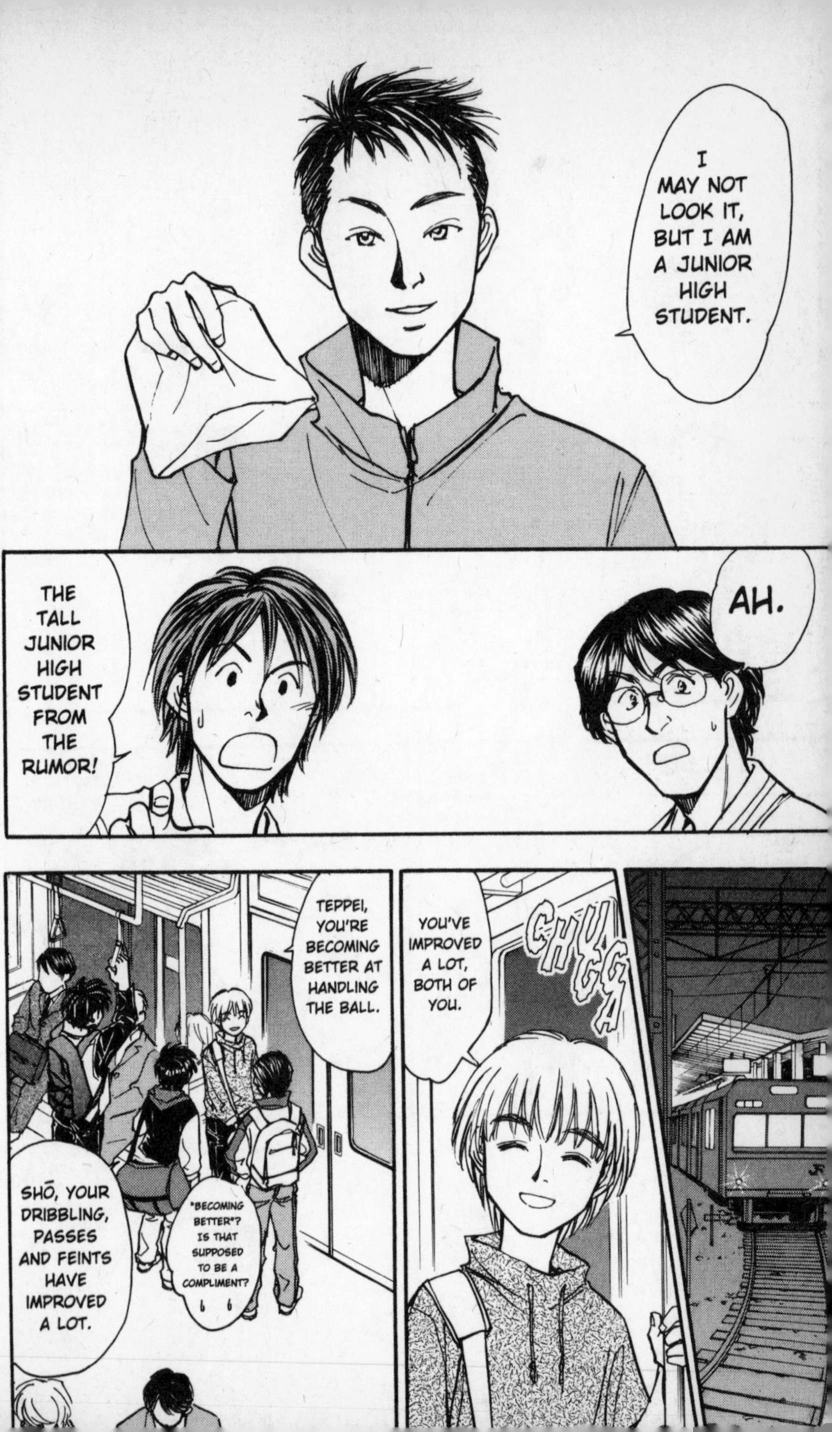
I MAY NOT LOOK IT, BUT I AM A JUNIOR HIGH STUDENT.
AH.
THE TALL JUNIOR HIGH STUDENT FROM THE RUMOR!
CHUGGA
YOU'VE IMPROVED A LOT, BOTH OF YOU.
TEPPEI, YOU'RE BECOMING BETTER AT HANDLING THE BALL.
SHŌ, YOUR DRIBBLING, PASSES AND FEINTS HAVE IMPROVED A LOT.
"BECOMING BETTER"? IS THAT SUPPOSED TO BE A COMPLIMENT?

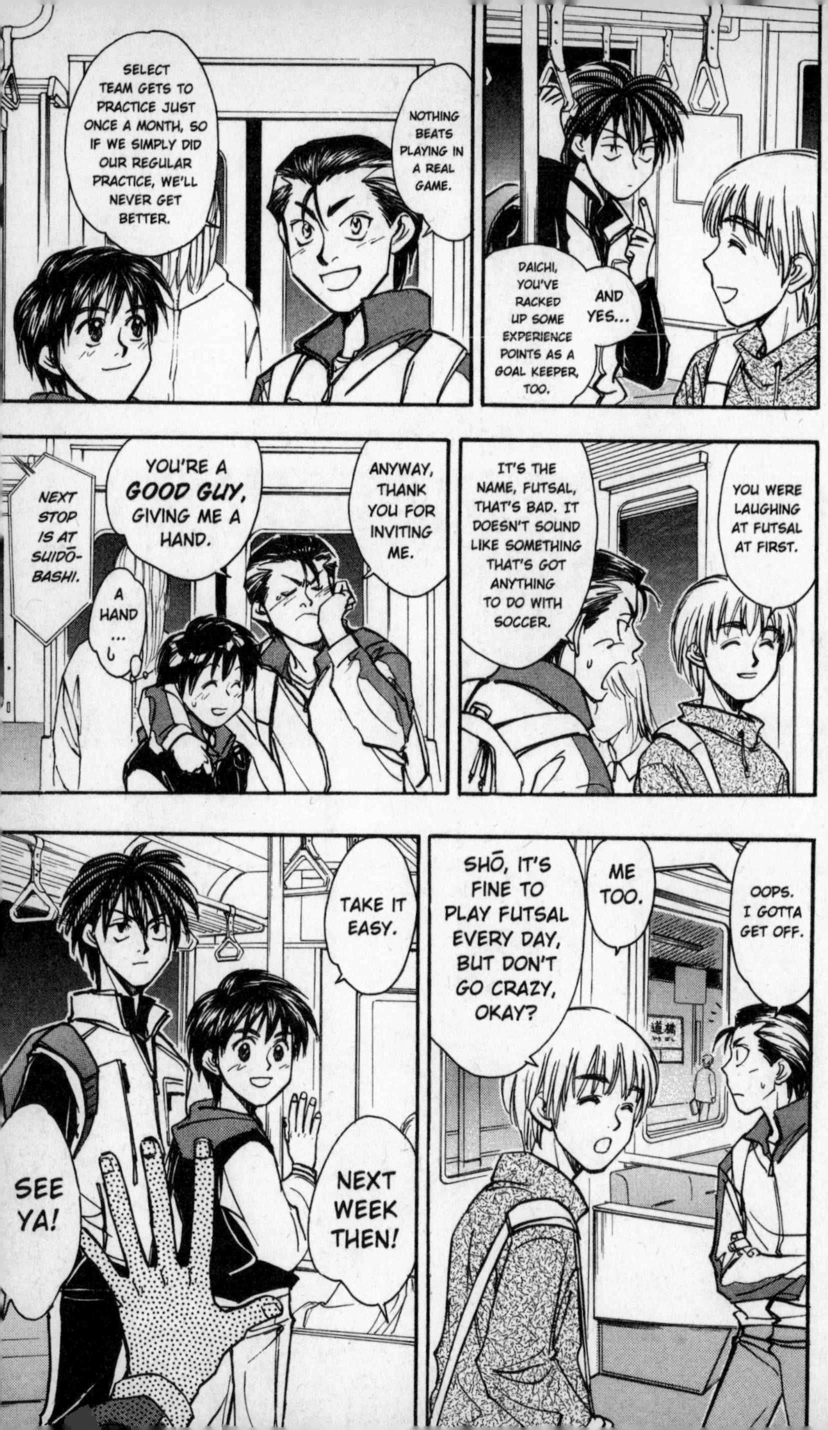
AND YES...
DAICHI, YOU'VE RACKED UP SOME EXPERIENCE POINTS AS A GOAL KEEPER, TOO.
NOTHING BEATS PLAYING IN A REAL GAME.
SELECT TEAM GETS TO PRACTICE JUST ONCE A MONTH, SO IF WE SIMPLY DID OUR REGULAR PRACTICE, WE'LL NEVER GET BETTER.
YOU WERE LAUGHING AT FUTSAL AT FIRST.
IT'S THE NAME, FUTSAL, THAT'S BAD. IT DOESN'T SOUND LIKE SOMETHING THAT'S GOT ANYTHING TO DO WITH SOCCER.
ANYWAY, THANK YOU FOR INVITING ME.
YOU'RE A **GOOD GUY,** GIVING ME A HAND.
A HAND ...
NEXT STOP IS AT SUIDŌ-BASHI.
OOPS. I GOTTA GET OFF.
ME TOO.
SHŌ, IT'S FINE TO PLAY FUTSAL EVERY DAY, BUT DON'T GO CRAZY, OKAY?
TAKE IT EASY.
NEXT WEEK THEN!
SEE YA!

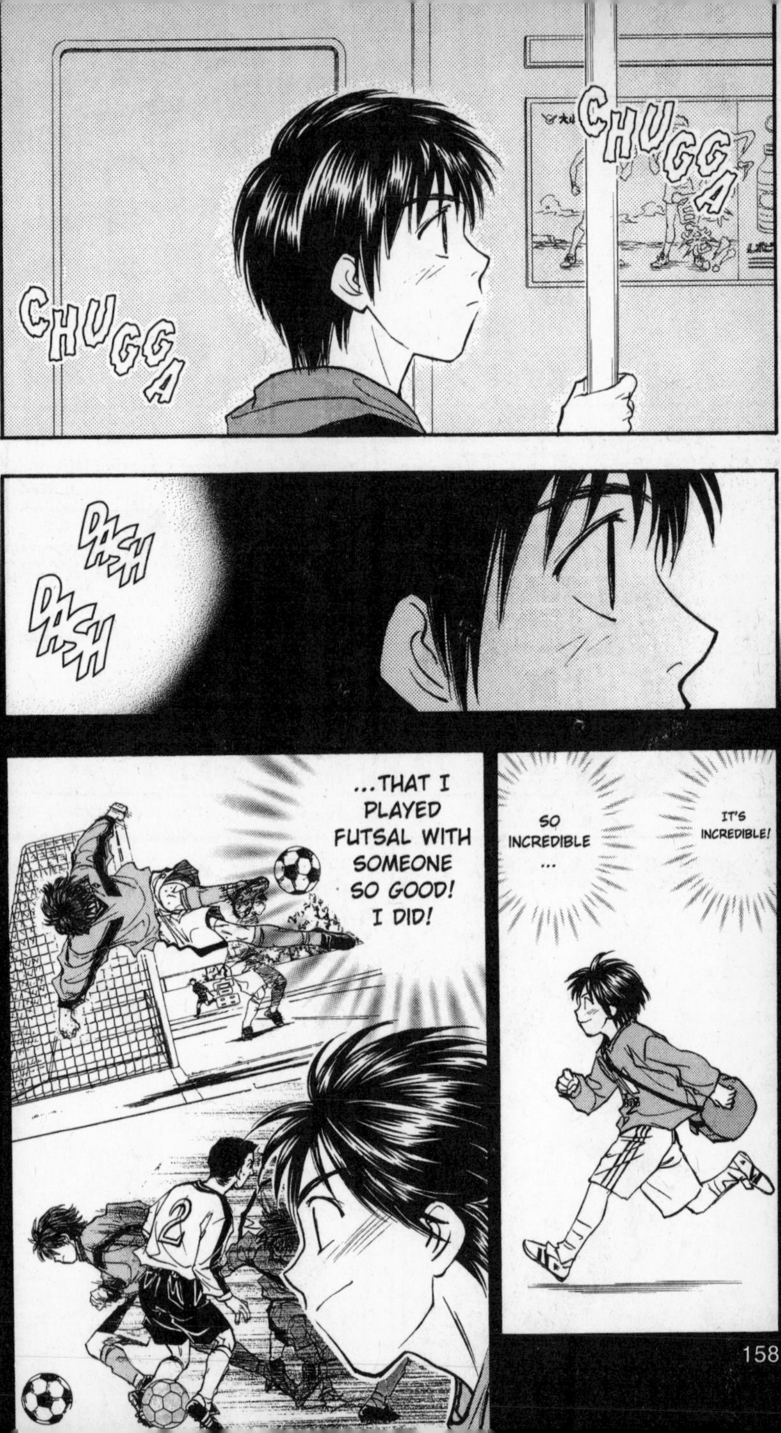
CHUGGA
CHUGGA
DASH
DASH
IT'S INCREDIBLE!
SO INCREDIBLE ...
...THAT I PLAYED FUTSAL WITH SOMEONE SO GOOD! I DID!

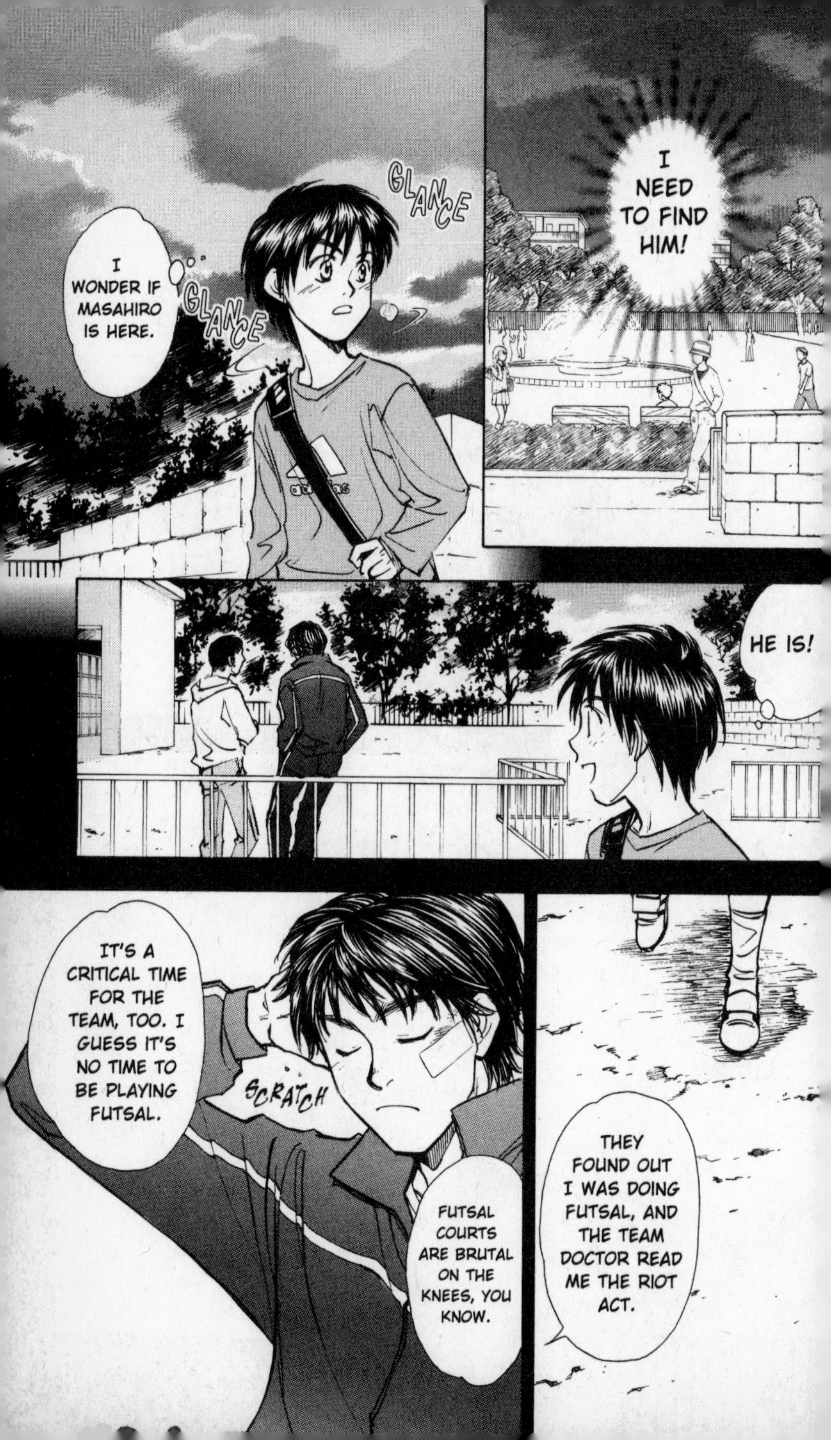
I NEED TO FIND HIM!
GLANCE
GLANCE
I WONDER IF MASAHIRO IS HERE.
HE IS!
THEY FOUND OUT I WAS DOING FUTSAL, AND THE TEAM DOCTOR READ ME THE RIOT ACT.
FUTSAL COURTS ARE BRUTAL ON THE KNEES, YOU KNOW.
SCRATCH
IT'S A CRITICAL TIME FOR THE TEAM, TOO. I GUESS IT'S NO TIME TO BE PLAYING FUTSAL.

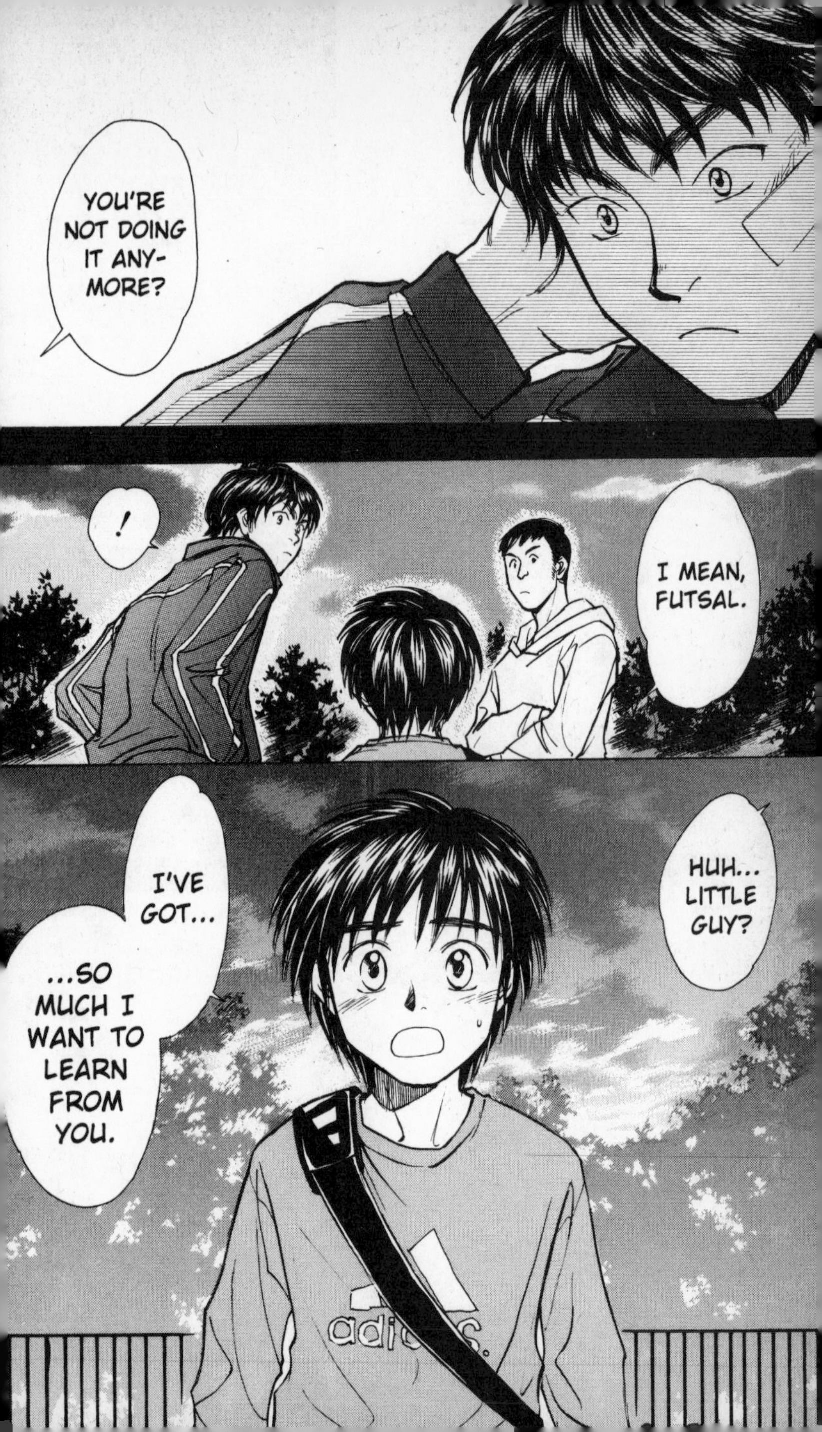
YOU'RE NOT DOING IT ANY-MORE?
I MEAN, FUTSAL.
!
HUH... LITTLE GUY?
I'VE GOT...
...SO MUCH I WANT TO LEARN FROM YOU.

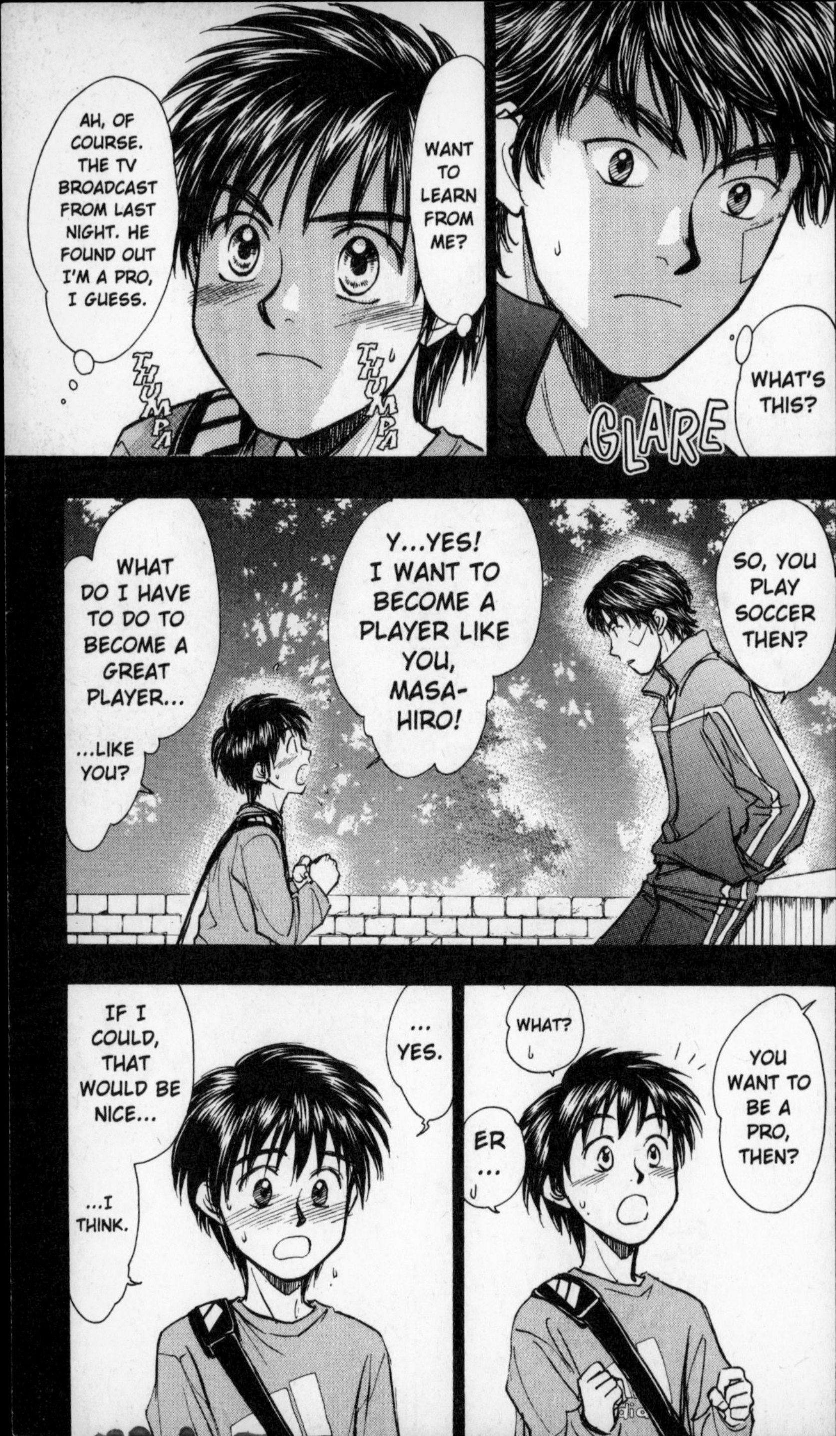
WHAT'S THIS?
GLARE
WANT TO LEARN FROM ME?
AH, OF COURSE. THE TV BROADCAST FROM LAST NIGHT. HE FOUND OUT I'M A PRO, I GUESS.
THUMPA
THUMPA
SO, YOU PLAY SOCCER THEN?
Y...YES! I WANT TO BECOME A PLAYER LIKE YOU, MASA-HIRO!
WHAT DO I HAVE TO DO TO BECOME A GREAT PLAYER...
...LIKE YOU?
YOU WANT TO BE A PRO, THEN?
WHAT?
ER ...
... YES.
IF I COULD, THAT WOULD BE NICE...
...I THINK.

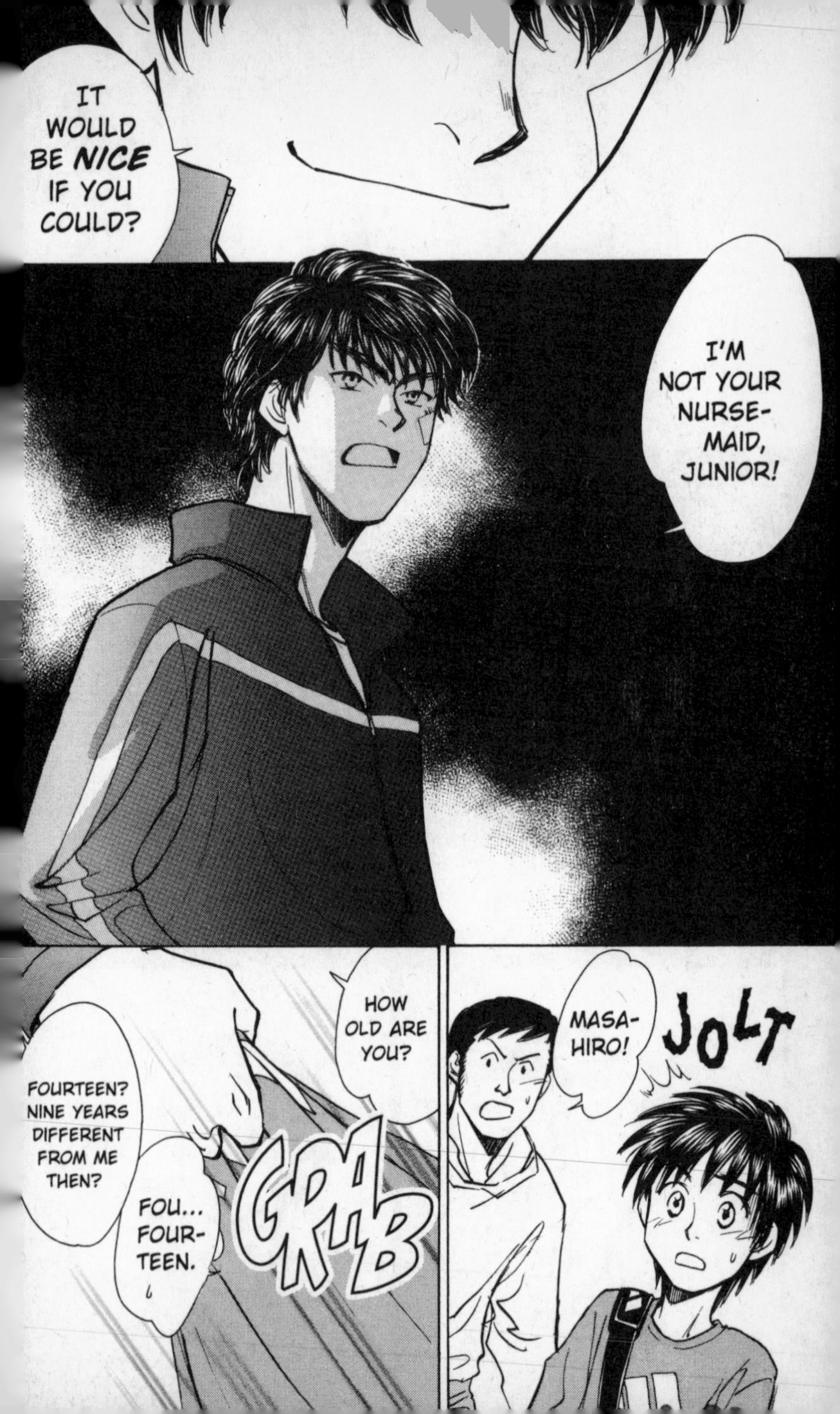
IT WOULD BE NICE IF YOU COULD?
I'M NOT YOUR NURSE-MAID, JUNIOR!
MASA-HIRO!
JOLT
HOW OLD ARE YOU?
FOU... FOUR-TEEN.
FOURTEEN? NINE YEARS DIFFERENT FROM ME THEN?
GRAB

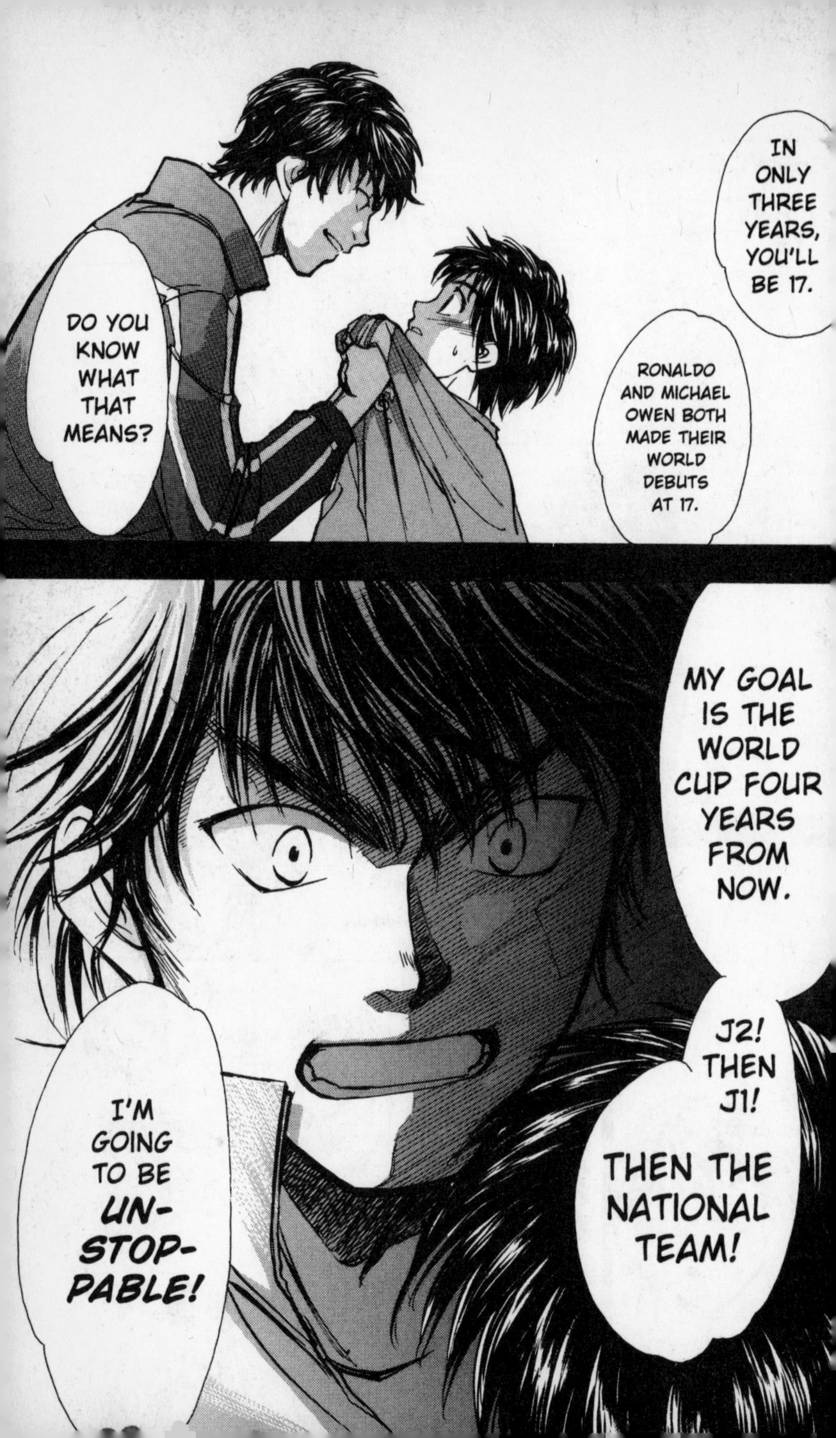
IN ONLY THREE YEARS, YOU'LL BE 17.
RONALDO AND MICHAEL OWEN BOTH MADE THEIR WORLD DEBUTS AT 17.
DO YOU KNOW WHAT THAT MEANS?
MY GOAL IS THE WORLD CUP FOUR YEARS FROM NOW.
J2! THEN J1!
THEN THE NATIONAL TEAM!
I'M GOING TO BE *UN-STOPPABLE!*

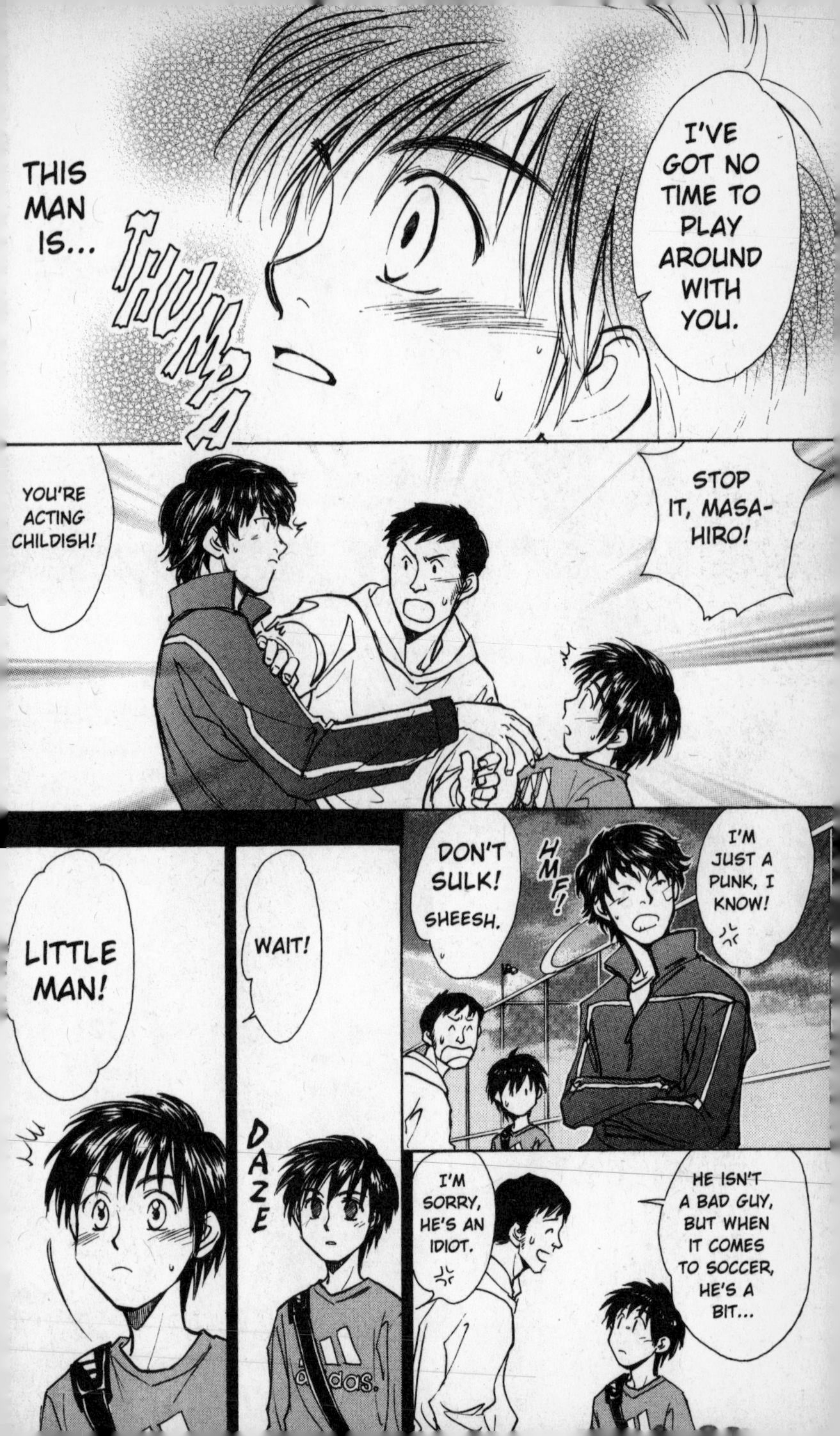
I'VE GOT NO TIME TO PLAY AROUND WITH YOU.
THIS MAN IS...
THUMPA
STOP IT, MASA-HIRO!
YOU'RE ACTING CHILDISH!
I'M JUST A PUNK, I KNOW!
HMF!
DON'T SULK!
SHEESH.
HE ISN'T A BAD GUY, BUT WHEN IT COMES TO SOCCER, HE'S A BIT...
I'M SORRY, HE'S AN IDIOT.
WAIT!
DAZE
LITTLE MAN!

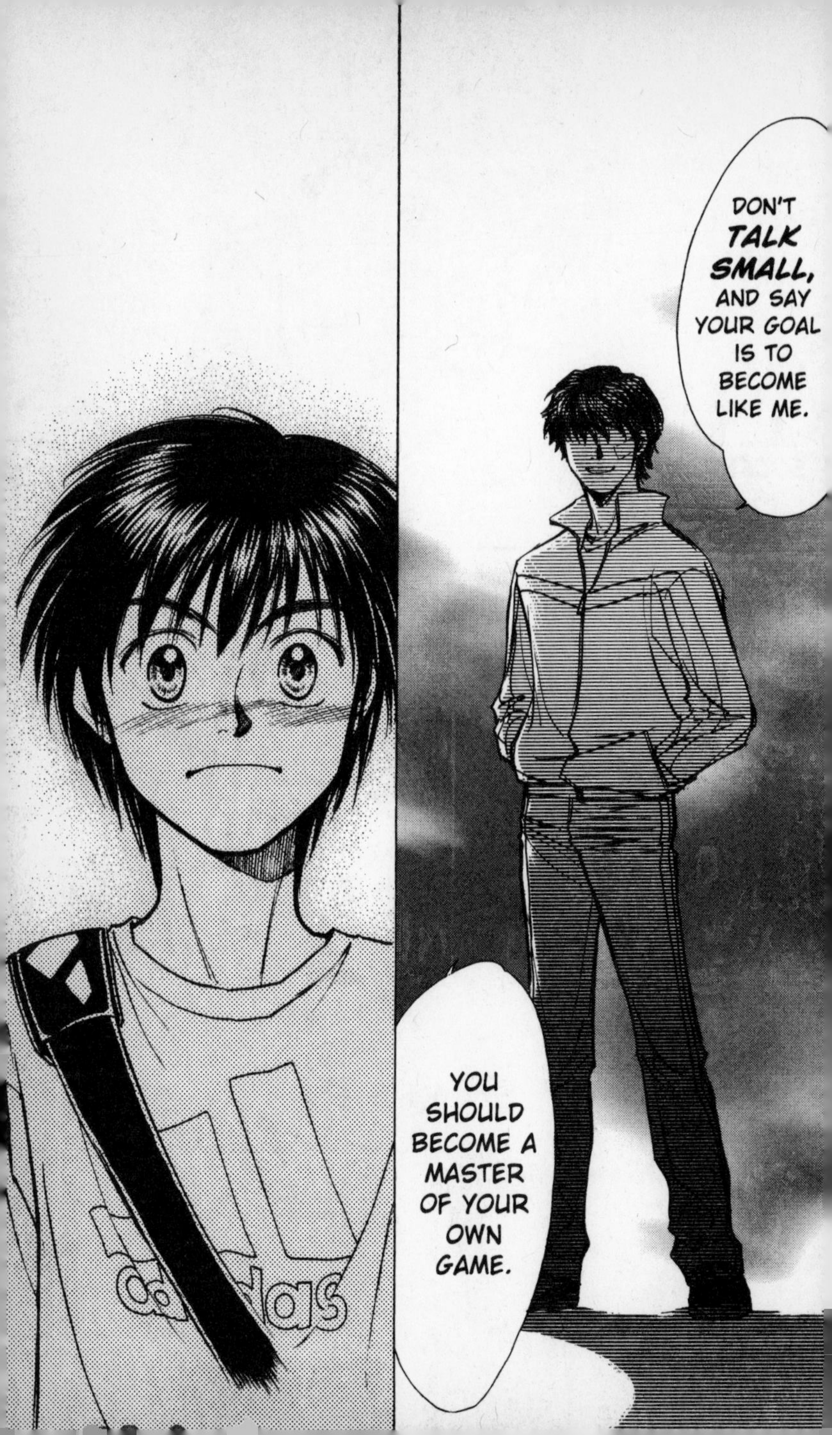
DON'T TALK SMALL, AND SAY YOUR GOAL IS TO BECOME LIKE ME.
YOU SHOULD BECOME A MASTER OF YOUR OWN GAME.

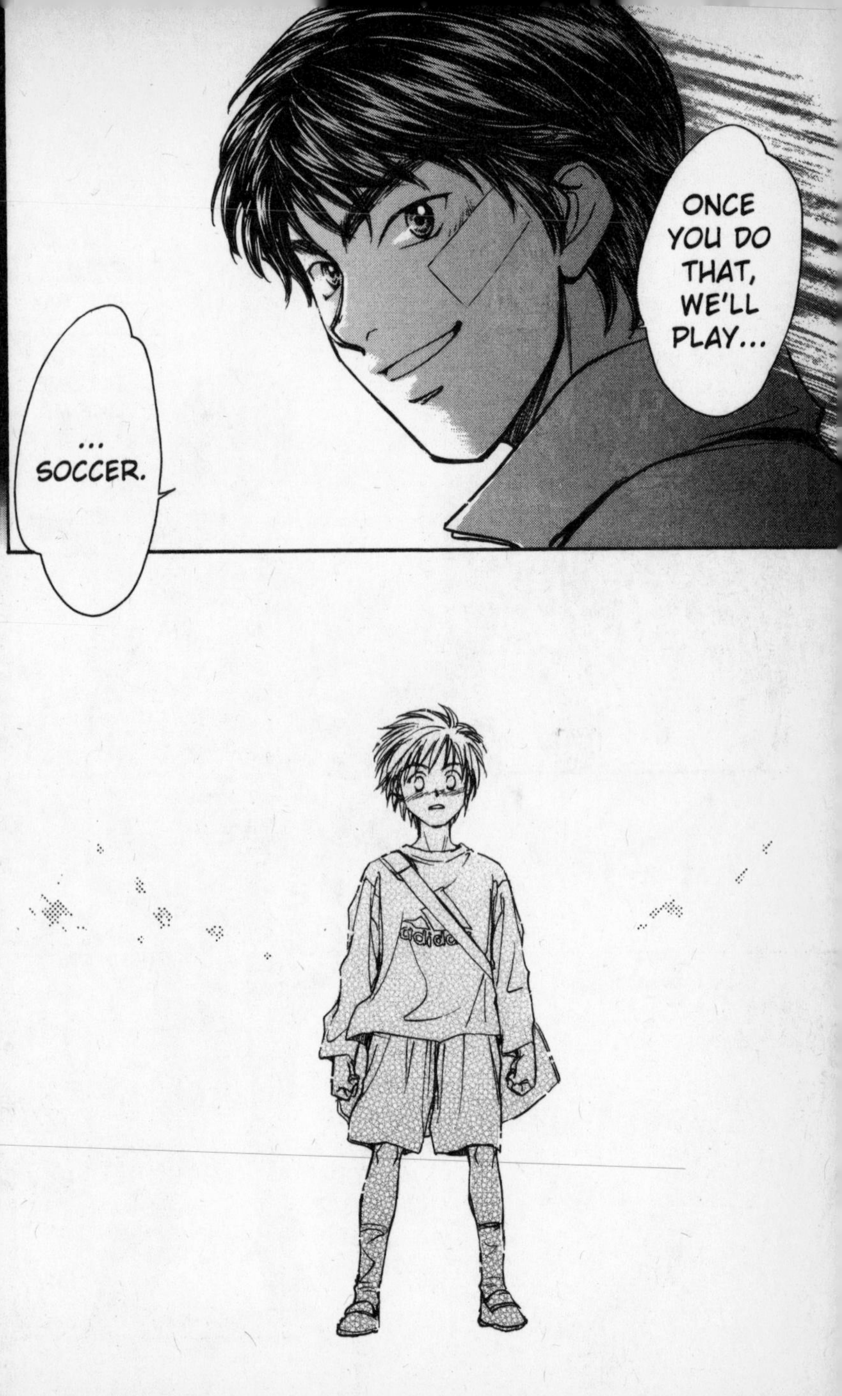
ONCE YOU DO THAT, WE'LL PLAY...
...SOCCER.

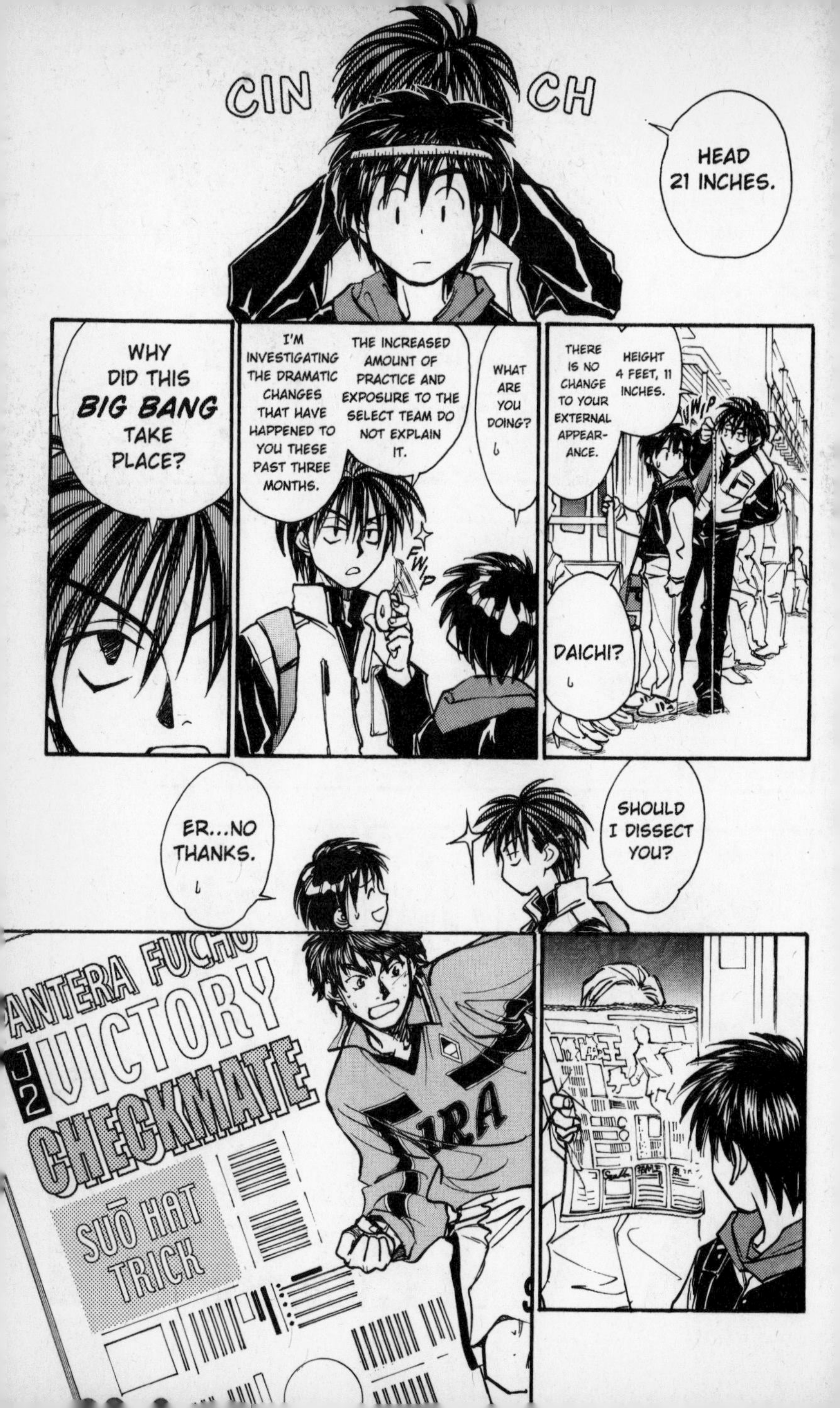
CINCH
HEAD 21 INCHES.
HEIGHT 4 FEET, 11 INCHES.
THERE IS NO CHANGE TO YOUR EXTERNAL APPEARANCE.
FWIP
DAICHI?
WHAT ARE YOU DOING?
THE INCREASED AMOUNT OF PRACTICE AND EXPOSURE TO THE SELECT TEAM DO NOT EXPLAIN IT.
I'M INVESTIGATING THE DRAMATIC CHANGES THAT HAVE HAPPENED TO YOU THESE PAST THREE MONTHS.
FWIP
WHY DID THIS **BIG BANG** TAKE PLACE?
SHOULD I DISSECT YOU?
ER...NO THANKS.
ANTERA FUCHU
J2
VICTORY
CHECKMATE
SUŌ HAT TRICK

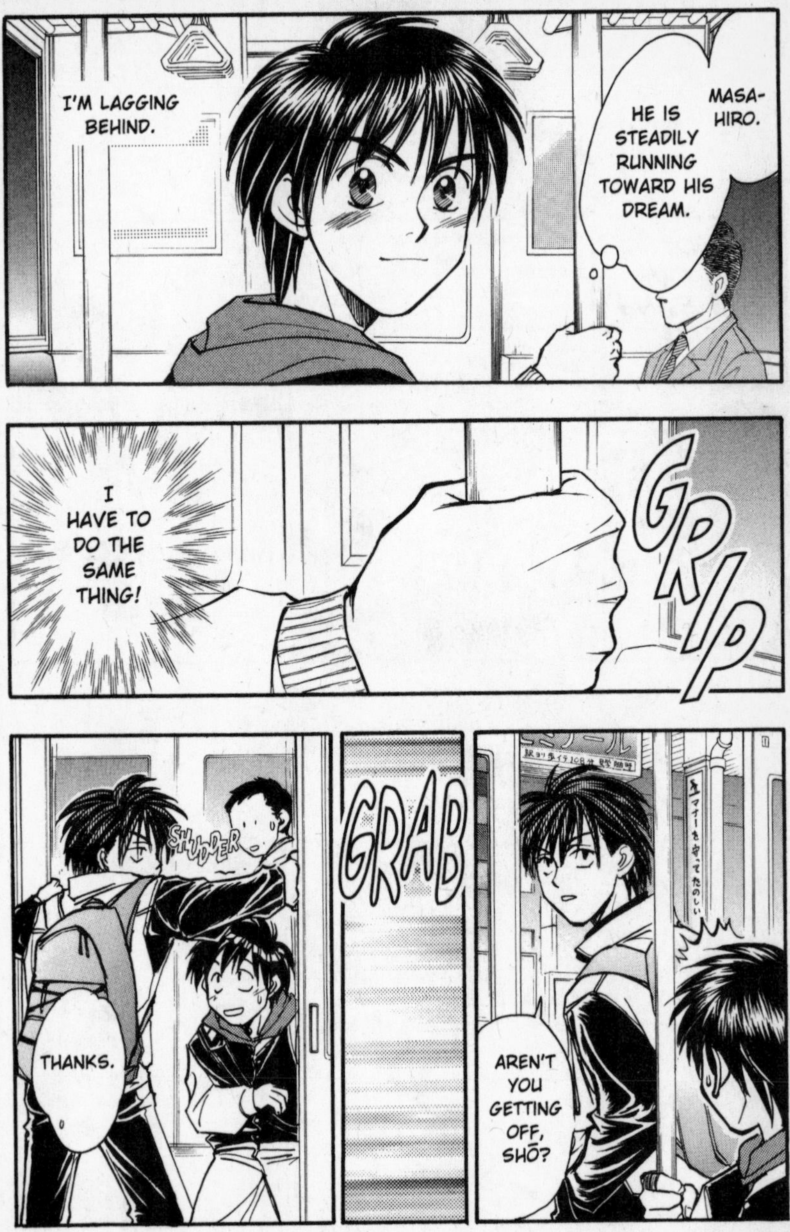
MASA-HIRO.
HE IS STEADILY RUNNING TOWARD HIS DREAM.
I'M LAGGING BEHIND.
GRIP
I HAVE TO DO THE SAME THING!
AREN'T YOU GETTING OFF, SHŌ?
GRAB
SHUDDER
THANKS.

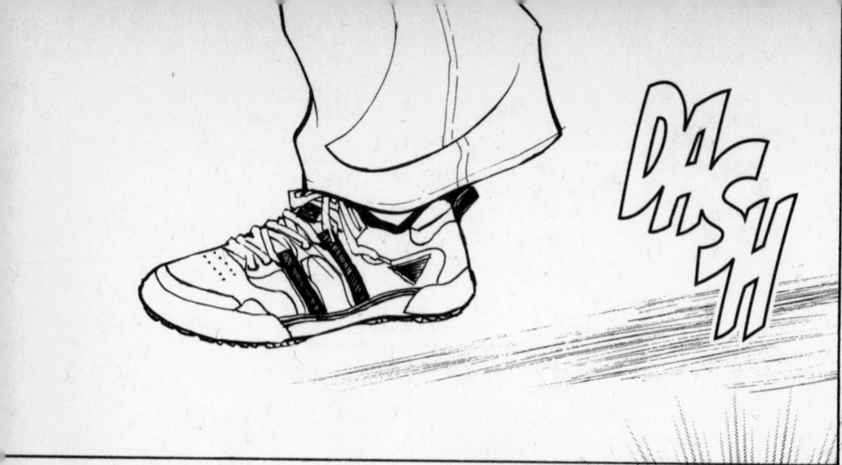
DASH
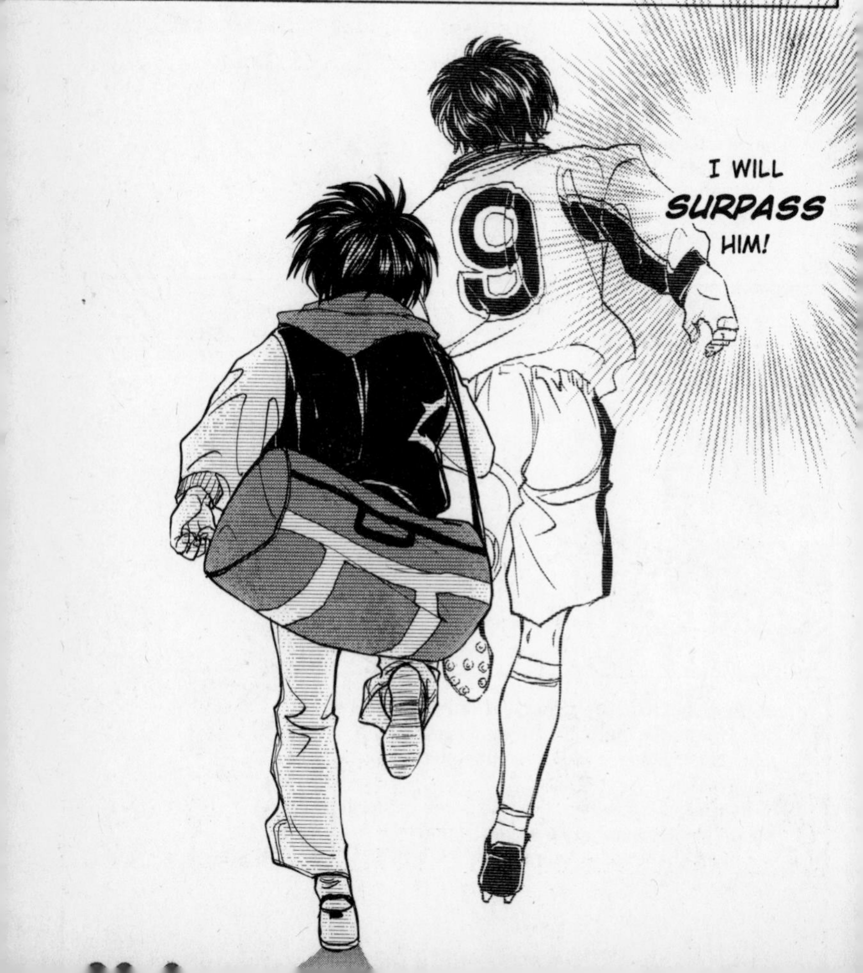
I WILL SURPASS HIM!

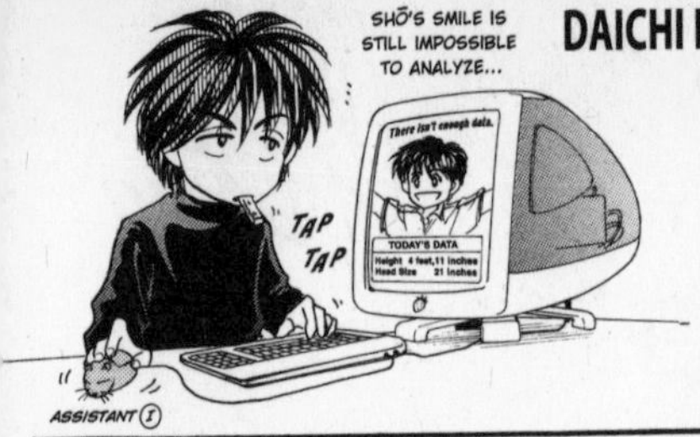
SHŌ'S SMILE IS STILL IMPOSSIBLE TO ANALYZE...
There isn't enough data.
TODAY'S DATA
Height 4 feet,11 inches
Head Size 21 inches
TAP TAP
ASSISTANT ①

DAICHI FUWA'S OBSERVATION REPORT

I am Daichi Fuwa, an 8th grader at Josui Junior High. At this time, I will make public a part of my report that details my observation and analysis of various events that took place around me. The report includes illustrations.

EDITED BY ASSISTANT K. HAMMER & OTHER PRECOCIOUS ASSISTANTS.

On the last day of the select team training camp, Tatsuya appeared to think he had failed when he was changed in the middle of a game.

As you can see in the illustration, not only were his eyes wide open, he was secreting his oily sweat profusely and his nostrils were also swelling up considerably.

Anyhow, it's easy to see how shocked he was.

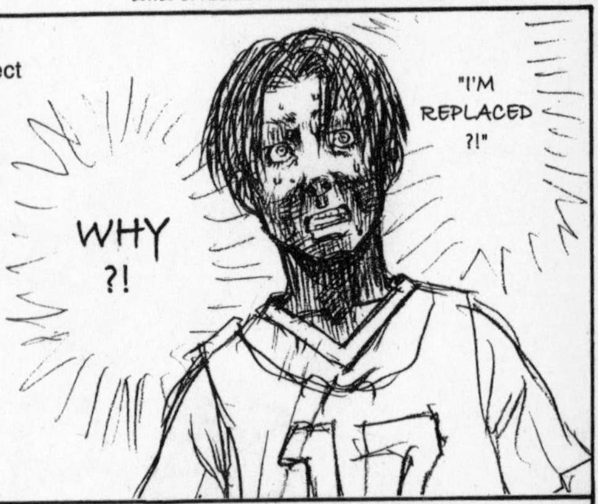
"I'M REPLACED ?!"
WHY ?!

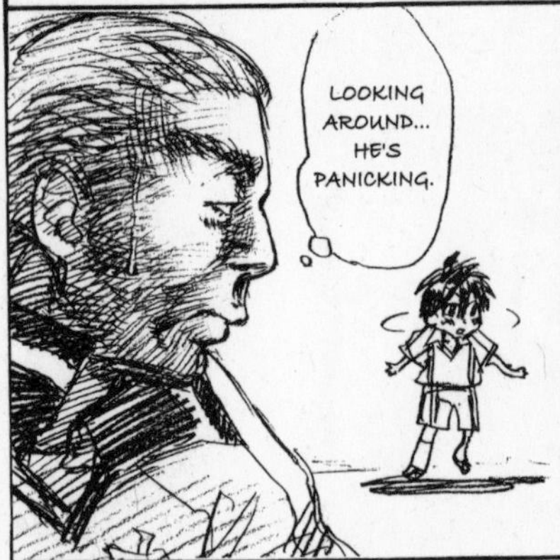
LOOKING AROUND... HE'S PANICKING.

Even though I failed the selection process, I ventured to observe the select team. It is quite interesting to note that Takashi thought Shō was losing his nerve when Shō was only looking for space to attack and was fully aware of the state of the game.

By the way, there's a chance that the man known as Takashi Narumi may be falsifying his age.
My estimate suggests he's 25 years old or... oops, I'm deviating from my main point.

Well, I can surmise that Shō is in Takashi's mind quite a bit.

Sorry, but this illustration was drawn without good reference material. It's supposed to be a man called Shigeru who was chosen for the select team.

Ever since I saw him, I've had some misgivings about him. He sure has a strange face.

I must spend more time studying his bizarre countenance.

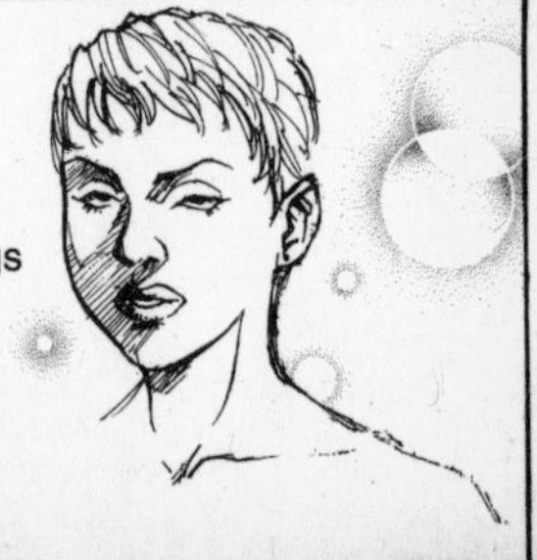

STAGE.143
The Heart in Another Country

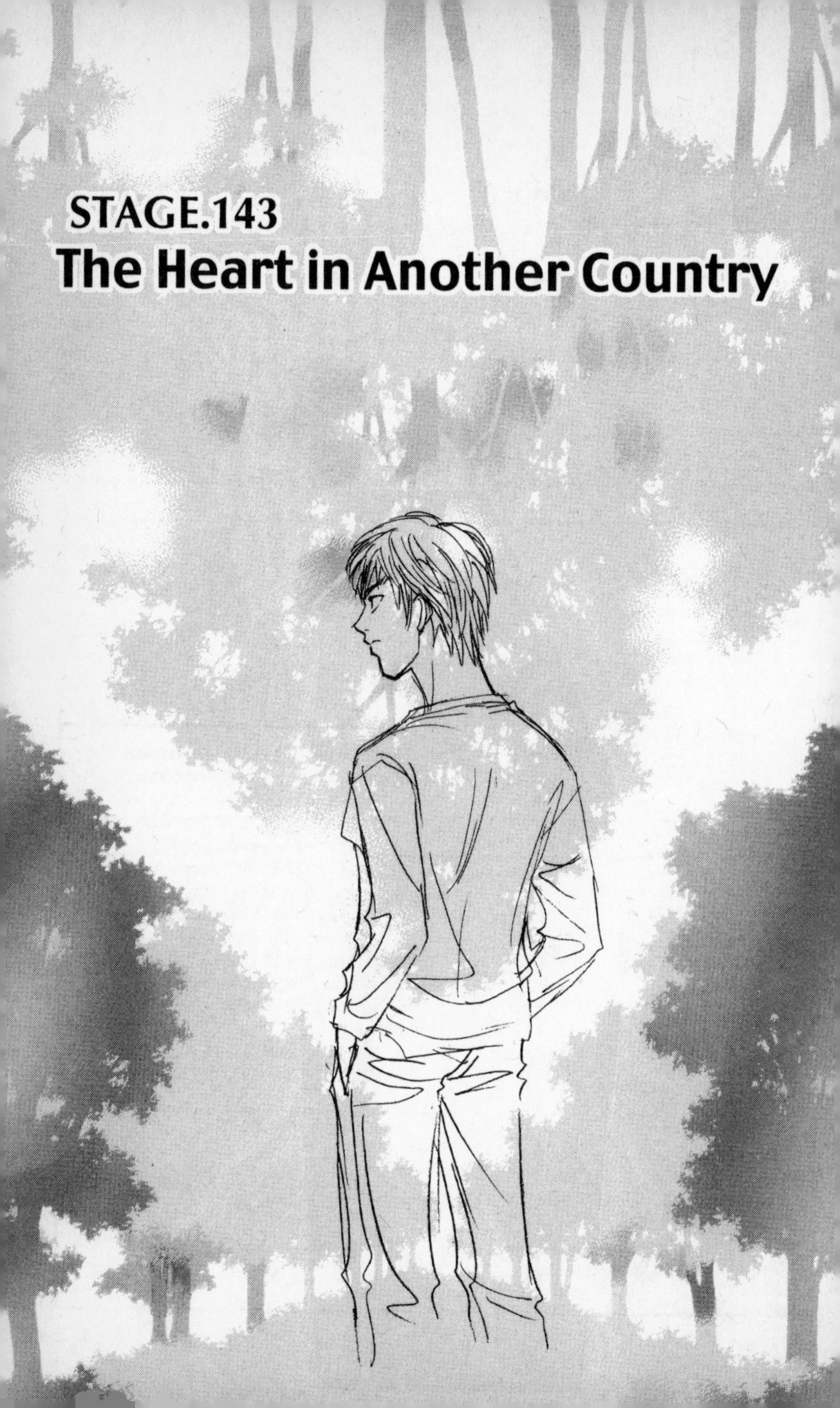

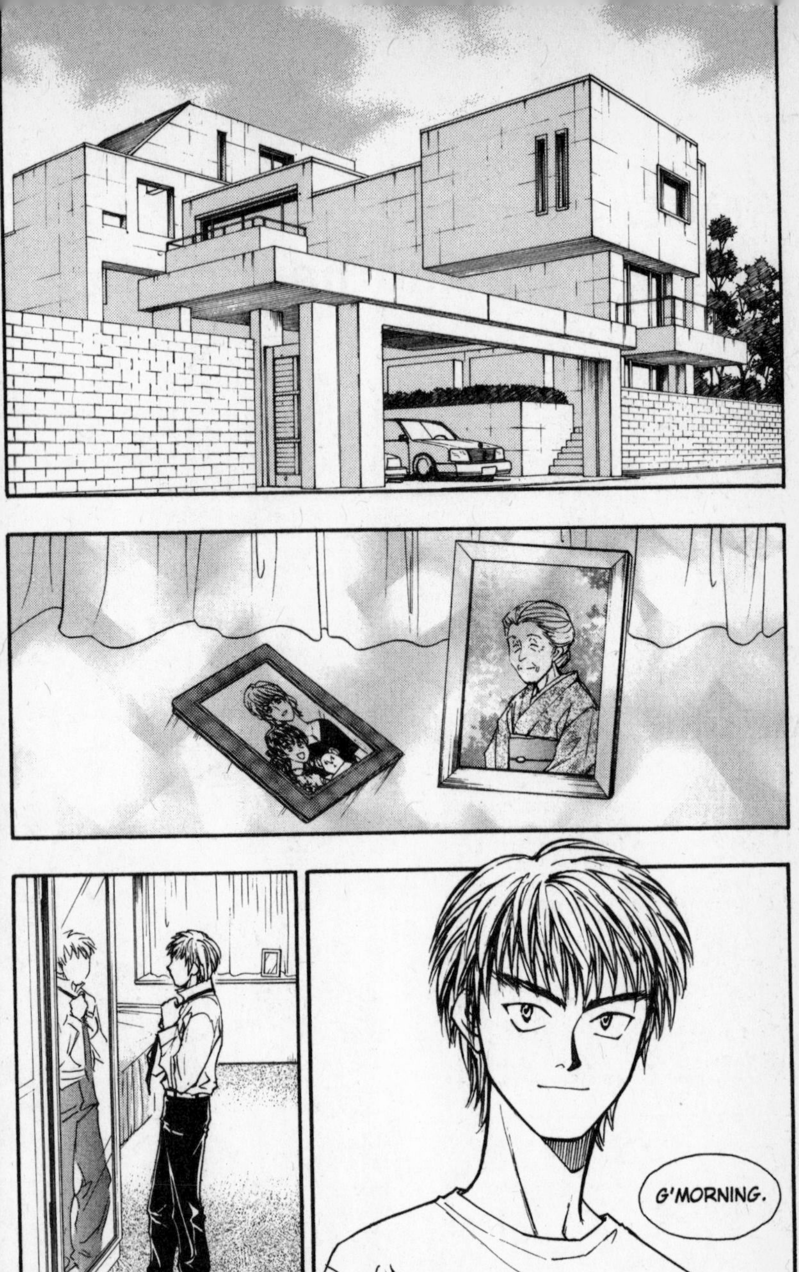
G'MORNING.

READ THIS WAY

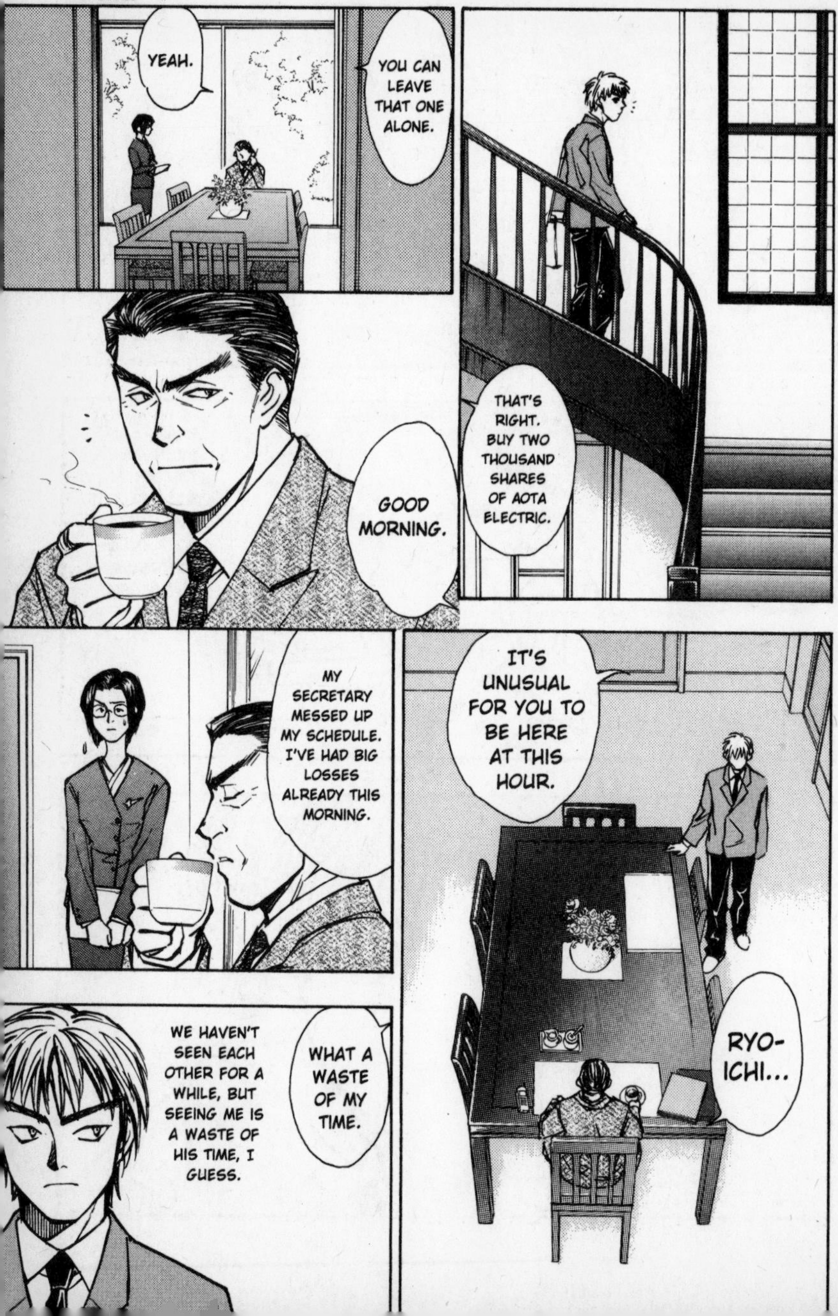
THAT'S RIGHT. BUY TWO THOUSAND SHARES OF AOTA ELECTRIC.
YOU CAN LEAVE THAT ONE ALONE.
YEAH.
GOOD MORNING.
IT'S UNUSUAL FOR YOU TO BE HERE AT THIS HOUR.
RYO-ICHI...
MY SECRETARY MESSED UP MY SCHEDULE. I'VE HAD BIG LOSSES ALREADY THIS MORNING.
WHAT A WASTE OF MY TIME.
WE HAVEN'T SEEN EACH OTHER FOR A WHILE, BUT SEEING ME IS A WASTE OF HIS TIME, I GUESS.

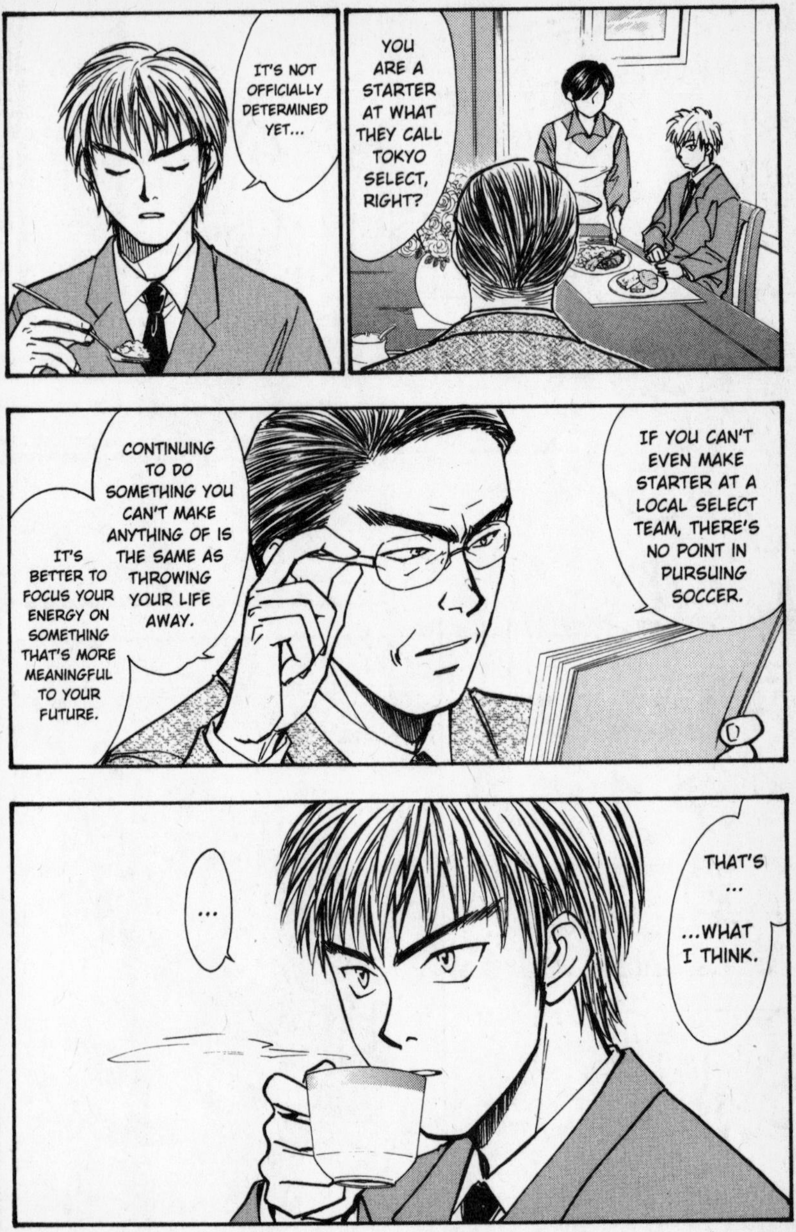
YOU ARE A STARTER AT WHAT THEY CALL TOKYO SELECT, RIGHT?
IT'S NOT OFFICIALLY DETERMINED YET...
IF YOU CAN'T EVEN MAKE STARTER AT A LOCAL SELECT TEAM, THERE'S NO POINT IN PURSUING SOCCER.
CONTINUING TO DO SOMETHING YOU CAN'T MAKE ANYTHING OF IS THE SAME AS THROWING YOUR LIFE AWAY.
IT'S BETTER TO FOCUS YOUR ENERGY ON SOMETHING THAT'S MORE MEANINGFUL TO YOUR FUTURE.
THAT'S ... ...WHAT I THINK.
...

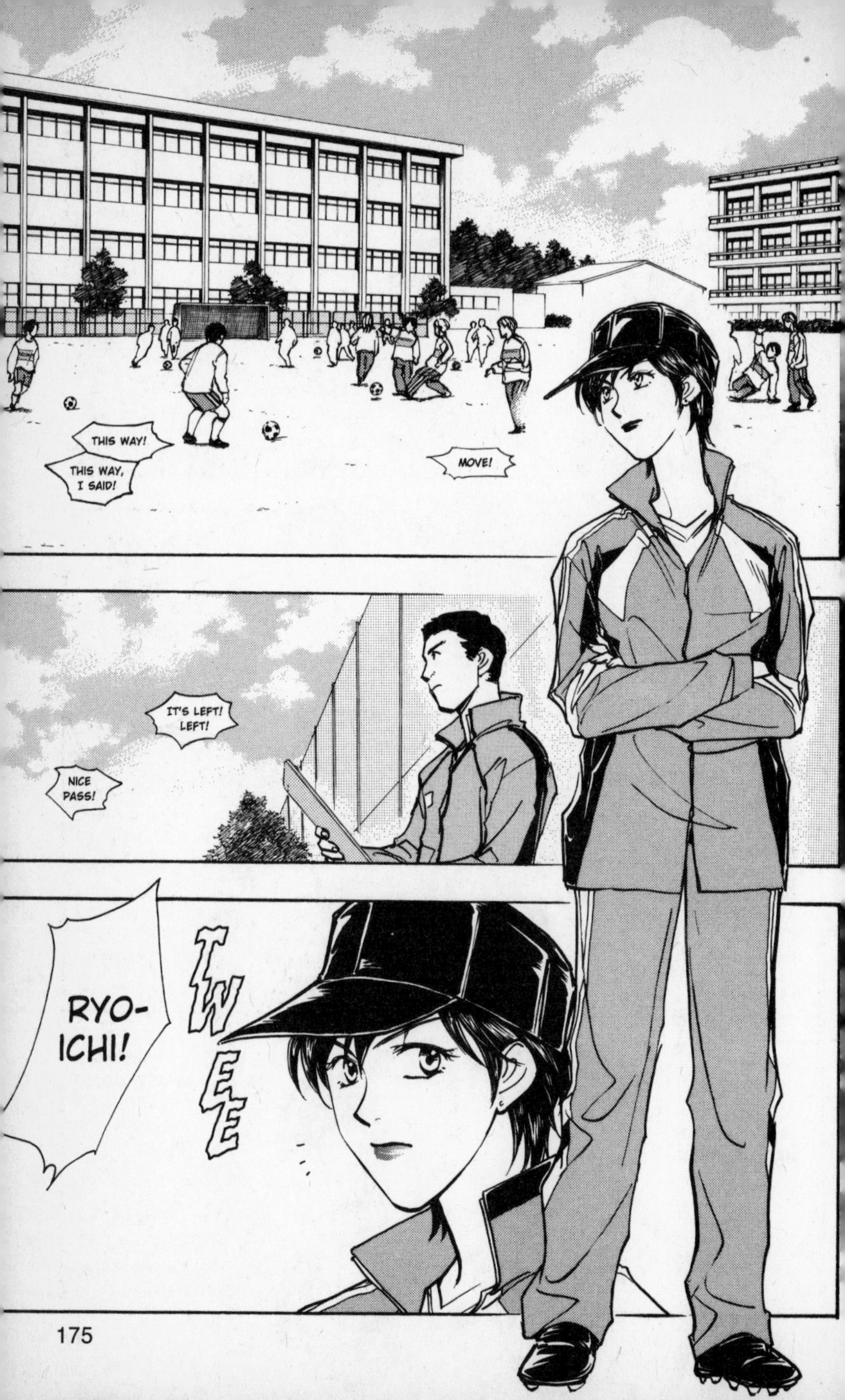
MOVE!
THIS WAY!
THIS WAY, I SAID!
IT'S LEFT! LEFT!
NICE PASS!
TWEE
RYO-ICHI!

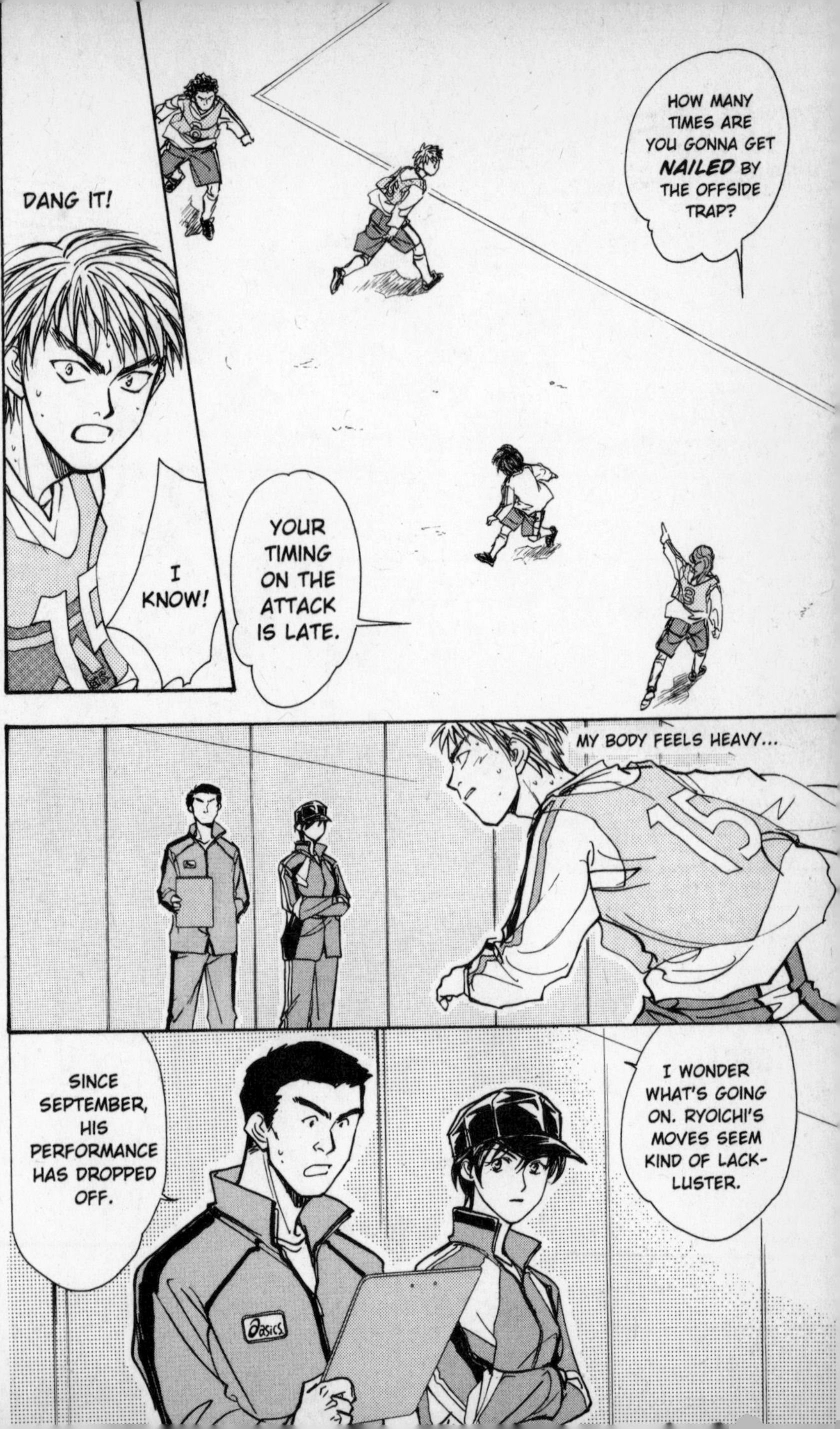
HOW MANY TIMES ARE YOU GONNA GET NAILED BY THE OFFSIDE TRAP?
YOUR TIMING ON THE ATTACK IS LATE.
DANG IT!
I KNOW!
MY BODY FEELS HEAVY...
I WONDER WHAT'S GOING ON. RYOICHI'S MOVES SEEM KIND OF LACK-LUSTER.
SINCE SEPTEMBER, HIS PERFORMANCE HAS DROPPED OFF.

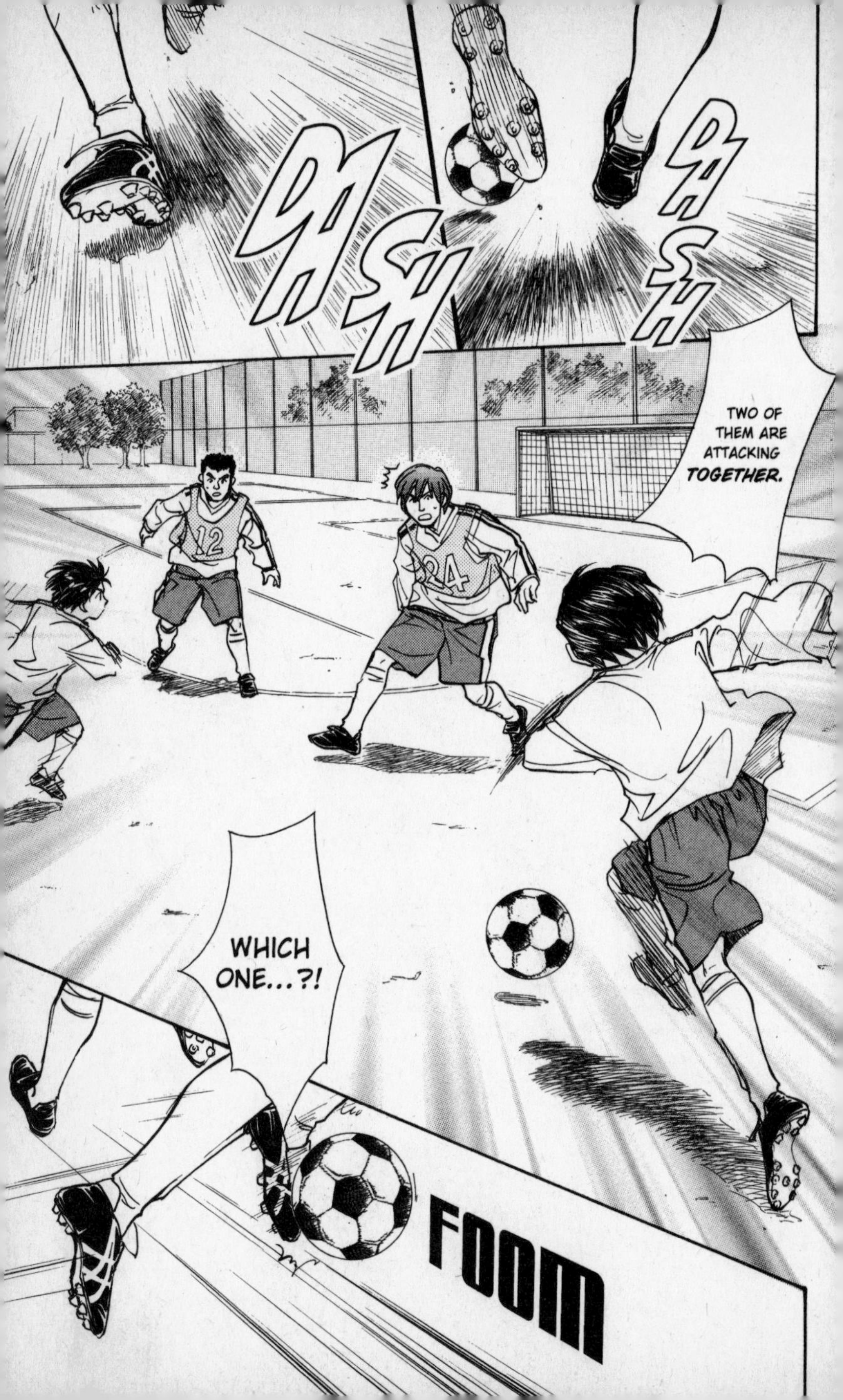
DASH
DASH
TWO OF THEM ARE ATTACKING TOGETHER.
WHICH ONE...?!
FOOM

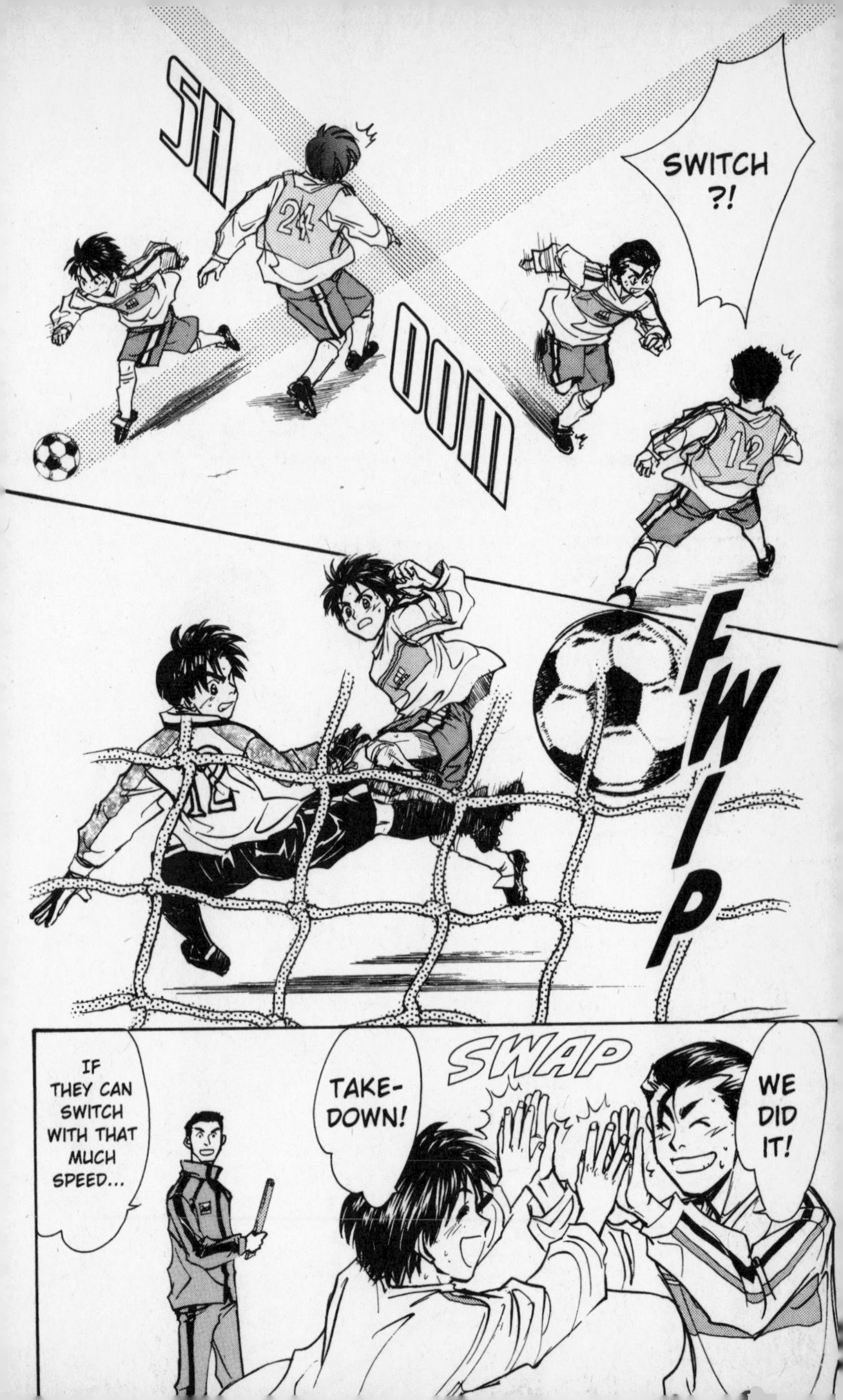
SWITCH ?!
SHOOM
FWIP
WE DID IT!
SWAP
TAKE-DOWN!
IF THEY CAN SWITCH WITH THAT MUCH SPEED...

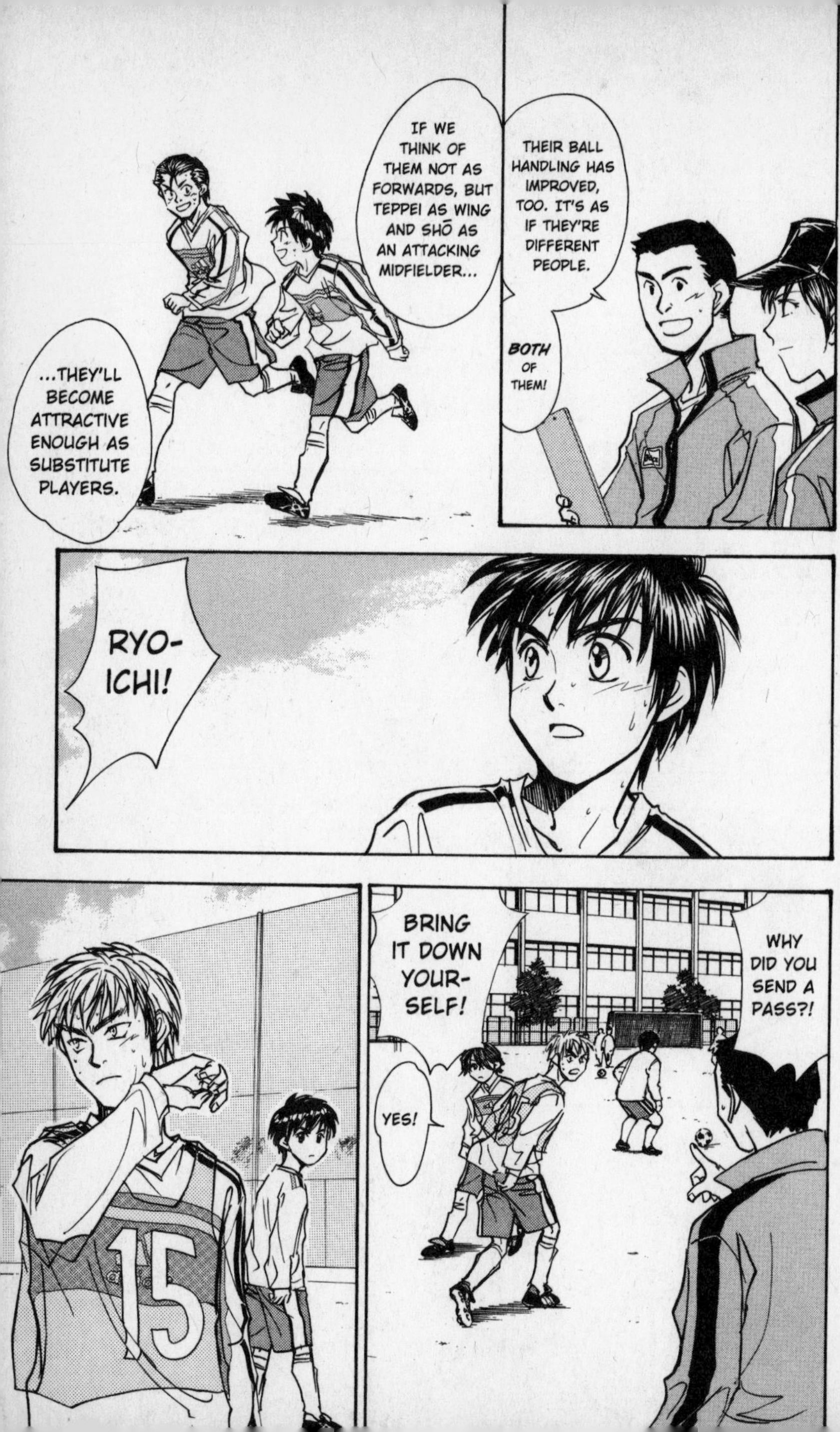
THEIR BALL HANDLING HAS IMPROVED, TOO. IT'S AS IF THEY'RE DIFFERENT PEOPLE.
BOTH OF THEM!
IF WE THINK OF THEM NOT AS FORWARDS, BUT TEPPEI AS WING AND SHŌ AS AN ATTACKING MIDFIELDER...
...THEY'LL BECOME ATTRACTIVE ENOUGH AS SUBSTITUTE PLAYERS.
RYO-ICHI!
WHY DID YOU SEND A PASS?!
BRING IT DOWN YOUR-SELF!
YES!

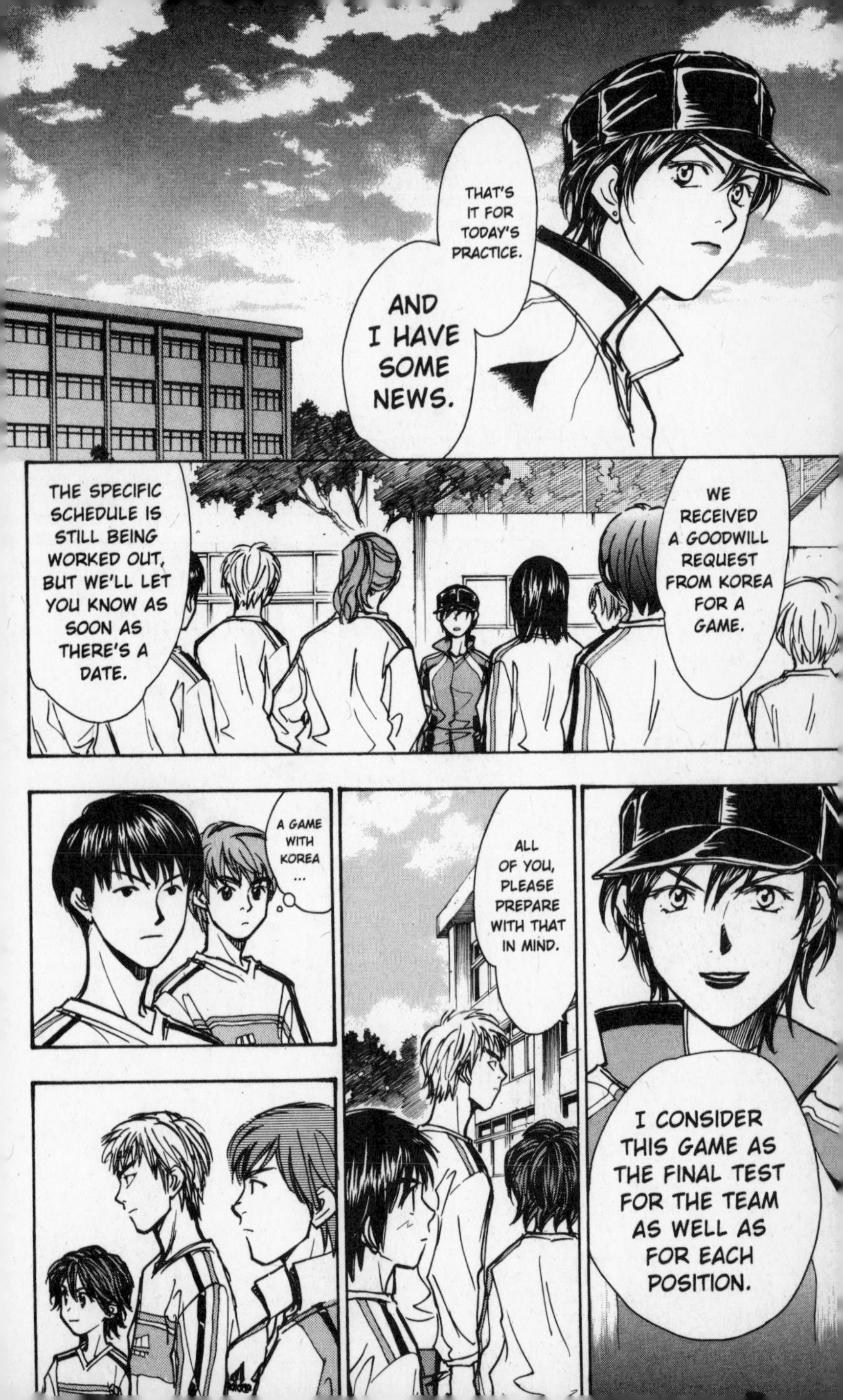
THAT'S IT FOR TODAY'S PRACTICE.
AND I HAVE SOME NEWS.
WE RECEIVED A GOODWILL REQUEST FROM KOREA FOR A GAME.
THE SPECIFIC SCHEDULE IS STILL BEING WORKED OUT, BUT WE'LL LET YOU KNOW AS SOON AS THERE'S A DATE.
I CONSIDER THIS GAME AS THE FINAL TEST FOR THE TEAM AS WELL AS FOR EACH POSITION.
ALL OF YOU, PLEASE PREPARE WITH THAT IN MIND.
A GAME WITH KOREA ...

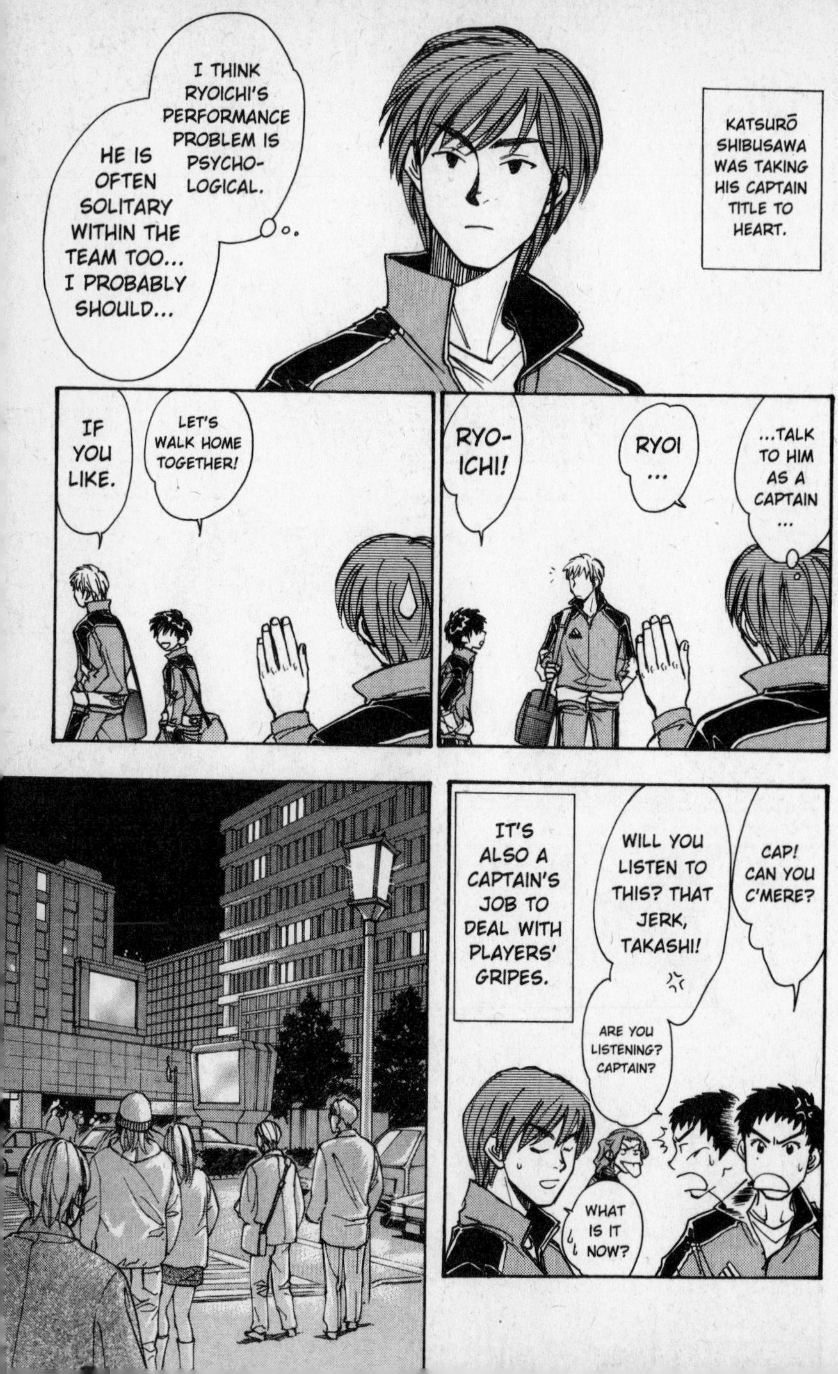
KATSURŌ SHIBUSAWA WAS TAKING HIS CAPTAIN TITLE TO HEART.
I THINK RYOICHI'S PERFORMANCE PROBLEM IS PSYCHO-LOGICAL.
HE IS OFTEN SOLITARY WITHIN THE TEAM TOO... I PROBABLY SHOULD...
...TALK TO HIM AS A CAPTAIN ...
RYOI ...
RYO-ICHI!
LET'S WALK HOME TOGETHER!
IF YOU LIKE.
CAP! CAN YOU C'MERE?
WILL YOU LISTEN TO THIS? THAT JERK, TAKASHI!
IT'S ALSO A CAPTAIN'S JOB TO DEAL WITH PLAYERS' GRIPES.
ARE YOU LISTENING? CAPTAIN?
WHAT IS IT NOW?

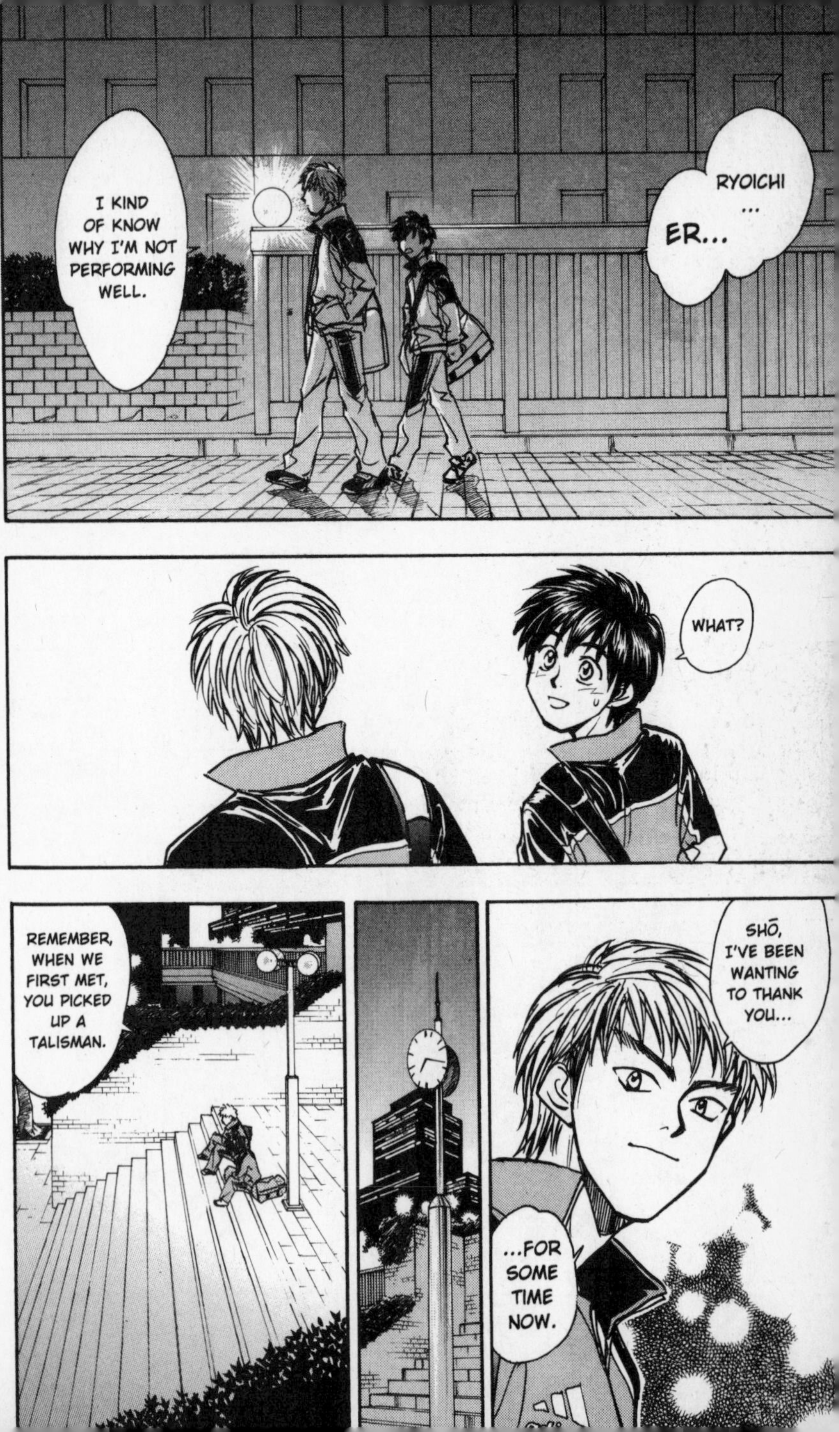
RYOICHI ... ER...
I KIND OF KNOW WHY I'M NOT PERFORMING WELL.
WHAT?
SHŌ, I'VE BEEN WANTING TO THANK YOU...
...FOR SOME TIME NOW.
REMEMBER, WHEN WE FIRST MET, YOU PICKED UP A TALISMAN.

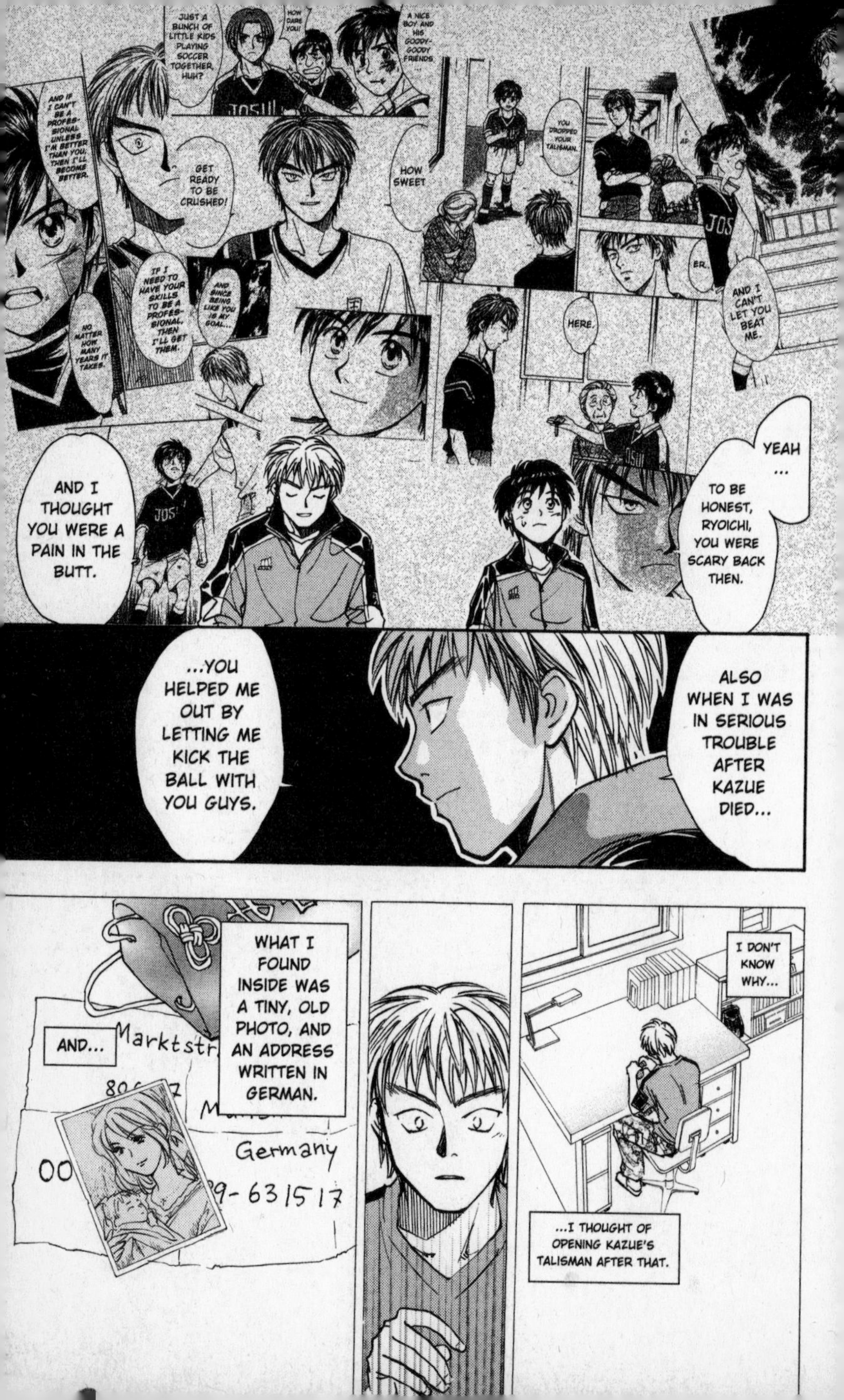
ER...
AND I CAN'T LET YOU BEAT ME.
YOU DROPPED YOUR TALISMAN.
HERE.
A NICE BOY AND HIS GOODY-GOODY FRIENDS...
HOW DARE YOU!
JUST A BUNCH OF LITTLE KIDS PLAYING SOCCER TOGETHER, HUH?
HOW SWEET
GET READY TO BE CRUSHED!
AND IF I CAN'T BE A PROFESSIONAL UNLESS I'M BETTER THAN YOU, THEN I'LL BECOME BETTER.
AND SINCE BEING LIKE YOU IS MY GOAL...
IF I NEED TO HAVE YOUR SKILLS TO BE A PROFESSIONAL, THEN I'LL GET THEM.
NO MATTER HOW MANY YEARS IT TAKES.
YEAH... TO BE HONEST, RYOICHI, YOU WERE SCARY BACK THEN.
AND I THOUGHT YOU WERE A PAIN IN THE BUTT.
ALSO WHEN I WAS IN SERIOUS TROUBLE AFTER KAZUE DIED...
...YOU HELPED ME OUT BY LETTING ME KICK THE BALL WITH YOU GUYS.
I DON'T KNOW WHY...
...I THOUGHT OF OPENING KAZUE'S TALISMAN AFTER THAT.
WHAT I FOUND INSIDE WAS A TINY, OLD PHOTO, AND AN ADDRESS WRITTEN IN GERMAN.
AND...
Germany

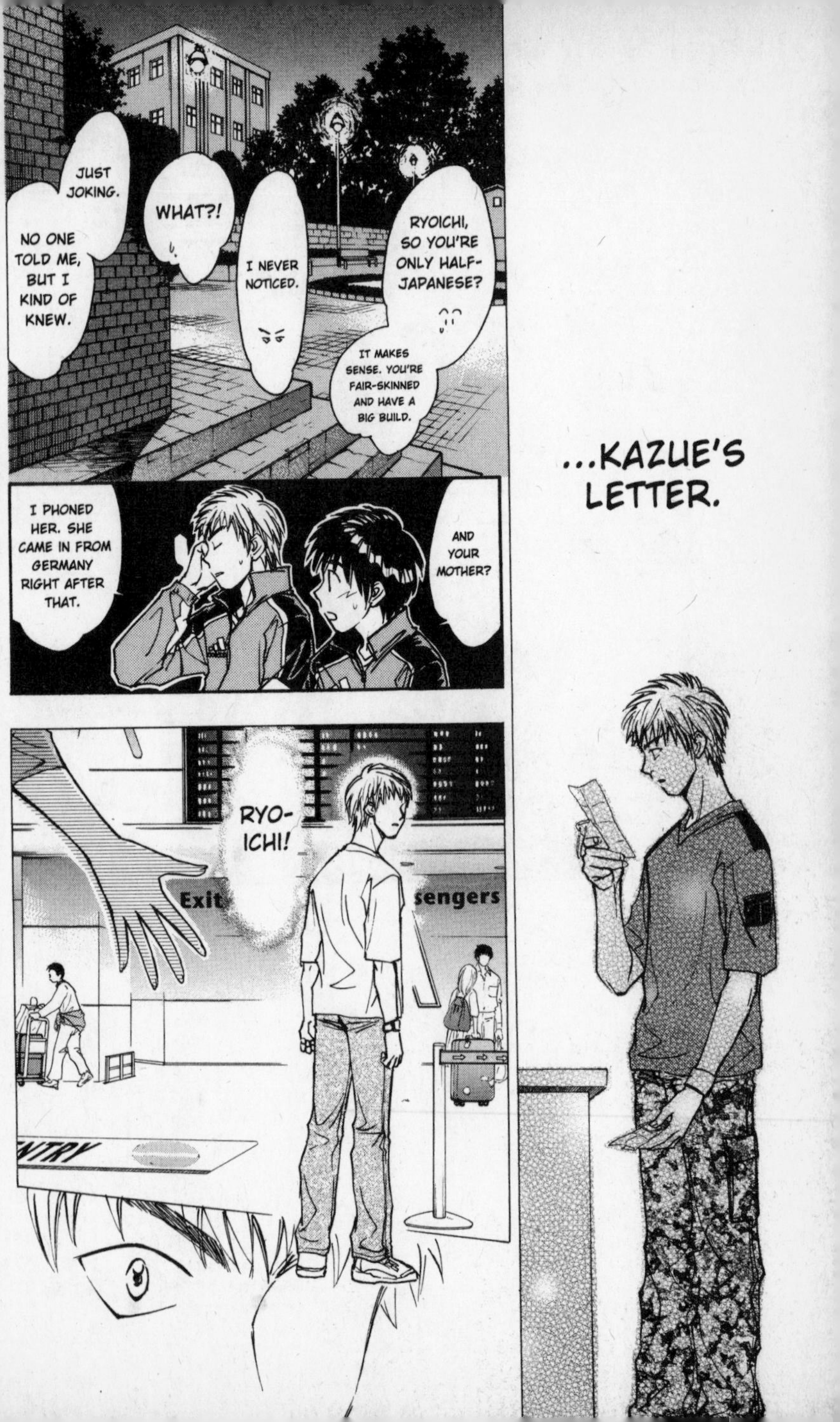
...KAZUE'S LETTER.
RYOICHI, SO YOU'RE ONLY HALF-JAPANESE?
IT MAKES SENSE. YOU'RE FAIR-SKINNED AND HAVE A BIG BUILD.
I NEVER NOTICED.
WHAT?!
JUST JOKING.
NO ONE TOLD ME, BUT I KIND OF KNEW.
AND YOUR MOTHER?
I PHONED HER. SHE CAME IN FROM GERMANY RIGHT AFTER THAT.
RYO-ICHI!
Exit

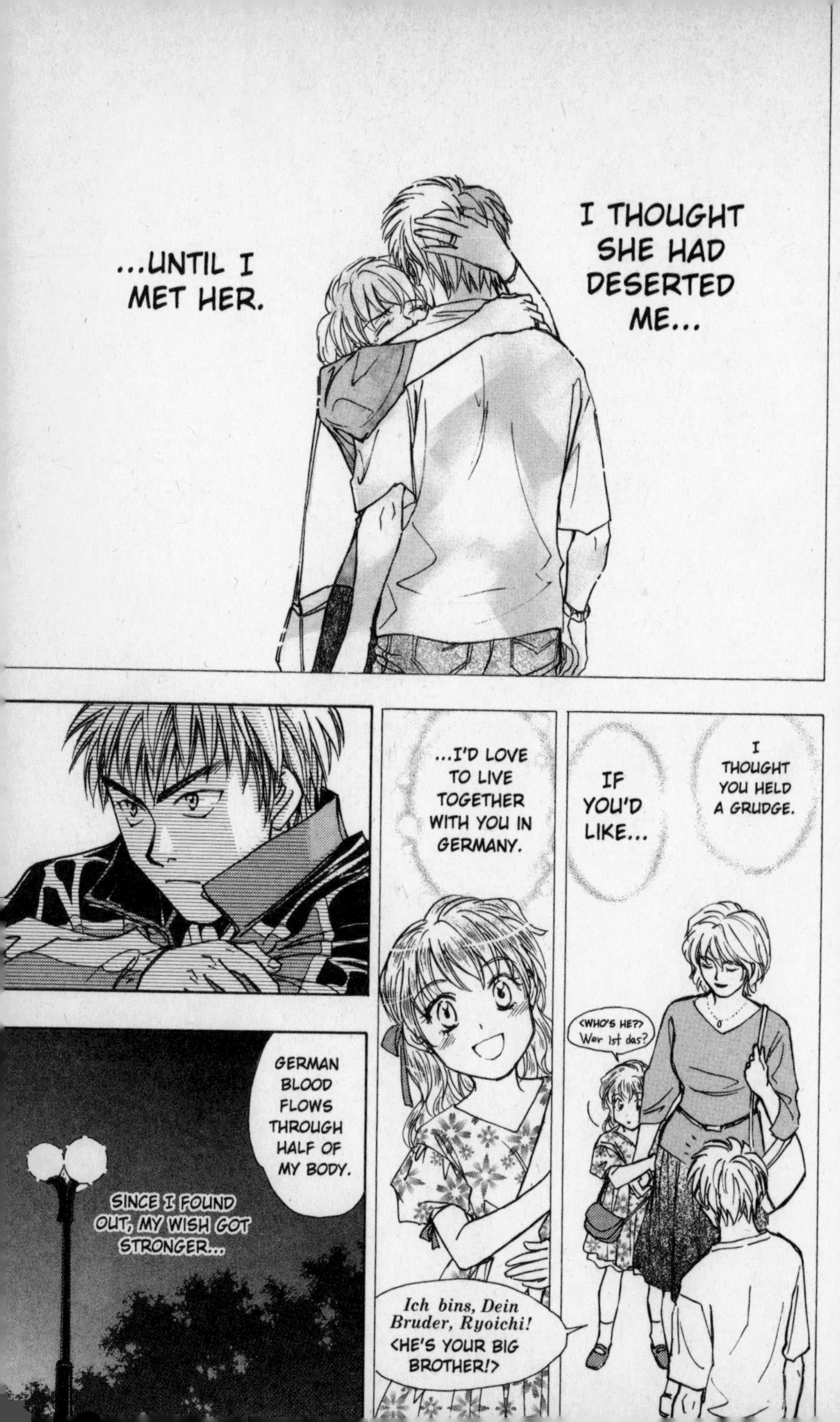
I THOUGHT SHE HAD DESERTED ME...
...UNTIL I MET HER.
I THOUGHT YOU HELD A GRUDGE.
IF YOU'D LIKE...
<WHO'S HE?> Wer ist das?
...I'D LOVE TO LIVE TOGETHER WITH YOU IN GERMANY.
Ich bins, Dein Bruder, Ryoichi! <HE'S YOUR BIG BROTHER!>
GERMAN BLOOD FLOWS THROUGH HALF OF MY BODY.
SINCE I FOUND OUT, MY WISH GOT STRONGER...

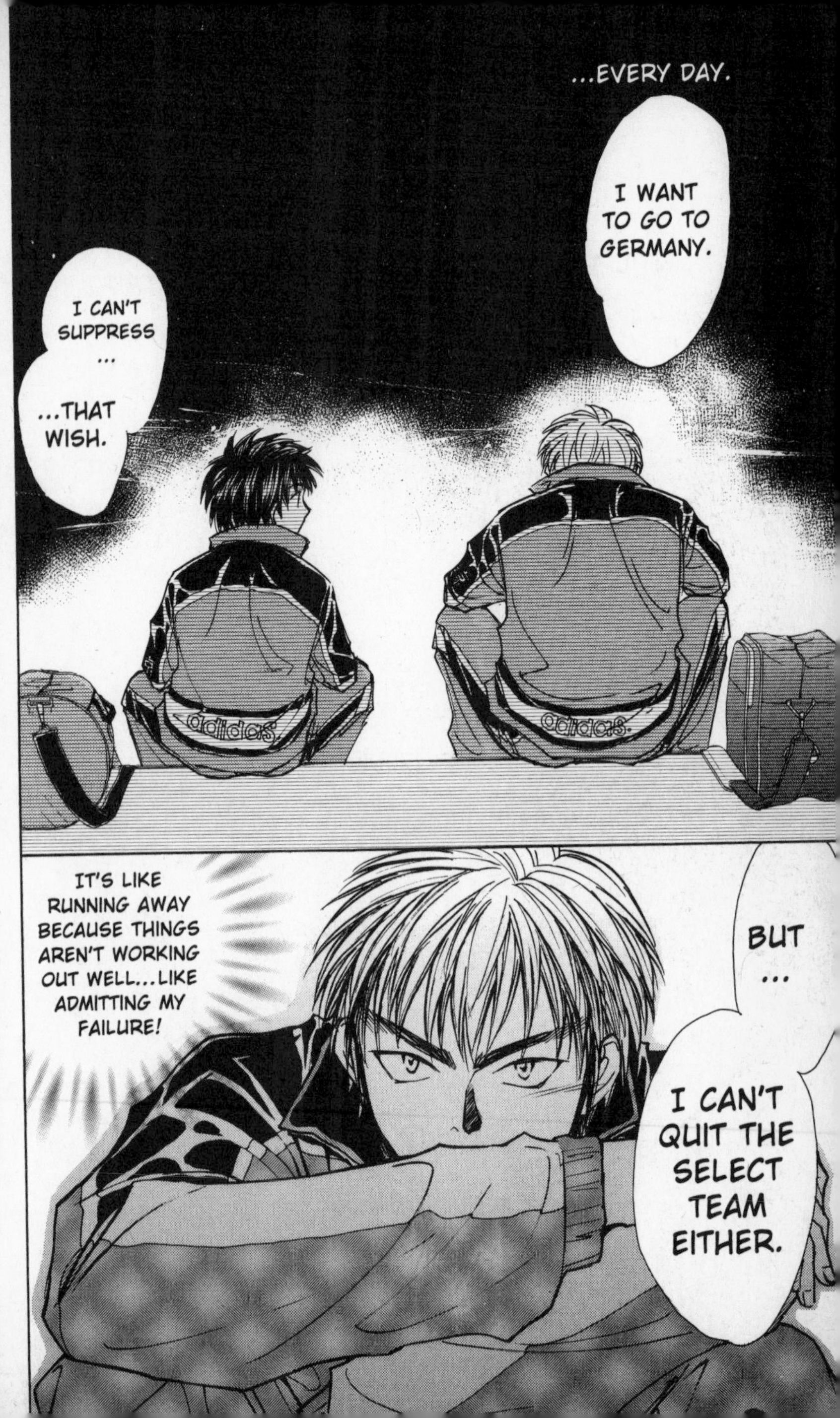
...EVERY DAY.
I WANT TO GO TO GERMANY.
I CAN'T SUPPRESS ...
...THAT WISH.
BUT ...
I CAN'T QUIT THE SELECT TEAM EITHER.
IT'S LIKE RUNNING AWAY BECAUSE THINGS AREN'T WORKING OUT WELL...LIKE ADMITTING MY FAILURE!

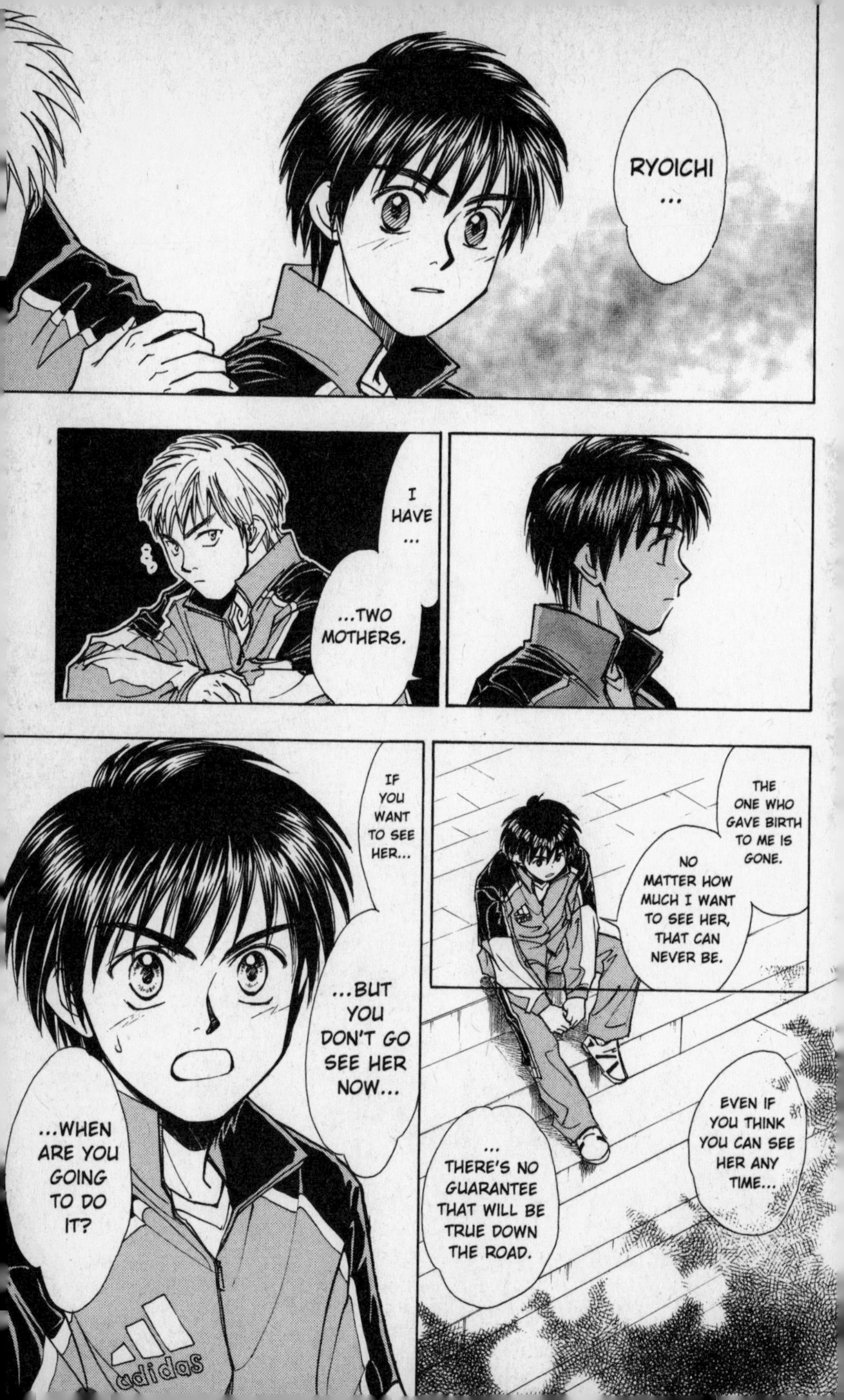

RYOICHI ...
I HAVE ...
...TWO MOTHERS.
THE ONE WHO GAVE BIRTH TO ME IS GONE.
NO MATTER HOW MUCH I WANT TO SEE HER, THAT CAN NEVER BE.
EVEN IF YOU THINK YOU CAN SEE HER ANY TIME...
...THERE'S NO GUARANTEE THAT WILL BE TRUE DOWN THE ROAD.
IF YOU WANT TO SEE HER...
...BUT YOU DON'T GO SEE HER NOW...
...WHEN ARE YOU GOING TO DO IT?
adidas

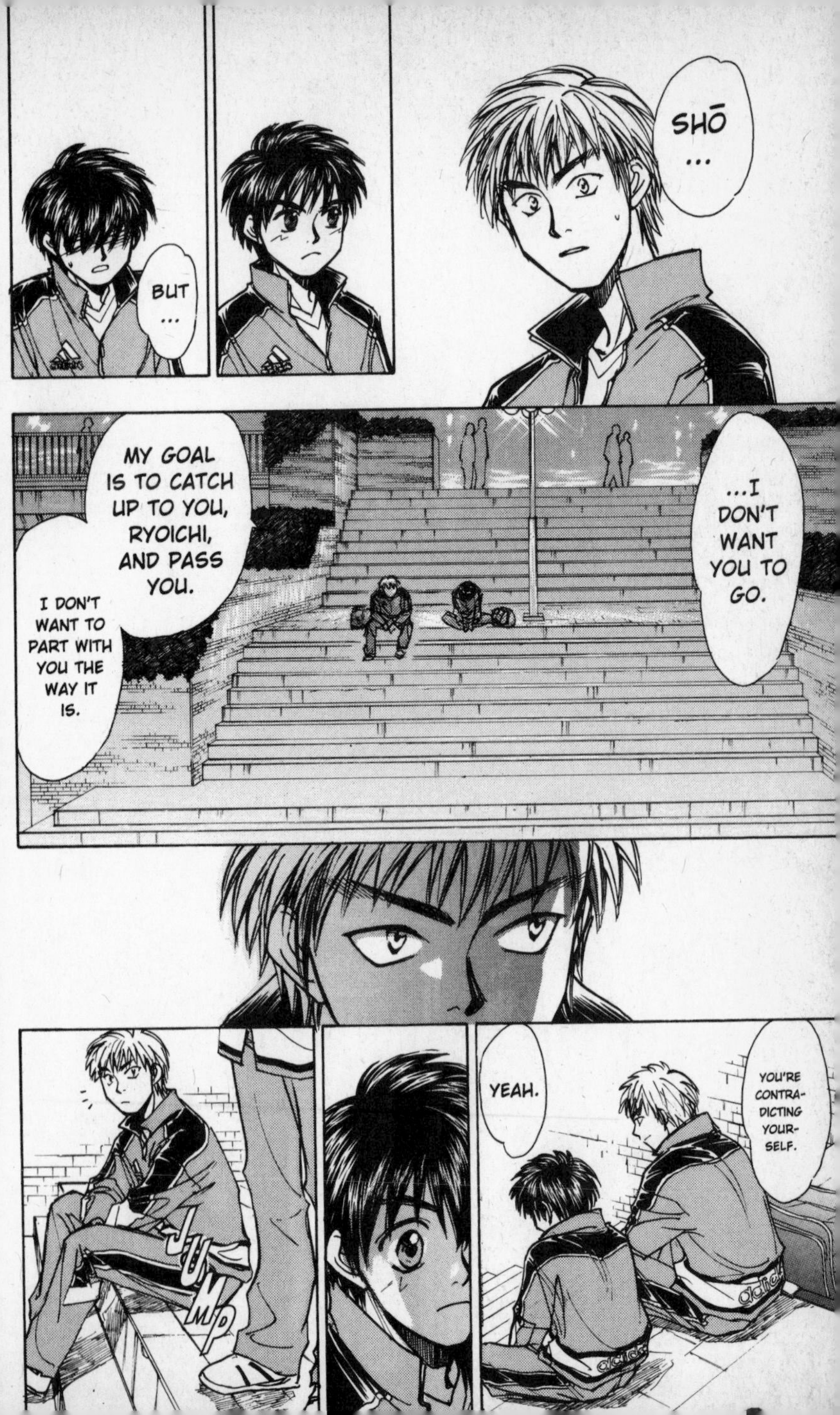
SHŌ ...
BUT ...
...I DON'T WANT YOU TO GO.
MY GOAL IS TO CATCH UP TO YOU, RYOICHI, AND PASS YOU.
I DON'T WANT TO PART WITH YOU THE WAY IT IS.
YOU'RE CONTRA-DICTING YOUR-SELF.
YEAH.
JUMP

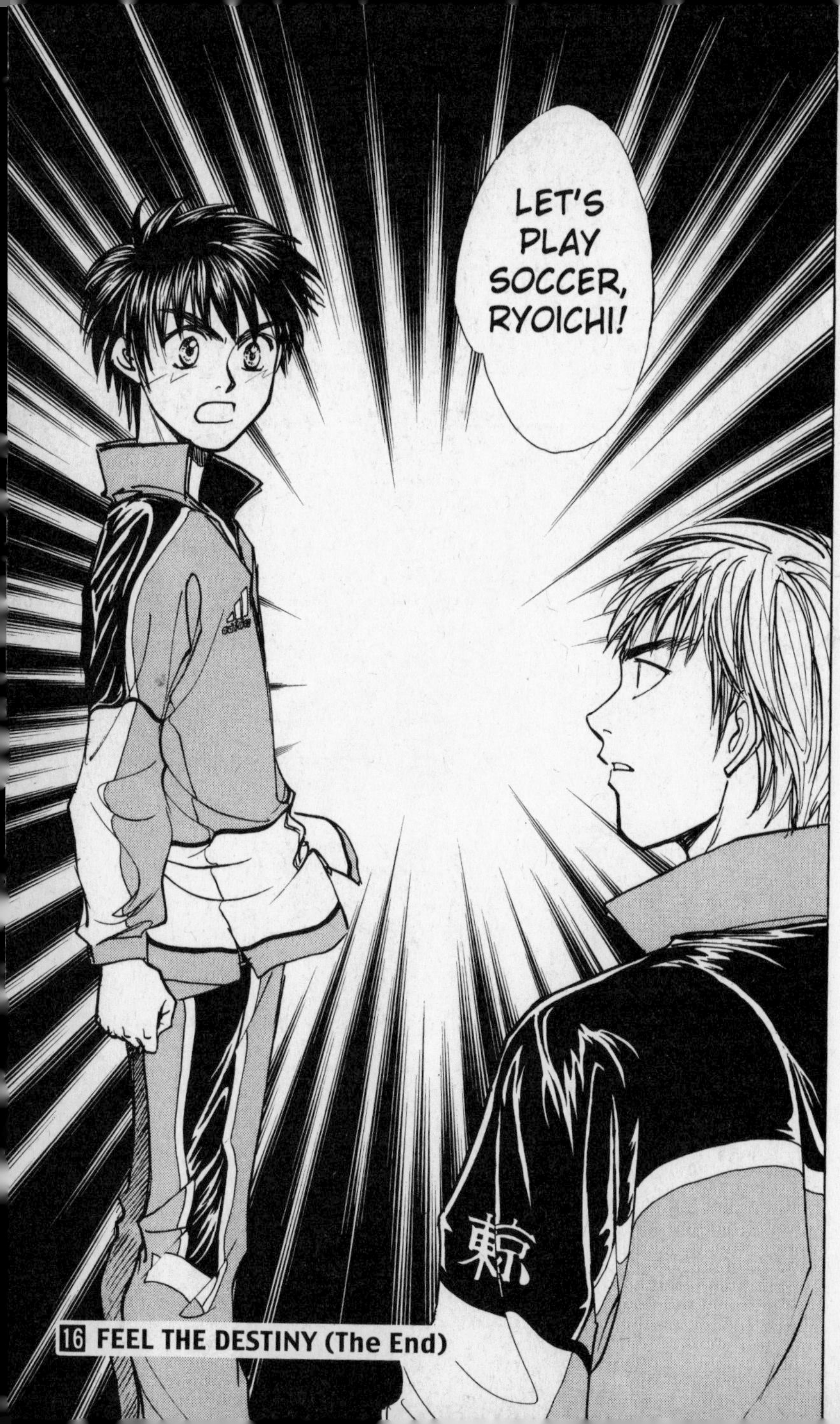
LET'S PLAY SOCCER, RYOICHI!
16 FEEL THE DESTINY (The End)

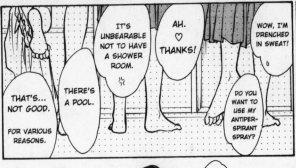

WHISTLE!

EXTRA STORY

Girls in Earnest

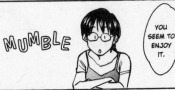

WOW, I'M DRENCHED IN SWEAT!
DO YOU WANT TO USE MY ANTIPERSPIRANT SPRAY?
AH. ♡ THANKS!
IT'S UNBEARABLE NOT TO HAVE A SHOWER ROOM.
THERE'S A POOL.
THAT'S... NOT GOOD.
FOR VARIOUS REASONS.
YOU SEEM TO ENJOY IT.
MUMBLE
HUH? WHAT?
WELL.
I NOTICED HOW FIRED UP YOU ARE.
TEE HEE ♡

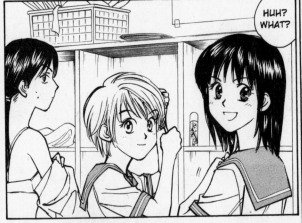

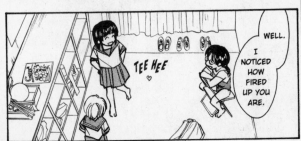

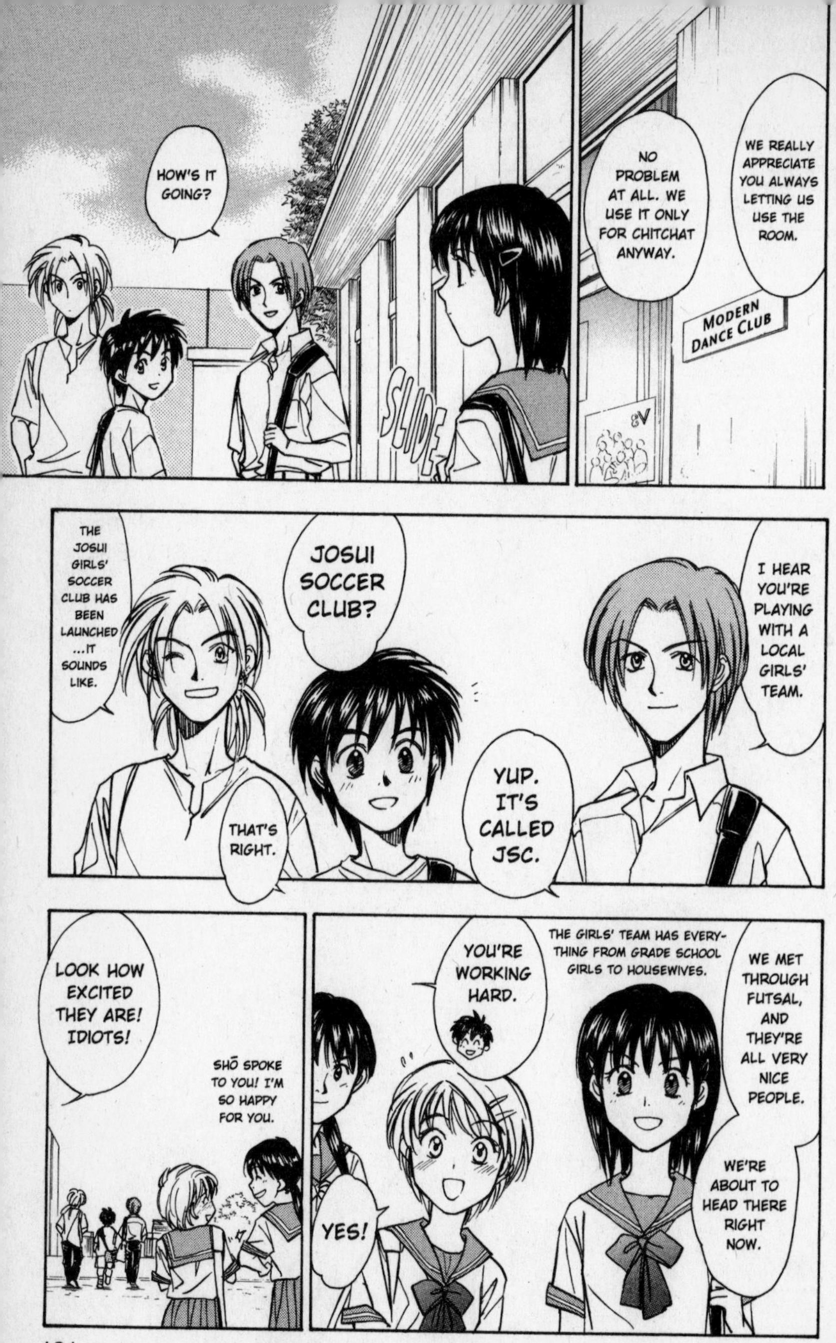

WE REALLY APPRECIATE YOU ALWAYS LETTING US USE THE ROOM.
NO PROBLEM AT ALL. WE USE IT ONLY FOR CHITCHAT ANYWAY.
MODERN DANCE CLUB
SLIDE
HOW'S IT GOING?
I HEAR YOU'RE PLAYING WITH A LOCAL GIRLS' TEAM.
YUP. IT'S CALLED JSC.
JOSUI SOCCER CLUB?
THE JOSUI GIRLS' SOCCER CLUB HAS BEEN LAUNCHED ...IT SOUNDS LIKE.
THAT'S RIGHT.
WE MET THROUGH FUTSAL, AND THEY'RE ALL VERY NICE PEOPLE.
THE GIRLS' TEAM HAS EVERYTHING FROM GRADE SCHOOL GIRLS TO HOUSEWIVES.
YOU'RE WORKING HARD.
WE'RE ABOUT TO HEAD THERE RIGHT NOW.
YES!
LOOK HOW EXCITED THEY ARE! IDIOTS!
SHŌ SPOKE TO YOU! I'M SO HAPPY FOR YOU.

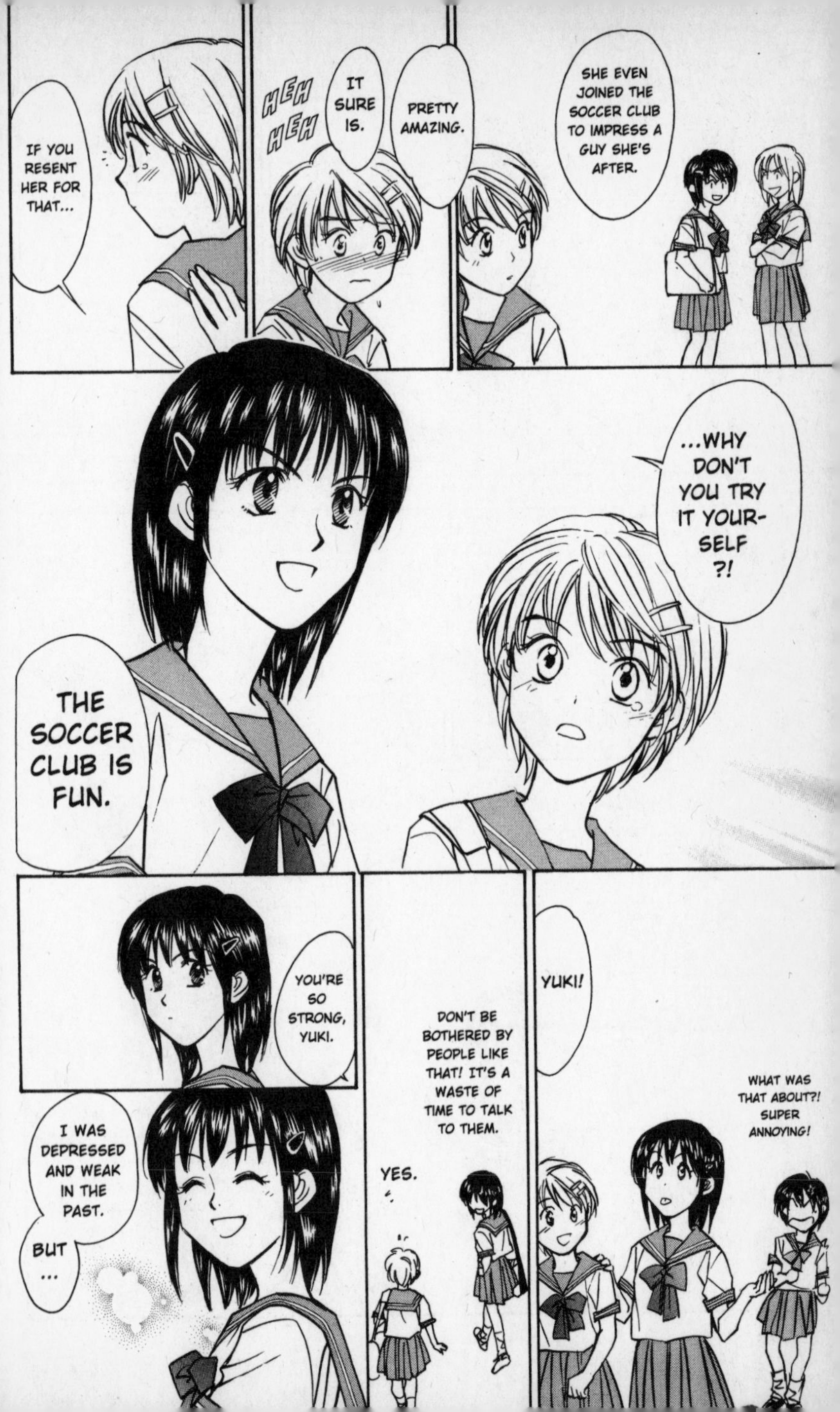
SHE EVEN JOINED THE SOCCER CLUB TO IMPRESS A GUY SHE'S AFTER.
PRETTY AMAZING.
IT SURE IS.
HEH HEH
IF YOU RESENT HER FOR THAT...
...WHY DON'T YOU TRY IT YOURSELF?!
THE SOCCER CLUB IS FUN.
WHAT WAS THAT ABOUT?! SUPER ANNOYING!
YUKI!
DON'T BE BOTHERED BY PEOPLE LIKE THAT! IT'S A WASTE OF TIME TO TALK TO THEM.
YES.
YOU'RE SO STRONG, YUKI.
I WAS DEPRESSED AND WEAK IN THE PAST.
BUT ...

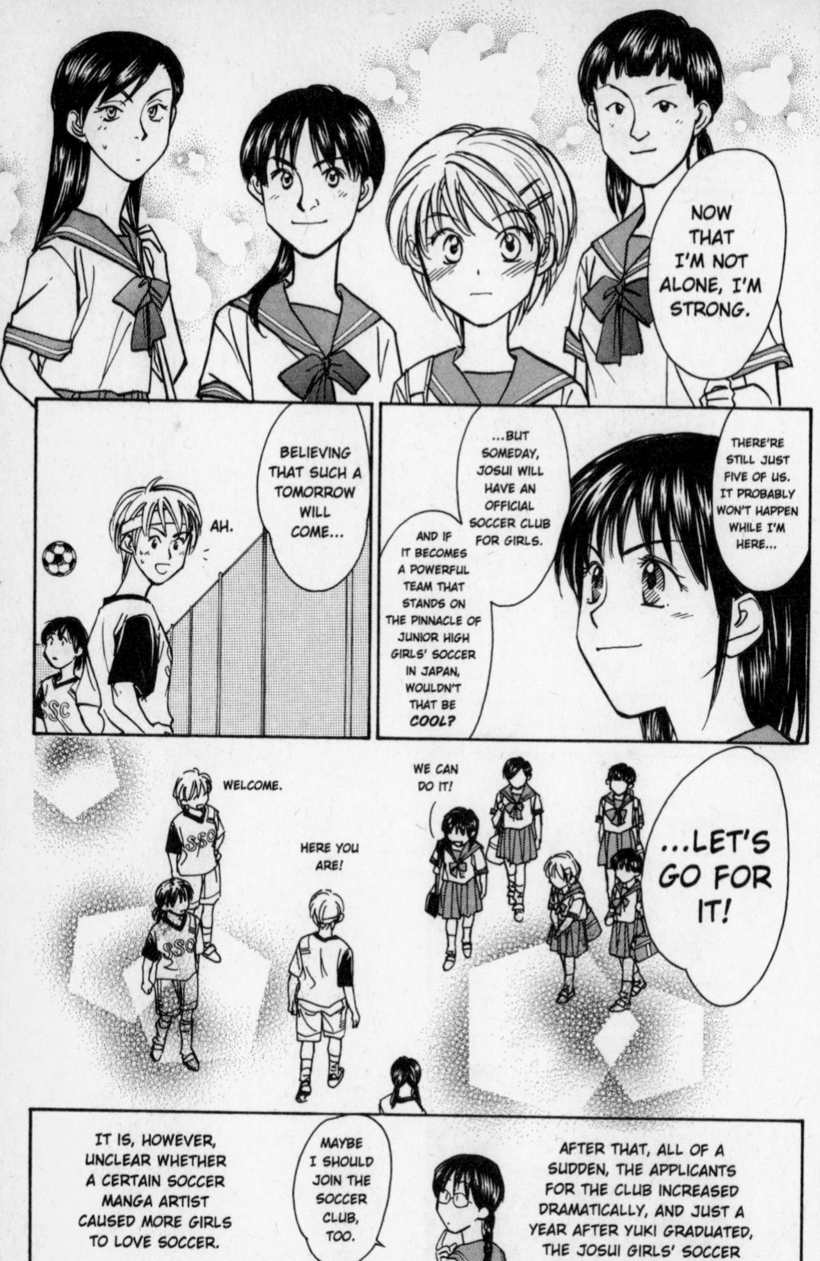
NOW THAT I'M NOT ALONE, I'M STRONG.
THERE'RE STILL JUST FIVE OF US. IT PROBABLY WON'T HAPPEN WHILE I'M HERE...
...BUT SOMEDAY, JOSUI WILL HAVE AN OFFICIAL SOCCER CLUB FOR GIRLS.
AND IF IT BECOMES A POWERFUL TEAM THAT STANDS ON THE PINNACLE OF JUNIOR HIGH GIRLS' SOCCER IN JAPAN, WOULDN'T THAT BE COOL?
BELIEVING THAT SUCH A TOMORROW WILL COME...
AH.
...LET'S GO FOR IT!
WE CAN DO IT!
HERE YOU ARE!
WELCOME.
AFTER THAT, ALL OF A SUDDEN, THE APPLICANTS FOR THE CLUB INCREASED DRAMATICALLY, AND JUST A YEAR AFTER YUKI GRADUATED, THE JOSUI GIRLS' SOCCER CLUB FORMED A TEAM.
MAYBE I SHOULD JOIN THE SOCCER CLUB, TOO.
IT IS, HOWEVER, UNCLEAR WHETHER A CERTAIN SOCCER MANGA ARTIST CAUSED MORE GIRLS TO LOVE SOCCER.

HUSTLE!

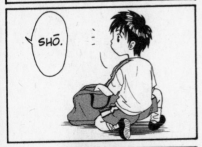

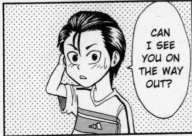

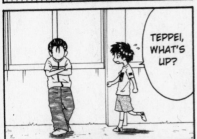

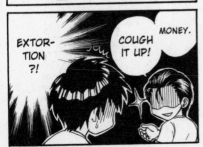

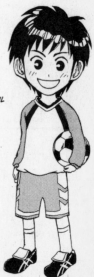

PRODUCED BY:
ASSISTANT F. JAGUAR
& OTHER WONDERFUL ASSISTANTS

Little Iron Foot's Invitation

SHŌ.
CAN I SEE YOU ON THE WAY OUT?
TEPPEI, WHAT'S UP?
MONEY.
COUGH IT UP!
EXTOR-TION ?!

Comeback Artist ☆ Shigeki

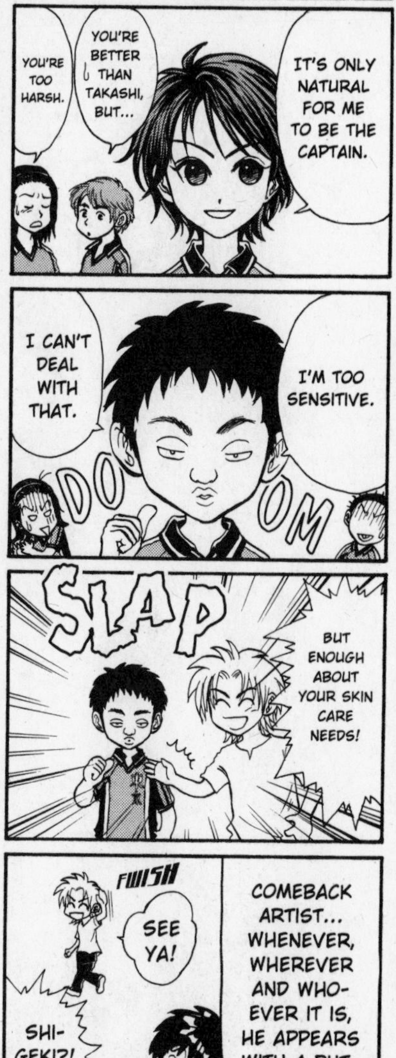
IT'S ONLY NATURAL FOR ME TO BE THE CAPTAIN.
YOU'RE BETTER THAN TAKASHI, BUT...
YOU'RE TOO HARSH.
I'M TOO SENSITIVE.
I CAN'T DEAL WITH THAT.
DOOM
SLAP
BUT ENOUGH ABOUT YOUR SKIN CARE NEEDS!
COMEBACK ARTIST... WHENEVER, WHEREVER AND WHO-EVER IT IS, HE APPEARS WITH A PUT-DOWN.
FWISH
SEE YA!
SHI-GEKI?!
WHY?

Akira Note Confidential!

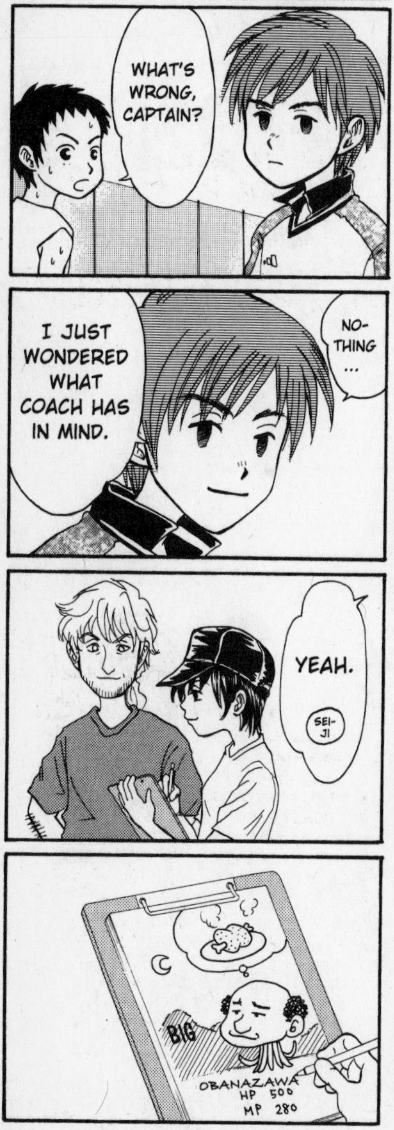
WHAT'S WRONG, CAPTAIN?
NO-THING...
I JUST WONDERED WHAT COACH HAS IN MIND.
YEAH.
SEI-JI
BIG
OBANAZAWA
HP 500
MP 280

A New Team

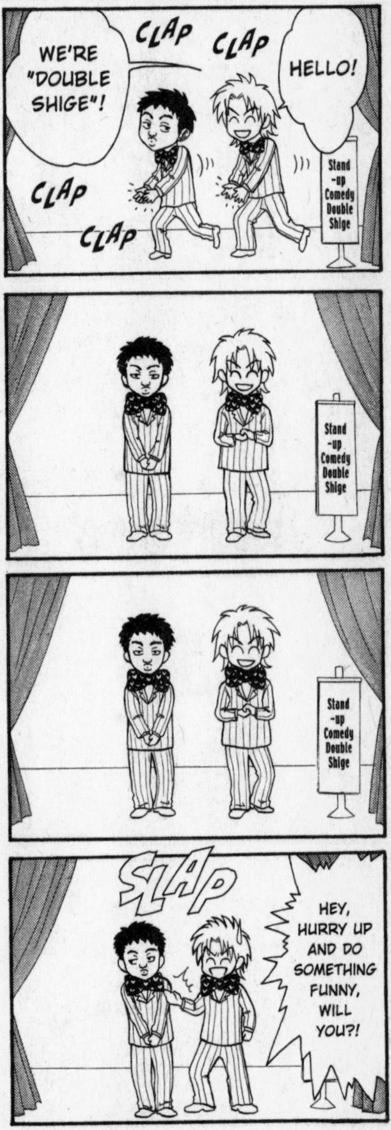
HELLO!
CLAP
CLAP
WE'RE "DOUBLE SHIGE"!
CLAP
CLAP
Stand-up Comedy Double Shige
Stand-up Comedy Double Shige
Stand-up Comedy Double Shige
SLAP
HEY, HURRY UP AND DO SOMETHING FUNNY, WILL YOU?!

I was just trying to encourage him...

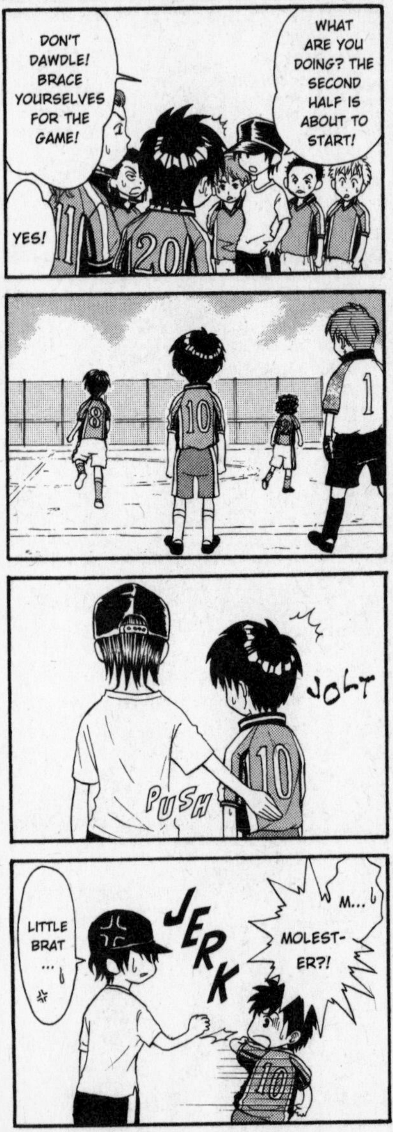
WHAT ARE YOU DOING? THE SECOND HALF IS ABOUT TO START!
DON'T DAWDLE! BRACE YOURSELVES FOR THE GAME!
YES!
JOLT
PUSH
M... MOLEST-ER?!
JERK
LITTLE BRAT...

Ahh, Tatsuya Mizuno ~ With ☆ Shige ~

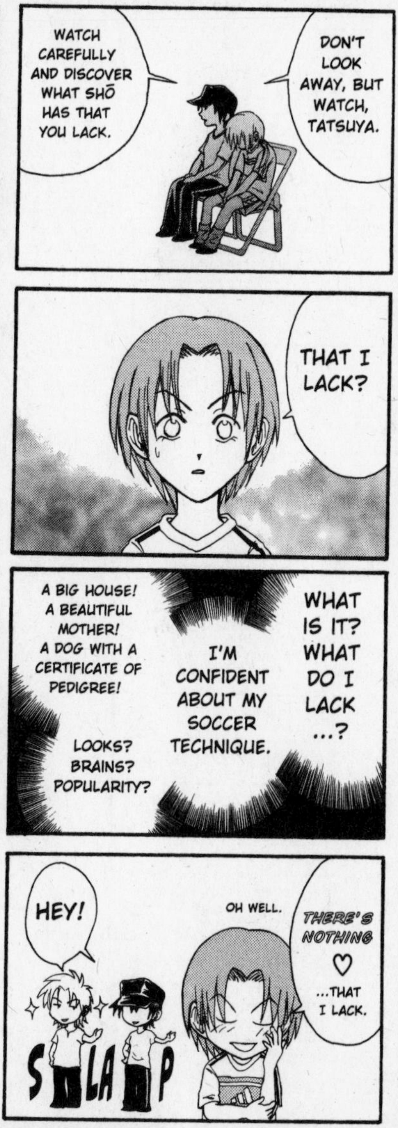
DON'T LOOK AWAY, BUT WATCH, TATSUYA.
WATCH CAREFULLY AND DISCOVER WHAT SHŌ HAS THAT YOU LACK.
THAT I LACK?
WHAT IS IT? WHAT DO I LACK ...?
I'M CONFIDENT ABOUT MY SOCCER TECHNIQUE.
A BIG HOUSE! A BEAUTIFUL MOTHER! A DOG WITH A CERTIFICATE OF PEDIGREE!
LOOKS? BRAINS? POPULARITY?
THERE'S NOTHING ♡ ...THAT I LACK.
OH WELL.
HEY!
SLAP

The Team Breaks Up

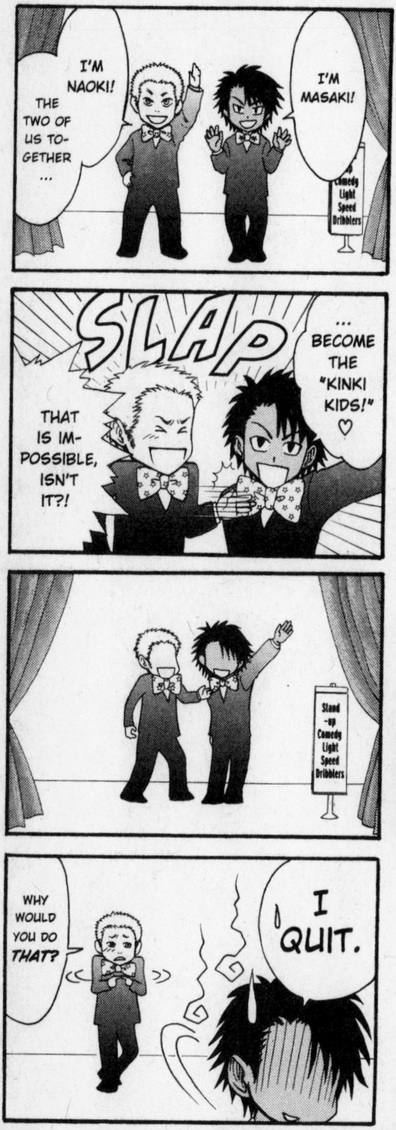
I'M MASAKI!
I'M NAOKI! THE TWO OF US TO-GETHER ...
...BECOME THE "KINKI KIDS!" ♡
SLAP
THAT IS IM-POSSIBLE, ISN'T IT?!
Stand-up Comedy Light Speed Dribblers
I QUIT.
WHY WOULD YOU DO THAT?

DAISUKE'S NOTES

MASAHIRO SUŌ

PERSONAL DATA	
BIRTHDAY	SEPT. 23, 1975
SIZE	6'0" 163 lbs
BLOOD TYPE	O
FAVORITE FOOD:	YAKISOBA
DISLIKES:	SQUID SHIOKARA & SHIITAKE MUSHROOMS
HOBBY AND SPECIAL SKILLS:	SOCCER

PERSONAL DATA	
BIRTHDAY	AUG. 29, 1984
SIZE	5'11" 147 lbs
BLOOD TYPE	O
FAVORITE FOOD:	SHRIMP IN CHILI SAUCE
DISLIKES:	MILK
HOBBY AND SPECIAL SKILLS:	FORTUNE TELLING & PICK-UP LINES

AKIRA SAIONJI

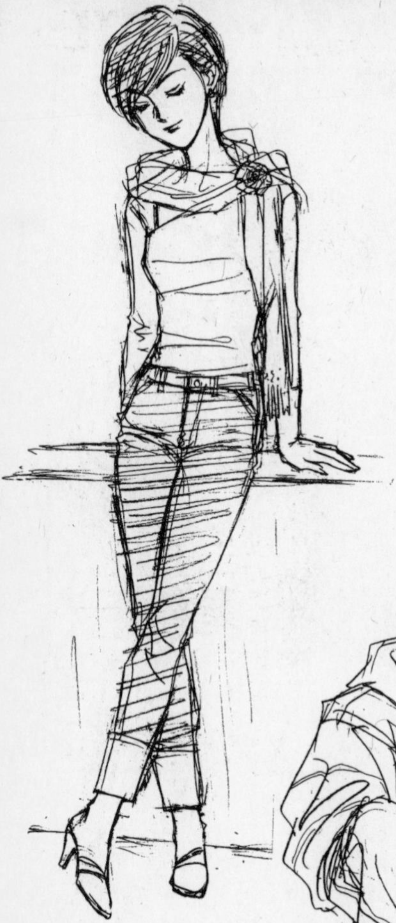

PERSONAL DATA	
BIRTHDAY	JUNE 7, 1970
SIZE	5'6" 110 lbs
BLOOD TYPE	AB
FAVORITE FOOD:	TOFU
DISLIKES:	MICE
HOBBY AND SPECIAL SKILLS:	COLLECTING TEDDY BEARS & KENDO

TAKASHI NARUMI

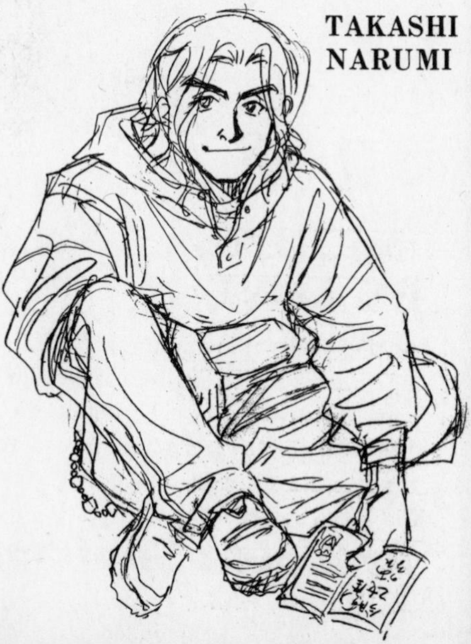

Next in Whistle!

BE ALIVE

As the weeks pass and the Tokyo Select Team gains more experience, the strengths and weaknesses of each player begin to surface, causing a shift in the team's pecking order. The players must learn how to deal with their issues before they travel to Korea to face their greatest opponent yet— the Seoul Select Team!

Available September 2007!

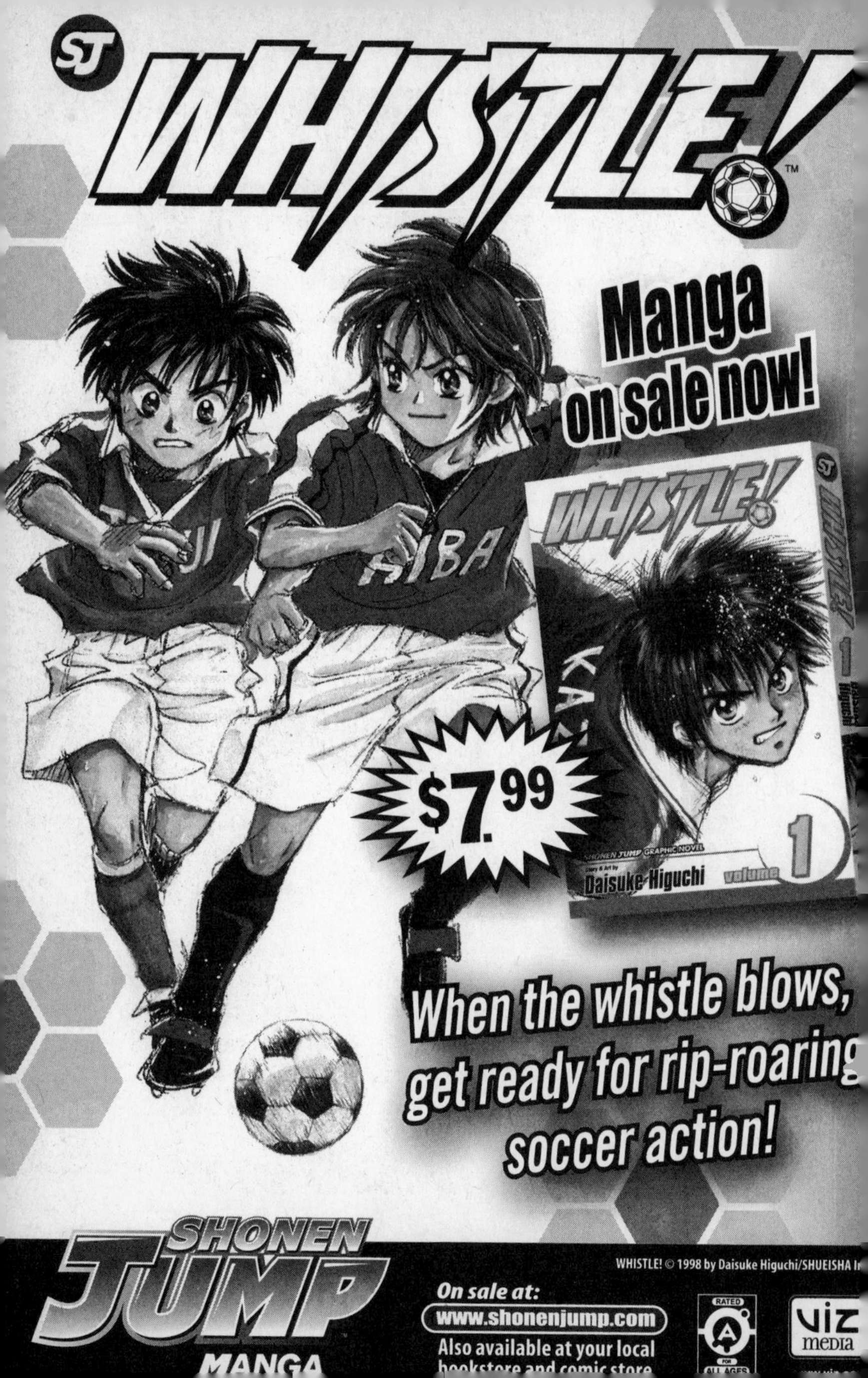

WHISTLE!
Manga on sale now!
$7.99
WHISTLE!
Daisuke Higuchi
volume 1
When the whistle blows, get ready for rip-roaring soccer action!
SHONEN JUMP MANGA
WHISTLE! © 1998 by Daisuke Higuchi/SHUEISHA Inc.
On sale at:
www.shonenjump.com
Also available at your local bookstore and comic store
RATED A FOR ALL AGES
VIZ media

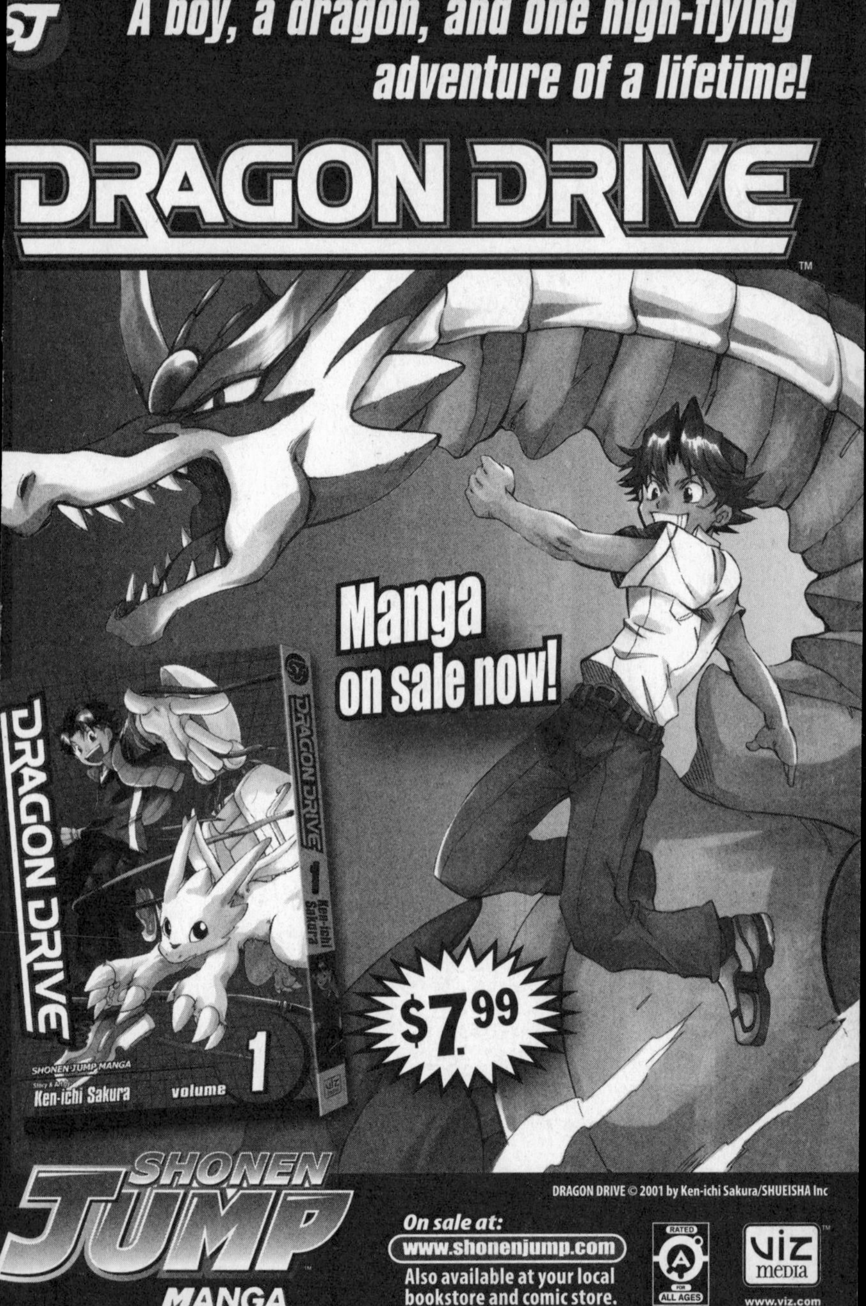
A boy, a dragon, and one high-flying
adventure of a lifetime!
DRAGON DRIVE™
Manga
on sale now!
DRAGON DRIVE
SHONEN JUMP MANGA
Ken-ichi Sakura
volume 1
$7.99
SHONEN JUMP MANGA
DRAGON DRIVE © 2001 by Ken-ichi Sakura/SHUEISHA Inc
On sale at:
www.shonenjump.com
Also available at your local
bookstore and comic store.
RATED A FOR ALL AGES
VIZ MEDIA
www.viz.com

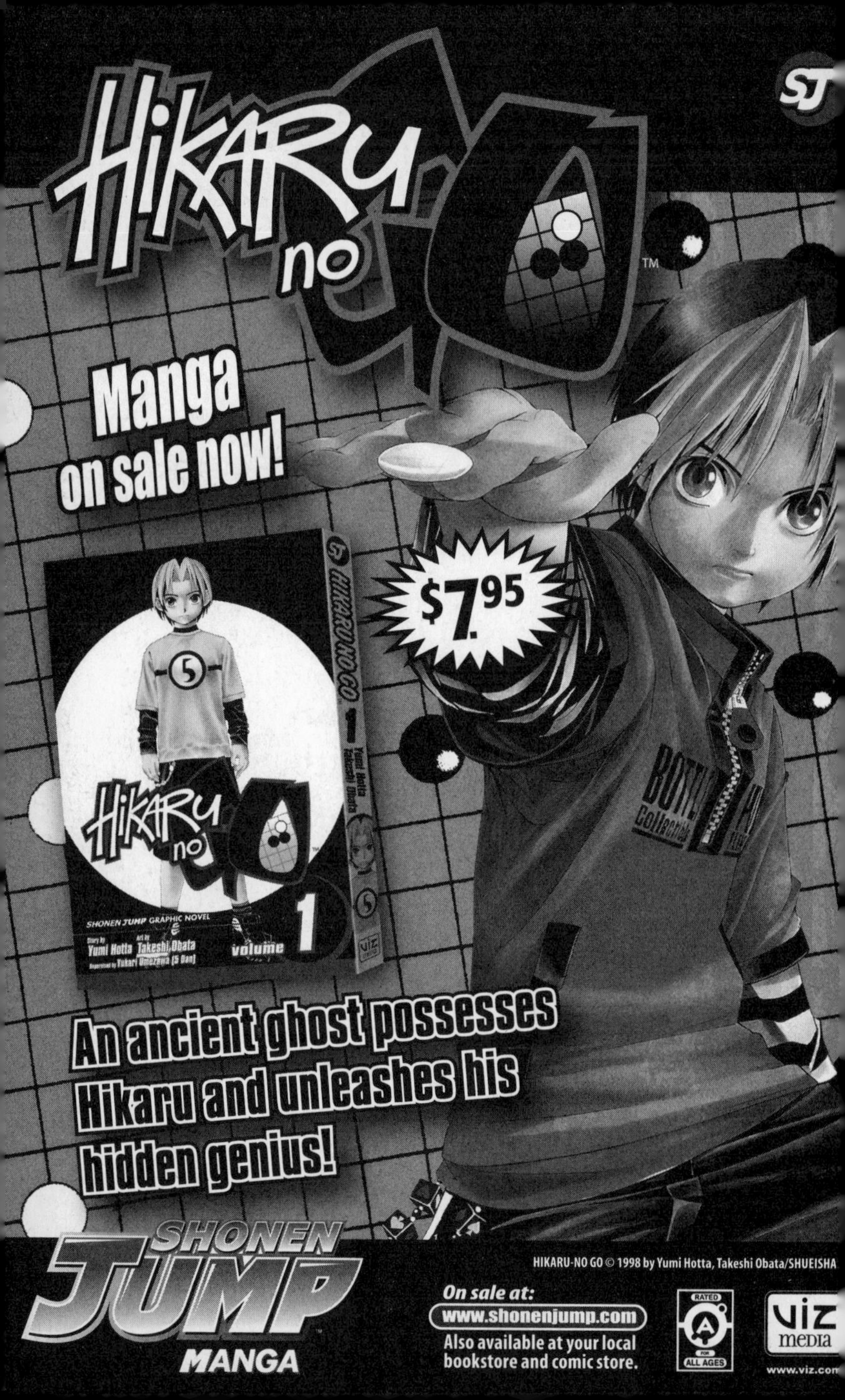
SJ
Hikaru no
TM
Manga on sale now!
SHONEN JUMP GRAPHIC NOVEL
Yumi Hotta Takeshi Obata
volume 1
$7.95
An ancient ghost possesses Hikaru and unleashes his hidden genius!
SHONEN JUMP MANGA
HIKARU-NO GO © 1998 by Yumi Hotta, Takeshi Obata/SHUEISHA
On sale at:
www.shonenjump.com
Also available at your local bookstore and comic store.
RATED A FOR ALL AGES
VIZ media
www.viz.com

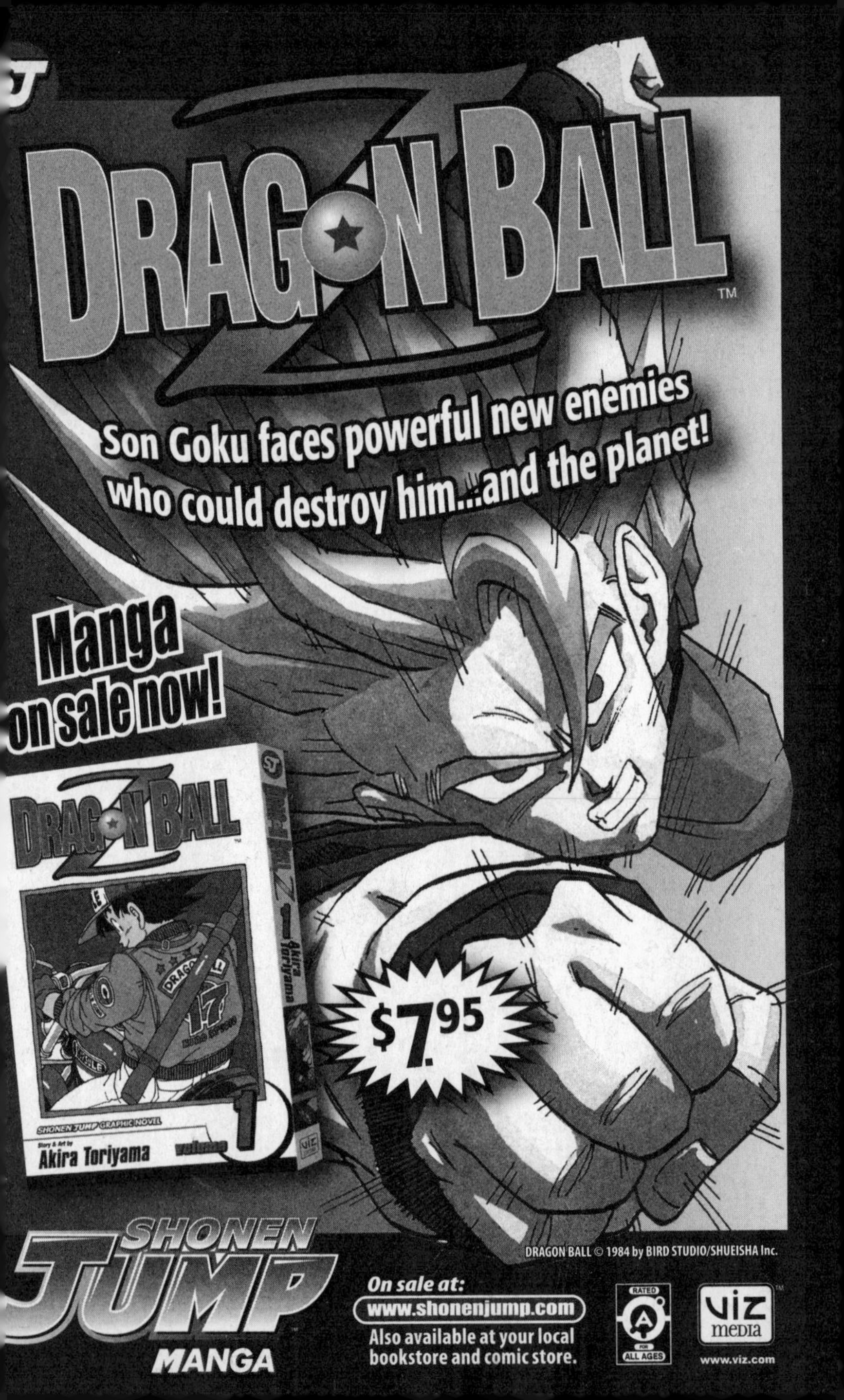

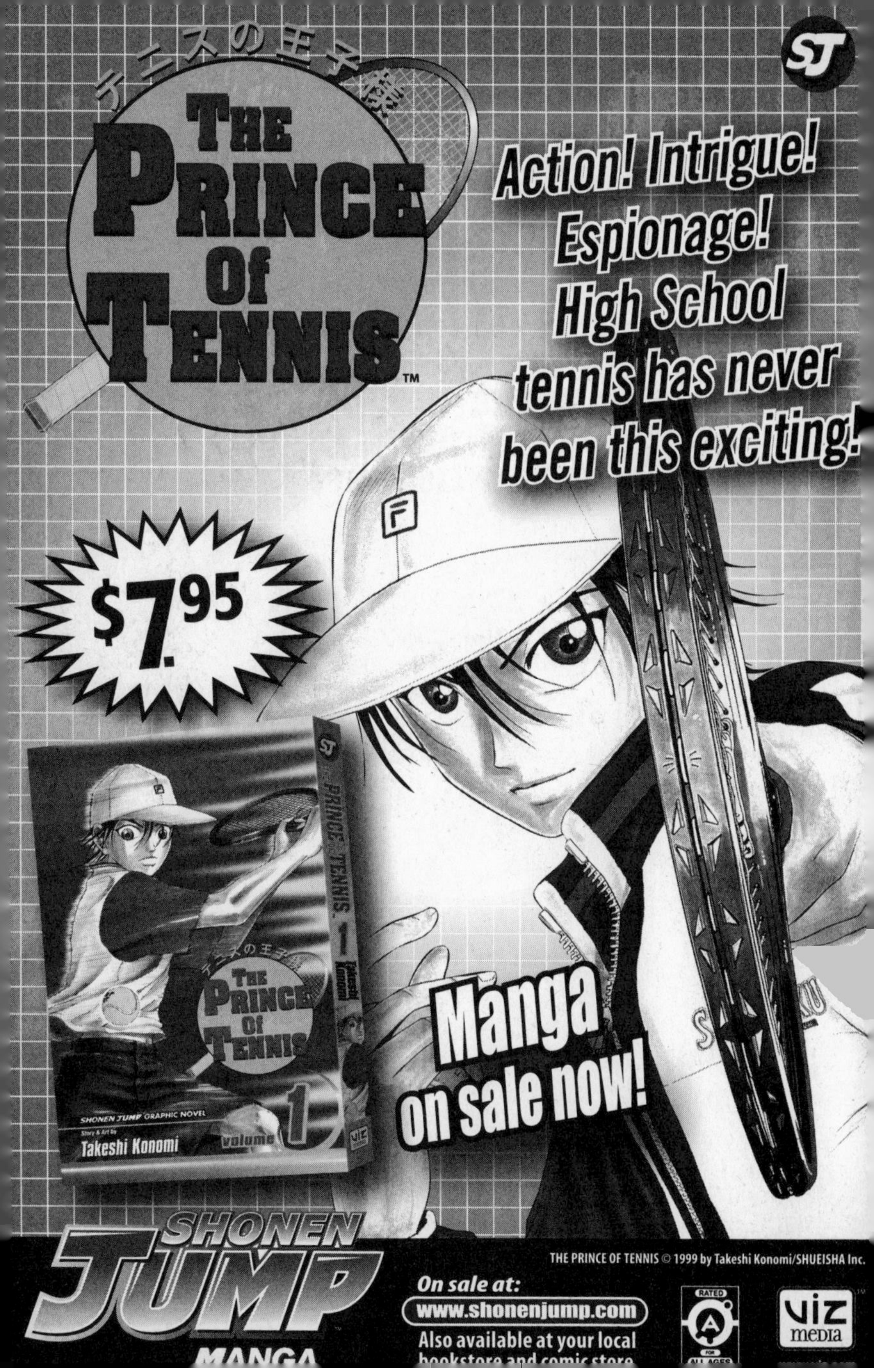
SJ
テニスの王子様
THE PRINCE OF TENNIS™
Action! Intrigue! Espionage! High School tennis has never been this exciting!
$7.95
SJ
THE PRINCE OF TENNIS
1
Takeshi Konomi
テニスの王子様
THE PRINCE OF TENNIS
SHONEN JUMP GRAPHIC NOVEL
Story & Art by
Takeshi Konomi
volume 1
Manga on sale now!
SHONEN JUMP MANGA
THE PRINCE OF TENNIS © 1999 by Takeshi Konomi/SHUEISHA Inc.
On sale at:
www.shonenjump.com
Also available at your local
RATED
A
viz media

Tell us what you think about SHONEN JUMP manga!

Our survey is now available online.
Go to: www.SHONENJUMP.com/mangasurvey